IN THE FIERY CONTINENT

IN THE FIERY CONTINENT

by

TOM HOPKINSON

052
H 77i

DOUBLEDAY & COMPANY, INC.
GARDEN CITY, NEW YORK, 1963

Parts of four chapters have appeared in *Holiday*, *The Twentieth Century*, *Photography* and *The Rand Daily Mail*, to which acknowledgments are therefore due.

All the photographs in this book are by Ian Berry with the exception of number four which is by Jurgen Schadeberg.

DEDICATION

TO THE PRESENT-DAY AFRICAN

and particularly to Sidney Andrews, Benson Dyantyi, Matthew Faji, Christian Gbagbo, Peter Magubane, Todd Matshikiza, Casey Motsisi, Nathaniel Nakasa, Matthew Nkoana, Henry Ofori, Nelson Ottah, Mike Phahlane, John Taukobong, Can Themba—and others with whom I worked in South and West Africa.

CONTENTS

CHAPTER I

FAIR WARNING

WE WERE LIVING in a quiet London backwater known as Stanhope Place, not much more than a very long stone's throw from Marble Arch. We had the top two floors of an old Regency house. From the curved front windows one could look down into Hyde Park, where I went nearly every afternoon for a walk. Our back windows looked out over the gardens of the Tyburn Convent in which every day, from quarter to one to one o'clock, a dozen or so nuns came out to giggle and chatter during their short spell of freedom. We had lived there for more than five years and were just thinking of renewing our lease for at least as long again.

After two years as Features Editor of the *News Chronicle*—which I left when finally convinced that the paper preferred slow suicide to the attempt to work out some fresh journalistic formula—I was making my living as a free-lance. I reviewed novels for the *Observer* every fortnight, wrote short stories when I could, did occasional articles for American magazines—doubly welcome because well-paid —and worked when the chance came along for radio and television.

There was always something to keep me busy, or at least to give me the feeling of being busy, and I enjoyed being able to work at my own times—between breakfast and lunch and again between five and half-past seven in the evenings—and to take a walk round the Park, or occasionally watch cricket or football in the afternoons. It was an agreeable life; I was keeping my head above water; and if sometimes I felt it was rather pointless, and that there was not much to show at the end of a year's work, I consoled myself that there might be a bit more progress in the next one.

Occasionally some magazine owner whose properties were wilting away more rapidly than those of his rivals would take me out to lunch with a view, I supposed, to suggesting that I should try and revive them. But any intention he may have had did not survive the meal; I was aware, of course, that, having once refused to toe the line for one proprietor, I must be permanently suspect to the rest. There were not many of them, anyway, and by the end of 1957 I must have had at least one lunch with them all.

A friend and ex-colleague, Simon Guttman, worked hard to have me entrusted with the moribund body of the picture magazine *Illustrated*.

"We think it would be taking too big a risk," the representative of the management informed him. A few months later Simon rang me to say that *Illustrated* was dead.

It began to be clear that I could not expect to edit another magazine in Britain, which was the work for which I felt myself to be best suited.

At the beginning of November, 1957, I had been up to Westmorland for a memorial service to my father who had lately died. The morning after I got back I had to go down to Bristol to give a talk at a school I visited from time to time. It was an early train and, as I ran out of the house to look for a taxi, I crammed into my pocket the letters put out for me on the hall table. I read through them in the taxi, but found nothing of special interest.

That same evening, when I got home, I showed them to Dorothy, my wife. There was one which she read with particular care, an airmail from South Africa.

> DRUM, "Africa's Leading Magazine",
> 176 Main Street,
> Johannesburg.
> 30th October, 1957.

Dear Tom,

Thank you for your letter of 12.10.57 which I have just received on my return from East Africa. I regret you have not been able to find an editor for me.

We are building here a really very fine and important instrument in *Drum* and the result of it is that it becomes very difficult to find a man of sufficient expertise to play it.

If we can play it right, and that demands of us considerable knowledge and discretion, we can do a great deal by the inhabitants of this continent. I know that you, Tom, possess eight* children and innumerable ties in London town. Would you not, however, consider seriously taking on this venture of ours for several years and see what you can do with it. For a great deal can be done once there is skill and understanding here.

> Best wishes.
> Yours sincerely,
> JIM.

---

* This was a considerable overstatement. However, the combined families of I[ ] and myself did amount to eight, or very nearly.

Having read the letter through, Dorothy looked at me: "Well, what are you going to do about it?"

The words rang ominously. "You don't mean that you'd consider giving up our home and . . . and everything . . . and going out to South Africa?"

"I will, if you will," Dorothy replied, and I could see at once that our fate had been decided.

This letter was not my first contact with *Drum*. It had been launched in 1951 under the editorship of the dashing cricketer-tank-fighter-author Bob Crisp. However, its formula had been too much built on the white man's picture of the black, and too little on the black man's picture of himself, and the magazine had failed to catch on.

Among the original backers and directors of the project was Jim Bailey, a younger son of the semi-mythical South African figure, Sir Abe Bailey. Either in hope of profit, from altruism, or a mixture of both, Bailey had sunk an odd thousand or two into the venture. His money had soon gone, and it was apparent that he would either have to write it off, or else put in more, and assume responsibility for the magazine. Bailey had taken it over and sent for a young man, Anthony Sampson, whom he had met casually at Oxford, to come out and assist him. Sampson accepted, was shortly appointed editor, and in his three-year term of office had made a success of the magazine, as well as a reputation for himself.

Though personally daring, alert in mind, and with a strong natural sympathy for the African, Sampson had started journalistically from scratch—with no previous training or experience. Either he himself or Bailey, the proprietor, had had the idea of sending me—at that time the recently discharged editor of *Picture Post*—copies of their magazine each month. I, in return, would write a long letter of criticism back—hampered considerably in this by having no idea of the conditions under which the magazine was produced, and whether indeed the points I criticised could possibly be altered or improved with the available resources.

Drum was a lively, bustling, vigorous production, full of gimmicks and stunts, shovelled together anyhow and peppered with photographs, mostly nondescript, but with every now and then one which stood out from the rest as the work of someone with a mind and eye. The writing was Americanised slang, bursting at the seams with gusto.

"Brothers . . . I've got smashing news for you. Real hot-poker stuff. The kind of dope that you get once in a blue moon. D'you know

King Force? Hey? The big, broad-shouldered hawk-eyed veteran sax
maniac? Hey? The chap that's the life blood of the great Jazz Maniacs
Orchestra of Joh'burg? You should know who I'm talking about, man.
The fellow that lots of recording firms have begged and begged with
big bags and bundles of dough to make discs for them. And he always
said, 'Nix'. The great guy that gulps giggle water by the gallon and
makes greater and greater sounds with every additional drop. What a
man! Everybody that's ever heard this sax giant has been raving mad
about him. If you've never had the upper-tune-ity, well it's here,
because King Force, alias Wilson Silgee, has gone and made a disc at
last. Yes man, King Force is now uptainable on record. He's gone and
taken a few fine birds from Jazz Maniacs Ork, put them plumb in the
middle of Gallos Studio and cut 'Sibatatu' and 'King Force Drag' on
Gallotone GB 1953.

"He calls his combo 'King Force and his Jazz Force'. For a label
nothing could be more suitabler.

"King Force once chased a man around a whole block of houses with
an axe. The man had broken one of King Force's discs. He has over
1,000.

"That famous chase just shows you his character. Powerful, forceful,
hot, dripping with go. His music is just like that. Man, I can't describe
music when it's great. Can you describe what you heard when it made
you mad when you heard it? If you can then I'm loony. . . ."

The writer of that highly original record review was the musician,
Todd Matshikiza. His name and those of other writers on the staff—
Can Themba, Casey Motsisi, Arthur Maimane, Ezekiel Mphahlele—
soon became familiar to me, as did the photographers, Peter Magubane,
Bob Gosani, Jurgen Schadeberg. Month after month I wrote letters off
into the blue, urging *Drum* to tidy up its lay-outs; to give more space
to the good photographs and throw away the bad; to use larger body-
type; to cut out the comic headings and splashes of crazy colour; to
push the advertisements, which were spattered over almost every page,
out of the way; to print on better paper, even if it meant fewer pages.
Occasionally, but not often, an answer would come back—two or
three sentences of thanks or explanation.

Twice I had met Jim Bailey. The first time had been a telephoned
invitation to lunch. It must have been the summer of 1954 or 5. I met
a tall gangling man with a slouching walk and a mop of fair hair which
he was continually pushing or tossing out of his sharp blue eyes. His
manner was a mixture of boyish charm and steely scrutiny. Ignoring
his food—he told the waiter to bring him whatever I had ordered, and

didn't even seem to take serious notice of the drink—he questioned me closely and constantly about magazine production.

I told him everything I thought might help, and he made notes of it on the backs of envelopes and all over a cheque book. He was acute and forceful; but for someone who had owned a magazine for some years and invested, presumably, a good deal of money in it, he appeared strangely ignorant of basic principles. I couldn't make out whether he saw to everything himself, down to the smallest detail, or whether he left everything alone to run itself, and then suddenly burst in with a long list of suggestions and complaints. Occasionally when something amused him, he flung back his head and laughed; not as though he were enjoying a joke, but as though he were savouring a situation. Once again the idiocy of mankind had been confirmed. The baying laugh died down—and we were back to business. He struck me as a man who kept every appointment knowing precisely what he intended to get out of it, and—with his mixture of charm and persistence—probably getting it. My only interest, however, lay in helping *Drum* to look more like a magazine, and I was quite content to be squeezed dry over the lunch table. My second meeting with Jim Bailey took place at our flat a year or so later, shortly before I left the *News Chronicle*. Jim called in the evening for a drink. A day or two later Dorothy and I were asked to a cocktail party given by his sister, after which a whole group of us went out to dinner.

These had been casual contacts. If I were to work with Bailey and for *Drum*, I had now to think the matter out more carefully. It appeared to me then, from what I knew of both, that *Drum* would be a magazine worth working for, and that Jim Bailey would be a proprietor with whom I could hope to reach a reasonable working understanding. Above all I looked forward to meeting, getting to know, and working with, the African staff. I knew my job. They knew their people. Between us we should be able to produce a magazine.

By Christmas all arrangements had been made. It was agreed that I should fly out to South Africa, stopping off in West Africa where *Drum* had a separate edition selling in Ghana and Nigeria, for a couple of weeks on the way out. I had agreed to go in the first place for two years, and Jim Bailey had agreed to pay our fares home if we wanted to leave within that time.

Talking it over with Dorothy, however, we decided to sell up our home and go for good. If we kept one foot in England we should be all the time looking back, comparing South Africa with England, and wondering whether we really wanted to stay on. Whereas if we gave up our flat, packed up the furniture and pictures we regarded as our treasures, and sold the rest, we should go to make the best of what we found and would be more likely to settle down. If my stay at *Drum* should prove a flop, I was fairly sure I could find other work, or else start in again to free-lance.

I was due to leave at the end of January. Dorothy took over the work of packing up our belongings, letting the flat, deciding what to sell and what to take. She was to follow by boat at the end of March. In the few weeks that remained, there were two or three functions or celebrations I had been asked to attend. We belonged to an organisation called the Progressive League, which gave a small party in our honour. Members of the League were in the main warm-hearted and serious-minded people who assumed their full share of responsibility—sometimes even rather more than their full share—for the sad state of the world.

At the party someone said that he thought it a very good thing for us to be going out to South Africa, but he was quite sure that I should not last six months as editor of *Drum*. Long before that time I should be in prison—which was probably, he added, the proper place for anyone of progressive opinions in that country. Dorothy spoke out on my behalf. "If Tom is going out to South Africa, he's going out to do a job of work. He can't work if he gets himself shut up, so you can be sure he won't get shut up."

The staff of my former magazine *Picture Post*—it had been defunct since the previous May—also gave a dinner for me at the Cheshire Cheese off Fleet Street, a favourite haunt of us all ten years before, when our paper had been in its prime. It was painful to see again the members of a hand-picked staff who had once felt ourselves on top of the journalistic world. Being men and women of marked ability, most of them were now successful either on other papers or in other fields, such as television. But there were one or two who had never really managed to fit in anywhere else; one whose peculiar temperament no normally-run newspaper would tolerate; another who had thrived in the special atmosphere of *Picture Post*, and seemed now at a loose end, as if, though still active in journalism, he no longer really knew what he was doing, and had abandoned hope of getting anywhere.

As I watched them greet one another I experienced a sudden sick feeling. Until this moment I had always felt that, in leaving *Picture Post* as I did on an issue which I felt to be one of principle, I had taken the only course I could. I had, as we say, "been right". Now I suddenly wondered if I had been irresponsible. Wouldn't it have been better to have swallowed both pride and principles—inseparable for most of us as oak and ivy—in order to keep such a team together and give them the chance to go on functioning? As the evening wore on, and many things were said, the one which stuck in my mind came from Ted Castle, my former assistant editor, now on the *Daily Mirror*, who declared with bitterness and intensity: "Why all this sympathy? Tom's a lucky devil, and he knows he is. Any one of us would give an ear for the same chance he's got."

I must have spoken myself, though it was late on in a well-lubricated evening, and I have no recollection of what I said. There was someone from the *Manchester Guardian* present, however, for I find in an old cutting:

"The hosts, who toasted their guest, drank to the coloured people of South Africa and deplored the failure of Fleet Street to find a use for Hopkinson. His reply was typically prosaic. The new job, he said, will be his first real opportunity since *Picture Post* to function on all four cylinders. He hoped they were still in working order."

I could not blame Fleet Street any longer for not finding a use for me, for in the interval between making up my mind to go out to South Africa and the fact of my going becoming public, I had suddenly been offered a job—and one which I should particularly have liked to take. But the offer had come a week too late.

Another celebration was more private, and had for me a rather ominous ring. One of the first people I had told of my new job, once I was free to do so, was Anthony Sampson, the former editor of *Drum*, then working on the *Observer* as its columnist, Pendennis. Sampson had proposed to get together the other two former *Drum* men in London— Anthony Smith and Sylvester Stein—and entertain me to dinner at the Savile Club. Anthony Smith, who had lately become scientific correspondent for the *Daily Telegraph*, had made a name for himself when in charge of the *Drum* office in Accra by a mixture of endurance and eccentricity. The office itself is one of a singular dusty bareness, like the administrative offices of a tropical prison. Its only concession to human needs was a dark closet half-way down the stairs, where a lavatory without water was freely and constantly bespattered, both by the workers from the many offices inside the building, and by anyone else who happened to drift in off the stifling, crowded streets.

When he was not travelling by "Mammy-Wagon"—decrepit lorry—all over Ghana, building up *Drum's* circulation, Anthony had made his home in this *Drum* office out of a desk, a suitcase and a broken-backed settee, a life compared to which passing one's days in a railway-station waiting-room would be one of luxurious self-indulgence. Finally, when his term of service was over, he had travelled down to South Africa, borrowed an overcoat from his proprietor, Bailey, and bought a motor-bicycle. Provided thus with everything he could want in the way of warmth, transport and protection, he had made his way back to England overland.

Sylvester Stein had succeeded Sampson as *Drum's* editor when Sampson came back to England at the end of 1954. Sampson had survived three years, and Stein—who had notably improved the magazine's looks—a little less. The cause of his leaving had been a dispute with Bailey over the use of a picture on the cover. The picture showed Althea Gibson, the 1957 negro champion of Wimbledon, being embraced by her white opponent after the final. Stein had chosen this as his cover; Bailey had thought the use of it likely to outrage South African sensibilities. The resulting row, it was said, was the cause of Stein's departure, and he was now working on the Sunday paper, *Reynolds News*. Meantime a young man, Humphrey Tyler from Durban, had taken over from Sylvester, and was holding on until I came out.

The three former employees entertained me hospitably, and made many polite enquiries as to my plans. When I, in turn, enquired as to what I should find when I got out, the replies seemed strangely evasive. From half-sentences and odd remarks, above all from occasional looks exchanged, I formed the impression that, in the opinion of my hosts, I didn't half know what I was in for. In particular when I asked about my employer and my future staff, the attitude was clearly—"You'll find all that out only too soon." I felt myself to be an odd mixture between guest of honour and sacrificial pig.

A week or two later, Anthony Sampson wrote a short piece in his Pendennis column:

"Picture magazines in Britain, confronted with television and waning advertisements, are having a difficult time: but there are parts of the world where they have an exciting and growing role to play in developing the self-consciousness of half-literate people. One of them is Africa; and it is appropriate that Tom Hopkinson, who was editor of *Picture Post* in its heyday from 1940 to 1950, should have been appointed last week as editor of the monthly picture magazine *Drum* in Johannesburg, of which 200,000 copies are scattered all over the continent.

"Tom Hopkinson is about as far from the conventional picture of a journalist as anyone could be. Gentle-looking and soft-voiced, with large melancholy eyes and an air of infinite patience, he has a habit of entering a room without anyone noticing.

"But he has been one of Britain's most original and enterprising editors: his quick, sensitive knack with pictures, and his strong integrity (he resigned from *Picture Post* when he was not allowed to print an exposé of atrocities in South Korea) showed through in every issue of his magazine.

"It had always been part of his principle that pictures should concern themselves with ordinary people, doing ordinary things—without condescension or stunts. His feeling for ordinary people was obvious in the famous series of B.B.C. broadcasts which he recorded in Rotherhithe, where he lived in a pub for three months talking to locals. It is this kind of warm sympathy, together with his vast experience, that is likely to make his contribution to an African magazine particularly important."

I am not one of those many people who—if their statements are to be believed—find any kind of publicity about themselves distressing. On the contrary; I only find it distressing when it is unfavourable. I read Anthony Sampson's piece with pleasure. But as I read it through a second time, and recalled the hints and glances which had sailed past me at the Savile Club dinner, the kindly words took on a different light. I saw that in fact they were more in the nature of an obituary than an introduction.

What they were really saying was: "Hopkinson was a journalist of vast experience, who understood his job on magazines—and *Drum* was a magazine. He liked people too, and there were plenty of people to be liked in Africa. However, there was something dim and self-effacing about him. He had got by, it is true, in the world of civilised convention. But the world of Africa called for a tougher, more aggressive, attitude. Particularly the world of *Drum*. The poor chap just didn't know what he was in for. Let us treat his memory with respect."

CHAPTER II

FIRST CONTACT

I FLEW OUT BY way of Rome and Tripoli, where we were called out of our 'plane at 3.30 in the morning to sit drowsily sipping tepid Coca-Cola in what appeared to be an enormous empty garage. It was the first time I had set foot in Africa, and it looked just like anywhere else or worse. Two hours or so later, I was woken up by the sunlight on my eyes.

One side of the experience of Africa has been for me to meet, in reality, scenes and impressions I had read about or frequently imagined. But now the clichés stand and face one. "Everything seemed to quiver in the heat" . . . "It was just like stepping into a Turkish bath" . . . "The village must have stood unchanged since the beginning of time" . . .

And then the detail—the enormous thorn tree, with its grim suggestion of impalings. The bald and pinkish vultures flapping round the huts for scraps. The figures in long garments resting from the sun in groups. The dog starting to scratch fleas, then flopping down into the dust exhausted. An orange-necked lizard raising itself on its elbows and scuttling away into the shade. Seeing them all on this journey for the first time, they were already as familiar as the brazen oak-trees or crying sea-gulls of my own country.

Now I was looking down from the 'plane on to just such a new-familiar scene—"Sunrise over the Sahara". Hundreds of miles away lay the horizon, level as the ocean rim. Below the 'plane was a mist of bluish darkness, for we were flying over night and looking towards day. Lifting slowly up from the horizon shone a band of yellow light, merging as it climbed into orange, red, violet, blue. The blue was still the night, and full of stars. Suddenly from the centre of the yellow band there shot up rays, distinct as the rays from behind God's head in paintings, then the rim of the sun rolled up, and day had started.

I was looking down now on to a world of rock and sand—bluish or rosy in the shadows, camel-coloured in the light of day. The desert was not flat, though there were great lakes of level sand within it, but moulded into ridges and soaring into bluffs and eminences. Perched on the summits were what looked like rock-built towns and castles—what indeed I was sure must be towns and castles—until, as the 'plane dragged its small fly-shadow over them, they melted back into the tumbled desert, and new shapes emerged; new towers, new cities, new delusions. Long after I had become used to these deceptions, my eye would light on a whole town of cliff-built houses grouped round a sandy fortress. This I was *sure* was solid. A minute later, touched by our flying shadow, it too had vanished into nothing.

Now and then a road appeared, a broad highway, scored with what seemed clearly to be wheel-marks, running mile after mile over the desert ranges. Just as I expected us to overtake the dusty convoy, the road ravelled down to nothing, petering away into the sand like a river that goes underground.

In mid-afternoon, after stops at Kano and Lagos, I reached Accra and got my first sight of *Drum*, being met by the manager in West Africa, Ian Pritchard. He took me to my hotel, where, over drinks and platitudinous enquiries about the flight, we slowly summed each other up.

Pritchard was a tall, rather sallow South African, somewhere between 25 and 30. He had large brown eyes, which sometimes in the middle of discussion would go vague and moony; he wore glasses and, when he took them off, his face had the innocent, defenceless look of the spectacle wearer lacking his accustomed barrier. I soon found, however, that he was anything but defenceless. What he wanted to know—naturally enough, since he was responsible for the whole business and financial side of the enterprise in West Africa—was what I intended to do with the magazine, and what changes I was going to make. Above all, how I intended to put up the circulation, and make the paper pay.

My intention, just as naturally, was to appear as though I knew what I was about, but to avoid committing myself in a situation where I still understood so little. Secondly, I wanted to see whether Pritchard was a man with whom one could stand together when things went wrong, for I had been long enough in journalism to know that in an enterprise of this kind some things are quite certain to go wrong. If, when they do, the two halves of the business—management and editorial—start blaming one another, then the energies of both are wasted and the situation must get worse.

Assisting on the outskirts were a white journalist—to whom I will give the name Agnew—and our local editor, Henry Ofori, a Ghanaian. Henry was a rotund figure with a sudden barking laugh which seemed more an explosion of nervous energy than an expression of enjoyment. He had a wispy moustache and beard, and the habit of selecting two or three long hairs from his eyebrows or moustache and twirling them into a point between his fingers. The points always came untwisted, so the exercise was never-ending. Sometimes, as the pain of twisting became acute, he would contort his jolly face into a scowl. Occasionally when spoken to he would delay answering until he had completed one of these homemade corkscrews. At least, I supposed, the exercise must give him time to think.

On the table before us were a number of tall bottles of Dutch beer, the moisture from the cold bottles making pools of water on the painted table. We sat with our coats off, but I felt that, if it were not for our soaking shirts and socks and shoes, there would be pools round our feet as well. Now and then one of the air-conditioning devices from the bedrooms in the hotel above us would gulp hoarsely and discharge a quantity of accumulated water down the baking wall. Black and white crows flapped overhead, and lizards scuttled across the soft tarmac of the road.

Among the moisture on the table were the three latest copies of West African *Drum*, issues for January, February and March, 1958. Even in the heat they gave me a cold shudder; was *that* what we were trying to put across? I had seen copies of the West African edition before, but never under circumstances which made me feel personal responsibility for its present and future. Pritchard must have noticed my brooding gaze, because he asked me rather sharply what I thought of them.

"I'd rather say nothing," I replied. "It's no good criticising what's been done till I know what it's possible for us to do."

Pressed to "come out of my shell", I added: "One thing I'm certain we can do is to clean the magazine up."

"How d'you mean 'clean it up'?" Ian asked. "What's unclean about it?"

"Have one big picture on the cover instead of four little ones. Cut down the number of pictures inside, and use the good ones big. Decide whether a feature is to be pictures or text—and lay it out accordingly. Sort out the ruddy muddle!"

"But four pictures on the cover gives an idea of the contents," objected Agnew. "If you only use one picture, you're not displaying the goods you've got to sell."

"If you try to display more than one picture on a cover you won't sell any goods at all," I answered. "The cover's the poster. Make it attractive enough—and people will buy. When we get the paper known, they'll take the contents on trust."

Agnew grunted. I couldn't be sure if the argument was right under such changed conditions; but I knew we could never make anything of magazines like the three I was looking at now.

"How far," asked Ian, "d'you mean to incorporate material from South Africa into the West African edition?"

I felt the others eyeing me. It was clear this had been a subject of argument inside the firm, and probably with Bailey. However, if there were strings to the question, I couldn't see where they led.

"Very little, I should think. Won't your own material sell better? It must be fairly lousy if it doesn't. Secondly, shan't we have trouble in South Africa if we supply it?"

"Once you start on *that* line," said Agnew sententiously, "you're dished. It's no good calculating the odds. We should print what we want from anywhere—and be damned!"

"But I don't want to be damned yet," I said. "I haven't even started. And journalism is nothing *but* calculating the odds. However, the one who has to answer Ian's question must be Henry."

Henry sat up with a jerk and let go his eyebrow. "Me? Why me? How *can* I answer it? I don't know what goes on in South Africa—ha! ha!"

"The question is, Henry—can you supply enough good material from here so that we don't need to pad the paper out with material from elsewhere?"

"Why yes," Henry replied, in a voice which seemed really to be saying "No!" "I'm sure we can. What we need is transport—a decent office car—and another cameraman. With that—and a really good assistant—I think I could supply enough. Not this month," he added hastily, "it's too late."

"If everyone works all out," declared Agnew, "there's no reason why we shouldn't do it for this month. But they don't—that's *Drum's* trouble."

"If they don't, *you should see they do*," said Ian with unexpected bluntness. "And as for more transport, Henry—you know I haven't a hope in hell of getting you more transport. We haven't paid for the last pile-up you had yet. You can take it that the shaky old Morris *is* your transport, and Christian is your photographic staff. Now, what can you do?"

So we went on, probing and sizing each other up under the guise of a general discussion. Sticky from twenty-four hours' travel, I was longing to go upstairs for a cold bath, but have learned to trust a lot to first impressions—particularly of people with whom I am going to work, where the impression so soon gets overlaid by the surroundings —and I did not want to cut these first impressions short. I was struck by Ian's grasp and his refusal to be put off by evasions. "Yes—but what exactly do you mean by a good photograph?"

"It's difficult to explain."

"Well, you have to explain it to the photographers, don't you?"

He was accustomed, I could see, to those about him going out of their way to please him; but I was not sure whether he was conscious of this power, or counted on it without thinking. With Henry he had an easy joking manner, and he was friendly—though not at ease— with Agnew. He gave me a sense of over-calculation; of someone who thought four times before taking a step; and, though he had clearly acquired the capacity to control those below him, I doubted if he had yet an equal capacity for standing up to those above. Lastly, I could see that he either found the climate of the West Coast trying— as, God knows, it appeared to be—or else habitually lived on the edge of his nervous resources. Particularly courteous to staff and waiters, he flared up suddenly when a large gin was brought instead of the small one he ordered, and took quite a time to slip back into his normally smooth skin.

About Agnew I felt less happy. No discussion remained general for more than a few sentences. Once it reached him it turned into: "Well, that's just what *I've* been objecting to all along", or, "Out here I have to keep an eye on everything". His talk alternated between extreme self-assurance—"I've got a pretty good name myself in Fleet Street"—and a painful lack of it. "I've been doing the best I could under impossible conditions," he told me, when the others had walked over to the car to fetch some back issues of *Drum*. "Now you've come out here, I shall expect to get some real support—can't say I've had much up till now. Life in this country's tricky enough, without having to worry the whole time about one's position in the firm as well."

"*Do* you worry about your position in the firm?"

"Have to—in this place. You'll soon see."

Henry I liked as a person, but as a journalist he gave me little confidence.

"What about a series of profiles of the local great men? Not only Cabinet Ministers—Ghanaian businessmen, sportsmen and so on. Would that be a good idea?"

Henry shook his head. "They'd be sure to give offence to some-one."

"Well, make them flattering."

Henry released his laugh-explosion. "Ha! Then they'll give offence to the people we *don't* write about!"

Summing him up, when at last I got up to my room, I thought, "Henry is a writer, not a journalist." I had read some of his pieces in the magazine. The best of them were humorous descriptions of village life, with an easy flow and a quiet inventiveness such as might suit a West African *Punch*, if such a thing existed. Temperamentally he was, I felt, a jolly clubman and a good companion. A journalist needs sharpness, something critical, almost hostile, in his make-up. He needs to be suspicious, and not too careful if he gives offence. He must enjoy a fight, even while trying to keep out of them.

The world's great men maintain an increasingly elaborate system for informing us of their merits and achievements; they do this just as thoroughly in Africa as elsewhere. With a little organisation, they can whip up a crowd of admirers and applauders out of nowhere, to shout their names and yell abuse of their opponents, but it is no part of a journalist's task to make one of the applauding crowd. It is much more his task to look for chinks in the armour, to detect the failures and half-failures which the great men are trying to cover up. And though newspapers ought not to live on scandal, it is their function to nose out what is faulty rather than to spread cloaks for the powerful to walk on.

Of the new black Africa, Ghana is the highly self-conscious centre. It would take a strong man and a determined journalist to live in Ghana, I thought, and not succumb to the general atmosphere of adulation and self-satisfaction—a doubly strong and determined man if he were, like Henry, a Ghanaian.

*   *   *   *   *

For the next few days, in the intervals of office work, I breathed in Africa through open nostrils. I would wake early, dripping-wet under a single sheet, though the fan and the air-conditioning had been running all night long. Going to the window, I looked out on to the early morning scene—unending lines of men and boys on their way to work, winding through the long grass by tracks invisible beneath the trees. Nearly all wore white sleeveless vests and shorts, a few wore flowing robes like the figures in Bible paintings.

The men were lean, and walked with a high athletic step. The women, plumply swathed in loose robes of Kente cloth or dark printed cottons, swayed slowly along with rotation of their ample hips and buttocks. The men flowed purposefully as ants, cutting their lines across the landscape, coming in from the suburbs or outlying villages to work, hurrying to be there on time. The women swung easily around, as if they had only just got out of bed, and would probably be going back there before long.

My hotel, in its competence and lack of personality, resembled any other big hotel throughout the world, but even here small glimpses of Africa crept in. Passing down the corridor on Sunday morning, my way was stopped by a green star—five little maids in their green uniforms lying on the polished floor to gossip, heads to the centre, neat figures radiating out, pink soled bare feet on the outside. Cautiously I stepped in and out between their slender bodies. Half-way down the staircase a shiny centipede was journeying slowly from an open window; it looked like a coil of dark metal swayed on a ripple of hair-legs. Two minutes later, when I came up again with a newspaper, it was expanding and contracting in death agony, as dozens of small fierce ants devoured its stomach.

Among the waiters in the dining-room was one I always looked for. Tall, lean, with strong features and skin a boot-polish black, he had an air of shyness, wildness; a creature of the woods and the lagoons, I felt I had seen him wild-fowling in an Egyptian frieze. His eyes, set towards the sides of his head, showed clear white triangles in each corner, like pieces of mosaic; I could imagine him carrying—like the man I had seen at Kano—a pile of board-stiff leopard skins on his head, or a huge sheaf of arrows, not bringing the marmalade or eggs and bacon from the kitchen.

One evening Ian and the rest of us went dancing. We sat in the gallery of a decayed but picturesque hotel down by the fishing harbour of Jamestown. The hotel had been a "Barracoon"—a depot or barracks for slaves waiting shipment to America—and its stucco arcades gave an odd suggestion of New Orleans and the Southern States. We drank cold beer, which grew warm before you could finish the bottle, and watched the High-Life dancers. From a small pavilion to one side of the cement courtyard, a five-piece band blasted away its lips and lungs and skinned its fingers, hotting up the same melody faster and hotter, for ten minutes on end.

In the High-Life the dancers separate, usually the man pursues or circles round the woman, who undulates along in front of him, tossing her head, snapping her fingers, throwing provocative glances over her shoulder, occasionally gazing down in fascinated approval at the rhythmic movements of her own breasts and stomach. Meantime her partner steps it out behind her, to one side, perhaps for the moment out in front. Occasionally with manly independence he mingles with the shuffling, swaying crowd—to appear on his own on the far side of the courtyard. With a look of humorous annoyance and a toss of her black oiled hair, the woman summons him to her side.

One young man, not more than twenty, was with a mountainous woman in purple—a rich "mammy" or trader from the markets with her "scholarship boy". In repose the mammy must have seemed immovable, a gigantic barrier of solid flesh—but here she was dancing gaily, lightly even, with the rest. Behind her pranced her boy—a depleted-looking lover—but with gestures of admiration, half-humorous, half-bawdy, emphasising for the onlookers the voluptuous contours wobbling before him.

"You like the little girl in pink, sah?"

I looked round. It was a junior clerk from the office—Jordan—whom I'd met for the first time that morning.

"I do. Is she your friend?"

"She name Comfort, sah. She cost two pounds. She ask three pounds—you say 'one pound'. Then she say 'all right'. Perhaps she say 'all right' for nothing for you, sah." The voice pattered on in a paroxysm of flattery and insinuation.

"Have a beer," I said.

The beer came, but my eyes must have wandered, because the voice began again.

"You like little girl in yellow trousers, sah? Her name Chastity, sah. She *very* nice girl, sah. Very smart. She cost five pounds, sah. But perhaps she go with you for two pounds. You like me fetch Chastity dance with you, sah?"

"Chastity looks well worth five pounds," I said. "Why should I say two?"

Jordan gave me a sickly look which said: "I can see I'm wasting my time, but if you choose to make silly jokes I suppose I have to lump it"—swallowed his beer, and vanished.

"Is Jordan a pimp?" I asked Ian, pointlessly.

"He's on your staff," said Ian. "You should know."

"He was taken on before I came out here," I answered. "I'm asking whether he has other qualifications—or whether you took him on for those he's been showing."

Ian laughed. "He's not a whole-time pimp. I expect he was just anxious to be on easy terms. If you'd wanted yellow-pants or pink-dress he'd probably have collared a small cut afterwards. Maybe he'd have had friendly treatment himself at a reduced rate ... How about a couple more beers?"

* * * * *

I got a shock when I first went into our office in Accra. Down a crowded, bustling side-street, dodging the sun and the women selling food, over a stinking gutter, through a yard, up a flight of stone steps at the head of which a knot of women in dark cottons sat ceaselessly gossiping, turn to the right and you had reached *Drum*.

Three concrete-floored rooms opened off a corridor on which stood a table for the telephone operator. The middle room was Pritchard's. The far room was for the accounts and circulation clerks. The near room was the editorial office over which Henry held sway. At the far end was an empty space in which unsold copies of the magazine were stored, and bundles which had been dropped into the sea and spoiled while being brought ashore in surf-boats were laid out to dry, before being dusted down, repacked and sold up country.

On the first available day I called a conference of the staff. There was Henry, Agnew, a young reporter, Julian, our cameraman, Christian Gbagbo, and Jordan prowling on the outskirts. While I waited for them to assemble, I nosed around the office. At one end was a board, on which were a few pin-ups, none quite in focus, and three or four notices. I began to read them.

NOTICE

There has been a tendency on the part of the editorial staff to turn up late in the mornings. This has got to stop. Staff hours are 8.30 a.m. to 4.30 p.m. These hours will in future be strictly adhered to. Only those to whom I have given special permission may arrive at the office late, or leave before the appointed time.

(Signed) J. J. Agnew.

NOTICE

It has been brought to my notice that on several occasions the office car has been used for private purposes. In future the office car can only be taken out on receipt of a signed order from myself. The driver has received instructions to this effect.

(Signed) J. J. Agnew.

There were others. I found Agnew standing by me as I read them.

"Does it help?" I asked. "Can't you just explain what you want over the table?"

Agnew frowned, then smiled a little patronisingly. "That sort of method doesn't work out here. Got to put it all down in black and white—and *keep on* putting it down."

The staff had now assembled. I looked round with a sense of despair. Agnew was looking important, like a sergeant-major ready to silence interjections; Henry was twirling his moustaches; Christian and the young reporter gazed hopefully at me, as much as to say: "Please make us journalists!"

"I'm going to introduce some changes," I began. "*Drum* is going to become a picture magazine. Yes, I know you've had a lot of photographs in it in the past, but now the photographs are going to *be* the paper. People are going to buy *Drum* for its pictures. This means a tremendous amount of work for the cameramen, and it means quite a new attitude in the writers and reporters—they've got to go out of their way, a long way out of their way, to help the cameramen. If the reporter comes back with half his story, there is always something he can do—telephone, look up cuttings, consult authorities. Somehow he can make up for what he missed. But if the cameraman has missed his pictures, the whole story is a flop."

For half-an-hour I went on talking, trying to point out what the new way of working would involve, explaining that, from now on, the cameramen would have to think as journalists, the journalists would need to see in terms of pictures. I had noticed already that Christian, our only cameraman, was treated as someone of a lower status. This, I said, would have to change. All were now journalists. All were equal. And, because everything hung on our getting good pictures, writers would often have to assist and even protect the cameramen, help them handle their equipment, keep cops and intruding authorities at bay.

As I was talking I remembered how, years ago, Denzil Batchelor had joined the staff of *Picture Post*, coming over as Sports Editor from the *Leader*. After one or two outings with our cameramen—in which they had told him freely what sort of help they expected from him, and complained bitterly when they didn't get it—Denzil said to me disgustedly: "You treat your bloody photographers on *Picture Post* like Royal Children." Christian was a long way from being treated as a Royal Child. I finished by saying that the office would subscribe regularly to *Paris-Match* and *Life*, and that I expected them all to look carefully at every issue. Within a few months from now we had all to be thinking, breathing and living pictures. . . . And now, had they any work prepared which we could look through together? What was there in hand for the next issue?

Henry scratched his head, rummaged around in the confusion of old newspapers and typing paper on his desk, finally fished in his pocket and fumbled out a key.

"Christian," he said. "Go along to my car. It's parked just round the corner. You'll find a folder on the back seat—get it and bring it up. . . . And mind you don't drop the papers on the way!"

*   *   *   *   *

After the conference I went through Christian's photographic equipment with him. He had only one camera, a very old Rollei, originally a good instrument, but now in the condition of an exhausted pre-war car.

"The shutter doesn't seem to be working properly," I said, fumbling to test it.

"It's the dust," Christian apologised. "We travel over these country roads. I try to keep the camera covered up on the journey." He fished a plastic bag out of his pocket to show. "Then we get to a village. All the people are dancing and the dust is rising. You can hardly breathe. I have to take the camera out of the bag to get my pictures."

We went into the dark-room; it was a corner of the editorial office roughly separated off by a partition which did not reach the ceiling. I looked around. Cracked dishes. One enlarger covered with dust. Strips of negatives still moist, hanging where anyone coming in or out must brush against them.

"Put some of your pictures into the enlarger."

"What pictures?"

"Any strips of negative you've taken lately. The negatives of that girl on the beach."

Christian fished them out, put them into the enlarger, and focussed it on a sheet of paper.

"But it's only sharp in the centre," I said. "Round the edges it's all woolly. How can you make decent prints with that thing?"

"It's the fungus," Christian explained. "Fungus on the lens. The damp brings it." He looked round almost tearfully. "The air's so full of moisture. Nothing's ever dry in here. I carry my camera in a plastic bag. I suppose I ought to fix something up to cover the enlarger—but the damp would get in anyway."

I looked closely at the hanging negatives. They were covered with dust and bits of hair.

"You'll have to wash these all over again," I said, "before you can make prints. Why don't you hang them in the drying-cupboard?"

"We have no drying cupboard. People walk about in the office outside. They stir up all the dust—it comes in over the top. I sometimes have to wash my negatives three times. The only time I can work properly is late at night—or over the weekend when there's no one moving in the office."

I patted his shoulder. "We'll get things fixed up," I assured him. "Just do your best to turn out this month's work."

I tried to fix things up with Ian over a beer. He was sympathetic, but he had his budget to consider—and after all, he argued, they had always managed to produce some kind of magazine, even with the present set-up. In West Africa alone the paper was losing £2,000 a month. As a business man his main anxiety was to see it paying; all costs had to be cut to the bone. I pressed my side of the argument; *Drum* was to become a photographic magazine—you couldn't make such a magazine without some sort of equipment.

Christian, he finally agreed, should be given a new camera. New dishes to replace the filthy cracked ones would cost only a pound or two, they also could be ordered. The partition would be carried up to the ceiling to keep out the dust "as soon as we can get a carpenter". The enlarger lens would be repolished to get rid of the fungus, and another one borrowed from somewhere in the meantime.

A drying cupboard for negatives would cost £20, so that would have to wait. It was in fact two and a half years—by which time *Drum* West Africa would be well out of the red—before Christian got his drying cupboard.

CHAPTER III

OVER TO LAGOS

BEFORE LEAVING GHANA for Nigeria, where I was to spend a week looking over our office in Lagos—*Drum's* control centre for the whole West Coast—I managed to obtain one or two glimpses into the countryside. I was anxious to get all I could, rightly foreseeing that, once I reached Johannesburg, I should be entombed in a concrete city. For my last weekend I had arranged to drive up with Henry Ofori to Kumasi, capital of the ancient kingdom of Ashanti, focal point of the Ashanti wars, and centre of such opposition to the Nkrumah regime as still struggles thinly on. Henry called for me soon after breakfast with his shaky Opel, which he drove with a mixture of rage and apprehension—fearful that it was planning to let him down, and determined to punish it in advance for its ill intentions.

The journey was my first chance, since I had arrived a week ago, to sit back and look, without trying to understand, alter or impress. We ran most of the morning through what Henry called "forest"; however, this was not the impenetrable green mass which that word conjures up, slid through by snakes and panther-haunted. It was a rolling wooded landscape, dotted with trees and shrubs. Patches of reddish soil showed here and there, but overgrown with weeds and creepers, looking to English eyes as though someone had begun the task of cultivation, but despaired of it half-way. Sometimes these patches were a recognizable crop—cocoa, plantains or cassava. More often it was hard to distinguish whether a roadside tract were part of a farm or of the background forest. Here and there trees had been felled and a stretch of the undergrowth cleared with fire; in other parts the land looked as though it had been worked out and was lying idle to recover.

"What *is* all this, Henry? Is it wild country or cultivated?"

Henry twisted his eyebrow and looked sideways at me in bewilderment.

"I mean—does it belong to anyone?"

"Yes, it belongs to the chiefs. That is, the chiefs decide who can use it."

"Is it all being farmed?"

"Of *course* it is," said Henry, waving his arm. "All this is farmland. Very *good* farmland."

I looked at the enormous cotton trees, towering up to twice the height of English elms, at the tangled mass of vegetation, the absence of anything that looked like a field, an orchard, an evenly planted crop.

"Does a farm—a piece of land—belong to a family? Or how is it organised?"

Henry scratched his head. "The land belongs to the village. Nominally the village is ruled over by the chief. He tells the people which bits of land they have to work. Some lots belong to the village as a whole. Some bits the farmers work and take the crops off for themselves."

"Why d'you say 'nominally'. Surely that *is* ruling?"

" 'Nominally' because the chief has to act in accordance with custom. If he didn't, he could be de-stooled—put off his throne, or stool."

"If I wanted to come and live here, could I?"

"Live where? *Here?*"

"On this hillside. If I wanted to live here, what should I have to do?"

"You'd have to go and ask the chief."

"Would he let me?"

"Probably he would," said Henry, obviously fearful of what commitment he might be making. "Of course, he'd have to talk it over with the elders. They'd decide whereabouts you could make a house. There'd probably be somewhere where a stranger would be allowed to live. That is, unless they'd got anything against you."

We were driving along a dusty laterite road. The car swung heavily from side to side as Henry switched course to avoid the deepest ruts and pot-holes. Sometimes on the loose surface the car seemed to be skidding continuously for hundreds of yards. Behind us we dragged a bridal veil of reddish dust which soared up among the tree-tops. Wild hooting every now and then showed that we were being overtaken. Swaying and bucketing, a lorry would swing past, packed with goods, animals and humans. Goats' heads peered out over the sides in the fore part of the truck; a row of human behinds shaved perilously along the Opel's swaying roof. Painted on the back were cryptic signs or slogans: "Beware Woman", "Even Me", "Samuel Smiled", "Still Nkombi he Devil Boy", "People will Talk of You". One lorry marked "All Shall Pass" rattled ahead of us down the crown of the road for several miles, swerving across to edge us out into the jungle whenever Henry, his hand pressed firmly on the hooter, tried to force his way past.

"Damn these mammy-wagons," muttered Henry. "*Bloody* mammy-wagons! They do nearly all the inland transport in West Africa. We send *Drum* out by them. The staff travel by them too—whenever they can't avoid it."

At the foot of a steep hill Henry's curse seemed to have taken effect. One of the wagons was lying across the middle of the road, belly upwards like a shot rhinoceros. Dark pools and streams were flowing away from underneath it; however, they seemed to be its life-blood—oil, petrol and water—not that of its passengers. Another mammy-wagon had drawn up, and the driver was bargaining with the stranded group for the remainder of their journey. Further on another—but this was old and rusted, a last year's disaster—had pitched straight off the built-up road into the jungle; the shock, as the heavy body rammed itself between the trees, had torn the engine off its mountings and shot it, nose-first, a foot deep into the ground. "I Am the Way" still saluted the passer from its broken tail-board.

From time to time we passed over a muddy river; one such had been dammed with a pleasant stretch of grass, almost a lawn, beside it. A dozen small naked boys were splashing wildly in the water, their shirts and shorts sunning on the bushes. Scarcely ten yards away a group of vultures squatted; stretching out their quivering wings to catch the sunshine, they looked as though they had just been bathing too.

We stopped at a hotel for lunch. I knew by now what we should get—a leg of extremely stringy chicken, scales, claws and all, in a thin yellow sauce, with boiled potatoes and tinned peas. This would be followed by half a tinned pear floating in condensed milk. However, the cold beer was welcome. After a couple of bottles I went out to the back to relieve myself. Seeing no door that looked like a lavatory, I walked up the yard. At the far end was a rubbish heap with a seedy vulture hopping awkwardly around it; I aimed a kick at the vulture, and had just begun, when the manager came running up to me and took my arm. I supposed I was offending some local by-law, but he led me with great courtesy to a door marked WOMEN ONLY. Inside was a clean wooden lavatory with a notice PLEASE SIT ON THE SEAT—BY ORDER.

After our frugal lunch we drove on to Kumasi. I was eager, as always, to see wild animals; I imagined a forest should be full of them, and so far had seen nothing more exciting than a toucan. But when I questioned Henry:

"Just a few monkeys," he told me. "That's all till you get to the very far north. A few monkeys and some grass-cutters."

"What are grass-cutters?"

"Cane-rats. Very big rats, the size of dogs. Last time I was coming down from Kumasi we killed one with the car. We were delighted—they're very good to eat. We use them in our ground-nut stew. So we pulled in to the side and jumped out to run back and pick it up. But there was another car coming along behind us. They saw the grass-cutter, and, before we could grab it, they'd put it in the back of their car and driven off," and Henry gave one of his laugh explosions. "It all happened in a moment! Ha! I wondered if the grass-cutter were really dead, or whether it woke up in the back of their car and started to play hell."

Though there were no wild animals to see, we passed herds of humped cattle with great scythe-like horns. The beasts were gaunt, slow-moving, pale in colour, dusk grey, biscuit and white. Driven by immensely tall, thin Moslem herdsmen from the north wearing loose white robes and round caps, the beasts came wandering down hundreds of miles towards the coast and slaughter, browsing the edge of the forest as they came. Henry cursed because they wandered in front of the car and kicked the dust up off the road, but I leaned out to catch their sharp animal smell, the sound of their hooves slapping in the dust, the wild slew of their eyes and the rattle of their great horns.

Our hotel in Kumasi was on a hillside. The city itself lies in a hollow, a huge tangle of rusty corrugated iron roofs—replacing over the last fifty years what must have been a similar tangle of grass roofs, and soon to be replaced, as elsewhere in Africa, by a tangle of shiny roofs, as aluminium comes in instead of rusty iron. Strong green of foliage and the dull red of the roofs, however, are today the colours of Kumasi, over whose bowl among the hills a swarm of scavenging vultures hovers all day long, like the swallows above an English village.

*   *   *   *   *

A couple of days later Ian and I flew to Lagos.

Lagos, built on the lagoons, is a vast, sprawling pullulating city. It has no heart, no focal point. People pour into it to work and to make money, living, eating, sleeping where they can. Those who can afford to get out every night, and even drive back into the open, comparatively sweet-smelling suburbs, for their lunch. Now the only good hotel was full, and I had to get in where I could. Down by the harbour there was a hotel with rooms to spare. A tiny reception clerk, his face scarcely visible above the counter, booked me in, and called to a boy to carry my suitcase. He led me up three flights of stairs; on every landing a group of Nigerians squatted, playing cards, drinking, arguing.

As the boy fiddled with the lock and then flung the door of my room open, I stepped back with a gasp. A horrible stench came gusting out of it in waves; even the card-players on the landing moved aside, pinching their offended noses. The boy pulled the plug in an invisible bathroom and after a minute or two I followed him inside. In the bedroom the curtains were close drawn, the only light coming from a naked bulb, scarcely strong enough to penetrate the fly-spotting on the glass. The boy switched on the air-conditioner and went into the bathroom to tidy up. I pulled the bed-clothes back. They were filthy, but not quite so filthy as I thought at first; it was only his pipe knockings that the last occupant had left between the sheets.

"Clean it up," I said. "Get some fresh sheets"—and, looking round the bathroom—"wash the bath out. Then bring me some soap and towel."

While waiting his return, I pulled the wardrobes open, meaning to hang up some clothes. One door fell off, and a cloud of mosquitoes volleyed up from among the fluff, dust and stubbed-out cigarettes. When the boy came back I asked him to spray the room out.

"No need for spray, sah! This kills all mosquito." He pointed proudly at the air-conditioner which was rattling away as though its guts would fall out any minute, but which contrived to send a jet of icy air across the room. In time, I supposed, it would drive out the stink and force the mosquitoes, chilled and embittered, back into the wardrobe.

Going downstairs to find food, I wanted to lock my room, not unnaturally in view of the groups playing cards and drinking on each landing, but the key spun idly round. The lock was shattered. I had a sharp impression of the room's last occupant, knocking his pipe out in the bed, pouring an old bottle of hair-oil on the floor (it was slimy from wall to wall), refusing to pull the lavatory plug, and then finishing the lock off with a savage kick.

"No need for key, sah," said the tiny man from behind his ledger. "All man this hotel good-good man. All master's things stay safe this hotel."

"It's your worry," I told him. "If anything is missing, it's you who'll have to pay. I ask for a key. You give me no key. You say my things safe—now see you keep them safe." Whether because of this warning, or because of the uncommon honesty of the clientele, I lost nothing in my short stay.

The hotel, I knew, was not far from the water. Wherever I am I never miss an opportunity of getting close to the sea and looking at ships, so after dinner I walked out in the direction I knew would lead me to the harbour. The streets seemed empty, but in a moment, from nowhere out of the darkness, appeared a swarm of youths, barefoot in white shorts and singlets.

"You want nice girl, sah? I take you see my little sister, sah. Very young, very sweet-sweet girl, sah. Very clean. Just sixteen years, sah. You come see my sister, sah."

I walked fast and tried to throw them off. I turned round and told them all to go to hell. It was no use; any white man walking in that part of Lagos must be a sailor, anyone else would have his own car. Sailors, it is well known, only want one thing. It could only be bashfulness or hypocrisy that kept me from admitting it—unless I was holding out for a lower price. The most persistent boy—he drove me back at last to my hotel—kept saying, in pedantic words and with a dignified manner: "Kindly to remember me, sah. I am original boy who approach you first. You obligated to consider me. I make you first proposition, sah. Not these poor boys"—dismissing them with a wave of his hand. "I conduct you good-good house, sah. Very fine house. Very clean. Only five minutes' walk, sah. Good healthy exercise —come, sah. I accompany you to good-good house." He might have been a curate advising a bishop as to an appropriate lodging for the night.

I endured my hotel for three nights, thinking of all that travellers must have endured in the past on ports of the West Coast, and grateful for the week of comfort I had spent in Accra. But on the fourth evening, when I got back after the day's work, I found someone else's luggage on my bed. I rang for the boy and asked him what it meant.

"Other master come stay hotel, sah. Other master share this room with this master."

"He can't share this room. It's mine. I booked it."

"Hotel manager say this master share room with other master. No more room this hotel. New master very nice; he good-good man. Master be happy share room with other master."

I went downstairs and rang the flat where Ian was living, since returning with me from Ghana. It was a small flat on one of the main roads out of town, rented by the firm for the use of Ian and his second-in-command, Roy Paulson. I asked Ian if he would drive over at once and help me find a new hotel.

"Certainly not," said Ian. "You must be fed up with hotels. We'll squeeze up and make room for you in here."

"Sure that's all right?"

"Of course it's all right. I'll be over in ten minutes."

Having assured myself of an escape, I could explain to the manager what I thought of him and his hotel with an easy mind.

*   *   *   *   *

The Nigerian staff of *Drum* had just been reconstituted; how often this had happened previously no one could now remember. A trusted employee had been allowed a number of loans to help him out; when suspicions as to his honesty first arose, he could not be fired because he owed the firm so much already. He had wisely made use of this respite to get his hands on a further £200—which he did not trouble to ask for as a loan, knowing it would be refused. In the clean-up which followed his departure, a new start had been made on both the management and editorial sides. My editorial staff, I found, consisted virtually of two men—Nelson Ottah, who had lately been brought in as local editor, though subject to the authority of Agnew in Accra and a young cameraman, Matthew Faji.

Ottah was young, slim, handsome in a demoniac way, with a lazy drawl and a continual smile—a smile which I quickly learned should not be interpreted as bland good-nature. Faji, though he had already had years of experience on Nigerian papers, looked little more than big schoolboy or a student. He lacked Ottah's command of language and at first when we talked I could never be sure whether he had understood me, or I him. The three of us held what might be called a "conference", at which I outlined my plans, much as I had already done in Accra. Matthew sat with his head in his hands gazing at me either because he did not really follow what I was saying, or perhaps because he did, and found it wonderful. Ottah's smile became both sweeter and more contemptuous as I described my intentions for the paper.

When I had finished, he asked me politely: "Sir. Is that all you have to tell us?"

"Yes, that's all."

"If I understand you correctly, sir, what you are saying is that you intend to turn *Drum* into a well-known and respected picture magazine—something almost on the lines of *Paris-Match* or *Life*?"

"Well, in time . . ." I nodded.

"May I enquire, sir, where is the staff to produce a magazine this nature? Here in Lagos there is only Faji and myself. How in the circumstances are you proposing to begin?"

"I'm proposing to begin with you and Faji."

Ottah laughed. "Allow me to point out, sir, that we have here territory as big as Germany—and you are suggesting that we two cover all that happens which is of interest in that territory. Are you aware, sir, that we are not even provided with a car by the management?"

This was dangerous ground; however willing I might be to provide transport for the staff, I had no authority to do so.

"A magazine," I said, "is not a newspaper. We are not obliged to cover everything of interest and importance that happens in Nigeria. All we have to do is to make, once a month, a magazine people want to buy. It's true that later on we shall need to have journalists and cameramen at least in the main centres—but at this moment we've not got them. And *still* we have to make a magazine that will sell."

Nelson thought for a moment. "But where will we begin?"

"Where would you?" I asked. "It's your country."

"Where I would begin, sir," said Nelson, rather irritably, "is not the point. Perhaps I would never at all begin an undertaking of this kind. It is, as you say, my country—but to make a magazine of this sort is not my idea but yours."

"Very well then," I said, "we will begin with pictures, and we'll begin in Lagos. Tomorrow we meet again, and we'll each have three ideas for stories, and on these we shall get to work."

But the matter was not to be so easily disposed of. "You spoke just now," said Nelson, "of making a magazine such as *Paris-Match* or *Life* —is that not so?"

"Yes, I did."

"That means that you admire these papers and the sort of stories which they publish?"

"I admire *Paris-Match*, and I used to admire *Life*. Why do you ask?"

"Because since this is what you like, and since we have never made such stories in this country, I presume you will be bringing out some white journalists from England or America, and some photographers from Italy or France. Then these people will tell us what to put into *rum* in order to interest Nigerians?"

"No," I said sharply. "I don't mean to do that at all. I'm sure you know best what will interest Nigerians, and it will be for you and your staff to decide what stories you mean to work on."

"In that case," Nelson remarked, springing with a particularly sweet smile the trap to which all this had been leading up, "perhaps you will explain to me, Mr. Hopkinson, why a white man—Mr. Agnew in Accra, who has never been in Nigeria for a whole week in his life— has been put over me to tell me what to do, and to instruct me in what will interest my own people?"

"Look, Nelson," I said. "I'm new to this organisation. I believe
you're fairly new to it too. I'm not prepared at this moment to argue
in favour of every arrangement that's been made. There may be some
which ought to be altered. Equally, I'm not going to undertake to
make changes until I know the capacities of everyone involved."

"You imply, sir, that I may be no good at my job. In that case, sir,
you ought to sack me."

"What I am saying is that I don't know one way or the other. You
may very well be the best journalist in Nigeria—or the worst. We
haven't worked together yet, so I don't know. I can promise you
that, if you are good, I'll support you to the utmost. If I think you're
on the way to being good, I'll do everything I can to help you become
better. If I find you're lousy, I shall say so."

"Very well, sir. Then there remains only one question to be discussed. May I ask if you are in favour of the current system as regards
salaries?"

"What system?"

"That a white clerk is paid far more than the editor of the Nigeria
edition?"

"What I believe myself, Nelson, is that everyone should be paid
according to the contribution he makes—irrespective of his colour,
his age, his sex, the number of his children, or the grandparents dependent on him for support. However, I didn't invent the system of
payment used on the West Coast. I didn't even invent the system
used by *Drum*—for which I haven't yet been working a whole month.
All I can say is this: if you'll help me to build up this paper in Nigeria,
I'll do my utmost to see you get a fair return."

"Do I understand that you are asking me to trust you, sir? On the
understanding that if I make a success of editing this edition, you will
support my application for improved payment and conditions?"

"Exactly."

"Okay, sir. Then I shall trust you. . . . When do you wish to see
the material we have collected for the next issue?"

"Now."

As I looked slowly through the material Nelson had assembled I
felt, for the first time since I came out, a glimmer of hope for the future
of our magazine. The writing was sometimes long-winded and
repetitive. There were passages of involved irony which could have
been understood and accepted nowhere, except in an 18th-century
House of Commons. But there were flashes of brilliance; phrases of
revelation. Above all, the choice of subjects was first-rate; in Ot-

we had stumbled upon a natural journalist. I could feel Nelson's sharp
eye on me as I looked through the work.

"It's good," I said. "Between the three of us we can make a
magazine."

"Good, you mean, for a West African, for some strange fellow that
you meet in Lagos? Not good for a graduate of Oxford, or for a correspondent of *The Times*."

"Oh, hell," I said. "Just take it that it's good, will you, and that I
look forward to working with you? We're both journalists; we should
be able to understand each other."

Nelson gave me a smile from which, for a moment, the demoniac
gleam was missing.

"Okay, sir," he said. "Now what?"

"Now a drink."

*   *   *   *   *

Next morning it was Matthew's turn. Nervously he led me to the
darkroom. Outside was a chair and a desk, the only territory marked
out as his own. With some difficulty he found a second chair and sat
down facing me.

"Well," I said. "Let's have a look at your pictures."

Matthew fished out a big bundle of prints, and we started slowly
going through them. Nine out of ten were useless—pictures taken in
the open air by flash, so that even the West African sunshine looked
artificial. Portraits of Nigerian politicians flashed indoors, black faces
against dark backgrounds, made still darker by the false shadows of
the flash. Just every now and then, however, a picture with real life
and charm. Slowly I began to explain: "The flash gives an effect. You
see?—an easy result. It's a technique for someone who can't take
pictures properly. Someone who can take pictures doesn't need this flash.
It's not for you, Matthew. You've got to learn to work without it."

"But what about light, sir? Often there is no light."

"You work by whatever light there is, indoors or out. And you use
your knowledge and your camera to make the utmost of that light."

"But——"

"Look, Matthew," I said. "You live in Nigeria. You live in bright
sunshine. Good cameramen are working this way in Sweden, Finland,
England, North America. In countries where they don't have half the
light you've got . . . Do you mean you can't be *half* as good a cameraman as they are?"

Matthew smiled, and we continued. To Matthew what I was saying
seemed all upside-down. Flash equipment was the badge of the

professional. His flash-gun marked him out for what he was—a man of the press, far superior to amateur snapshotters. Now I was wanting him to leave this mark of honour behind.

"See it this way, Matthew. You started as a boy when you first left school. You had a schoolboy camera—a Box Brownie. You took a few pictures, maybe at school sports meetings, and you sold some to a newspaper for ten shillings each. Is that right? Is that what you did?"

Matthew's face broke into a grin. He nodded.

"After a time you sold more pictures. You concentrated on one paper. They got to know you. Then there was a vacancy—at first it was a vacancy in the darkroom. You asked for it and got it. Is that right?"

Again Matthew smiled.

"So you worked there for a year or two—and someone left. Now they started sending you on jobs. You knew the sort of pictures they wanted—faces with a big smile and the teeth showing—and you took them. Before long you were the best man they had for big smiles and teeth. It was Faji they sent to photograph even Prime Ministers with big smiles and all their teeth showing. Am I right?"

Matthew giggled. "Mr. Ottah tell you all this."

"No," I said. "I'm reading it in your pictures. Now you've come here—to *Drum*. This is going to be something new too—another step in the career of Matthew Faji—see? I don't *want* you to go on as you have been doing, photographing big smiles and teeth. That's over now. You're going to take photographs the modern way. If the sky is gloomy, your pictures will show it dark and gloomy. If the room's smoky, your pictures show that too. Your skill will be this—in spite of the dark sky and the smoky room—people will see what's happening. They'll see the men fighting under the dark sky. They'll see the couple kissing in the smoky room—and they'll be *really* kissing, not staring into a camera with startled eyes. D'you see what I'm telling you, Matthew? I want the dark room—*and* I want the couple kissing."

"But what must I do if there is *no* light? In Nigeria lots of our houses are small and dark. It isn't like the big houses in America...."

At the end I gave Matthew an assignment; it was one which I thought would appeal to him. He was to go out into the streets of Lagos and photograph all the pretty girls he saw. If there was a girl who looked pretty from the back, but had an ugly face, he was to photograph her from the back. If there was a girl with only pretty ankles, he was to photograph just her ankles—or her hair-do—or her body down to the waist—or whatever it was about her that attracted him. He was to use whatever light there was, sunshine, street lamps, an open door—anything except flash. In two days' time we'd go through what he'd taken, and we'd talk again.

* * * * *

In the flat where I had moved in with Ian and Roy, a cheerful bachelor existence was maintained. "We took it really for the bar," Ian explained. "We're on the main road, so it's hellishly noisy, and there isn't any air-conditioning. But we liked the bar. David! Get the master a cold beer. Bring us three cold-cold beers!"

Our life here was a mixture of the uncomfortable and the lordly. The noise of traffic was so great we would often have to suspend conversation for a minute, and sleep after daybreak was impossible. In the tiny bathroom we had some difficulty in getting ourselves all bathed and shaved before half-past eight. But the service was princely. We would call out to the boy—David's assistant, a child of twelve—to bring us a glass of water, the evening paper, to go to the bedroom for a book, or run out into the street to fetch a taxi. We ate our dinner on stools drawn up to the bar, and afterwards would lie back in easy chairs with our legs sprawled out, drinking bottle after bottle of cold beer.

"I suppose you know what you're in for with Nelson?" Ian remarked one evening.

"I think I do."

"He'll resent your criticism—at the same time he's too shrewd to work for anyone who doesn't give him criticism. He'll insist that he's in the right, yet he'll keep on putting himself in the wrong, in order to put you there too."

"Look," I said, "I don't know how it is in business, but as an editor I'll put up with *anything*—if only I can have people of talent to work with. I'd crawl round Lagos on my hands and knees tomorrow to find one more good journalist or cameraman. And if anyone tries to get rid of the two we've got, I'll strangle him with my bare hands. I'll work all day for years with the most exacting and difficult people you could find, provided they'll give me what I want."

"It must be a hell of a life," said Roy, who wore shorts, raising one of his long handsome legs and examining it thoughtfully.

"What must?"

"Crawling about on hands and knees looking for journalists."

One evening when we came home late, a figure peeped out from under the stairs and saluted us. Looking closer, I saw he had made himself a kind of home beneath the staircase. There was bedding, a light, and a cooking stove. A barrier of hanging sacks secured his privacy from people passing up and down.

"What's he doing?" I asked. "Is he supposed to be there—or has he just wandered in?"

"Who? Haji? He's our night-watchman," Ian answered. "The flat was broken into once, so we took on Haji for protection."

"And does he live here?"

"I should say so. He not only lives here, he makes a thriving business out of it."

"How so?"

"Lagos is crowded out. Every hut or shack you see has got two or more families living in it. People rent the cracks between two shops or houses. Thousands of people haven't anywhere to sleep at all. Haji lets out the pavement in front of the house as sleeping quarters. It's a wide pavement, he gets in three rows. The rows nearest the house pay most because they're furthest from the traffic."

"How much do they pay?"

"Probably a shilling a month, or something of the sort. The second row down pay sixpence. The bottom ones—who are liable to be walked on by everyone and have their legs run over by bicycles or lorries—he probably takes a penny or two off when he can."

"And this is a business? This is Haji's living?"

"Oh—he's out all day, so I've no doubt he's got other business interests, fiddles on the side. But he'd be happy to be night-watchman even if we never paid him, in order to have a corner under the stairs for himself, and bully the people who sleep outside on the pavement."

I thought of Haji's staircase retreat in a new light. Compared to sleeping on the pavement and having your legs run over by bicycles it was clearly luxury.

"What happens when it rains?"

"When it rains they all vanish. God knows where they go."

"That explains," I said, "what I saw on my first evening."

"What was that?"

"Well, I was walking round the town—down by the docks where there are big offices. Most offices have a sort of verandah on the ground floor, a tiled space surrounded by arches."

"Yes?"

"Each of these tiled spaces had a family or two in it. They'd got a lamp, and sometimes a bit of fire, and they were settling down for the night—some of them talking, and the children nestling under coats or rugs. I wondered where on earth they came from."

"Same as ours do here. They'll pay a few shillings a month to the night-watchman, and he'll allow them to keep their own space free. By daylight they all have to be gone, before anyone turns up at the offices."

It was my last night in Lagos. Next morning I would fly to Kano, the ancient walled city in the far north of Nigeria, and from Kano I should catch the plane, by way of Leopoldville and the Belgian Congo, to Johannesburg.

Ian called for two more cold beers; Roy had gone out somewhere for the evening and would not be back till late.

"Well?" he asked. "Now you've seen the whole set-up. What are the prospects?"

I thought for a minute. "Until I came to Lagos I honestly didn't see how we would ever get a paper out at all. I couldn't see where the raw material for making one could possibly come from. You haven't got the staff, and what staff you have isn't properly equipped—it hasn't even begun to be equipped. And for me the biggest headache is that I shall have no real contact with them. Stuck away there in Johannesburg, I can do nothing but praise or bellyache. If the stuff I'm sent is lousy, as far as that month goes, I've just got to put it in the paper—or most of it—but what I ought to do is chuck it back, explain why it's wrong, and start again. I'm not surprised the edition has been all bits and pieces—a couple of stories from Ghana, three from Nigeria. An account of something in South Africa which nobody has ever heard of. A life of Jack Johnson—who's been dead since God knows when, and some jokes and Pen Pals to fill in the holes. I'm much more surprised that some sort of a ruddy issue has pitched up regularly each month."

"It hasn't been as regular as all that," Ian said. "It often pitches up weeks late."

"Well, it's going to pitch up in time from now on. That's certain. But since coming down here I think it's just possible the magazine may have something in it. Nelson's a find, and I believe Matthew may be too, if only he can trust himself and not just work the way all the other photographers in Lagos will be doing."

"How did that story he did for you turn out?"

"It had two fairly good pictures in it. But . . ."

"But what?"

"The point is he could see which were the good pictures. Oh hell, I wish I could stay up here six months."

"H'm," said Ian, reaching for his beer and ignoring my last remark.

"So you reckon you'll be able to give the sales out here a pretty good tonk?"

"Put up your sales? I don't know about *that*. I just mean I can see it may be possible for some sort of magazine to be produced."

"Well, we *know* it's possible to do that," said Ian, "because we've been doing it. If you can get good work out of Nelson and Faji and Christian, then we ought to be able to do something more than just bring out a magazine. We ought to steam ahead. We ought to start making dough."

"Maybe we shall. . . . However, you've got to lay out a little dough first, before you start raking it all in."

"How's that? What's up? What d'you want now?" Ian sounded alarmed.

"A new camera for Faji. He's working with a worn-out Rollei, just like Christian. Matthew's ready for something better—a high-speed miniature camera. A Leica for choice."

"And what's that going to set us back?"

"About a hundred and twenty, or a hundred and thirty."

"God Almighty!" exclaimed Ian, horrified. "We can't spend *that*. I should be torn in pieces."

"Well," I said, "we could get him a Japanese imitation for around sixty. It won't last as long, but he can take photographs with it."

"But we've only just bought a new camera for Christian. That' knocked us back sixty, plus a few quid for dishes and so on."

"I know. But Christian's too far away for them to pass the camer across."

Ian looked at me suspiciously.

"I tell you what. I can sneak one camera through my budget, bu I can't possibly get two. It's more than my life's worth. You fix it a up with Jim when you go down South. You tell him it's necessary fo Faji to have a new high-speed camera. Cameras are cheaper dow there anyway. You buy what you want in Jo'burg, and, the next tim anyone's travelling this way he can bring it up."

"Okay," I said unwittingly. "I'll fix that." Then, suddenly remen bering how Faji had crammed all his negatives away into a dus drawer, I added: "Provided you'll get Faji a filing cabinet for h negatives—on your budget."

CHAPTER IV

WELCOME TO SOUTH AFRICA

My PLANE WAS due out of Kano at four in the morning, but planes are not so punctual over the continent of Africa as they are in Europe, and it was the following midnight before I got away on the twelve-hour journey to Johannesburg. On the way down I thought a lot about the last two weeks, and also of what lay ahead.

I felt committed in my mind to the *Drum* staff in West Africa; to Matthew Faji and Christian to help them become photographers; to Nelson for encouragement, and whatever guidance he would accept in his drive to soar to the summit of West African journalism, dragging —as I hoped—our paper after him; to Ian, to try to help him achieve his ambition of a West African edition which made a handsome profit.

All these wishes and ambitions could be realised, I felt sure. My difficulty would be to do enough to help them forward at a distance of several thousand miles. It would be like editing, from the Urals or a city in the Middle West, a magazine to appear in Manchester. However, I had at least seen West Africa and I now knew our own people here—which was more than any previous editor had had the chance to do. If I were to come up two or three times each year, and keep constantly in touch with them all by letter, it might just be possible to work effectively. Meantime I felt all my real troubles and difficulties lay ahead. West Africa was a lotus-land, where black and white could be friends, enemies—indeed lovers if they wanted—without the race-aries being invoked, from inside themselves as well as outside; and an editor could take his staff round the corner for a drink. Things were likely to be very different in Johannesburg.

Jan Smuts, the Johannesburg airport, was speckled with black and white storks as our plane flew in. They were rummaging for food in the long grass, and stepped with long-legged dignity out of the plane's path. Inside the airport buildings passengers were collected into a lounge, from which a number of small offices opened out along one wall. When a light shone outside the door of one of these offices, the name of a passenger was called, and he or she went forward to be interviewed.

"Mr. Hopkinson?" The official turned my passport over. "We've been expecting you."

"How did you know I was coming out here?"

"I saw a paragraph about you in the evening paper. There was a picture, and I never forget a face. Well, that's all in order," he said genially. "Just go through and pick out your luggage."

Outside in the main hall a young man came up to me—short, sallow, a hatchet face and a mop of dark hair over one eye. He was wearing a sports shirt and slacks.

"I'm Humphrey Tyler," he said gruffly. "What about a cup of coffee before we go up to the office?"

I didn't want any coffee, but I was glad of the chance for a talk which might help me find my feet. Tyler was a South African from Durban. When Sylvester Stein—the editor who succeeded Anthony Sampson and whom I had briefly met in London—parted company with Jim Bailey, Tyler had been sent for to take over, and had been in charge for the past six months.

"Had you had much to do with picture magazines before?"

"Not a thing," said Tyler cheerfully. "Not a single ruddy thing— though I'd worked for a bit in the *Drum* office in Durban. I guess they just couldn't find anyone else."

"I think you've kept it going extremely well."

"Thanks. All the same, it's been hell. Pure bloody HELL! Thank God you've come out. It'll be your baby now," he added with some relish.

"What's been the trouble?"

"Trouble? The lot! Printing. The staff. The bloody West African edition—don't know what they want and always complaining when they get it. And of course the management. I could manage all right if I were left alone—but just to keep the paper ticking over with the staff we've got is one hell of a job. Trying to do it with one hand and fend off proprietors with the other is too much. However, it shouldn't be so bad for you," he added reassuringly. "You know photography, I suppose you know what you want, and you'll have the authority to get your own way."

"Maybe," I said doubtfully. "My worry is not knowing the country. Being new, I won't know which way I want to go—or whether it possible or safe to go that way. Thank God you're here! I shall rely on you for what we can safely say and what we can't."

"For a while," Humphrey explained, a little uncomfortably. "For as long as I'm around."

"How d'you mean 'for a while'? You're not leaving, are you?"

"Yes. I'm going to the *Rand Daily Mail*. I pack up at the end of this month."

"In a fortnight? But who do I take over from then? How do I pick up the routine, get to know the staff and so on?"

"There's a couple of weeks yet," said Humphrey philosophically. "You'll get the hang of things all right in that time. At least I hope you will."

*   *   *   *   *

Drum offices, when we reached them, were a small block of about a dozen glass-partitioned rooms on a first floor. Fat blue-painted pillars carried a low white-washed ceiling. The linoleum on the floors was new, but so thin that it showed heelmarks everywhere as if it had been tar. I was shown into the glass box which would be my office; it held a desk, two chairs, a bookshelf, a filing cabinet and a square blue carpet. I opened the top drawer of the filing cabinet. It was crammed with papers in confusion; stuffed there, I guessed, by my departing predecessors—in an ecstasy of relief that it would never fall to their lot to answer all those letters, weigh carefully those applications for jobs, or read through those sprawling hand-written articles or poems.

Rashly I tugged at the lower drawer. It stuck: gulped, rattled—and flew open. Bursting out over the floor came hundreds of folders, entries for a *Drum* short story competition, each with a stamped addressed envelope, an entry coupon, and a form for the judges to register their opinions. I picked up a handful. "I consider this one of the most promising entries. It should certainly receive careful consideration in the final judging," signed "Ezekiel Mphalele". Underneath was written "So do I", signed "Can". With difficulty I levered the forgotten entries back into the drawer, telling myself I'd go through them when I got a quiet day.

Outside my door was a large office into which seven or eight desks and chairs were being carried.

"What's going on?" I asked.

"We're moving in," said Humphrey. "This is our first day in our new home. You can think yourself damned lucky. You couldn't scratch you neck in the old office without knocking someone else's typewriter off his desk."

As the morning went on I was introduced to any of my staff who were around, to some of the staff of our sister paper *Golden City Post*—Sunday tabloid—to the advertising and circulation managers, and finally taken in to see Jim Bailey. He smiled, shook hands and turned

back to the set of photographs he was being shown by Jurgen Schadeberg. I knew Jurgen by name for my years of commenting on *Drum*
by letter. He was a fresh-faced, heavily-built young man with a friendly
manner, who had not quite lost his German accent. He took photographs for *Drum* and did the lay-outs—that is, planned the arrangement
of pictures, headings and typematter on the pages.

I took one of the pictures from Jim. They were photographs of a
riot. There had been a strike of clothing workers at a place along the
Reef called Benoni. Black cops, well clad and helmeted, were laying
into the strikers with long wooden clubs. One old man on his knees
raised up a hand appealingly to the cop about to strike him; you could
see that seconds from now the old man would be dangling a broken
arm.

"Thank God!" I said.

Both Jim and Jurgen looked at me with astonishment.

"Are these yours?" I asked Jurgen.

"No. They're being offered to us by a free-lance—Ian Berry. He
does odd jobs for us now and then."

"Okay," I said, "we'll buy them," and I made a mental note of Ian
Berry's name.

In the daily haze and muddle in which we spend our days, never
fully aware of what we are doing or thinking, only half-conscious of
ourselves or anyone around us, there are occasional lucid intervals
like gaps of vision in a wall of mist. For an hour all one's senses are
awake; every word and scene makes a direct impact on the mind; and
one lives for a moment as we are meant to live continually. Such an
interval came to me on my first morning in Johannesburg.

Jim Bailey had kindly booked me a room at his club; I could stay
there for a week, he said, while I found somewhere to live. He
suggested now that we go there for lunch, and offered to drive me in
his car. During the short journey from *Drum's* office to the club—
journey I have made hundreds of times since on foot and seen nothing
calling for a second glance—everything impressed me like the introduction to a film, in which every incident is full of meaning for the
story that will follow.

A building was coming down. African convicts, in what looked
like red-striped football jerseys, were demolishing the walls in clouds
of dust. At strategic points among the rubble stood white police,
rifles resting in the crooks of their arms. Further on three Africans were
walking; suddenly the middle one dived, turned, twisted and bolted
away into the traffic. The others were after him, and in a minute he

grabbed him from in front of a car and were marching him off with his wrists behind his shoulders. The "Ghost Squad" cops, Jim Bailey explained, and their prisoner pulled in for some 'pass' offence.

On the pavement was a little crowd, blacks and whites stopped on their way home from work to listen. In the middle were three ragged black boys, playing a penny-whistle, a guitar and a tea-box 'cello fitted up with a broom handle and a piece of string, while two smaller ones walked around in the roadway on their hands.

I was struck by the casualness of Jo'burg manners. At a traffic-light turned green, a driver in front held up a long line of cars while he hooted insistently for a paper to be brought out to him by a street-seller. Vans would double-park in busy roadways, their African drivers walking casually away, leaving following traffic to sort itself out as best it could.

There were some odd surprises. Having parked the car to walk the last fifty yards to the club, we were forced to step into the road for a group of overalled African workers. From their intense and bending forms I supposed there had been an accident. But no—they were an audience, leaning over to give advice and encouragement to a couple of draughts-players seated on the kerb. The men played their game with drama and aplomb, thumping each piece down or sweeping it aside with defiant or triumphant gestures. It was a busy street, the midday rush-hour, but nobody shouted at them or moved them on. They just sat there on the pavement in this supposedly rough-neck town, their supporters taking up what room was left, and everyone must step into the roadway to get past.

After lunch Jim asked if I would like a quick run round to see the city before he drove out to his farm for the weekend. At a turn of the road on a hill outside we got out and looked back. A long row of sky-scrapers set down on the open plain was framed by a number of arti-ficial, flat-topped hills, a yellowish-grey in colour—the renowned "mine-dumps" of Johannesburg, huge mounds of sand from which most of the gold had been extracted, but which might one day, by newer methods, be worth sifting through a second time.

"It's nothing but an overgrown mining-camp," said Jim, looking with proprietary affection at the city. "And the life is just mining-camp life too."

*   *   *   *   *

Johannesburg is a city of a million people—but the million is made up by all the whites who live in the rich suburbs to the north, where almost every house has its big garden, tennis-court and swimming-pool, and the locations to the south and east where the African workers swarm in endless rows of tidy hen-houses. The actual heart of the city is tiny—one can walk across it in ten minutes either way.

The gaunt new building housing the *Drum* offices stood at about the far end of that ten minutes, in a district where the skyscraper centre dwindles down into a shambles of small factories, arid waste patches, and the half-bare, half built-over lots of second-hand car dealers, displaying their unconvincing clichés in both Afrikaans and English—"Uitgesoekte Gebruikte Karre", "Quality Used Cars". Southwards, across a couple of streets and a dusty stretch used as a car-park, is the Native Affairs Department for the City of Johannesburg, its name changed later by a masterpiece of official tact to "The Non-European Affairs Department". Outside this building there was usually a queue, Africans hoping for passes, permits to remain, houses to live in; and it was hardly possible to walk from the car park to the office without being asked: "Any job for a boy, baas? Any job for a good boy, my baas?"

Wandering around the streets at lunch time, I became gradually familiar with the area and its particular sprawling squalor. SPORTY CAPS, HI HO TYRES and HI HO BANDE ran the notices painted on the walls. HEAR LUTHULI, FREEDOM SQUARE, SUNDAY, someone had chalked up. Solly's café advertised HAMBURGERS and FIREWORKS. The dirty yard behind the general store was a shebeen, an illegal drinking-den. When any of my staff were missing, this was the first place to enquire. One could ring through and ask for "Can" or "Casey", and the voice at the other end would say they knew no one of that name; then, after five minutes or so, Can or Casey would drift quietly back into the office.

The only building of any style or oddity was the bogus castle down the road—a stucco battlemented fortress, painted in the colours of tomato soup and rancid butter—in which it was said some now famous cigarette firm had begun its life. Now the castle had become the stronghold of Naomi Beauty Form Gold Medal Corsetry, and at midday a throng of coloured girls—visibly not purchasers of the company's products—would hang round the doors, giggling, pushing one another, and teasing the van-drivers as they went in and out.

On stretches of waste ground lean horses browsed, nuzzling for blades of grass among fragments of iron bedsteads, brick-bats and rusty cars. On one was a gambling school for Africans; they looked suspiciously at me for a time or two and then must have recognised that I was harmless. On another stretch in the evenings an old tyre was always burning. This, as I later got to know, was the headquarters of a gang of African boys who lived wild throughout the summer. Having observed them for some time, we one day rounded up a dozen into the office and talked to them. They perched on desks and tables, wide-eyed, suspicious, ready, I felt, to soar off through the ceiling like a flock of starlings at a sudden noise.

They slept, they said, in the derelict vehicles of a car-breaking firm just opposite my office windows, but they could not take possession of their sleeping-quarters until the last of the workers had gone home. So they would gather at the same spot each evening, set fire to an old tyre which they had either cadged or stolen, and sit round the evil-smelling blaze on old buckets or upturned oil-drums. Once or twice, as I went past on the way to collect my car, they looked, in the blaze and drifting smoke and flicker, like a collection of child-demons struggling to pickle and roast themselves into full-grown fiends. I knew already how they made their living. I had seen them prowling in the half-light on the edges of cinema and theatre queues. "Tickey* for bread, please, baas." "Tickey for supper, please, baas." "Tickey for bread," they chanted.

Having acquired a pocketful of pennies, they would dart away to a lonely corner in an arcade. Here, in a spatter of torn and dirty playing cards, they gambled away their takings to each other. The gang were easy to recognise from their practised beggars' voices, their bold expressions, filthy fragments of torn clothing, and the fact that, as they scuttled off down the street, two would hang back for a cripple who came limping after. We asked how they managed to survive the winter.

"Too cold winter-time," they said. "All go back home."

But weren't their parents angry? Few of them had parents. Nearly all lived with "an auntie". The auntie beat them for running away, but not hard, because she'd been rid of the bother of them for eight months. Now they would be a nuisance around the place for the short winter, and with the summer they'd be gone again. When we asked about school they shook their heads; the word seemed to convey no meaning to them.

Dotted around the back-streets and on the edge of the waste land were what looked like hen-houses, or stores for workmen's tools. Green-painted as a rule, balanced on low brick supports, each had a flap which let down towards the street. These were the so-called "coffee carts", where many of the African workers got their midday meals, big plates of porridge with lumps of meat in it, bowls of thick

* "Tickey" is South African for a threepenny bit.

soup or stew, and cups of tea or "coffee". None of them had running water. Plates were washed by dipping in a bucket. Every now and then there would be an outcry against the coffee carts in the white press; white authority would declare they were unhygienic and should be swept away; letter-writers would hold out the threat of an epidemic which "might easily affect white areas as well". However, the coffee-carts survived, providing midday warmth for the stomachs of the hungry, and a living for the plump soft-voiced African women who owned them—and who were treated with the same good nature and consideration by their clients as a popular barmaid in an English pub.

"Good-bye, my sister*" I heard one man say, wiping his greasy mouth on a still greasier sleeve. "Thank you, my sister, for the food."

Though we were on the edge of the city centre, some sidewalks only were paved. On others there would be nothing but a kerb with an enclosure of red dust—or slime in the rain of summer afternoons—with rank weeds struggling for life along the edges. When a lorry was driven up on to the pavement, cracking a dozen paving-stones to fragments, they remained cracked for good. When a manhole cover was stolen from the crossroads near the office, the manhole stayed open for six months; stray horses stepped carefully around it, cars bumped their way over, and laughing boys threatened to push one another down.

"Won't someone fall into that after dark and break a leg?" I asked naïvely.

"If you stick around here after dark you'll get worse than broken legs," was the reply. I stuck around many evenings, however, and met little except the dark and silence. Coming out late from the office one evening to pick up an old Ford lent me by Jim Bailey "till you can get some transport of your own", I found the bonnet prised up and two Africans busy over the battery. They ran off, leaving an old jacket and the set of tools with which they had been busily unfastening the connections.

I threw the jacket on the ground for them to pick up later, but kept the tools for my trouble—and in the general interest of the motoring community.

*   *   *   *   *

I had hoped to have two or three free days to look round at the office and get to know my staff, but I was at once in the thick of every-thing. The South African edition had just gone to press, and it was necessary to start in straight away on the West African.

* "Sister" is used among the Africans without any sense of family relationship, much as an English workman might say "duck", or an American "honey".

Drum's arrangement as regards editions was a curious one. The South African edition for, say, May would be on the streets around the 20th April—in the normal manner of magazine publishing—having been printed four or five days earlier; the few intervening days being needed to get the magazine distributed throughout the country. In South Africa, therefore, we had to be thinking only a week or two ahead. But the West African edition, printed in Johannesburg from material air-freighted down from Ghana and Nigeria, had a long and complicated journey before it could meet its readers. The printed copies had to make their way by train for several days to Cape Town; be unloaded in the docks; get on board a steamer to West Africa; be unloaded again in Lagos and Accra; sorted and repacked in appropriate quantities; and then distributed over vast territories by train, mammy-wagon, bicycle, canoe, or whatever means might be available. All this meant that, instead of working on the May West African edition during April, we were busy on the one dated July, which would not go on sale till the end of June.

Because of this long delay, we could of course cover nothing topical, and in spite of all our caution we would sometimes be caught out—perhaps because someone died or a Minister went out of office. But in the absence of better-organised competition, and in the general dearth of reading matter on the West Coast, *Drum* somehow managed to go ahead. With our tiny staff, most of whom in any case did not work on the West African edition, it was a strenuous two weeks' work to get the magazine planned, laid out, set up in type, corrected and put to bed. Meantime it was essential for our reporters and cameramen to get busy locally, so that I should have something ready for the next South African edition. On the first Monday morning therefore, after a short talk with Humphrey Tyler, I sent for the assistant editor, Can Themba.

Can (his full name was Daniel Canadoce Themba) was a tallish, lightly-built African in his early thirties. He walked with a springy step, wore a bright red shirt, and a small knitted cap was perched on top of his unusually round head, giving him a jaunty knowing look. He seemed to have been hurrying to reach the office, for sweat poured like water down his forehead, forming fresh drops and rivulets which he brushed away as he talked.

"Cripes, chief! Am I glad to meet you! I remember the letters you used to write us from England. I never thought we should really see you out here. Welcome to South Africa!"

"And I'm happy to meet you, Can," I said, shaking hands. "I've read and admired your stories. D'you manage to do any writing now?"

"Off and on, chief. Off and on. But *Drum* keeps us all pretty busy—you know how it is."

"Later on," I said, "we'll have a meeting, and I'll get you to introduce me to the staff. But we may have to leave that for a day or two as the printers are shouting for lay-outs for West Africa. What I suggest is this. Humphrey and Joe and I will get down to the West African stuff—and you get the rest of the staff organised and busy, so there'll be something in the bag when West Africa's cleared out of the way."

"Okay, chief. What do you want us to get working on?"

"Whatever stories you've got in hand. I suppose you make out a list each month, don't you? You've probably got various ideas half-finished, and others you were planning to do later. Just pick the ones it's easiest to complete, and get everyone started on something. We can fill the gaps in later."

Can mopped his forehead doubtfully. He had a habit of chewing a pin and switching it from side to side of his mouth as he talked.

"What system are you working on now?" I asked. "How d'you get the month's work planned and organised?"

"Well . . ." Can answered, switching his pin. "We've really been waiting for you to come out, to see what system you prefer. At present we all just go out from day to day according to the news."

"What were you going to do this morning?"

"Have a look through the papers, chief, and see what's cooking."

"Good," I said. "And let me know by lunch-time what everyone has started on."

Can smiled cheerfully and went out. "Be seeing you later then, chief. . . . Come on, boys," he called to the others. "We've got to work out some stories and get busy."

In the course of my first full morning's work I had a couple of surprises. The first was pleasant. I had long since made up my mind that the very first thing we had to get for *Drum* was a lively, properly-printed cover, in place of the existing confused and muddy mess. A young man, Claude Davies, who had been general manager for the past few months, had, I found, done all the preliminary work for exactly what I had in mind. Samples and estimates were all set out in a folder. After some discussion in Jim Bailey's office, the plan was agreed to, and I felt we were off to a lucky start.

The second surprise was not so reassuring; it concerned the new camera for Faji. Ian had already warned me back in Lagos that I should need to get agreement for this purchase in Johannesburg. I mentioned it therefore to Claude Davies, supposing that, as general manager, he could quickly give me his agreement.

"What's that going to set us back?"

"A hundred and fifty for a Leica . . ." then, seeing the expression on Claude's face, I fell back rapidly on my second proposition, ". . . or about £50 for a Canon. We can buy it here cheaper than in Lagos. Clyde Sanger can take it with him when he goes up next week."

Claude let out a whistle. "Fifty ruddy quid! My God! You'll have to get Jim in a good mood for that."

Without waiting for signs of a good mood, I went in to Jim Bailey's office and told him we needed the new camera in Lagos in order to get Faji working in time for the next issue. Could I ask Jurgen to buy it at whatever discount we were allowed, and send it up when Sanger travelled there next week?

Jim's eyes narrowed. A particular concentrated look came into his face, a look which I was going to know well during the next few years. It was the look of a general rallying his mental forces, when he perceives the enemy are closing in.

"Didn't you buy a new camera for Christian Gbagbo when you were up in Accra just lately?"

"Yes," I said, thinking that small piece of news had travelled very rapidly.

"Well, we certainly can't afford to give another new camera to West Africa so soon. Faji must manage with what he's got. It isn't so very long since he was taken on by *Drum* and completely fitted out with new cameras."

"The 'fitting-out' appears to me," I said, "to consist of one worn Rolleiflex. Faji is really promising. He'll make a first-rate cameraman in time—but he must have a camera with which he can take action."

"In *principle*," Jim answered, "I'm sure you're right. But on *Drum*, you know, we can't operate by your lavish *Picture Post* standards." He smiled wryly. "You'll find an entirely different *kind* of organisation is needed on this continent. We must do things in our own way, which means making the best use of the equipment we've got. You've ordered a new camera for Christian. It's bought now, so we must let that go. In a few months' time, when I go up there myself, I'll see what we can do for Faji."

"This isn't a piece of Fleet Street extravagance," I urged. "It's a question of giving each man the working tools he needs. It's wasteful to have either of our only two West African cameramen functioning at half-cock. I realise it seems a lot to have to order two new cameras in one month—but the fact is both should have been bought long ago."

"Out in this country," Jim explained patiently, "you'll find that you have to take a much tougher attitude. There are a lot of things we should like to have in the way of equipment, but which we simply have to do without."

"But surely," I persisted, "if we employ a man at all, we can afford to equip him for his work—otherwise why employ him?"

"Our staff," said Jim, "might get through more work if we gave them all fast cars, but we just can't afford to do it. That's all. I have to finance two papers, and I can only do so much at a time. There are many other claims from other departments which have also to be considered. *Drum* is losing money—very heavily in West Africa—and we've *got* to take the economics of the magazine seriously."

"But this isn't a matter of fast cars for the staff to rush about—it's a matter of fifty quid so that Faji can take pictures. We intend to make *Drum* a picture magazine, and so far as Nigeria is concerned Faji's our one and only source of pictures."

"We'll look into it . . . we'll look into it," Jim answered, "as part of the general financial position of the paper. One of the things I particularly want to do in the next few days—when you've found your feet —is to work through the whole of the editorial costings of *Drum*, and decide where we can cut down."

I leaned back in my chair. I had been preparing in my mind a list of what seemed the absolute priorities, both as regards staff and equipment. These were beginning now to look remote, as Jim continued: "The outside contributions, too, will certainly have to be cut back. We need a very much tougher attitude towards these. It's absurd to be spending £85 a month on outside contributions when we've a staff of our own not fully occupied."

Long years of journalistic struggle had made me familiar with the technique of counter-attack; also with the need for an occasional strategic retreat. This was one of those occasions.

"I can't say anything useful about editorial expenses," I said, "until I've made one or two issues of the magazine, and see what possibilities there are for saving—also what additions and developments the magazine may need. Nor do I know enough about the staff to say whether anyone can be spared, or who will have to be promoted. I'll go through it all with you when my own mind's clear. Now I can see that people are waiting to talk to you"—Eprile of *Golden City Post* had put his head round the door four times in the last five minutes—"and we can come back to the question of the camera later on."

When I looked for the staff just before lunch-time in order to find out what assignments they'd fixed up, there was no one to be seen; I concluded they must all have gone out on their respective jobs. On my way out to lunch with Humphrey, I told him of the difficulty I was meeting over the camera, and my surprise that so small and necessary an expense should be causing such a battle.

Humphrey let out one of his deep laughs, which seemed to rack his whole frame like a cough. "Ha! Ha! Ha! You haven't a hope in hell of getting that camera. Not a hope. Faji'll be using his little old Box Brownie when he retires as an aged citizen with a grey beard. It'll be the oldest camera still in use, and he'll be the only man alive who knows how to work it. Thousands of people will come each year on special trips from California to see Faji take a picture, and when it finally packs up, Jim Bailey will sell it for hundreds of pounds to go into a camera museum. . . . People pay huge sums, you know, for early Colt revolvers."

CHAPTER V

THE NEW MAGAZINE

It was half-past nine in the morning, and in the big office on to which my own room opened, Can had just arrived. He still had on the red shirt, but today for some reason he was wearing a sock on top of his head in place of his usual knitted cap.

Can's morning entries were always dramatic. He would come in with his sliding, cat-like walk, head held forward to seize attention, eyes sparkling with anticipation and excitement. He would address himself usually to Casey, but in a minute or two everyone had stopped work to listen, two or three clerks and drivers from the circulation department were leaning across the barrier which separated their office from ours; one or two of the reporters from *Golden City Post* would have drifted over to join them.

"Jeefies, Casey," Can began, his high-pitched voice half lost in an explosion of laughter. "Jeefies, man! You ought to have been there last night. What a night, man! What a night! Everyone was shouting for their little Casey. You remember that big girl we met the other night in Orlando? She was jumping mad, ready to swallow you up alive. 'Where's that Casey-man?' she kept saying. 'Where's that honey-man Casey? What you all done with my man Casey?' . . . And what were you doing while the girls were all hungering after you? Prowling around at home, feeling married!"

Casey, a slim frail figure with the face of a worldly-wise choirboy, looked up and smiled. "Some of you boys never grow up. But where was this party anyway?"

"The Nurses' Home. That new Nurses' Home on the other side of Diepkloof. We were christening it, man, christening it. I've never seen so much hooch in any one nurses' home—even the matron was pughead. Oh what a time for the evil-doer! Half those patients must have perished by this morning, man. I swear they have! Rows of patients all passed out in their beds—one lot will have died because the nurses never attended to them, and the other lot will have died because they did. Jeepers! I could do with a bit of attending to myself this morning. . . . I think I shall just . . . very quietly. . . ."

Through the open door I called out, "Can!"

He danced in, beaming. "'Morning, chief! What can I do for you?" He leaned over me, and it was like the opening of a furnace door—that certainly had been a party.

"How's it all going, Can? What stories are being worked on for the new issue?"

"Hang on a sec., chief . . . I'll just go and rough you out a list."

Later in the morning we held our first conference. The *Drum* office was always short of chairs, and the staff had to perch on tables, filing-cabinets, or lean against the wall and bookshelves. We looked each other over from these points of vantage, in the manner of men who have heard a good deal of one another in the past and must now, for an indefinite future, face close contact. We might have been a ship's crew signing on. Besides Humphrey, Can, Casey and myself, there was Jurgen and our African cameraman, Peter Magubane; a bearded reporter known as "Butch"; Joe Blumberg, our chief sub-editor and the only other white on the editorial side; and a junior reporter, Nathaniel ("Nathan" or "Nat") Nakasa.

Peter was a sturdy, thick-set figure with an open face and determination in every line. He had a habit of wrinkling up his brows when talking, as if all speech were a matter demanding concentration. At twenty-six or seven, he was one of the older members of our staff, having made his way up by way of being, first, a driver, then a dark-room assistant; he was fond of good clothes, and always drove a big American convertible. African cameramen were not popular with the South African Police, and his big car marked him out for the attentions of gangsters in the townships, so that in his three years as a *Drum* photographer Peter had already survived more rough handling than many professional fighters take in a career. He would no doubt have met with much more trouble, but he possessed one quality almost unique among African journalists: he did not drink.

Butch had not been with *Drum* long. He was a friend of Can's, and like him had been a student at the university college of Fort Hare, and later a schoolmaster. Butch was big and burly. I presumed he must be a good news-getter, since, having read carefully through all recent issues, I could see he was no writer.

Nathan Nakasa was short, rather light-skinned, with a lively look and a quick response. The others, I noticed, tended to shut him up when he spoke, as being too young to know anything of life. He could hardly be more than twenty-one, but had already some years' experience as a reporter, partly on *Drum* and partly on a Zulu paper in Natal.

Joe was around thirty, patient, hard-working, passionately interested in jazz. Mysterious figures were always hanging around his desk, bringing furtive packets out from beneath their coats, the latest pressings, straight from the factory backdoor. Either he must have a special warehouse for his record collection, I thought, or else he just drops them all down a grating on his way home, for he was always too good-natured to refuse to buy. Joe's long sad face concealed a sharp sense of humour. He would not be put upon by proprietors or managers, but was endlessly patient with the rest of us, by whom because of his good nature he was also constantly exploited.

"What about coming along to a jazz party this weekend, Joe?" Nat called out to him one day, the voice sailing in through my open door.

"Good. Where at?" asked Joe with interest.

"Your place," Nat answered. "We're always well looked after there."

Four whites then—one soon to leave—and five Africans, we assembled in my office, together with our office-boy or messenger, Sidney Andrews, whom I insisted should be brought in too.

*   *   *   *   *

From now on, I told them we were all starting out on something new. I had great admiration for what the paper had done in the past, but the time had come for a step forward. We were going to make *Drum* into a picture magazine famous for its photographs, but famous above all for its straightforward presentation of African life and the African point of view.

Great picture papers—such as *Life* or *Paris-Match*—enjoyed resources of money and staff, compared to which our own were tiny. But, compared to them, we held one advantage—we could concentrate on what we knew.

This closeness of contact, I said, could not possibly come from me, a stranger unfamiliar with the country. It could only come from them. But if they would pass on to me the picture of our readers' lives and interests, I would undertake to give it shape, to set it out in the most telling way. In the writing, I did not want correct and ponderous English; I wanted the vivid phrase, the fragment of conversation, the breath of life. Every article, every heading, every caption must be made to tell—even the choice of readers' letters must be thought of as important. Our photographers were the basis on whom everything would depend. All our efforts must be directed towards finding them

[1] Nat Nakasa (seated) and Can Themba.

[2] Hopkinson talking over one of Peter Magubane's stories.

the right jobs, the fresh ideas to work on, and—once out on the job—
to helping them take and bring back their pictures.

I had no idea, I said, on what terms they had worked with previous
editors. My idea of editing was that everyone would know exactly
what was going on, and say just what he thought about every issue.
We would operate through conferences—like this one—where we
would all put forward our suggestions for next month, and our
criticisms of the last one. Everyone would be expected to bring ideas
of his own, and to discuss or criticise the ideas of other people. When
each conference was over, Can and I would work out the assignments
—subject to all the changes which would come from the movement
of events. The essential thing was that, with our tiny staff, everyone
should be busy throughout the month. The last thing we wanted was
a kind of tabloid scrambled together at the last minute; there could be
no excuse for a monthly paper unless it was more thoughtful, more
original, better written and much better pictorially than a daily or a
weekly could be.

As regards the running of the office I should do my utmost to get
to know and bring out the abilities of each one. The paper could only
grow if we all grew. If in time it appeared that any one of us had no
abilities, or those he had were not suited to the paper, I should sack
him exactly as I would a fellow-white. No one would ever be sacked
for telling me what he thought of me or the paper; but anyone would
be liable to be sacked who let us all down by not doing his job—
particularly if the failure came from neglect or carelessness. No one
would be treated any differently for being African; equally no one
need expect any special favour or tolerance for being African. We
were all journalists together.

I should rely a great deal, I said, on the Assistant Editor, Can Themba.
The work of making-up and laying out the magazine would keep me
busy. Once our plans for the month were agreed, it would be Can's
task to drive everything ahead. If they felt he was driving them too
hard, they could blame it on me, but each day had got to bring the
paper one stage forward. I hoped everything was clear, but, if not,
anyone could ask whatever he pleased. The fact that my door was
always open meant that any member of the staff could walk in and
out at any time.

When I had finished there was a silence. We then went on to our
ideas for the month's work.

*   *   *   *   *

A couple of days later Jim Bailey gave me a buzz on the inter-office telephone. I had already begun to know when he was calling, though there was no apparent difference in the sound.

"'Morning, Tom. You busy?"

"You want to speak to me?" I asked, and went into his office.

"How's it all going?"

"Slowly. We haven't got a system yet. Also I don't really know what each person's capable of. But it'll come in time."

He nodded. "Look, Tom. There's just one thing I ought to have told you when you took over—however, I can tell you now. I don't know how things are in Fleet Street—they must obviously be different when you have so much ability all round you, and the resources of the world to draw on. But it isn't like that in our little community out here. You can't ever, for instance, *sack* any of our chaps. You just mustn't, because you can't find replacements for them. Some of our chaps, I know, are only half-trained—possibly by your standards they seem hardly to be trained at all. All the same, there's an enormous difference between the half-trained and the completely untrained—as you'll find out. Here we have to get first-rate work out of the half-trained."

"I certainly hope I shall never have to fire anyone," I said. "My tendency is rather the other way. . . . But if you make it a principle that nobody can be fired, how d'you maintain discipline?"

"We don't want 'discipline' in the usual meaning of the word. We want everyone to work together harmoniously. That's how we manage things on *Drum*."

"Y-e-e-s—but you do want everyone to *work*. At least I do. With only two reporters and two photographers, we shall get no paper unless they do. At the moment I'm not sure everybody does work. And I see in my basket a memo from the management saying that staff are habitually coming in late, and that in future everyone has to be in the office by eight-thirty every morning unless he has some very good reason. Also that people are not to disappear out of the office during the day without permission. . . . Supposing no notice is taken of your memo—what do you do?"

"That's *your* problem," Jim replied. "Every head of a department must be responsible for seeing that his own staff members conform to the regulations which the management lays down." He smiled. "It's quite simple really. Just a matter of exercising proper control through ingenuity and tact."

*   *   *   *   *

I had found myself a room in a business hotel not far from the office. This meant that I could be at my desk by eight-thirty before most of my staff began to show up. I used this time in the morning, and time in the evenings after they had gone home, to work out my plans for the paper. I was gradually getting some idea of what I wanted to do, but could not be sure yet whether what I wanted would prove successful, nor how far I should be able to carry others with me. I decided therefore to make changes only by degrees, when I was sure the next step was the right one.

As regards West Africa, I had fixed on two to start with. Hitherto it had been the custom to insert a number of the South African pages straight into the West African edition. This arrangement was welcome to the staff because it saved time and trouble, and to the management because it cut down costs. I was determined this should stop. It was obvious the West African must prefer—like anyone else—pictures and stories about his own life. Secondly, my visit to Ghana and Nigeria— short as it was—had showed me that the two countries were different from, and not entirely sympathetic to, each other. Therefore the sooner we were printing a quite separate edition for each territory, the better.

In South Africa also big changes were required, and I had roughed out the form they would take, with a priority. To make *Drum* into something approaching a modern magazine would require half-a-dozen important alterations in production, which would have to be introduced step by step. These were:

1. A decently printed cover on good paper—this we had now got.
2. The advertisements must be rearranged, so that instead of straggling all over the magazine, they would be mainly confined to the front and back. This was all the more important because the advertising in *Drum* actually took up from 50 to 60 per cent of our total space.
3. We must enormously improve the appearance of the magazine so that it became something people would be proud to carry around. The fact that ours was a black man's paper was no reason why it should look like a poor relation of a white man's.
4. We must improve the printing.
5. We must get the magazine on to a better quality of paper, so that good photographs—when we got them—could be seen.

Beyond these plans, which I imagined might take twelve months to complete, lay others—such as putting up the price of the advertising pages, so that in time we should carry not 55 per cent or more of advertising, but 50, 40, and one day even 30 per cent, in return for the same or a larger revenue. But this, of course, meant building up the circulation. . . . I dreamed continually of a new *Drum*, better-printed, better-produced, combining prestige with popular success. It would have a larger staff, better-paid, better looked-after, better-equipped—for all of which our present tiny organisation was to be the germ.

* * * * *

Hours of talking to the management; hours with the circulation department—the smallest and most ill-organised section of our office; hours with the printers; hours of argument with the advertising side —who bitterly resented any changes in the make-up of the magazine and in particular the changes I was planning.

"We'll have no advertising in the paper at all in six months' time, I'm telling you—not a single bloody page!" declared Fred Brewis, the tall, despondent Afrikaner who was advertising manager for *Drum* and *Golden City Post*.

"Advertisers aren't going to stand for this," he hammered my suggested make-up on his desk, "having their ads. packed away in the front and back. You don't seem to realise—they're paying good money for this lot. Far more than they're paying our competitors. And they won't pay money to be pushed away out of sight. Another thing, all these big photographs you're planning, instead of type and little pictures. Why—they'll dominate the bloody paper!"

"That's the idea, Fred."

"Well, they may stand for that in England and America or somewhere, but they'll not stand for it here. I've had two cancellations already this morning. Two whole pages cancelled!"

"Come off it, Fred," I said. "The first number isn't even out yet. You saw that make-up yourself only this morning—and you're telling me two advertisers have cancelled because they don't like the look of it. What they don't like is the look of the old paper; when they see the new one, they'll probably come back."

"I'm *warning* you—that's all!" Fred maintained grimly. "I'm giving you a friendly warning. Advertising's not easy to get. It's a damn sight harder this year than last. Your salary and mine and everyone else's depend on the advertising. You'll get nowhere with this paper if you put the advertisers' backs up. Nowhere! Now you'd much better take this make-up back and start again."

He held it out to me across the desk.

"Look, Fred," I said, not taking it, "I'll promise not to worry about my salary, if you won't worry about yours."

"This is no bloody joke!" Fred answered hotly. "I'm going right in to see Jim Bailey now."

*   *   *   *   *

Hours of discussion with Humphrey and Can about what should go into the first issue, hours of talk with each member of the staff, trying to see what we were going to draw out of each. At first I sometimes mistook one for the other.

"Nat," I began. "I want you to go out this morning . . ."

The slight figure before me smiled. "It isn't Nat, Mr. Hopkinson. It's Casey. That's Nat over there talking to Peter."

"Okay, then, Casey. Here's something I'd like you to work on . . ."

One such mistake was enough, and I wrote down a descriptive phrase about everyone, not only those on the editorial staff but throughout the office, and would memorise this in the evening after I got home.

I made other, worse, mistakes.

Operating the telephone board was a cheerful round-faced African called Daniel, with whom I would always exchange a few words on the way home. One evening I noticed that he had his head shaved bald.

"What's this, Daniel? A new style of haircut? It looks very smart."

Daniel showed an embarrassed face, then: "Shaving the head is an African mourning custom, Mr. Hopkinson. I have just lost my youngest brother."

"Excuse my clumsiness, Daniel. Put it down to ignorance. And I'm very sorry to hear about your brother."

Problems of inefficiency plagued me, till I got used to managing without efficiency.

"Where are the letters?" I asked a temporary secretary one day—our own was away on holiday. "I'm expecting something urgent from West Africa."

"I don't know. They haven't been brought round yet," she replied, looking up despondently from her knitting.

"Well, can't you go and look for them? It's eleven o'clock already."

Wearily she laid her knitting down—to return in a minute or two triumphant.

"There isn't any post this morning."

"But there must be *some*."

"No there isn't. They haven't been to fetch it from the Post Office."

"Why ever not?"

"Patrick's away ill."

"But if Patrick is sick, does that mean that the whole office gets no post?"

"Yes."

Another day all the prints from the dark-room came out yellow. They were put down on my desk without a comment. I sent for the dark-room head.

"What the hell's happened here?"

"The prints are all yellow, sir."

"Yes, I can see that—but why?"

"We haven't any more printing paper."

"Why not?"

"We've used it up, sir. I asked the accounts department for an order for some more—but they say we've used up our quota, and we can't have any more till June."

"And what's this you've been using?"

"That's some old paper we found behind the pipes. Sidney found it and fished it up."

Ten minutes arranging for the post to be fetched, half-an-hour struggling with the accounts department. . . . "But the management says we mustn't spend more than fifteen pounds a month on printing paper . . . it's always been enough before . . . If the printers cut all the sheets in half then they *would* last the whole month. . . . Anyway, if they weren't always printing pictures for themselves, there'd be plenty of paper to last out. . . . Okay! Then if you *insist* on getting more paper, you'll have to send out yourself and fetch it. We haven't any transport. . . ."

And at once, before I had been in the office a week, the problem posed by the hazardous, insecure life of the urban African was brought home to me, not just as a matter for sympathy but as a nuisance interfering with our work.

I was trying to piece together a story from an incomplete set of pictures, when Nat ran into my room.

"Got your car nearby?"

"Yes—why?"

"Then come along. Right away. The cops have pinched Sidney."

"Sidney pinched?" I looked up puzzled. It was Saturday morning and there were few of us in the office. "What on earth for?"

"Passes, I suppose. But hurry—please. Otherwise we may not get him back. He can be shipped off to a farm or something."

"Where is he now?" I asked, as we were half-way down the stairs.

"I didn't see him. One of the chaps on *Golden City Post* saw him—up by the station. He was sitting on the pavement with a lot of others. They were rounding them up as they came in off the trains."

At the corner where Sidney had last been seen, Nat made hurried enquiries. Yes, the vans had come, and they'd taken the lot to Marshall Square. Off we drove to Marshall Square, the main police station.

"Now, go in and say you want Sidney back. Say he works for you and that you need him at his job," Nat instructed me. "Play hell if you don't get him—it'll be easier without me there."

They were all collected in one room—thirty or forty depressed black faces, ragged clothes; a smell and a feeling of fear hung in the air. Life had suddenly turned upside down; when would they see their homes and families again? How could they let their bosses know? Would they be sacked, or lose pay, for being late? If they couldn't pay the fine, where might they be sent? Would their jobs be waiting when they finally got back?

I couldn't recall the face of Sidney, whom I had seen only a few times, but he caught sight of me at once and pressed hopefully forward through the crowd.

"This your kaffir?" a police sergeant demanded.

"He works for me," I said. "I want him back. Is it a fine? If so, can settle up for him?"

"You can wait in the office," said the sergeant. "I'll see to him in a minute. Now, you lot—get through that door there!"

After a quarter of an hour and a pound, I had got Sidney back. It was to be the first, and mildest, of several similar situations in which Sidney and I were to find ourselves involved.

*   *   *   *   *

As we got close to the printing date of my first issue, Jim Bailey called a meeting of the heads of the departments. How many copies were we going to print? Had the distribution been properly organised? When would the issue go on sale in Durban and Cape Town? How many posters should we need? Methodically he worked through every point.

"What about advertising?" I asked, after a while. "I suppose we can have a bit of a campaign to put the issue over half a page in the *Sunday Times*. Some 'nine across threes' in the *Rand Daily Mail* and the *Star*. Give it a bang the day it appears and for a few days after-wards."

There was a stunned silence, and one or two faces looked at me a though I had gone mad.

"Your new cover will have to be its own advertisement," Jim ex-plained patiently. "It's costing us several hundred pounds; it shoul be much the most striking thing on the streets. We can't afford adver-tisements as well."

Towards the end of a long afternoon, a new point came up. appeared that *Drum* had some tons of inferior newsprint (the paper o which newspapers are printed) in store. This had been bought as a jo lot for economy, and the purchase had turned out a disaster. The pape was yellowish, brittle, everything on one side showed through to th other, and the pages printed on it looked conspicuously bad—even b our very modest standards. Some eight or sixteen pages of this inferio paper were being run into each monthly issue; I could see that at th rate it would take seven or eight months before the whole lot wa got rid of.

"Would you like," Jim asked me, "to leave the bad paper out c your first issue? It might help in giving it a good send-off."

My first thought about this ageing newsprint had been to say "Thro the lot away—or sell it for whatever it will fetch"—since putting into the magazine would only be injuring ourselves twice over. How ever, I was slowly learning.

"Is there no way of using up this bad paper? You can't sell it? we don't put some in this month, then we'll have an extra month lat on when we've got to use it?"

"That's right."

"Then let's make a whole issue of the dud paper and use the lot at one go. The new cover can carry this issue because of its novelty and we shan't be handicapped for months to come. Also the stuff on deteriorates in store—in six months' time it would look even foull than it does today."

"That would be fine—if you're prepared to take the risk."

I nodded.

"Then that's agreed."

Half-an-hour later, as the others went out of the meeting, I hu back.

"I think we've got everything in hand for the first number," I sa "It won't be wonderful, but it should be fair."

Jim smiled, then: "That was a good move over the paper—i

save us quite a bit of money. If we keep it lying about, some might become unusable—and we're having to pay storage all the time."

We chatted for a few minutes, then: "One small point," I said. 'That new camera for Faji. Sanger's going up to Lagos on Friday. 've spoken to Jurgen, and he says he can get us a new Canon at a good eduction—can I go ahead and fix it?"

Jim gave me a shrewd look, then laughed. "Well, y-e-e-s, I suppose ou can," he said.

CHAPTER VI

GETTING STARTED

In March of this year, 1958, South Africa was preparing for a General Election and, once the April issue was safely at the printers, I started to go round and listen to the speakers. I wanted to get a clearer view of what South African politics were all about, and I felt that a General Election would give me the opportunity to learn. In the course of one week the leaders of the two chief political parties—Strijdom, the Prime Minister, leader of the Nationalists, and De Villiers Graaff, leader of the opposition, the United Party—both held evening meetings at the Johannesburg City Hall. I went along to watch and listen.

The Prime Minister spoke to an audience rapt, intent with an almost religious fervour, sombre as if at a church meeting. Moving with difficulty and with his throat muffled, he spoke for an hour, but it was with the voice of a sick man, often dying away and then suddenly when the listener expected it to fail, coming out strong; a mute "Lion of the North". Only a small part of his speech was in English and that, it appeared, not the most important.

The Ministers of his government had been attacked, he said, for the misuse of the official cars. The Prime Minister argued that his Ministers had not used official cars improperly, or if they had, they had only been using them in the same way as their United Party predecessors. He even went back ten years to discuss the use once made by Smuts when he was Premier, of an official aeroplane. The main part of his speech, however, was more significant. It was devoted to arguing that the United Party showed itself unsound on that cornerstone of all South African politics—race relations.

"From the leading articles of the United Party press, and from speeches made by United Party spokesmen, hostile non-White* organisations like the African National Congress can come to only one conclusion, and that is that the United Party is supporting them in their action against the Government." ("Shame" growled the audience.)

---

* It is the custom, significantly, in South Africa, to give capitals to the adjectives "White" and "Black". In quoting newspaper reports I have followed this custom though not in my own writing.

"The intention of the United Party, if it should come to power, is to give the non-White a stranglehold on the Whites, and to put White civilisation at the mercy of the non-Whites.

"The African National Congress (encouraged by the United Party) are now demanding a minimum wage of £1 a day for every African worker and are threatening to dislocate the entire country by strikes. The United Party and its press, who are continually telling the Natives that their wages are too low, must take responsibility for this.

"The Government will deal with every contravention of the law in this connection by Natives with the full weight and authority of the State."

The Prime Minister then went on to speak of the United Party's proposals to reform the Senate, calling them "the most serious attack on White South Africa we have ever come across. . . . A vote for the United Party is a vote for the Senate Plan—which is a dagger-thrust in the heart of White South Africa . . . a diabolical threat to the continued existence of the White race".

To describe this plan, as the United Party had done, as "a guarantee of the rights of the White people", was, he declared, "the greatest piece of political fraud and dishonesty ever known in South Africa".

Though the Prime Minister said nothing that was original or inspiring, though his whole appeal was to fear and not to hope, the depths of bitterness and scorn out of which he spoke called to an answering feeling in his audience. The meeting gave a formidable impression of tense and impassioned solidity.

His references to the Senate Plan aroused my interest. It seemed so utterly unlike everything I had heard and read of the United Party that they should be sharpening daggers to thrust into their own hearts, and issuing diabolical threats to their own continued existence; I therefore got a copy of the plan and studied its proposals. The Nationalist Party had recently flooded the Senate by the appointment of a mass of their own supporters. This had been done to obtain the necessary two-thirds majority, in a combined meeting of both Houses of Parliament, which would allow them to remove from the voters' roll some 50,000 Coloured citizens in Cape Province who traditionally enjoyed voting rights. As these rights had been "entrenched" in the constitution, they could not be abolished by a mere parliamentary vote.

The determination to remove the Coloured voters was due partly to the conviction that the possession of a vote is a purely white prerogative, and partly to the fact that a majority of the Coloureds regularly voted against the Nationalists. Their removal from the roll, with the intended addition to it of white youths from the age of eighteen to twenty-one, were steps in a long-term plan to ensure that the Nationalists should dominate South African politics beyond any possibility of change.

The so-called "Senate Plan" of the United Party consisted of proposals for reforming the "Enlarged" Senate produced by this Nationalist manœuvre. In brief, the 50,000 Coloured voters would get back their lost votes, plus a certain number of new Coloured voters with high property and educational qualifications. In place of four white senators—who at that time represented the interests of the Union's ten million Africans, and who were abolished altogether two years later—two extra, making six in all, were to be elected by "qualified" Africans. Duly qualified Coloureds would also elect five or six white Senators to represent them, in place of the one then nominated by the Government. These eleven or twelve whites, therefore, out of an all-white Senate of originally 50, and at that time 89, Senators, constituted that "diabolical threat to the continued existence of the White race", that "dagger-thrust in the heart of White South Africa" of which Mr. Strijdom had spoken so passionately.

A day or two later, in the same place, the Johannesburg City Hall I was able to hear Sir de Villiers Graaff, the leader of the opposition He was handsome, imposing, agreeable, fluent and bi-lingual—but he aroused no emotion, outlined no policy and called for no action His concern was manifestly, not to expel his opponents from office take over their authority and reverse their policies, but to proffer himself and his followers as a reasonable alternative against the day when destiny should decide to drive his opponents out on his behalf Then—since his programme was almost indistinguishable from their —it would be natural for the voters who had supported them to rally behind him.

"The voters will be asked to vote for the continuance of co-operation between the White races in South Africa," he said. "The Afrikaners i the United Party—and there are many—have seen fit to sink thei differences and co-operate in the interest of a greater South Afric Both English and Afrikaans-speaking want to build a united Sout Africa. . . .

"The United Party cannot—and will not—ignore the contribution of the Afrikaners to South Africa—their language, their religion, the idealism. . . .

"The absence of harmonious race relations in recent years has caused South Africans to think all is not well in South Africa. It is the realisation of this that has kept the United Party together . . ." And so on.

Outside in the roadway stood a section of the audience who had come to ridicule and make trouble, but in a bored rather than angry way, shouting "Kaffirboetie!"* and similar warcries whenever any phrase annoyed them, or there was a pause in which they might be heard. An Afrikaans-speaking sailor who had difficulty in standing threatened two black men who were listening quietly beside me—though any comfort they got from what they heard must have been slight. The black men stood their ground for a minute to show they were not intimidated, then, with a glance at one another, melted backwards into the crowd. The loudest storm of jeers and booing from the objectors in the road—they looked like a group of wealthy farmers—came when "Div" declared: "We cannot indefinitely govern a majority of eleven million people of other races without some degree of goodwill and consent."

In these two speeches I had been given the main pattern of white South African politics, and I never afterwards made the mistake of underestimating the grip on the whole machinery and process of government which the Nationalists had secured, nor that of expecting any change in the situation to be brought about by political action from English-speaking South Africans through their chosen instrument, the United Party.

The Nationalist party lived and grew by brandishing the "swart-gevaar", the black menace, and calling on all who feared extermination by the black masses to rally behind them. They had the edge on their opponents because, going themselves to the limits of extremism, they left no room for any party more extreme, and from this vantage they could always denounce the small degrees of progress hesitantly proposed by the United Party, as an alliance with "the evil of black nationalism". A couple more white senators could become, on these terms, "a diabolical threat to the continued existence of the White race".

Meantime the United Party, unwilling to propose any real alternative to "White Man's Rule", was left trying to think up such super-

* "Kaffir's brother", "Kaffir-lover", "Friend of the Kaffirs", a stock term of abuse for people of liberal or progressive opinions. It is interesting that the term "Kaffirboetie", applied by whites to any fellow-white who has friends among the Africans, has now produced a parallel term of abuse applied by blacks to a black who has friends among whites. He is known as a "sell-out".

ficial advances as its followers might accept—but which were no sooner put forward to the electorate than they were "exposed" by the Nationalists as "diabolical threats" and "dagger-thrusts". It was obvious that a party which had put itself into the position of the United Party could *never* gain power from its opponents. Change, if it was to come, could be brought about only by a change of heart in the ruling party, or by some unparalleled disaster, or perhaps by the change of heart resulting from an unparalleled disaster. As for the United Party, it must be doomed to a slow disintegration, like that of an army which spends its whole time in barracks.

★ ★ ★ ★ ★

Not many days afterwards I drove out one Sunday afternoon to Sophiatown, for a meeting organised by the African National Congress to hear its leader, Chief Luthuli. Luthuli lives some hundreds of miles away near the Natal Coast, and, enjoying at the time a short interval between successive sentences of banishment, was paying one of his rare visits to the Reef.

Inch by inch, foot by foot, Sophiatown was being demolished in order to be turned into a white area. Whole streets were already in ruins, and as fast as the families could be got out of any house, it would be bulldozed down, leaving the neighbours on either side to wait their turn. On the central patch of waste ground, known as "Freedom Square", a crowd of some hundreds had collected. It was not a static mass of listeners; people drifted up and moved away. On the outskirt little groups of men and girls were jiving to a mouth-organ. Men selling pea-nuts or copies of the Communist weekly, the *New Age* pushed in and out. Occasionally a procession of Zionists would go by, dressed in their blue and white robes, on their way to hold religious meeting that would last till nightfall. From time to time straggle of youths would march past singing, following a leader who had nailed a piece of cloth on to a stick as a flag. Once a fight started but was quickly hushed.

The Chief spoke from a wagon into a microphone. Behind him in a row sat half-a-dozen supporters and organisers, including one white From the descriptions white politicians regularly gave of the A.N.C as a violent and militant organisation—a number of its leaders were at this time being accused in the Treason Trial of plotting to overthrow the South African Government by force—I had expected an excited rabble-rousing exhortation. What listeners got was just the opposit The Chief spoke in English, slowly, humorously, discursively; no arguing to a brief, but seeming to draw up what he wanted to say out of his mind as he went along.

He ridiculed the position of the black man in this white-run country. He condemned the whites for their greed and ruthlessness, and for failing to take seriously the noble religion which they preached. But he insisted that the white man was to be distinguished from white policies. "Hate the things he stands for, but it is wrong to hate the man himself. Whether he is willing to recognise it or not, the white man is our brother. In the end in South Africa all races will have to live together. Because our own people are in the vast majority, one day we shall be in power—then we must show that the black man knows how to use power fairly and with justice. When that day comes we must not be looking for revenge."

Luthuli kept his audience occupied and entertained for a full hour, pausing from time to time to mop his shining face with a huge handkerchief, and there seemed no reason why he should not go on entertaining them for two hours more. Occasionally he told an anecdote, or rather a fable with a political allusion. Once he sang a song—explaining that he always sang at least one song in the course of any speech. When he stopped, the chairman came forward, ordered an old sheet to be laid out over the stones and rubbish, and called for contributions to help pay "Chief's" fare back to Natal.

There was a shower of small coins, and I stepped forward to put my own contribution into the sheet. As I did so, I was aware that a white man in a sports coat and flannel trousers had pushed through the crowd, stepped out in front, and taken several snaps of me with a miniature camera. I turned away and walked off to my car which I had left a couple of hundred yards up the road.

"Tickey for bread, please, master." A small black boy, in a pair of shorts with one brace running diagonally across his chest and his peppercorn hair full of dust, was trotting beside me. I fished in my pocket for the tickey.

"Who was the white man taking pictures?"

The child looked at me with astonishment.

"He Special Branch cop, master. Take pictures of all white men come to meetings, and write down numbers of cars. 'Nother tickey, please, master?"

I shook my head, and he scuttled back to his companions.

*　　*　　*　　*　　*

Towards the end of April I went down to Cape Town—a beautiful and dignified city, with an atmosphere more relaxed and tolerant than Johannesburg. Dorothy was coming out by sea, and I had arranged to meet her and bring her back by train to Johannesburg. She arrived on a misty daybreak at the quayside where—in my eagerness to catch the first sight of her after our three months' separation—I had been waiting since four in the morning.

We stayed just outside Cape Town in the suburb of Sea Point, at an hotel called "Arthur's Seat", and in the week we were there I got some glimpses of the English as we appear to Afrikaners. The people staying in the hotel were not in the main South Africans; they had come out from England to visit their married nieces and to escape the northern winter. Sitting in lounges and sun-porches after meals, while pretending to drink coffee, I listened to their talk.

The election was just over, and the Nationalists confirmed in their power for another five years. It probably meant the end of all hopes—not merely of political power but of any serious political influence—for the English-speaking people in South Africa for good. But I never heard them speak once about the election. Further north, Black Africa was beginning to boil—but I never heard them speak, either of the liberation or the menace, of Black Africa, only about the merits of Salisbury or Nairobi as shopping centres. All around us, in the streets and shops, and waiting on us in the hotel, were the fascinating mixtures of race known as the Coloureds, a spectacular people, full of vitality and interest, containing some of the most strikingly beautiful and some of the most ingeniously hideous variations of the human face. But our companions never once spoke of the Coloured people and their problems.

They spoke about Guildford, Bournemouth and Redhill, and how their gardens would be looking when they got back home. They spoke about "shows" they had seen in London six months earlier on their way out. They spoke of the prosperity of their married nieces' husbands, the number and progress of their children, and the comparative comfort and discomfort of hotels they had stopped in on the way to see them. They spoke with friendly patronage of Mr. Macmillan and with contemptuous hostility of the Labour Party and the Trade Unions, who were "all out for what they can get"; and they remarked how very curious it was that April in Cape Town should not be spring but autumn. Above all they talked about their coming journey home by Union Castle; how many times they had done the trip before, how wise they had been to reserve cabins on the "right" side of the boat, and how fortunate that they had made certain, twelve months back, of having a separate table to themselves for meals—though, from the way they looked and spoke to one another, I should have thought any stranger's presence would have been welcome as relief.

*   *   *   *   *

Drum staff in Cape Town consisted at that time of a Coloured reporter and a Coloured cameraman. Neither had sent me up anything of interest in the past two months, and I wanted to find out whether they were able to supply what was needed or, if not, what new arrangement I could make.

Besides working with them in the office during the day, I therefore spent two or three evenings in their company, going round to meet people of interest in the Coloured community, and learning all I could about their views and aspirations. I was received with great courtesy everywhere, and my hosts as a rule talked freely. The visit which left the most lasting impression was one to a professional man, a Coloured socialite. He was young, light-skinned, with an exaggeratedly neat moustache just fringing his upper lip; he had proved useful, the reporter said, as a contact for finding model girls for fashion photographs.

The members of some society were meeting in his living-room, so he led us through to his own little study at the back. On the wall over his desk was a fruit-drink poster of a near life-size American cutie in scarlet brassière and panties, and another of a drum majorette in top boots, military tunic and no skirt. We chatted for a while, and then I asked our host the question I had put to everyone I met: what could we do with *Drum*, or in it, that would increase its appeal to Coloured readers, or be useful to the cause of Coloured progress and development? We were prepared, if it would be of value, to set aside so many pages every month.

Leaning back in his swivel-chair, and pressing the tips of his fingers together: "If you wish, Mr. Hopkinson, that your *Drum* magazine should have any appeal at all to Coloured readers, you must first get rid of what I call 'the African taint'."

On the way back to my hotel, I asked the reporter if this attitude were typical of most Coloureds.

"It's typical of the socialites," he said, "and some of the sporting people. The politicians think differently, of course—but then politics is almost a dirty word with us Coloureds nowadays. Our leading people—schoolmasters, professional men, better-off business people and so on—don't like to be mixed up in politics. They're too dependent on official goodwill for promotion, permits, import licences, or whatever it may be. They just want to get on with their work, and to be accepted socially. You might say that the real aim of every Coloured is somehow to work his way out of the class he's in, and into the class just above. And that's a wholetime job."

"You talk of 'classes'. How many classes are there? And are they degrees of riches, or of whiteness?"

"Well, really you could say that we have six." He looked across at the cameraman, who nodded. "At the top are the 'Off-Whites'—they're light enough to 'play white' if they want to, and many of them do. Probably at least one member in every Off-White family is a Play-White. Same thing goes for most of the second class—the 'Fairs'. Then come the 'Mediums'. Then 'Blush', 'Coffee', 'Dark'. That's just about the picture. Some people might give them different names, but most of us recognise the same six classes."

"And does any Coloured know at a glance to what class any other Coloured belongs?"

"Within reason. That girl you were talking to in the office this morning—the very pretty one—is an Off-White. So is the fellow you've just met. Daniel's a Medium, Rodney's a Fair—and the liftman's a Dark."

"Is there much mixing among the different groups?"

"Yes, mixing goes on all the time. Many of us go to the same schools. We meet at work, at dances, at big sporting or political affairs—but on the whole each group has its distinct social life. Some rugger teams, for instance, will be all, or almost all, Off-White. You might manage to play for them if you were a Medium, but you'd need to be a damned sight better player to get in."

"So not only are the Coloureds on the whole antagonistic to the Africans—or at least not in sympathy with them—but they're also very much split up among themselves. Is that right?"

The reporter nodded. "That's how we are."

"Has it always been like this?"

"Far as I know."

"Could anything change it now?"

The two men looked at one another. Then: "I suppose the Nats might change it," the reporter said.

"The Government change it—how on earth?"

"By making it clear that there's no future at all for Coloureds in white society—that way they could force us into an alliance with the blacks."

"Can't really see it happening," objected the cameraman; he was a shade lighter of the two. "Can't see us ever allying ourselves with *them*. Doesn't seem natural somehow."

*   *   *   *   *

Looking after the affairs of *Golden City Post* in Cape Town was a white South African—Dennis Kiley. Tall, bearded, athletic, he had lived in many parts of the country and adventured his living in a variety of ways. He was a shrewd observer with a dry, despondent attitude, a sardonic sense of humour, and a flat, dead voice. I went out to dinner with him once or twice, and he talked with understanding of the Coloureds and their life.

"They're the worst off of any group in the country. They've got all our tastes and inclinations, which they have to keep up on about a quarter of our means. They've got much more than our touchiness and sensitivity, and none of our prestige to defend it with. They don't know where they belong, all they know is where they don't belong, where they're not allowed to belong—which is where they want to belong. They've got no history, no ancestry, no genuine political representation, no focus for their life—they haven't even got a name, because 'Coloureds' isn't a name, it's a description. They've got no art of their own, no literature, no science and they get a second-class education. All they've got is a sort of in-between status, some odd patches of land allotted to them under the Group Areas Act in order to get them out of the white areas, and a terrible rivalry with one another.

"They've never produced a great leader who could bring them all together, and I don't think they ever will. They've got some excellent men on a middle-level—schoolmasters and so on. And they make wonderful craftsmen—carpenters, plasterers, bricklayers, moulders, shoemakers—when they're sober. We owe them, through their streak of the Malay, whatever decent cooking is to be found in this country. They've got high spirits, good temper, and a marvellous turn for mimicry, like cockneys. They adore singing and dressing-up, and they'll splash a whole month's pay on an outfit for the Coon Carnival—their annual lark at the New Year—which is either magnificent or pathetic according to your point of view. They produce the loveliest girls in the world, with skins that actually look like the bloom on peaches—only smoother. . . . But they're utterly lost and rootless—like children without a family, a home and background, a destiny, or even any origin.

"The Afrikaners make a great deal about having 'nowhere to go' except South Africa; but first of all they *have* South Africa and are hanging on to it bloody tight; and second they're the most united and concentrated group in the whole world—except possibly the Eskimos or Jesuits. But the Coloureds are allowed no real position in South Africa—and as for their community, or group, their one aim is to get out of it.

"You know that free-lance who used to bring us in pictures—Ernest Bransby, the thin chap with the yellow face? He's been in and out of the office several times while you've been there—well, Ernest's a very good example. Ernest likes everything you and I like. He likes good food and drink. He likes to dress well. He likes books. He's mad to own a car. He likes taking his girl-friends out—one of these days he'd like a pleasant home. If Ernest were a shade whiter, he'd have all these things almost as a matter of course. He'd be earning £80 or £90 a month, with more to look forward to. But because he's a Coloured he earns £25 or £30—and he can't live on it. He's got tastes and aspirations—but he hasn't any prospects, hardly any hopes. And he can't afford even one single principle. There's hardly anything he wouldn't do if you promised him £50—and you can't blame him. He's in a desperate situation, fitted out for a kind of life which he's forbidden to live.

"I've been a friend of Ernest's. He's been out to dinner with me a few times. When things've got too awful I've lent him a few quid to keep going. One night when I came back late to the office unexpectedly, he'd got in with the cleaner's key and was going through all my papers. I caught him at it fair and square. God knows what he hoped to find—some hold on me, I suppose, some means of getting himself on in the world. . . . He can't have expected to find any boxes of cigars or bundles of £5 notes."

"What did you do?" I asked.

"Told him to clear out and not be a bloody fool. Not long after he sent a long letter to Johannesburg accusing me of telling libellous stories about him, and not giving him proper chances to get on. God knows, he hasn't got proper chances to get on—but not because I fixed it that way. . . ."

I liked our two staff members, and enjoyed my day or two with them, but I was convinced that we had to make a change. They were both so much part of the Coloured community that they had become incapable of looking at it objectively, and seeing which of its activities would have journalistic interest; also, I saw, they were Coloureds first and journalists second. They didn't believe it possible to treat controversial subjects without offending their friends, and their social lives and contacts meant more to them than the progress of the magazine. The attitude was understandable, but it was not much help to me. I was therefore glad when they said of their own accord that they had had enough of *Drum* and Cape Town and were going to try their luck elsewhere. Casting round in my mind for someone to whom the Cape Town scene would not be unfamiliar, but who would be able to look at the life with a new eye, I thought of Ken Mackenzie, a young South African I had known and worked with on the *News Chronicle* two or three years ago, and I decided to talk over with Jim Bailey the question of bringing him out.

CHAPTER VII

IF BUGS WERE MEN

BACK IN JOHANNESBURG, Dorothy and I took two furnished rooms in a block of so-called "Mansions". We could live there without discomfort and get meals in the restaurant, while Dorothy got to know the town and decided where she would like to make our home. We were going to take a flat and not a house because, with visits to West Africa and elsewhere, I might often be away for two weeks or more at a time. Houses in Johannesburg are continually being broken into—burglary insurance is many times what it is in most parts of the world—and I could not go away contentedly and leave her on her own. We needed a flat big enough to house our furniture when it came out from England, and it had to be a place where we could entertain *Drum* staff without having too many rows on that account with our neighbours. From this point of view some parts of the city or its suburbs would be much easier than others, and Dorothy needed time to look around.

Meantime at the office I was still struggling to get the staff and our work organised. I believed that lack of organisation was the main reason why the standard of our work was not higher, and why the output of each man was comparatively low—an article or two being accepted as a fair month's work. I was sure that, once I got a proper system going, everyone would be happier, the work would go on more smoothly, and the staff themselves would make more rapid progress.

One change I made which worked out well; it concerned Casey Motsisi. Turning over the back numbers of *Drum*, which I did often, with feelings of mingled admiration and horror, I came across the following piece. It was one of a series built round the same chief characters—bugs.

IF BUGS WERE MEN

It was the year 1758. Two bugs were sitting and chatting in a nook of the wall in the House of Discussion. One bug yawned and confessed it was feeling sleepy. But it dared not sleep. It always enjoyed listening.

A leading official had just remarked that half the members of the Opposition were asses, whereupon someone asked him to withdraw. He withdrew by saying that half the members of the Opposition were NOT asses, whereupon he was roundly congratulated for being the first person to withdraw a remark instead of stamping out of the house like a bull.

"Do you believe in evolution," the yawning bug asked its friend.

"Yes. Why do you ask?"

The first bug scratched its head and said: "Well, I was just thinking. Last night I bugged that chap who calls himself President. His blood is flowing in my veins, so I'm his blood relation in a way. Maybe some centuries to come I might evolve into a human being, and who knows I might be elected President too!"

"What will you do when you're a President?"

"I will make laws. Humane and human laws. Nothing but laws."

"That means you will forget your bug brothers, even me?"

"Nix, chum. I will appoint a Minister of Squalor, whose sole business would be to see to it that every human being stays dirty. I will ban all disinfectants; encourage bug immigration; and tighten up on emigration. Anybody who disagrees with me, even on such a small matter as weather, will be named a bugomist and banished to a concentration camp for an indefinite period. By Bugs, I'll make such laws bugs will build me a monument after I'm dead, for being the one bug who fought relentlessly to uphold Bug supremacy."

"You wouldn't escape criticism from other democratic countries if you carried on like that."

"Woe unto those who dared point a finger at me! I would of necessity have to be tough. After all, my problems would be unique. What with a President who was once a bug."

But the other bug was bored with all this kind of rambling. It stifled a yawn and said: "Stop talking like a human being and let's sleep. Wake me up at midnight."

The two bugs fell asleep immediately, and dreamed of human beings.

The piece was signed "Casey Motsisi". I was beginning to know Casey fairly well by now, and I thought he was being wasted in his present job—as a clerk looking after the files of prints and negatives in the picture library. It is true that a good library is vital to any picture magazine, and that Casey was the only person in the building who had any idea at all as to where, in the chaos of our dozen or so rickety filing-cabinets, any particular picture might be found. But important as a picture library is, it is still as it were only a second rank in the line of battle, and *Drum* had not got a front rank yet. I talked the matter over with Jim Bailey, telling him that Casey was a writer of humour and originality, and deserved something better than to spend his days filing negatives and prints. On the other hand he was a peace-loving character, and I did not think he either wanted to be, or would make, a very good reporter.

At this time I was also anxious to relieve the strain on Joe Blumberg. Since Humphrey Tyler had left, Joe was carrying the whole burden of "subbing" every edition of the magazine, and his patient back was beginning to crack. If he should fall ill, get fed up with constant over-work, or take some of the holiday due to him, the paper would come almost to a stop. I had therefore been asking for some time for a second sub-editor. Now Jim suggested that Casey should be given a desk beside Joe Blumberg and should learn the whole business of sub-editing from him. I liked the idea. Though it meant more work for Joe for a few weeks, in the long run Casey would be a great help to him; and for Casey it meant his learning a professional technique which could always be useful in the future.

Sub-editors on a magazine dealing with current affairs have a highly responsible job. They have to take over articles written by the reporters or sent in from outside—cut them to fit the space available, and provide them with suitable and telling headings. They have to make sure that the articles are coherent, concise and accurate; it is for them to query with the writer or editor anything which is wrong, or which may land the paper into trouble. This is an arduous enough job in any country, where the danger to be guarded against is chiefly that of libel; in South Africa, with its complex and stringent laws about "incitement"— where every issue is political in one way or another, and where extreme touchiness on all political issues is taken as a matter of course—the task is many times harder.

Under Joe's patient tuition, Casey quickly got the hang of the work and became a right-hand man. In addition to this new arrangement, was determined that Casey should write a regular column of his own in which his humour and knowledge of his special world should b expressed; for if Can was the man of the world, of intellectual interest and intrigue, Casey was the authority on sport, the underworld and drink. Of boxing he had an almost professional knowledge; he wa well up in football and athletics; but his chosen field of interest was the life of the shebeens, and I would often hear him through my open door describing what had happened the night before in one or other of these centres of social life.

I therefore suggested to Casey that, though the pieces on bugs had been ingenious, the range of activities open to a bug hero was too confined—he could only talk and bite. Instead could he not write us a monthly piece in the form of an anecdote or very short story, centring round location life, catching its flow, its tension and humour, introducing from time to time, under disguised names, real characters or types whom everyone would recognise?

After one or two prods, Casey came up with a column which we called "On the Beat". It was immediately popular, brought him fame around the townships and a warm welcome in shebeens, and, except for a month or two when its author was away on holiday, ran continuously for the whole three and a half years in which I continued to edit *Drum*. The following—one of the later pieces in the series—is a fair example.

On the Beat

The other day the phone rings and a voice I can't recognise says to me how about having a little drink somewhere in Western after five pee-em. It is only when this voice tells me the address where the booze session will take place that I get to know who is on the other side of the line. It's Kid Jailhouse Blues.

Kid Jailhouse Blues explains that he's throwing this little "do" to celebrate his recent release from the jug. I go to this place after five pee-em, and I find Kid Jailhouse Blues with a dozen other guys in his room. I settle down and lick my lips in anticipation for the hooch which I reckon will flow like malten lava.

But it turns out that Kid Jailhouse Blues has invited more people than he can get happy and high. Whoever heard of Veterans of the Bottle getting happy and high, all twelve of them, on a poor nip? Which is what Kid Jailhouse Blues pulls out and announces like follows: "Gents, this is all I could organise."

Well, Kid Jailhouse Blues comes with twelve glasses and a teaspoon which he uses as a measure to pour droplets of mahog* into the glasses. We all lick at the droplets in the huge glasses and sing, "for he's a jolly good fellow", although I wish he drops dead.

* Mahog=mahogany=brandy (from the colour).

After the licking and singing we settled down on some benches, whereupon Kid Jailhouse Blues starts playing us some real cool jazz. Anyway, the music is good, and I'm just beginning to forget that I was wanting for Kid Jailhouse Blues to drop dead, when he comes to me and whispers something which nearly makes me wish I had a jawbone of an ass and do a Samson on him.

What he whispers into my ears is that—can't I loan him a fiver so's he can go and buy some hooch for the boys. He explains that he had the boodle that same morning when he went to town to gweva some bottles for the party, but that when he tried to get the boodle from his hip-pocket, it wasn't there.

That kind of jazz coming from an accomplished pick-pocket like Kid Jailhouse Blues is not easy to swallow. I can smell that he's just up to one of his confidence tricks again. And what he says after I tell him I have no mazuma, proves that I am right.

He says loudly to me: "Hao! But you *Drum* chaps got paid to-day." When he says this, everybody's head in the room jerks in my direction and I am just in time to see one of the boys nudge at the guy sitting next to him. These two guys stand up and walk out.

Everything begins to dawn on me. I was invited here by Kid Jailhouse Blues just so his pals can roll me and unload me of all my hard-earned boodle. I'm sure those two blokes who walked out are waiting for me at some dark corner just ready to pounce when I go out.

I'm just wondering what I'm going to do when who should walk in but Kid Hotwater Bottle carrying his inevitable hotwater bottle! He goes about with this thing on account he carries his hooch in it. He is no end pleased to see me and he offers me the hotwater bottle and tells me to take a swig. I take my swig and then stash all my boodle into it while nobody is looking and give it back to him.

He puts the hotwater bottle back into a leather case such as photographers use for their cameras and walks out. I say so long and follow him. Suddenly some guys attack me and go through my pockets. They find only tuppence and I hear one of them curse that Kid Jailhouse Blues sent them on a false alarm.

I go to Kid Hotwater Bottle's place, explain everything, and after some struggle manage to retrieve my booze-bathed boodle out of his hotwater bottle. . . .

*   *   *   *   *

There were two other staff changes I was anxious to make, but about which I was disappointed. I wanted to persuade Todd Matshikiza to come back on to the staff. Todd had been on the paper some years before, and I was struck by the brilliance of his writing; he handled his typewriter, as someone said, as if it were a cross between a saxophone and a machine-gun. At the present time Todd's energies were divided between working on the music for "King Kong"—due for its first production in Johannesburg early in 1959—and selling razor-blades. As a successful razor-blade salesman, I was informed, Todd's earning would be greater than *Drum* could afford to rival; and, though I took this argument with a pinch of salt, there was further opposition to him in the office on the ground that he would never produce his work to time. Later on, when I managed to persuade him to write a regular monthly column for the paper, I found this charge to be quite untrue; but the objectors had known Todd for longer than I had, and I was obliged for the moment to let the project drop.

Secondly, I wanted to take on another photographer, Bob Gosani. Bob was a tall, frail, willowy Coloured, whose work I had followed from the days when copies of *Drum* used to be posted over to me in England. He worked with a shaky Rolleiflex of his own, composing his pictures with some care. I was eager to work with Bob, feeling he could be trained to take the softer, more human, pictures, and he might develop an eye for fashion photography and for covers. His height, dreamy eye, gentle manner, and habit of always hesitating before answering, made Bob appear vague, until you talked to him. Then he was quick to understand what you were after, and if at first he didn't often produce it, I thought that with more confidence and a new camera—which I intended the firm should buy him—he would before long establish a position for himself.

Like others of our staff, however, Bob had an enemy: it was the same enemy—drink. His easy-going nature led him to say "Yes" to any offer, and his frail health meant that he was quickly affected by a few drinks. Some years before Bob had been involved in a disastrous car smash with Can and others, from which they had all been lucky to come out alive, and this had further weakened his physique. More than once Bob had been fired and taken on again. At the moment he was out of a job, and I decided to take him on, at any rate for a three-months' trial. I told Jim Bailey of my intention.

A couple of days later, Cecil Eprile, editor of the firm's Sunday tabloid, *Golden City Post*, called in on me. He spoke with a stutter.

"I h-h-h-hear you're thinking of t-t-t-taking on Bob Gosani?"

"Yes."

"I d-d-don't think that's right."

"Why not?"

"I f-f-f-fired Bob for drinking. W-w-what's the good of my f-f-f-firing a man, if you take him on directly afterwards?"

I had to accept the force of this argument, and agreed that Bob should work for the time being as a free-lance, resolving that—if he could make out successfully for the next few months—I would then give him a regular position. I called Can in and told him of my intention, urging him to do all he could to keep Bob working successfully, also to pass the word round among the others that, for the next few months, everything for Bob depended on his keeping sober—at least in office hours. Though I had failed to secure Todd and Bob, Peter Magubane and Jurgen Schadeberg were producing sets of pictures—Peter indeed had just won a £25 prize in a competition open to both whites and blacks; Nat Nakasa and Can were getting busy as reporters, as also was our Durban editor, an Indian, G. R. Naidoo; and Ken Mackenzie had accepted my offer to come out from England and take charge of things in Cape Town.

The first two issues of *Drum* for which I was responsible had sold fairly well, and a third was on its way. I felt I had reached a working understanding with Jim Bailey, and, to strengthen the situation further, we had now a new general manager. He was a South African, bilingual, of considerable experience and some authority, whom I will call Mr. Weatherstone. With Mr. Weatherstone installed, and a better system for producing the magazine worked out, I felt by the end of May that we were slowly beginning to find our feet.

CHAPTER VIII

DEMON ALCOHOL

It was a Monday morning. I walked into the office in good spirits. We had got both the West African editions to press on time the previous Friday. Today we should reap the benefit of our new system—a number of stories completed by the staff, who had been working away on their own for the previous two weeks. As I passed through the main office to my room, there was no one about. However, I had come in early and, since it was quite often nine o'clock before some of the staff pitched up, particularly after a weekend, I started to look through the papers for ideas, and then to turn out letters which had accumulated in my basket, ready to dictate answers when the secretary appeared.

At half-past nine she phoned to say she was unwell, and would be at home for at least the next day or two. By ten there was still no one but myself, Jurgen Schadeberg and Joe Blumberg. Jurgen was reading the paper in his favourite attitude, leaning back with his feet up on the desk, a pose which always drew critical glances from Jim Bailey when he walked through our room on his way to the lavatory. Joe, who was incapable of idling, had started to sort out the readers' letters, "pen pals" pictures, enquiries from the lovesick and other bits and pieces which filled in the magazine's odd corners.

At half-past ten Butch rolled up, red-eyed, bleary and unshaved.

"Where the hell *is* everyone, Butch?" I asked irritably. "We've got to get started today on the new issue."

Butch rubbed his bloodshot eyes and looked doubtfully around, though expecting that one or two members of the staff, invisible at the moment, might reveal themselves to a more careful inspection.

"Casey's not in," he said, "and Bob's not in. Can's not in either, Mr. Hopkinson"—Butch always used my name in speaking to me. "Perhaps they'll all be turning up a little bit late this morning, Mr. Hopkinson."

"All out on the piss most likely," Jurgen suggested. "Probably won't see any of them at all today—or tomorrow either."

"But I fixed up with Can on Saturday that we'd have a meeting first thing this morning, so as to get everything moving for the August issue."

Jurgen smiled and turned over to the sports page. Joe went on busily sorting through the letters.

"Butch," I asked, "d'you know where everybody lives? Can, Bob, Casey—and the rest?"

"Yes, Mr. Hopkinson. I think I know."

"Okay then, we're going out to bring them in. And you can come too, Jurgen. Joe, if anyone rings, say I'll be back at lunch-time."

"All right," said Joe. "I'll tell them you've passed out in a shebeen. What about Bailey? Supposing the big boss wants to see you?"

"Tell him I'm seeking his lost sheep."

We drove first to Sophiatown, the African "Latin Quarter", where most of our staff were still managing to find somewhere to live. We sat, all three of us, side-by-side on the front seat of my car. It puzzled me that, as we drove through the battered streets, avoiding pot-holes swerving past lumps of concrete, straying children and skinny dogs Butch kept leaning out of his window, smiling at passers-by as if we were on a Royal tour, and bellowing "Hi, Samson!", "Hi, there Wilson!" or "Hey! Man!", to anyone he knew.

Jurgen noticed my surprise and whispered: "Butch is afraid his buddies'll think he's with two cops. He's shouting to show he's jus driving round town with his friends."

"Do we look like cops?"

"In the townships all white men look like cops."

We went first to Can's house, round to the back, and hammered on the door. At last a face at the window, and a girl let us in. Can, lying across rather than in bed, was in a sleep from which no shakings o shoutings could recall him. Once his eyes rolled up, and it seeme that the dying man might recover consciousness, but a second later h had slid back into the pit.

"It's no good waiting," said Jurgen. "You could pull the whol house away from round him and he wouldn't know about it."

We left word with the girl to say who we were, and that Can shoul be told to come into the office as soon as he could be told anythin at all.

At Bob's house his young wife and baby helped our efforts, and be fore long he was apologetically on his feet—but it was clear he woul not look through any viewfinders or click any shutters today. His wi began making him some tea.

"What about Casey?" I asked.

"Oh, Casey lives a long way off, Mr. Hopkinson. A very long way off. Do you want to go and look for Casey too?"

But it was already half-past one, and I'd had enough of trying to collect my staff. Butch saw my hesitation:

"Would you like a drink, Mr. Hopkinson, before we go back?" he suggested and, when I agreed heartily, he took us to the home of a girl-friend who, he said, was a part-time amateur shebeen-queen. The part-time queen proved to be a large good-natured brown girl, with a pleasant voice and dignified manner. The room into which she led us was neat and well-furnished; she pulled a curtain over the bed alcove, and drew chairs for us to a table in the window. Leaning out over the sill, she called to a child playing in the road, whom she sent off to bring a half-bottle of gin and some beers. As fast as we drank, Butch kept filling up the glasses, and our hostess, mellowing, turned her attention to Jurgen. His youth and good looks obviously interested her, but being thoroughly married, Jurgen was unresponsive, and the hot afternoon sun had made him drowsy—which annoyed her too.

"Why are you not at ease, Mr. Schadeberg?" She said it as all one word, "notatease". "Mr. Tom here is at ease. Butch, we know, is always at his ease. Only you are notatease. Why is it, Mr. Schadeberg? Why cannot you be at ease, too?"

"I'm quite at ease," declared Jurgen, then—since it sounded unconvincing even to himself—he added, "I'm very happy."

"No. You are not happy, Mr. Schadeberg. You are not happy and you are notatease." She poured us all out another slug and repeated, "Only Mr. Schadeberg is notatease."

I looked across at Butch to say I thought it was about time we were moving, but Butch's face was no longer where I had last seen it. He was lying full-length along the window-seat, passed out cold.

Our hostess looked at him with disgust: "That *Butch*!"

To my surprise, however, I found I was looking at Butch with a new sympathy; he lay there in the window, legs apart and mouth wide open, visibly at peace with himself and all mankind. His habitual nervous, rather guilty, expression was all smoothed away; the doubts about his competence, which forced him to say "Mr. Hopkinson" appealingly with every sentence, had all vanished. Butch drunk was clearly a lot happier—and for himself at least much better company—than Butch in possession of his senses. This glimpse of Butch in his drinker's paradise remained with me long after, and the weakheadedness of those—of whom I was to know many—who "drink in order to get drunk" and pass out after the first few swallows, appeared to me now to have something innocent about it, even touching, like the ability of small children to fall fast asleep in the middle of a game.

The voice of the part-time queen brought me to my senses: "You can leave him here if you want to," she said, but she didn't seem at all anxious to keep him, so we decided to take the body along to Bob's house and leave it there. Bob's gentle, kindly wife would make Butch a cup of tea when he woke up, and most of our staff—as I had begun to realise—were able to stay more or less indiscriminately in one another's homes in time of need. Before lifting Butch up, Jurgen and I shook hands with our hostess, thanked her for entertaining us and asked her to allow us to pay for the drink. She waved our offer aside, saying we were her guests and could certainly not be allowed to pay.

It was after four by the time Jurgen and I got back to the office and sent out for some sandwiches and tea. The day was gone. All I had achieved by my ill-tempered expedition was that the one member of the staff who had been partly sober when we set out, was now as drunk as the rest.

* * * * *

I was still puzzling over what steps I could take to ensure having staff sober enough to get the paper out on time—and still have energy left for learning more about their various jobs—when a small incident occurred which showed I had better get a plan put into force without further delay.

For the editorial needs of the two papers, *Drum* and *Golden City Post*, we had only two small cars, which at that time were battered Morris Minors. One or both were continually going wrong or breaking down; the rough township tracks—often more like dried-up water-courses than roads—and the clouds of dust which rose and covered everything out in the country, would have tested much stronger, newer cars than ours. In addition they regularly carried half a-dozen or more home at night, and, since they belonged to "the firm" and no individual driver was attached to any one car, there was little inducement to keep them in good order. In fact there were certain drivers who were only too happy, I could see, when a car was laid up for a week and it was impossible for them to do anything but hang around the office and draw pay. There was one good driver, Jo Taukobong, but he mainly worked for *Post*, and it was proving a long slow job to secure his services for *Drum*.

Then one week, while John was away on holiday, *both* our cars were smashed up. This was not a case of breakdown; one had been driven straight into the back of a stationary car in broad daylight, not a hundred yards from the office. The other was telescoped head-on into a telegraph pole, ending up in a ditch in one of the townships. The driver at first could not be found, but while they were looking for him, he crawled out, still drunk, from the boot of his wrecked car where he had been sleeping while awaiting rescue.

Shortly before this the new manager, Weatherstone, had instituted a regular weekly meeting for the heads of the different departments, at which all our problems were supposed to be thrashed out. "Transport" came up at every meeting, and both Cecil Eprile and I used to moan that our work was being made impossible by lack of adequate transport. With a weekly paper to produce, I don't know how Cecil managed to get by at all; I only kept our side going by constantly using my own car for office work—which Cecil was too cautious and experienced to allow.

On this occasion there was an enquiry into the two accidents. The driver in the first case was sacked out of hand. He had only been taken on that morning as a replacement; it seemed doubtful if he had ever driven before, and he had no doubt made up the various references he gave. But the driver of the second car had a long story in his defence. He had, he said, been driving quietly home through the township after his day's work, when he was suddenly stopped and set upon by gangsters. They had knocked him about, and then forced him to drink a whole bottle of gin. Such a thing had never happened to him before, and—if only he could be given one more chance—he was quite sure it would never happen to him again.

I found the story improbable, to say the least, but I was still under the influence of my British background, in which consideration had to be given to anyone's statement in his own defence, and I was uncertain what we should do. Cecil Eprile, however, cut through the knot of doubt with a few quick-fire sentences: "The chap's story is a ... an obvious lie. Gangsters *like* gin. They go to very great lengths to obtain it. They spend all their time taking gin away from other people. When these gangsters get hold of any cases of gin, what they do is to drink it all up themselves. They don't go round forcing other people to drink *their* gin. So—sack the driver, and have the car repaired as soon as possible."

*   *   *   *   *

One evening as I sat at home in our new flat, pondering the problems of our paper and looking with envy at the sumptuous magazines produced in America and Europe, I had what I thought was a good idea. Next day I called everyone together.

"Look," I said, "what you do in your own time is your concern, not mine. But what you do when you're on the job or in office time is the concern of all of us. I'm determined that between us we're going to make a first-rate magazine, and I've seen enough of you in the months we've worked together, to know that we can do it. But we've got one big obstacle in the way. We can only make a good magazine with a staff we can depend on—that means a staff that stays sober while at work.

"From now on we're going to have new regulations about drink. From today, anyone who gets drunk on a job or in office hours will be sent home for a week without pay. Anyone who's drunk on a job or in office hours for a second time, will be sent home without pay for a month. Anyone who does it a third time—has had it. He's out!

"I want everyone to understand that there's no discrimination about this. It applies to whites just as much as to blacks. If anything it's milder than you'd find in Fleet Street or the States. I hope none of us is going to be sent home—even for one week. But those are the regulations from now on."

* * * * *

A week or two later Can suggested a story for the paper; he wanted to go down to Kimberley to cover a conference of the combined African churches. The churches were just beginning to become politically vocal; no one was better than Can at getting a grasp of a complicated situation, and he could also be a convincing talker, which should surely go down well with the clergy. I knew how well Can could talk from having driven him up a couple of times to give lectures to groups of students at the Witwatersrand University. One such talk he had given—delivered mainly over his shoulder as he walked up and down in front of a blackboard—was one of the most brilliant lectures I had ever heard.

I could see Can had a clear idea of what he was after at this conference; his piece—with a dozen or so interesting groups and portraits such as Bob was well capable of taking—would give us something in the bag for the next issue. I agreed therefore that Bob and Can should go to Kimberley for three days in the new Land-Rover, with John—whom we had at last secured for *Drum*—as driver.

The Land-Rover—the first new vehicle ever bought by *Drum* Publications—was the product of deep consideration. It was costing us something around £1,200–£1,300, and was expected to be the answer to our transport problems. Designed for farm work and hard military service, it would surely make light of the township roads and the rough handling of our drivers.

One Saturday morning there it stood, bright and gleaming outside the office, and we all went out into the roadway to admire it. It was to be assigned to *Drum*: but we were told that, before it could actually be entrusted to us, two capable whites—Dick Pierce, the Circulation Manager, and Bert Ryley, the Company Secretary—were to take it away for the weekend and give it a "thorough tryout". No one anticipated that they would test the new vehicle so thoroughly as in fact they did. In the course of the weekend they turned it completely over; it had to be lifted back on to the road and towed home, and the rest of its first month of service was spent in being repaired and over-hauled. It never again looked as it had that first sunny morning, and a little more than a year's time the accounts department was glad to accept £100 for it. It looked by then as if it had gone through the whole of the Korean War. Now, however, the Rover was newly back in service; ready to carry our team to Kimberley.

Before they left, I took Can aside and urged him from now on to be doubly careful—first, because the last person who ought to be sent home under the new system was the Assistant Editor. Second, because of Bob Gosani. I had just been successful in arranging for Bob to be-come a regular member of our staff—after serving his period of probation—but his life must hang by a thread until he had built up some reserve of credit in the firm. If he were found drunk at work even once, he would be out.

As it happened, their road lay through the town of Potchefstroom, and, as it also happened, there was a fire in the middle of the town. Woolworth's was burning, and they stopped to get some pictures. Next door to the blazing Woolworth's was a bottle store; a white man was carrying bottles from it into safety, and they went across to help him. According to their account, which I accepted, he told them to take half-a-dozen bottles for their trouble. They picked up the bottles—which happened to be brandy, their favourite drink—climbed back into the Land-Rover, and drove off.

From this point on, the stories diverged. The driver, who had been commonly put in charge of the new vehicle, said he wanted to throw the bottles out, but that the others refused to do this and insisted

on his drinking with them. Can and Bob said that they all dran]
some part of five bottles of brandy, chucking the bottles out whe:
they were finished. Before they could start on the sixth bottle, however
they were arrested by the cops who had been following them eve
since they left Potchefstroom. They denied that they were drunk a
the time, and clearly felt it an injustice that their efforts to help on
white man should have landed them in trouble with other whites—
first with the cops, now with the editor.

There was a further confusion in the story, because the incident c
the fire was supposed to have happened around midnight, yet the
were not taken up by the cops till between seven and eight the ne:
morning. When I asked for an explanation of this, the stories diverge
and became more involved than ever; all agreed, however, that the
had been fined £7 a head on a charge of being drunk; that they ha
never reached Kimberley or the church conference; and that on
more we had got neither story nor pictures from our expedition.

This event caused a big stir inside the office. Everyone on the sta
of both papers soon knew all about it, and before long it reached t]
management. Apart from my responsibility as editor, I was personal
involved in two ways. I had argued many times that, if we were giv
decent transport we should know how to take care of it, and I h
undertaken, if allowed to bring Bob on to the staff, to ensure that
kept sober. Now we were all in the cart together. I was hoping t
matter might be solved on the basis of sending all those concerned ho:
for a payless week, but just at this moment there came into the Gene
Manager's hands a copy of the local newspaper—the *West Transv*
Record—which, besides casting doubt on some particulars in the sto
I had passed on, added one which I had not passed on since I kn
nothing about it. There had, it appeared, been a fourth passenger
the car, who was not on the staff and had no business to be there.

Very shortly I was sent an instruction by the General Manager th

1. Can's salary was to be reduced, and he was to be deprived of
   title of Assistant Editor.
2. Bob was to be dismissed.
3. Can was to be told that any incident of the kind in future wo
   mean immediate dismissal.

Though much disturbed by these instructions, I did not find t]
unjust, and accordingly passed them on.

*   *   *   *   *

Tom Hopkinson and Nat Nakasa discussing an article.

So closed what had been a grim month—except for one final incident in keeping with all that had gone before. Butch was found incapable in the office on a Monday night after the rest of us had gone home, and the white who found him at once reported the matter to the management.

"What a bloody fool you are, Butch," I said to him the next morning. "Why can't you keep clear of the office when you're drunk? If you hadn't come back here, nobody need have known anything about this. Is it true that . . ." and I repeated the story that had been passed on to me with indignation by the complainer.

Butch hung his head and looked very downcast. "I can't remember doing anything bad, Mr. Hopkinson."

"Were you sober enough to remember if you *did* do anything bad?"

"No, Mr. Hopkinson."

Before any worse fate could overtake him I ordered Butch to go home payless for a week, warning him that his journalistic life would now hang by a thread. Then I told the General Manager what I had done. To my surprise, instead of calling for worse punishment on Butch, he said: "But you can't sack Molotse in any case." (Molotse was Butch's official name.)

"I certainly don't want to sack him, but why can't I, if he keeps on getting drunk?"

"He owes the firm £30. He's paying it back at £5 a month. You mustn't sack him till he's paid his debt off."

"God Almighty!" I objected. "If a chap causes trouble or is inefficient, surely it's better to get rid of him and lose thirty quid, than to have him hanging about the place when he isn't wanted, and receiving far more than thirty quid in pay?"

"I have got to keep order in the books," Weatherstone explained to me severely. "Jim Bailey has instructed me that there are to be no more office loans at all—except in the most special circumstances. And if ever there are loans, they have got to be repaid in full by the appointed time. Molotse had this loan before I took over—how am I going to explain it to Jim Bailey, if he clears off owing the firm thirty quid? No—if you want to sack the man, sack him—but not till he's settled up his loan account."

I went out relieved so far as Butch was concerned, but also scratching my head. The way to survive, I thought, if only the more troubled members of my staff knew it, was to get the largest loan possible out of the firm on any pretext, and to fix the slowest possible rate of payment. Then, when any part of the loan got worked off, they would think up a powerful excuse for borrowing some more.

CHAPTER IX

SIDNEY IN DISTRESS

AN ODD FEATURE about life at *Drum* was the way things seemed
to go in cycles. For weeks I would be worried over the circulation,
which was rising far too slowly in South Africa. All interest would
be concentrated on the 15th of each month when the figures for the
previous month were due in. If they were satisfactory, all was momen-
tarily well. When they were not, the struggle to find likely stories—
and the drive to get them done, completed and into print—became
more acute than ever. Then for weeks there would be the struggle
over drink—all the stranger for me because I enjoy my own drink
as much as any man, and the role of an apparently teetotal ogre sat
heavily on my shoulders. Every time the telephone rang in the evening, I would fear it was someone else in trouble, a new row brewing
with the management, fresh penalties to be enforced.

For weeks, later on, life would become a succession of disturbance
with the police—then these particular difficulties would fade into the
background, and for a month or two a new set would take their
place. Similarly for weeks on end I would see a great deal of one
member of the staff, then his activities would lead in another direction
and I would find myself involved day after day with someone else.
For the last weeks it had been all Can. Apart from constant contact
in the office, he had been out several times to the flat for supper and
talk with us in the evening, and Dorothy knew him by now almost as
well as I did.

"And how's Can today?" she would ask sometimes when I got
home in the evening, after her usual greeting: "How's my Hoppy?"

And now suddenly it was Sidney, our office messenger, with whom
my life had become entangled. Sidney was a short slim man in his mid-
twenties; with his jet-black skin, protruding lips, big teeth, head
narrowing to a point, he looked more like the conventional image of
the negro than any African I had met. Though the position he filled
was a modest one, Sidney was touchy, with a sense of his own dignity.
Every now and then he would start an argument with the secretary,
Edna Wilcox, because he claimed she was sending him about too
much—though to be sent around was in fact what he was there for.

Once or twice I had come out of my room, intervened in the dispute, and told him to get cracking.

Sidney's usual expression was one of harassment. His eyes were narrow with worry and his brow furrowed, though he could smile cheerfully and, when something happened which really tickled him, his face became one vast ear-touching grin. In contrast with Casey, whose unobtrusive air and friendly smile carried him intact through most of the hazards of life, there was about Sidney something plaintive, expostulatory—combined with a repressed aggression—which attracted violence and harsh treatment. He went about reacting to the blow before it fell, and fate—in the form of tsotsis, cops, or personal misfortunes—too frequently obliged.

One Friday evening on his way home, as he got near to the notorious Noord Street area just by the station, a group of tsotsis (small-time gangsters and teenage thugs) surrounded Sidney and began to jostle him. They pushed him into a dark doorway, tripped him up and went through his pockets, taking his week's pay and his few belongings. In the end, on his urgent plea, they gave him back his precious pass-book, after tearing it in half.

When I heard about this on the Monday, I gave Sidney something to see him through the week. It was no use appealing to the management who would reply, quite justifiably, that robbery was a natural hazard in the life of Africans, and that if once they started making good such losses, they would soon be paying everybody twice a week. I also told Sidney it was silly to carry his money where anyone could find it, and that on future pay-days he must take care to pin it inside his pants or hide half of it in each sock. Casey, who was standing by, added the sage advice: "Just leave ten bob or a quid where they can get it easy. If they find that they won't be so mad. If they get nothing at all they'll more likely carve you up." From that time on, before going home on Friday evenings, Sidney would half undress to dispose money about his person, with the advice—helpful or improper—of anyone who happened to be present. Not long after this pay loss, however, came a worse one.

I was busy going through a set of pictures, trying to make up my mind how much space they were worth, how they could be built into a connected story, and which were the key pictures in the set. Such work demands concentration, since it is only when one has virtually memorised all the photographs, that—as one stares at them again and again—the feeble ones drop out, and the best ones gradually begin to arrange themselves effectively. Suddenly you decide to put one here, another there, cut a section out of this one and combine those two together—and the whole thing has worked out like a children's puzzle. But to be interrupted in this process means that you must go back to the beginning and start afresh, submitting yourself to the impact all over again.

Just at this moment a plan was beginning to form, a lay-out which would be both explanatory—in the sense that anyone looking at the pages would see at a glance what they were all about—and striking, in the sense that the pictures hit the reader in the eye, making it impossible to turn over till he had understood what they were trying to tell him. While pursuing this half-apprehended pattern, shuffling the photographs around and throwing away those which contributed nothing, I became irritably aware of a slight figure on the far side of my desk. I did not look up, hoping he would go away. He stayed— and I now saw that he was holding out a paper. I flung the pictures down: "Well? What is it?"

It was Sidney proffering some kind of printed form. "This was my trouble, sir."

The odd phrase struck me at once. However, I knew Sidney had come in late that morning, and supposed what he was holding out to me was a doctor's certificate. I was just going to say "Oh, hell—don' bother me with that now", when I saw there were tears in his eyes. took the form from him: it was a death certificate. I went over an closed the door, and pulled up a chair for him.

"It's another one, sir. Another child dead."

"How did it happen, Sidney? Has she been ill for long?"

The certificate showed that the child was a girl, and had been ju under two years old.

"No, sir. It was only since last Wednesday. On Wednesday s brought up a small worm, so I took her to the doctor. He told me bring her back again on Monday—the day after tomorrow. Only s died, sir, in the night. Last night. He was very surprised himself hear that she was dead."

"Had the doctor seen the child since Wednesday?"

"No. I wasn't told to bring her back till Monday."

I looked at the certificate again. Cause of death was given as "bro chial pneumonia". No one would ask in the case of Sidney's daught when the doctor had last seen her, what treatment—if any—he prescribed, nor indeed anything at all about the matter.

"I've had so much trouble," Sidney burst out, the tears pouri down his cheeks. "It's been so hard. Five deaths in my family, c after the other, and three I've had to pay for. . . . I don't like troubling you, sir, but I'll have to ask if the firm can lend me some more money."

"How much do you need?"

"Seven pounds, sir. I've been to the undertaker, and now I'll have to go to the office that gives burial certificates."

"We'll send you up there in the car."

"It's too late, sir. The office closes at eleven on Saturdays"—I looked at my watch, it was eleven already—"that means I can't get a certificate till Monday . . . And now there's this hot weather come," he added distractedly.

I must have looked uncomprehending, because he added: "We can't have the funeral now till Tuesday. . . . Because of the hot weather, we must find somewhere to put the body."

"Can't the undertaker fix that for you? Hasn't he a special place? Would you like me to ring him up?"

"Yes he has, sir. Only they charge for it . . . I think the loan had better be a little more."

I arranged with the firm about the money and told Sidney to take Monday and Tuesday off. Three days later he was back at work, but fate, it seemed, had not finished with him.

It was again a Saturday morning, some three or four weeks after the earlier one, and we were all just preparing to go home, when there came a sudden shouting and scuffling in the street, and we all hurried to the windows.

"It's a pass raid," someone said.

"No it isn't, it's a shebeen raid. They've been raiding the 'Tree Tops'."

The photographers snatched their cameras and we ran down into the street. A mixed selection of humanity was already bundled into two police vehicles, squat metal cages on low wheels; eight or ten "flat boys"—household cleaners recognizable by their undignified uniform of dark-blue vests and sloppy knee-length shorts; a dozen labourers in ragged clothing; three or four well-dressed Africans in suits and ties, and a couple of hard-case whites.

These last were "mailers", purveyors of illicit liquor. They buy drink, chiefly brandy and beer, at liquor stores as if for themselves, and run it over to the shebeen "queens", who either pay them a profit or give them free drinks in return. After a few years all "mailers" look alike: red-faced, sandy-haired, filthy. They tremble, their eyes refuse to focus. They keep shaking their heads and blinking, as though somewhere far below the surface they are still hoping to understand what is going on. Degraded, sometimes brutal, but more often simply childish, there is something profoundly touching about them, as though they were muttering through inflamed and broken lips: "We're human, too, if only we could get at it."

Directing the raid were two white plain-clothes police, a tall thin one in a dark blue shirt, and a short round-faced man, little more than a boy, with the air of a debauched cherub. Under the strain of a good deal of heckling from the bystanders, they were growing exasperated. I nodded to the two cameramen to clear off. Shebeen raids are nothing new in Johannesburg, any pictures they took would be valueless, and, if the cops started pulling in the bystanders, the photographers would be the first to go inside.

At that moment I caught sight of Sidney. He had been helping all morning in the dark-room. Now, conspicuous in his long white coat, he was rashly shouting and jeering at the raiders. I was just about to order him indoors as well, when he was seized by an Indian cop who twisted his white coat and shirt into a tight knot. There seemed almost nothing left of Sidney's narrow chest and thin neck; it was all knot. From his wild look and angry splutter of protest I could see what was about to happen. "Keep quiet, Sidney!" I shouted, trying to push closer to him through the crowd.

Too late. With a shove and a twist he tried feebly to escape. In a flash the Indian pinned Sidney's arms behind him and he was thrust into the cage among the rest.

"What's this for?" I called out. "Where are you taking him?" No one took the slightest notice.

The Indian cop had made a further capture. The whites were giving orders to the drivers to get going. I ran round to the front and put my hand on the arm of one of the police, who gave me a puzzled look.

"That boy in there works for me. The one in the white coat. I want to know where you're taking him."

"Police headquarters."

"On what charge?"

"Assault."

Inside the packed cages men were clinging to each other for support, but I managed to catch Sidney's eye. "See you in five minutes."

I found Nat. "Let Sidney's wife know he is pinched. It may take a bit of time to hook him out."

"Shall I send the car out to his home?"

I nodded, ran off to get my own car, and followed the moving cages. When we reached police headquarters, I drove straight

behind the police vans and parked. The prisoners were ordered down
a corridor. I went after them and stood near a doorway. I felt sure
that in a few minutes someone in authority would ask me what I
wanted, and that anyone who did so must be partly sympathetic.

So it happened. A young man in sports coat and suede shoes approached me. I pointed Sidney out.

"That's all right," said the young man. "That lot was drinking in a
shebeen. They'll only have their names and addresses taken."

"No," said the blue-shirted cop, coming up at that moment. "That
boy in the white coat's booked for assault."

"Pity," said the first one, walking off. "Or you could have taken
him back right away."

"We've got to get them sorted out. Come back in an hour," the
tall plain-clothes cop explained in answer to my questions. "Ask in the
Charge Office. They'll tell you where to find us."

Back again after an hour. A sergeant ran his eye quickly down the
book. No sign of a Sidney Andrews. I must be mistaken. As a last
resort he told me to call in at the C.I.D., Room X.

Inside room X I found all the occupants of the police vans, seated
about in attitudes of apathy and dejection. There were also two women
—an enormous pale Coloured woman who I knew was the shebeen
queen, and her equally large African assistant. The tall cop beckoned
me over. "We're just coming to your case." He ordered an Indian
detective to bring me a chair, and I sat down beside the two police
as though making the third man on a tribunal. The policeman next to
me was slowly completing a long grey official form, asking questions
in Afrikaans, to which Sidney replied in the same language. I said
nothing, but watched the sheet laboriously filling up. At last we came
to "CHARGE". This, I was sure, was the crucial moment. If the charge
space got filled in, the case would have to go forward to the magistrate.

The tall policeman described the assault and said that, in addition,
Sidney had not had his reference book—or pass—on him.

"That's true," I broke in. "He hadn't his pass, but only because he
left it hanging up in his jacket. He ran out into the street in his white
coat. He could have brought his pass down in a minute. I could have
got it if I'd known you wanted it. As for the assault—well he did start
to wriggle about when he was seized, but . . ."

The short policeman cut in sharply. "This your Native?"

I nodded.

Suddenly he began to shout at Sidney. Shouting as if on a parade
ground. He was trying to get Sidney to admit that he'd fought back

and had hit out at his arrester. I thought: "I've got to let him shout a bit, but if he shouts too much Sidney will shout back. Then it's all up."

Under the storm Sidney suddenly began to tremble and his eye slewed wildly round like a horse that is going to kick.

I leaned across my two fellow judges. "May I say just a word or two?" I asked.

The shouter paused, grunted, hesitated, and let me speak.

"Look," I said. "It's true this chap ought to have had his pass, and he hadn't. He left it in his coat when he ran out into the street. And it's true that he wriggled around when your man seized hold of him—he shouldn't have done that either. But he *didn't* hit the detective who was holding him. I was there all the time—so were a dozen people from my office. If there's a charge of assault my firm will defend it. I shall go on from here and see the lawyer now. But does there have to be a charge? The fact is he's a nervous chap—quickly gets excited and upset. Especially if he's at all frightened."

I could feel Sidney flash me an angry look.

"He was trying to show off," asserted the short detective. "That's his trouble—trying to show off in front of the other Kaffirs. I know his type—make a row to show how brave he is when he thinks he's safe among a crowd."

"No doubt that often happens," I agreed, finding more truth than I cared for in his summing-up. "But there's something else as well. Sidney's very excitable. He's had a lot of trouble lately. Only last month he had his pay packet pinched by gangsters on the way home. He's had other bad troubles too. I know he shouldn't have struggled but it was a very natural thing to do." I caught a sympathetic glance from the tall detective.

"Look," I said, "I don't know if it's in your power to show leniency or whether this charge is already booked. But if it is in your power to be lenient, I think this is a case for it."

The two policemen looked at each other. The first passed the green form over to the second and they studied it for a minute. At last the tall one spoke.

"It's up to the detective who arrested him. He's the only one can withdraw the charge. If he likes to withdraw it, it's withdrawn. Otherwise it must go on."

He called the Indian detective over, and after a moment's talk declared: "If he"—nodding at Sidney—"will apologize to the detective, the detective will withdraw his charge."

I conferred for a moment with Sidney, thinking the Indian detective also had shrewd judgement.

"Apologize?" Sidney muttered angrily. "What for?"

"Look," I said, getting exasperated myself. "Either you apologize or you spend the weekend inside. Take your choice."

"But why?" Time was running away fast. I turned to the detective. "He says he is very sorry."

"He has to say so himself."

For a moment it all hung in the balance, then Sidney swallowed and brought it out, not looking at the Indian. His two words—"I'm sorry" —sounded more like defiance than regret.

However, I didn't wait. Thanking the two detectives and the Indian, I led Sidney off. The crowd from the shebeen looked enviously at us as we walked quickly through. I couldn't wait to get safely outside.

In the car I could feel Sidney's troubled eye on me, his lip once more a-tremble: "Sir, I wasn't really sorry. You shouldn't have said I was."

I switched off the engine and started to climb out. "O.K., then, back we go!" Sidney paused for a second in bewilderment. Then his face relaxed into a huge smile.

"I'm not sorry I tried to hit that cop. But I'm not sorry I'm outside either," he admitted.

*   *   *   *   *

When I asked Sidney where he wanted to be dropped he said he must go back to the office to pick up his pass—"Otherwise I may get pinched on the way home, and then you'll have to do this all over again."

Sidney ran off to collect his pass, but at the top of the office stairs I stopped. Over to the right, on a table which was used for sorting out entries for competitions and letters to the lovelorn, something was lying. I thought it would be one of the office staff, passed out, and had just time to hope it was someone from *Golden City Post*, not *Drum*, when I saw that he was half-naked.

I went over to the table. A youth was lying there face downwards. There was blood on his head and arms, blood on the table, smears on the blotting-paper and the wall, blood dripping down on to the floor. His shirt had been taken off, and a dirty face-flannel laid over the knife-wounds in his back from which most of the blood was flowing. The back of his khaki shorts was soaked in blood as well, as if he had also been stabbed in the behind. I remembered that at the big hospital Baragwanath there is a special ward with more than eighty cases of

Africans paralysed from the waist down, victims of gangsters who have planted their thin knives or sharpened knitting-needles with delicate skill between the vertebrae. This did not look like delicate skill, however, but rather the bungling of an amateur. Being Saturday afternoon there was no one around in the outer office, but after a while two *Golden City Post* reporters drifted in.

"Who is he?" I asked.

"Don't know. We found him staggering about in the street outside the office."

"How did he get like this?"

"He'd been to bioscope" (cinema) they told me.

"The bioscope?"

Patiently they explained. There were always stabbings in the bioscope. This kid was probably a tsotsi. He'd gone there with someone else's girl, then either the chap himself or some friends in his gang must have caught sight of the couple—so naturally they stabbed him. "After all," they ended up, "it *is* Saturday afternoon."

"Well—and what's going to happen to him now? Can't we take him along to the hospital? I've got a car here we can use."

"That's all right," they assured me. "We've rung for the ambulance. It's out on its rounds, but when it comes down this way they say they'll call in and pick him up."

CHAPTER X

IN THE SOUP

THERE WAS A stir in the outer office this morning. Through my
door came in Can's husky, urgent voice:

"Cripes, men! Listen to this. Nat, Casey, Butch. Listen to this!" and
he began to read.

". . . A patriot is someone who loves his country and his people,
and who is loyal to its recognized institutions. The true patriot is
also proud of his country and upholds its honour. He may differ
from his fellow citizens over certain points and may even quarrel,
but he will not permit outsiders to say derogatory things about
his country *even though there may be justification for this*. His attitude
is always: *it is none of your business*. If one of the country's own
citizens denigrates or criticises his own country to strangers the
patriot regards him with scorn and brands him as an unfaithful
renegade. There are naturally in all countries such unfortunate, unpatriotic people. . . ."

"Here, what the hell is all this?" cut in the voice of Nat. "People
abroad mayn't criticise because it's none of their business—whatever
that may mean—and people at home mustn't criticise because it's
unpatriotic. Who the devil *can* criticise?"

"Don't be silly, Nat," said Casey from behind his elderly typewriter, "nobody ought to criticise. Where the hell d'you think you're
living?"

"But I don't want to criticise South Africa," persisted Nat, always
ready for a good argument. "South Africa's all right. It's my country
anyway—so far as I'm allowed to have one. I want to criticise the
government!"

"Shut up, both of you," said Can. "D'you want to hear what comes
out of the horse's mouth, or don't you?" He continued reading. "Let
no one say that there is no place for true patriotism in our beloved
South Africa. We know that our composition is complicated and that
there are numerous groups of people which must co-exist. . . . We
are composed of at least ten different population groups of which each
retains its own identity, and despite the uproar which is often made
because of periodic demonstrations and slight commotions there is no

country in the world where ten distinct groups of people co-exist so happily as in South Africa. . . ."

Can paused. "Jeefies, man. D'you think he's living in the same country as the rest of us? He should have seen the distinct groups co-existing happily up at the station this morning when there was a big pass-raid. The cops must have rounded up at least fifty happy co-existers and pushed them all into the kwela-kwela."

"We were co-existing quite happily in Whitey's last night," put in Casey, "with half a jack and a few quarts of beer. Then the cops charge in—some guy just pulled me over the wall in time by my jacket. That's why it's looking the smallest bit frayed at the edges."

"Lewis and I were co-existing very happily with some guys and girls from the University at a house up in Parktown last Saturday night," said Nat.

"What happened?"

"One of these guys has a buddy in the cops who owes him money. This cop manages to phone our guy and warn him. By the time the cops blow in there's no dancing and no drink. We're all just sitting around talking philosophy."

"So what do the cops do?"

"Strut around for a bit and write all our names and addresses down in a book—then they cleared off. . . . But what *is* that stuff you're reading, Can?"

"Government hand-out for the teachers. You didn't know Butch had been a teacher? Well he was once, and they keep on brainwashing him. But you haven't had the best of it yet . . ." and he went on "There are the Whites, born and bred in this country with their Western language and culture but who differ vastly from other Europeans of the Western world in their character and ideals . . ."—"Too bloody true!" said someone—". . . in addition," Can continued skimming through the article, "we have various lower order Coloureds, Indians and the rest. Ah, now here we come to it . . Then there are the various Bantu . . . The various Bantu with their own interesting and charming ways of life and their languages of indescribable beauty. In a modern world their traditional economy and needs necessarily underwent a radical change. . . ."

"Oh come on," urged Nat. "I'm sick of this guy—I've got an article to finish by lunch-time."

". . . but the core of their national character remains unblemished something of which all of us, with them, are truly proud. . . . The different population groups of our country have over the years com to know one another intimately, and although it may not always appear so, the one has more appreciation for the other than for any foreign nation in another country. There are bonds binding us which cannot easily be described . . . The country offers a glorious challenge to the young Bantu, and their White friends stand ready to help where necessary."

"Oh, pack it in," urged Casey. "I don't feel too good this morning anyway."

"It's quite simple," Nat explained. "All the guy says is that we love him and his buddies more than anyone else on earth—in spite of 'periodic demonstrations and commotions'. Well, if he wants to believe that, we can't stop him."

There was silence in the outer office, then Can got up and came over to my room, carrying the magazine from which he had been reading: "Something here you might like to look at, chief."

"Yes, I heard you reading it."

We had now worked together for more than six months, and it was as easy for me to tell Can's moods as, I imagine, it was for him to tell mine.

" 'A glorious challenge to the young Bantu—and their White friends stand ready to help,' " repeated Can. "There's only been one white in this country who stood ready to help, and wasn't just out for what he could get."

"Who was that?"

"Father Huddleston. He's the only one. Why, in the townships today they know his name better than Verwoerd's, though it's years since he left."

"Why d'you think that is?"

"Because he really identified himself with us. No half-way house. He got up once and made a speech, saying, 'From now on I identify myself with the African.' "

"If he did," I said, "he shouldn't have."

"Why?" demanded Can fiercely.

"Father Huddleston's a great man," I said, "but if he ever said, 'From now on I identify myself with the African' then he was saying just the same thing in reverse as that fellow whose stuff you were reading out. That fellow says 'my country'—by which he means 'my Nationalist government'—'right or wrong, and let no one dare to criticise'. In other words, 'I prefer my own prejudices to the truth'. Equally, if Huddleston or anyone else identifies himself entirely with the African—which means he takes their point of view because it's theirs—then he's abandoning his own judgement and discrimination. I don't believe he ever said it, and I repeat—if he did, he shouldn't have."

"Nothing less is any good to us," declared Can flatly. "We don't want someone who supports us when he thinks we're okay, but withdraws his support when we do something un-Western or un-gentlemanly. We've had too much of this patronising liberal attitude—pat us on the head when you think we're going the right way, kick us in the pants when we take a different turning."

"Look, Can," I said, "if you want a hundred-per-cent all-for-the-poor-African-man, you've come to the wrong shop. I support the African in this country, and try to help him state his case, because I don't think he gets a square deal and isn't allowed a say in the country where he lives. Above all, he's not allowed to develop his talents and rise to the position he could occupy. But the fact that I think Africans get a raw deal here doesn't mean I'm willing to hand over my own judgement and support a man when I think he's in the wrong."

"In fact," Can protested, "you're another who goes just as far as it suits you. You don't side with us. We can go along together—but as soon as it's something we want and you don't, then you drop out. That's why I say—Father Huddleston was the only one who was worth a damn."

"Okay," I said. "If you want someone to swallow you whole, with no criticisms and no complaints—try someone else. I didn't come out here because I was fed up with England and couldn't stick the sight of my own people. I came here to make a picture magazine—which is a job I know and understand. If you can learn it from me, you're welcome to. But don't expect me to 'identify myself' with you or anyone else."

"Then you mean," said Can, "you'll always stand on the touchline? You'll always be an English liberal, half-way between everything and nothing?"

"Look, if you can't understand or don't like detachment, that's your affair. You're an African—if you weren't African, you'd be nothing. I'm an Englishman—if I weren't English I'd be nothing, too. I came here to work with you, not to *be* you. I'm ready to work on equal terms; the question is, can you take it?"

"Of course I can take it! That isn't the point. The point is—what's the basis on which we work?"

"The basis is for you to get everything you can out of me while I'm around—and for Peter and Nat and Casey and everyone else to do the same. You don't have to like me. I'm only asking you to *work*. If you learn how to make a paper—the day will come when you'll make it by yourselves. And when that day comes you'll know how to make it properly."

"There wasn't much wrong with the way we used to make it."

"I can tell you one thing that was wrong."

"What's that?"

"You can't make a paper without discipline. You resent discipline from anyone else. But will you take the authority, and exercise discipline yourself? I've offered you what amounts to the running of the paper, while I make up the pages—but you won't take it."

"I never said I wouldn't take it."

"I know you didn't say it, but you don't. With your position——" Can laughed bitterly. "—but I mean you to get your title of assistant editor and the pay back, *soon*, and in such a position, you *must* exercise authority. You can't help it."

Can paused, then: "But you can't expect me to discipline my own people." And, as he said the words, I saw that a six-months' battle had been lost. "As for your own position," he went on. "You won't always be standing in the middle. You won't be able to—not when the real test comes."

"What's the real test?"

"When the shooting war starts—which side will you be on then, black or white? Because the whites will start it one day for sure."

I made no answer, but Can pressed. "Which side will you be on?"

"Depends who starts it, what the issues are, and where I'm standing at the time."

Can snorted and went out. Our talk had been as unsatisfactory to him as it had to me.

*   *   *   *   *

During the months since his installation as General Manager, Weatherstone had introduced a new system into the office. This took the form of working out exactly what every item of expenditure for the magazine—e.g. photographic equipment, dark-room expenses, blocks for reproduction, motor-car repairs and so on—had cost in previous years. From the figure so obtained he subtracted a substantial amount and handed me the result—usually about four-fifths of the previous year's expenditure on any item—as what he called my "budget".

When I protested that the budgets took no account of rapidly rising prices, the changed character of the magazine, the steadily increasing number of pages, and the complete run-down that had taken place, for instance, in photographic equipment and transport, I was told: "The figures are only experimental. Do your best to keep to them, and next year we shall know just where we stand." In fact, however, the so-called "budgets" involved me in endless arguments and a flood of paperwork.

At the moment I had the following memoranda.

MEMORANDUM 24/A

TO: T. HOPKINSON   FROM: G WEATHERSTONE

Subject: CONTRIBUTIONS

1. Your position so far this financial year vis-à-vis your allocation for the year and your actual expenditure is as follows:

Allocation for all contributions for the year £1,400
July Payments (August issue)   £ 173
August Payments (September issue)   £ 191

2. If you continue eating into your allocation at the above rate there will be precious little left for April, May and June next year.

3. I suggest you give this matter your immediate attention and inform me what steps you intend to take.

MEMORANDUM 24/B

TO: T. HOPKINSON   FROM: G. WEATHERSTONE

1. I notice that you have paid the sum of £12 12s. for a story illustration. This in my opinion is too high.

2. I must point out that I also think that £16 16s. per issue for such material as that used on p. 57 is inexcusable.

3. If you continue at the present rate you will have spent your full budget for illustrations for the year by January.

4. This is not a situation which either the Proprietor or myself can contemplate without anxiety.

MEMORANDUM 24/C

TO: T. HOPKINSON   FROM: G. WEATHERSTONE

STAFF SALARY INCREMENTS

1. In regard to your recommendations for staff salary increment I am obliged to reject those in favour of XX and YY, because as told you the Proprietor has directed me to inform you that in hi

opinion these members of your staff are not necessary and should be retrenched.

2. Since we discussed this position it has been again raised by the Proprietor who reaffirms his view.

3. Kindly inform me what action you intend to take on the above, as the salary costs for your paper are threatening to be grossly in excess of the amount budgeted.

Such notes, though irritating, form of course the small change of office life, but on this occasion there was another, longer, note in my basket. The background to this note was that sales of the September issue had been bad. The month, from the staff point of view, had been exceedingly disturbed, work had suffered, and there had been a lack of vitality about the magazine. The long note came from Jim Bailey.

Drum is suffering from shortcomings which are partly due to your newness in this country, but which must be overcome quickly. It is urgent that we put on another 10,000 sales in South Africa, and they are fairly easily obtained.

1. *Drum* is quite out of touch with its public. The reason is obvious —you are failing to identify yourself wholeheartedly with the people for whom you are working.

2. The September *Drum* is middle-class respectable. This is lost on our public who are rough and tough. It is a safe general rule that if your white friends congratulate you on your paper, the less your real public will be interested.

3. Our presentation is not tough enough. Since we cannot improve the printing, and shall be handicapped for several years by semi-visible pictures, you must find ways to overcome this difficulty by bold display and editorial ingenuity.

4. *Drum's* staff of reporters are not doing their job. They collect 3rd rate stories, miss all the important facts and angles and write them in a soggy manner. *Drum* must have personality and guts. It must go all out for the tough stories. It is now several years since *Drum* led the field in S.A. journalism, and it is several years since your reporters did a day's work. They have for far too long formed a mutual admiration society.

To be constructive may I suggest:

1. You mix round the town with your readers here and in Cape Town and in Durban. They will give you contacts, angles, and the feel of public opinion.

2. You invite highly critical outsiders to a monthly post-mortem, telling you exactly what is wrong with every issue. There must be no holds barred.

3. Aim at fourteen important stories every month. They should be made up as follows: 4 good stories from G. R. Naidoo in Durban, 4 good stories from Mackenzie in Cape Town. This is a minimum. Three strong African Reef stories, of which one must be a tough crime story. These are all easily got. A list of all the "fences" in Johannesburg with the manner in which they receive and dispose of stolen goods would go down well. Also one Coloured story from the Transvaal, one story from the West African edition, and one up-to-date political news story from another part of Africa should complete the issue. This last should be written inside the office to avoid expense.

Complete *Paris-Match* style coverage is important, plus decent subbing so that the text is really alive.

I think that you know me well enough by now to realise that these comments are made with the best of goodwill and with full appreciation for all you have done for the magazine since you came out here.

Stage one, when you got into the saddle, is now over. Stage two, the exciting one, must start."

There are, I know, people on whom complaints exercise a beneficial effect. They think: "Those in authority are dissatisfied with me. I must do better and earn their praise." There is another type that is able to extract from criticism anything there may be of value and, for the rest, to shrug it off without another thought. For an editor this is the ideal temperament. There is a third type which, while resenting criticism, makes an outward show of accepting it, expresses gratitude for the advice, blames the weaknesses of colleagues, and undertakes once a month to turn over a new leaf, crack the whip harder in all directions, reorganise itself and everybody else, and show the results of all this effort and devotion very shortly.

I had examples of these types among my colleagues. My own reaction—and I do not defend it—is a different one. I can respond readily to anyone who says—"Look here, this is a bad situation. How are we going to sort it out?" But a flow of criticism, particularly in writing and from a distance, both angers and depresses me. On this occasion told Weatherstone that if he "retrenched" YY, or agreed to anyone else retrenching him, he could retrench me too, since YY was the most promising young journalist in the office; and I rang to see if I could have a word with my employer. Jim Bailey, however, had gone away to his farm, and it was not until ten days later that he passed me in the office, smiled cheerfully and asked if I had got his note. I said "Yes" and suggested we discuss it right away.

"I hope," Jim began, once we were inside the office, "that you took all the points I made in the right spirit. It's always been a tradition of *Drum* that there should be absolutely straight-from-the-shoulder criticisms. I want that to be kept up."

"Yes," I said, "I mean to keep it up. Which of us begins?"

"Which? I suppose we begin by going through my memorandum."

"All right. On the general point that the paper is missing fire, it is, and you're probably right in blaming my lack of knowledge. Only time can put that right. Time, and some guidance from those who know the readers and who live among them."

"This is crucial," Jim declared. "You must see more of your readers. The easiest way is to see more of your staff. Do you go out with them regularly after working hours?"

"No," I said. "By the time I've finished here they've very naturally gone home."

"But are you in *touch* with your staff? That's the point. The whole thing is really an attitude of mind. Do you identify yourself with them—or don't you?"

"No," I said. "I don't, but then I'm not . . ."

"Well, there you are! Until you do you'll never make a success of this paper."

"Can I finish what I was going to say? I'm not an urban African. However much I try, I can't become one. I like urban Africans; I think I can make a paper for them. But if I can, it won't be by pretending to be one of them, it will be because I know my job and can work with them."

Jim smiled dryly and threw a letter to me across the desk. It came from a professor at a Cape University, someone I had heard of but never met, saying how well he thought of *Drum* and how interested he had been in the last few issues.

"That," said Jim, "is the kind of thing we *don't* want. White approval for *Drum* is the hand of death. The bishop was speaking favourably of the paper the other day as well . . ."

"All right. I get your point. And now can I say a couple of things?"

"If you want."

"First, what you say about *Drum's* 'staff of reporters'. The 'staff' consists of three—young Nat, Butch who has been sent home, and Can. You tell me that they do no work and form a 'mutual admiration society'. In fact they no more admire one another than you and I do, but that's not the point. The point is that *you* picked this team. You instructed me that none of them were to be sacked whatever happened. You—or someone—has given them about as much discipline as a crew of pirates. For six months I've tried to get the roots of journalism into their minds—one, thank God, has the roots by nature. And now you write me a memo hanging the whole lot round my neck and blaming *me* because they 'haven't done a day's work for several years'. I've been here six months. What the hell were you doing up till then?"

"Look," said Jim. "There's no point in taking these things the wrong way. I realise you don't like criticism, but as proprietor of this firm I've got to have my say."

"You've had your say about me as editor. Now I'm having my say about you as proprietor. And the second thing is this. If we're going to work together, then we *have* to work together. You know the country, I don't, and I'm always ready to take your advice about it. I'm also willing to carry the responsibility for everything I do and the mistakes I make. But I won't carry responsibility for arrangements you—or someone—made before I came out. And the situation between us has to be that we're both in this together; not that I'm in the soup, or something worse, and you're outside pouring more over me with a ladle."

"All right, then," said Jim, recovering his good nature, "we're both in the soup together. But remember—the important thing is to *identify* yourself wholeheartedly. If you do that, everything is bound to work out all right."

CHAPTER XI

BACK TO WEST AFRICA

WHEN ONE THINKS of South Africa, one thinks naturally of warmth and sunshine, but in fact the winter—which corresponds roughly to the period of an English or American summer—can in some parts be sharply cold. Moreover, to a newcomer it is treacherous; in Johannesburg on a winter afternoon the temperature can fall ten degrees between three and four o'clock. At lunch-time, escaping from the office for an hour, one walks basking in hot sun. By the time an afternoon cup of tea comes round, one is cursing oneself for not having brought a sweater, and looking around to see who has pinched the electric heater this time.

The African staff in particular seemed to suffer from the cold. On a really bitter day one or two would sometimes sit in front of their typewriters in overcoats and woollen ear-caps, quite still, as if suddenly paralysed. Joe Blumberg also used to complain bitterly that the cold "comes up through the floor". When his pleas for a small piece of carpet were ignored by the management—which immediately saw itself as being asked to provide Persian rugs for everyone—Joe would sit with his shoes wrapped up in newspaper, and a look of exaggerated suffering on his face whenever I went past.

In addition to the cold which can be measured in degrees, there is something else which affects the newcomer for a year or two. The Reef on which Johannesburg is built, and from which it derived its golden wealth, is really a high range of hills. Johannesburg itself, nearly 6,000 feet above sea-level, is at an altitude far greater than that of any mountain in the British Isles. Because of this the air is thin and insubstantial, and in winter peculiarly dry and piercing. Moreover, the mine-dumps, or heaps of yellow dust from which the gold has been extracted, surround the city closely; some of them even press their way in towards its heart. Despite many attempts, no one has been successful in finding vegetation which can nourish itself on their aridity, and most are simply topless pyramids of yellow grit, scored with channels and rivulets from the thunder-rains of summer. When the wind blows strongly in the dry winter, a plume of dust swirls up from the top of every dump, and comes driving in over the suburbs and the city, maddening housewives; covering every desk, table, and flat surface in the office; inflaming eyes and irritating nostrils; causing throats to go septic and sinuses to flare.

By the middle of our first winter I had begun to suffer from a succession of sore throats and colds. I had great difficulty in breathing, and felt as though all the small corridors and winding passages—which I imagined as existing inside my nose and forehead—were continually inflamed. In addition, the thinness of the air—which visiting fighters and athletes find a great handicap to their exertions—handicapped me in the opposite way. I could not sleep. I would drop off normally, that is in about half a minute, only to wake again in an hour or two, gasping, and with the sense that my heart had missed a beat. For a couple of minutes, or an hour, I would doze off—then the same thing happened once more, and my head would jerk up with a start. When, as a result of colds and sore throats, I missed a day or two at the office, work piled up, difficulties increased, criticisms became sharper, rows more frequent—and again I found I was taking a couple of days off.

One evening, still feeling ill, I had to fly down to Cape Town. Ken Mackenzie was just arriving, and I was particularly anxious to meet him, and do whatever I could to settle him in. When his ship arrived, it was a long time before the passengers could leave, and Ken and his family were among the last. As I hung around the draughty baggage-halls or walked up and down the windy quays, I could feel my temperature mounting. Next day I was in bed at the small hotel where I had booked a room. Six penicillin pills from a doctor got me back to Johannesburg—and to bed once more. So it went on, far into September and the start of spring, spells of normal work interrupted by occasional days or half-days off.

One afternoon, which I had been dozing through uneasily, Dorothy came and sat down on my bed.

"I think you should make up your mind," she said.

"My *mind*? What about?"

"Are you absolutely certain you want to stay here—or would you rather go back and take a job in England?"

"Good heavens!" I sat up, disturbed at the thought that I might have shown—and must therefore be experiencing—any doubt on the matter. "I'm quite clear I want to stay here."

"I know you feel you have to—but that's not the point. You don't have to at all. The point is—do you *want* to? If you find you don't want to, I'm quite ready to pack up and go back. It would mean a b of trouble, but that couldn't be helped. It would be far better than staying on if you're not happy."

I thought for a minute. Then, "I'm quite certain I want to stay here," I said. "There are difficulties about work—some which I had expected but others which I hadn't—and I have the feeling they will get worse. However, all jobs have difficulties, and I like this country. There's more life to the square foot than we've had anywhere else. I'm not even sure I *could* go back—I mean settle down contentedly to something like the life we had before."

"You're sure you like it? *Sure* you want to stay?"

"Quite sure."

"Then why d'you think you keep on getting ill? You didn't get ill like this in London."

"I don't know . . . one thing is the air. When people have talked about the different air in different places, I've never known what they meant. Air's just air—the stuff you breathe. But I don't seem able to breathe this air properly—it's too thin."

"Thin or not, you can probably get used to it—if you make up your mind you're going to."

"How d'you suggest I do that?"

"Accept that it's all there is—just as you would if you were stuck down in the Arctic."

"And for another?"

"Well, you might try doing breathing exercises every morning. . . . And another thing."

"What's that?"

"Don't work so late at the office. Work's supposed to end at five—you finish at half-past seven or eight. Does the staff stay on until half-past seven?"

"No."

"Does Jim Bailey stay on until half-past seven?"

"No."

"Then don't you do it. You're making the same mistake with *Drum* as you made with *Picture Post*."

"Oh! What's that?"

"Identifying yourself with it, which is all to the good as far as the magazine's concerned, but not so good for you personally. That's why you're the first to arrive and the last to leave."

"It's the quietest time in the office. It's the best chance to work out what's to go into the paper, and I can do the lay-outs without being interrupted."

"But the result of all this effort is that you become identified with the magazine. Then when things go wrong, or you feel yourself let down, you get upset. But you know by now that things are *bound* to go wrong, and you're certain to be, or to feel, let down. I suggest you come home at six, have a drink and read for an hour before dinner—and read something that has nothing to do with work."

I felt, as all men feel, resentful at having my ways criticised, and at the implication that it was my own fault if I didn't remain well. However, I could see that what Dorothy said was true, and the mere thought of having some sort of plan encouraged me.

Luckily just at this moment came a break in the routine.

*   *   *   *   *

When I had been up in West Africa in February, I had promised to go back there in six months. For a couple of months now I had been anxious to make good my promise, and now there arose not so much the opportunity as the necessity of going. Agnew, our editorial adviser in Accra, had packed up and left. I had a good deal of sympathy with Agnew. He had never seemed to me well suited to his job; I guessed that he was happiest in a big office among a number of near-equals. He was not used to authority and had acquired no manner of carrying it easily. He stood on his dignity—and few of us have enough of that to support our weight. Also I suspected that in his heart he did not like Africans, or not enough. Jim Bailey, who had been up to the West Coast in May, and again in June and July, had hammered him. Agnew wrote me a long letter of defence and explanation—and cleared off. I haven't seen him since.

It was now clearly necessary for me to go there, sort matters out with Ian Pritchard, and evolve some new arrangement. As regards what such new arrangement might be, however, we had very little choice.

One of the handicaps under which we worked at *Drum* was that our staff being the absolute minimum needed to get through the month's work, no allowance was made for ill-health, holidays or accidents. Such absences, though they came round constantly—and indeed from the hazardous life of our Africans and the impossibility of their keeping in touch with us by telephone, occurred far more often and unexpectedly than in a European office—were regarded temporary embarrassments to be got over by everyone working a bit harder. The loss or absence of one man, therefore, immediately imposed an extra strain on the rest. More serious, from the point of view of the firm's future, was that we had no trainees. Neither on the management side nor on our own was there ever anyone who was learning a job, and could be promoted when the time came into a suitable vacancy. Everyone's salary had to be fully justified on his present work.

In view of the fact that the papers in the group were still running at a loss, economy was clearly necessary, but the effect of carrying it to extremes was that the departure of anyone in a responsible position rocked the whole organisation.

We had no fat on our bones on which we could live in times of emergency, and our normal leanness had been made more acute in the last months by a succession of "economy drives". Our cupboard being bare, the alternatives were to find someone new, who would be bound to take a few months accustoming himself to the position, or do without an adviser altogether.

*   *   *   *   *

After the harassment of the last few weeks in the office, the journey up was a day of peace. The huge plane rolled across the sky like a heavenly billiard-ball over a celestial table, and almost the only interruptions were the pleasant ones for drinks or food. We reached Kano late, and spent the night at the airport hotel. In the morning the plane which should have carried me on had broken down, and I was left with a whole day to spend. It seemed silly to hang about the airport, where the only things to see were lizards, and a man in handsome robes mounted on a camel, sounding a long silver horn to impress tourists whenever a plane came in. Luckily, however, I had the name of *Drum's* agent in Kano, and decided to take a car into the town and try to find his office.

Kano is an extraordinary city, one of the oldest in Africa, and for centuries a terminus of the great caravan routes across the Sahara. As I drove in from the airport, such a caravan was just setting out—forty or fifty camels swinging purposefully along through the dust in single file, head to tail, the camel-drivers in their flowing robes reminding me of the figures in Bible illustrations. To one side of the road was this scene out of the past, almost as odd as seeing a fleet of caravels leave harbour; on the other side the huge screen of an outdoor cinema rose up. Against the low white-washed wall which kept out the non-payers were piled rows and rows of broken-down cars and lorries, like the bones of some vast mechanised caravan that had collapsed and could go no further.

The Arab city, when we reached it, was a vast space four miles across, surrounded by protecting walls built—like the town and everything in it—of baked mud. *Drum's* office turned out to be a gap between two houses, with a piece of corrugated iron as roof and a long trestle table as equipment. *Drum's* agent was not there, but when I explained who I was, a tall Arab who said he was a friend offered to take me round the town. Swarms of children, darting in flocks like birds; Touaregs from French territory, tall and haughty, muffled in smoke-blue clothing; an Arab perched cross-legged on a donkey's rump driving a whole herd of donkeys—teetering on their tiny hooves as if on stepping-stones—before him with a switch; an occasional burdened camel swinging by with a sailor's rolling gait; Arab horses, out for exercise, stepping delicately as if accustomed to walk on carpets, tossing elegant small heads, and snorting through bloodshot nostrils....

My guide took me to the enormous palace of the Emir. Its mud walls, reddish-purple in colour, were scrolled with paint, battlemented, adorned with tiny turrets and cornices, and patrolled by guards. The gateways stood out from the walls, imposing as a mediaeval castle's. Close to one of the gates was a stone or cement platform with deep holes in, like narrow wells. The covers had been taken off, and squatting beside every hole were dyers who lowered long twists of cloth into the dye; at last, after many dippings, it began to take on the beautiful smoke-blue of the desert riders' clothing. A fearful smell rose up out of the dye pits as if they were filled with old bones, dog dung and sulphuric acid.

To one side, from a kind of tent, there came a rhythmical pummelling or beating; my guide led me to the tent and raised the flap. Inside in semi-darkness, a dozen or twenty forms were hammering newly dyed cloth with wooden cudgels: "That makes it soft," my guide explained, "and spreads the dye evenly all through." Thinking of life spent hammering cloth, I said: "I suppose the Emir still has enormous power—even in modern times?"

My guide put his fingers to his lips. "Two days ago," he said softly, "a man was ordered to be given forty lashes by the Emir's guards for speaking disrespectfully of him in the market place."

He took me to the mosque, then to the old market. This last was the strangest sight I had come across in Africa. It was enclosed, like everything else in Kano, by a baked mud wall, and approached by a kind of mud bridge over a dirty stream. Within its bounds were hundreds of stalls—not movable stalls but mud emplacements, rather like children's sand-castles set solid, or the nests of giant flamingos. Some had

mud roof; over others canopies were suspended, resting on posts or
pillars at each corner. The stalls had no fixed pattern, shape or size,
but seemed to have been constructed to the builder's fancy—usually
with a platform raised some two feet from the ground, on which the
owner squatted among his wares, with a low ridge all round to prevent
them rolling away. Between the stalls wound narrow tracks or alleys
worn by the passing of myriads of bare feet; every now and then a
drain, into which passers-by relieved themselves freely, cut an im-
placable straight line across the maze. A market-place, I thought, must
have looked like this in Babylon or Cunaxa.

The contents of the stalls were both fascinating and repellent. In
one huge ragged lumps of raw meat, black with flies. In another
different kinds of grain in little pyramids. In a third men sat spinning
cotton, using a spindle and their toes. There was a grocer's with a few
tins and packets, some flat brown cakes of sugar, like pieces of old
kitchen soap, and a bowl of honey—a muddy mixture full of drowned
insects and their wings. A beauty parlour sold antimony, a mineral
which the women soak to produce a substance for blackening their
eyes; henna, in which they dip their hands to make them red; and lye
for making soap. A chemist offered heaps of withered herbs, in piles
or hanging in bundles, as medicine; but also, as charms to ease the path
of life, magnify one's status, attract or satisfy the object of desire, and
harm the hated—were the ill-smelling skins of vultures, rats and hedge-
hogs; the heads of crows and herons; dried mice and weasels; powdered
rhino horn and teeth of leopards. Then suddenly, amongst the primitive and gruesome, a stall selling cheap Italian brooches, bracelets,
mirrors, strings of beads; a man who hammered kerosene lamps out
of condensed milk tins; and money-changers sitting cross-legged amid
piles of dollars, pounds, marks, francs and the currency of half the
world.

From this city of the past I flew down next day to Lagos.

"Well, Mr. Hopkinson," said Nelson, "I suppose you've come up
here to put someone in place of Mr. Agnew."

"That depends. Have you anyone in mind for the job?"

"There is no job for anyone to fill. I don't think we require a white
editorial adviser, telling us what to put into the Nigerian edition."

"It's sometimes useful to have a second opinion. I find it easy to
make mistakes about what will or won't interest the readers."

"For that we have Mr. Pritchard. He knows the country well. He
has good judgement. I am happy to have everything seen by Mr.
Pritchard. He can read it all through after it's ready to send down to

you—and if I've any doubts about anything I will talk it over with him before I start."

"Do you feel confident you can handle the edition yourself? You'd have no worries about taking it on?"

Nelson smiled his sardonic smile.

"Have you been satisfied with my work?" he asked. "You, as editor-in-chief, have you been satisfied with what I've been sending you down these last six months?"

"More than satisfied."

"Well, Mr. Hopkinson, I can tell you this—if I have been able to satisfy you when I have Mr. Agnew sitting on my shoulders and giving me advice I don't want, I shall much more than satisfy you now that he has gone." He paused. "That is, unless you put someone else on my shoulders in his place."

"And how's the staff been doing? How's Faji?"

"Faji is good. He is waiting in the other room to see you."

"And the two beginners?"

"They were more trouble to me than a help. So I have got rid of them."

"You'll need some help if you're going to be on your own."

"I always need good help if I can find it. But I shall not need it any more for being without Mr. Agnew. However, Mr. Hopkinson, you avoid the question. You haven't told me yet what you intend to do. Is there to be another Mr. Agnew—or not?"

"I can't give you a straight answer, Nelson," I said. "It doesn't only depend on me. I'm going over in a few days to Ghana to talk it over with Mr. Pritchard."

In charge of the business side at Lagos at this time was Roy Paulson, since Ian was living in Accra to keep an eye on everything after Agnew's departure.

"How's it all going, Roy?" I asked.

"Wonderful!" said Roy. "It's been the best six months up here the paper has ever had. We've put on 40,000 in sales since the beginning of the year. This last month, September, we've sold something like 145,000 copies out of 148,000 sent up to West Africa. The returns are fabulously low, two or three per cent. Why, even in Europe they reckon it's a 'sell-out' when they have six per cent returns, and here with our home-made distribution we're getting half that. I never thought it could happen."

"Thank God for a bit of success somewhere," I said. "What's the cause, d'you think?"

"Mainly that we're getting better stuff. Partly the idea of a photographic magazine has gone down well—people who can't really read enjoy the pictures, and get someone to tell them what they're all about. And partly separating the two editions. No one in Nigeria wants to read a life of Nkrumah or the story of a Ghanaian football team—and it must be the same, I suppose, in Ghana."

The fact of the magazine's success was, of course, common knowledge through the office, and it made an extraordinary difference to everyday life. Everyone was more cheerful, confident, better tempered. Requests for necessary equipment could now occasionally be granted, the golden hope of a pay rise loomed in many minds, and quarrels between departments had become less bitter. In place of the usual—"Why the hell can't you people get out and *sell* the paper?", answered by an equally indignant "Why the hell don't you give us a decent paper we can sell?"—there were congratulations and benignity, with a pleasant sense of benefits to come, when our success in sales should have been transformed into profits through an increase in the selling-price of the magazine. This operation was planned to take place early in the new year.

*　　*　　*　　*　　*

If the soft climate of Lagos was physically relaxing, the human climate was agreeably relaxing too. White and black met everywhere on equal terms; one could take the staff out for a beer, or be taken out in turn; we could all lunch together, or go out for an evening drinking and dancing with their wives and girl-friends. It was a glimpse of normal human life, and I wished the staff from Johannesburg were here to share it.

One such evening, getting on for nine o'clock, I was sitting in my hotel. I had expected Nelson and his wife to dinner, but either they or I had made a mistake about the arrangements. I had to have dinner on my own, and now there was a whole evening before me. For the past two days it had rained violently, deluges of water lashing down, flooding the gutters alongside the streets—and in Lagos they seemed always more sewers than gutters—and turning much of the low-lying city into a swamp. At lunch-time, when several of us went out together, we had got half-drenched in a ten-yard dash from the car to the hotel, and half-drenched again afterwards in the ten yards back. You could get soaked through as you fitted your car key into its lock.

But now, as I stood at the window of the huge empty lounge, I could see a full moon rippling up and down in silver slices on the waters of the lagoon, and the yellow light of the street lamps reflected in huge puddles along the causeway. The rain had stopped, a cool breeze had begun to blow, and I at once felt a longing to get out and walk around. I might, I thought, find a part of the town in which signs of life still lingered, and at least the walking would refresh me.

Down on the causeway a double line of traffic streamed to and fro, and there was a steady flow of cyclists circling the puddles on the muddy pathway where I slithered to avoid the cars. Of walkers, however, there were almost none, and certainly in half an hour I did not meet another white. White men do not walk in Lagos, or, if they do, they don't walk after dark; and many curious faces gleamed at me as I pushed on across the long bridges, past the railway station, in the general direction of the harbour where I still imagined the centre of this centre-less town must lie. Suddenly a large car drew into the pavement alongside, and a voice called out. I looked up. At the wheel was a uniformed chauffeur, and in the back were the imposing figures of two Nigerians in the loose dark-patterned robes which, following the example set by Dr. Azikiwe and other leading men, are increasingly worn in place of Western suits.

"Can we offer lift? Has your car broken down? Where can we take you?"

I hesitated; I had come out to enjoy a walk, but to refuse the offer seemed churlish. I climbed in, and sat down on a small seat facing my two hosts. In the light of the passing street lamps I could see that the one immediately opposite was a man of great bulk and presence, his loose stomach swathed in folds of bluish cloth.

"Where are we to take you? Is your home on the Island—or do you look for friends?"

"Neither. I was just taking a walk."

"Then where do you stay?"

"I am staying at the Mainland Hotel."

"But we go now *away* from the Mainland Hotel."

"Yes, I know, but I did not like to refuse your friendly offer. It doesn't make any difference to me which direction I walk. Put me down in a couple of miles and I'll walk back."

Both men broke into laughter, we shook hands and exchanged names. The big man's face was agreeable, even jolly, when he laughed, but sank into a heavy despondency as soon as the smile faded. The second man also introduced himself; he was of smaller build, with the round face and smooth polished features common in Nigeria. He

black and brown robes and the brown circular cap he wore gave him
a look of authority; I imagined he might be a chief or government
official.

"My name is Iwonu. I am petty trader," he said simply.

The big man was still curious about me. He seemed to think I was
concealing something, or perhaps that there was an opportunity for
profitable trade.

"You have car back at hotel? It is broken? It will not go? I make you
good price for old car, you trade it in against new model. Here is my
card," he said, fishing in some mysterious corner of his robes. "You
come see me. I treat you well, give you good terms."

"My car goes all right," I said, "but it's in a country a long way
away. Even for a good price, it wouldn't be worth fetching it up
here"—and, as we had now driven three or four miles, I suggested
that he put me down and let me find my own way back.

"No, not wise walk here by night," they both protested. "Are bad
boys in this town. You come up my place for a cold beer—then I
send you back to hotel by car."

I thanked my host and, after another mile through narrow streets
where a lot of selling was still going on in lighted doorways, we came
out into a quieter district. When the driver pulled in to the side in a
street of silent villas, I stepped straight out into a pool over my shoes.
My host led the way, hoisting his robes up round his knees, squelching
along through the mud to the back of a tall stucco building, then up
a narrow outside staircase with an iron railing. For a moment, as I
went up the stairs between the two, I had a twinge of fear; my host
looked so enormous, and the district dark and eerie. Doubt changed
to interest as we came out from the stairhead into a kitchen. Seated
together on the floor was a little group of people, a powerfully-built,
pregnant wife, a sulky elder daughter, a glum-looking child of perhaps ten, and a lively little thing of about six who at once came running to her father's arms.

After shaking hands all round, I was led through into the front
room. This was long and narrow like a converted corridor; yellow
walls well marked with finger-prints, thin cotton curtains on big
rings; half-a-dozen rexine-covered armchairs. My host sent out for
some bottles of cold beer and a little whisky, and pushed me down
into one of the armchairs, heaping an armful of photograph albums on
me. Then he went over to the radiogram and turned it on full-blast,
as if the demons of depression were to be driven out by force of sound.
I looked at this instrument with loathing, first for the appalling noise,

and then for its appearance; it seemed to be decorated with every kind of substance, varnished wood, brass, chromium, imitation marble.

Turning my head away to reduce the sound, I started paging through the albums. Most of the pictures were of himself and his wife, and many I had seen already in the form of glass and plastic-mounted cut-outs, decorating the tables and the top of the radiogram. The photographs showed that my host was a salesman or agent of some kind; that he worked for a big importing firm; that he had a number of white acquaintances who attended his parties—("That little party cost me £200")—and asked him back to their business entertainments at which they all posed together looking matey. Before I was half-way through the first album, my host had begun to doze.

When the drink came he sat up with a jerk and shared it equally, a tot of whisky and a bottle of cold beer each, then sent the child out once again with money. She, the ten-year-old, received all his orders with a cold impassivity, whereas the smallest girl sported gaily about and was clearly not afraid of him or anyone. She had greeted his guests charmingly by kneeling in front of us in turn and taking our outstretched hand in both of hers. Dressed in a tube of dark blue cloth she had a way of drawing herself up to her full three feet, opening the cloth out, and swathing it tightly round her tiny figure. She did this every minute or two, as some young men tap cigarettes on cases obviously thinking it a very grown-up gesture.

After a few minutes the ten-year-old came back with a dish of hard-boiled eggs. Having eaten two or three—they were only the size of bantam eggs, but I'd already had dinner—I refused any more.

"I don't know how you can drink without eating," said my host with good-humoured contempt, swallowing another handful.

Now, as the radiogram continued its rhythmic onslaught, he stood up. He had taken off his robes and was wearing only a vest and a dirty pair of beige trousers over which his stomach hung like an impending avalanche. Shuffling in time to the music, he tried to dance first with his little daughter, but she scarcely reached his waist, nor had she yet picked up the peculiar hitching rhythm, so he shouted at the elder. Facing each other, but not touching, they stamped and shuffled rhythmically, up and down the narrow room.

There was something both terrible and pathetic about this giant in decay, a human ruin without even the dignity of age. His only enjoyments, it was plain, were eating, drink and sex; he claimed to have fifteen children—"and perhaps some more". His wife—a powerful woman with a fine, but submissive face—was pregnant. A young woman, more pregnant still, made her appearance, knelt down, said a few words and went out. "That's the junior wife," the petty trader told me.

From the photographs I could see that he was successful in business; he made money; he competed with the white traders as an equal, imposing on them, no doubt, quite as much as they imposed on him. He had a big car and a chauffeur. Yet with all this, with prosperity, as much as he could eat and drink, as many women as he could cope with—enjoyment somewhere eluded him. He looked utterly bewildered and bedevilled. If he had been a European or American, the conventional answer would have been easy; he was repressed, cut off by guilt from his natural capacity for enjoyment; he was over-anxious, over-worked, troubled with ulcers. He needed analysis, hospitalisation, relieving of his burden of anxiety. But nobody could have been less repressed, less neurotically anxious than my host; he didn't need natural enjoyment, he needed interest in life. Inside him, he was bored to tears. He had hoped I might interest him, but I hadn't. Wearying of the dancing, and catching perhaps my speculative eye upon him, he turned the radiogram down slightly, so that it was at least possible to hear each other, and made one last attempt: "What do you do? What is your work?"

"I'm a journalist. I edit a magazine. You may know it—it's called *Drum*."

"Oh, do you? We all know *Drum*. But *Drum* is Nigerian magazine, and you are white. How you know enough about Nigerians to edit *Drum*?"

"Most of the work for the Nigerian edition is done by Nigerians. They decide what stories to cover. They write all the text and take the pictures."

"What then is left for you to do?"

"I decide how much to make out of each story. I plan and arrange the pictures on the page . . . I try to build a connected magazine out of all the material they send me. . . ." I was beginning to get interested, as I always do when I think anyone wants to hear about my work.

"Ah!" he rubbed his stomach thoughtfully. "I see how it is. The real work is all done by the Nigerians—it is still often that way in this country. But where you do this? I do not ever see you here in Lagos. And"—suddenly remembering—"you say your car is far away. Where is this place? Where you do all this work you say you do?"

"In South Africa. Our headquarters are in Johannesburg."

The big man drew a deep breath and looked across at his friend, who was already glancing up from the picture albums.

"So—you are a *South African*? You live there in South Africa, and you say you work for *Drum*? How is this possible?"

"That's where the magazine is made up and printed," I said. "The Nigerian edition as well. As it happens I'm not a South African, I'm English—but I live in South Africa and work there."

"You white people living in South Africa," my host declared emphatically, "we here know all about *you*. You oppress our people. You keep down the Africans. They are not allowed to work at this job or that one, to live in this place or that. They may not have education like white men. They must not go into hotels or restaurants. All of them are forced to carry passes . . . What is this way you treat our people? Why are you doing these things to us?"

The petty trader was also becoming heated: "If you wish to act in such way, why you now coming to Nigeria? In Nigeria we do not like such things—to treat our Africans in these bad ways."

"Not all of us in South Africa like these laws either. Many of us think differently. Many would like . . ." I began and stopped. Something was sticking in my throat. Although I had only lived in South Africa six months, I felt already a strong attachment to the country; much as I detested its official policies, I found it impossible to join with strangers in casual attacks. An argument, a discussion, by all means—but not just to echo the opinions of those who knew nothing at first-hand.

Secondly, even if I had wished to dissociate myself from my adopted country, what would be the good? Such claims were too obviously interested to be accepted. And how much justification would they have in any case? Must not everyone who lives in a country carry some responsibility for what goes on there, even if he doesn't like it? Hadn't we all—British, Americans, French, Russians, people of almost every nation—felt righteously indignant at the Germans who tolerated the Nazi regime, and contemptuous of their argument, "What could we do?"

"If you disagree with the policies of your government," my Nigerian acquaintances could argue, "then you must get them changed—or hold yourself responsible with everybody else for their continuance."

Encouraged by my silence, my host was continuing his angry speech: ". . . you won't be allowed to go on like this for long time. *We* will not allow it. Africa will not allow it. The whole world will not allow it. You better hurry up and change your ways."

"I would like us in South Africa to change our ways"—I said, then added, rather nettled—"but if we don't, what can you do? It's a great distance, almost without roads."

My host smiled triumphantly. "Do not worry! I tell you—you need not worry yourself over this. We find a way. One, two, three years— then we shall find a way!"

"But you've no ships. . . ."

My host leaned across and patted my knee, good humour returning as he thought of our coming disaster. "Do not worry, my friend. Dr. Azikiwe, Prime Minister Nkrumah—they soon find a way! They not allow things in your country to go on like this."

CHAPTER XII

A STRONG MAN ARMED

AFTER A COUPLE of days I flew over to Ghana. Accra, where there is so often a breeze blowing in off the sea, seemed delightfully fresh after the dank lagoons of Lagos. I took a morning off and, borrowing the office car, drove out to one of the beaches up the coast. Palms waved against a cobalt sea, on which anchored steamers hung far out, unloading their cargoes by swinging grabfuls into surf-boats. Though the sun was strong, a thin film of mist blew steadily in off the wave-tops, thickening the air, stickying face and clothes, and leaving a salt taste on one's lips. The crows which flapped heavily over had white collars and shirt-fronts, and a kingfisher big as a woodpecker with a speckled back and dull red breast, perched on a bough to snatch crabs from the muddy creek. As I lay under a palm tree, half in shadow half in sun, I thought: "This is the first morning I've done nothing since I came to Africa," and a voice seemed to answer, "Then it's your first really African morning."

Ian Pritchard was married now, and I stayed with him and his wife in the upper half of a house, rented by *Drum*, on the outskirts of the city. It was pleasant and roomy, with a border of tropical garden all round, but mosquitoes bred in myriads in the near-by ditches, full always of floodwater from the last rains, despite continued drainage operations; and the flat, quiet enough during the day, reverberated half the night to the noise of two nightclubs, one on each side, the Lido and the Tiptoe. The Lido had the better girls, but the Tiptoe band made the louder noise; it was like sleeping in the no-man's land between two armies which had not yet clashed, but were still summoning their distant followers to battle.

On the question of the editorial adviser, Pritchard had no hesitation. His one fear was that a half-baked appointment might be made and himself landed with someone in a position of authority who had no experience of journalism. The chances of getting an adviser who would really be useful were, he thought, about fifty to one against, since the few journalists with any knowledge of the country were all in good jobs and would not move, and those people who were available, and knew their way to some extent about the country, were not journalists

"I can make sure you don't find yourself landed with a wet," I said, "provided you can be sure of carrying on all right if you have no one."

"Suits me," Ian answered. "Nelson's quite able to manage on his own, and I'll be here to help Henry out with the Ghana end of things."

"So long as you *are* here, that should work," I agreed. "But what's going to happen if you shift over to Lagos or come down South?"

"Let's worry about that when it happens, shall we?"

And so the matter was decided.

*　　　*　　　*　　　*　　　*

A task which faced me during this stay was to pay a visit to one of the ministers in the Nkrumah Government—Krobo Edusei. Krobo had the reputation of being a tough negotiator, a forceful orator, and —if you caught him in a friendly moment—a genial, good-natured host. I should have preferred to see him informally at his home; however it had been arranged that I should go and talk to him in his office. He proved to be short, thick-set, voluble. I had come, accompanied by our local editor, Henry Ofori, to suggest that we run his life-story in *Drum*. Krobo was a man about whom lively tales were continually circulating, and everyone would be eager to read his story and see which, if any, of them had been printed; but we had first to obtain his permission and co-operation.

Krobo acted hard-to-get. "No, no. On no account! There are many more important persons than myself—many more interesting persons than myself. Many of them! Also I am a loyal member of the Convention People's Party. I am a loyal follower of Kwame Nkrumah. As a follower, I do not want the limelight. Others should be written about before me. I will not take anybody's place. . . ."

This is going to take a bit longer than I expected, I told myself, and began the slow manoeuvring familiar to every journalist, when a politician means to accept the proposal you're making, but has not yet found a satisfactory formula for doing so. At this moment Krobo's eye fell on a copy of *Drum* which Henry had brought and was just opening to place before the Minister. The issue contained part of the story of one such "more important person", Gbedemah, the Minister of Finance. It was possible—whoever had written the article suggested —that Gbedemah might become Ghana's next Prime Minister, when in course of time Kwame Nkrumah should vacate the post, perhaps by becoming the country's first President. . . . At this our host exploded:

"Mr. Gbedemah—the next Prime Minister? What nonsense! Who has written this stuff?"—Henry began corkscrewing his eyebrow with an agonised expression—"Why, for myself, I am certain that our great Kwame is immortal. I am convinced that He will never die. But if ever something *should* happen to him, or if he should one day retire of his own free will, it is not for you or Mr. Gbedemah to say who the next Prime Minister will be. No! That is not even for our great leader to decide. The Prime Minister does not choose his own successor; that is not the custom of democracy. The rank-and-file chooses him. Why even in South Africa, when your Prime Minister died, it was the rank-and-file that decided who should follow him. Am I not right?"

He spoke rapidly, in short sentences and with bold gesticulations. It was not conversation or discussion; it was the talk of an orator itching to get into his full stride and I felt we should apologise for the small-ness of the audience. To lead him back to the question we had come to settle, I remarked that we had important changes planned for the magazine in the coming year. From February it was going to be bigger, and better-printed; we should like to start this new improved edition off with the life-story of Krobo Edusei. It would mean a great deal to us; it would have enormous interest for the people of Ghana; it would perhaps not be without some value even to himself, that so many readers should have their attention focused upon him during so important a period. . . .

At this moment one of the telephones on his desk rang. From his indignant outburst we could pick up the threads of what was happening. Krobo, as Minister of the Interior, was in charge—besides much else—of the police. He was being called now from a police post near the Togoland border, to inform him that they had found men in the district selling party cards for the party of Olympio, the Togolese Prime Minister. What were they to do?

Krobo hammered on the desk. "Get me the police inspector! The inspector evidently could not be found. "The sergeant then—get me the sergeant! Is that the police sergeant? Bring the sergeant to the telephone." At last the wanted man arrived. "You know who I am? You know who is giving you these orders? Very well then—you are to get those men! Arrest them. Take them inside. Put them behind bars! Do you hear? Do you understand what I am telling you to do?"

But now, it seemed, the inspector had arrived in turn and the same instructions had to be repeated more emphatically. "Get them inside. Put them behind bars! Bring charges against those men." There was short pause, then . . . "What charges? You ask *what* charges? You can decide that later. There is plenty of time for that later on. Get them inside!"

He put the phone down and turned to us again. "That was an interesting talk," I said. "It brings up a question I was meaning to discuss. I hear very often from Government supporters that the opposition, the United Party, is extremely weak, and that it has no real footing in the country. Is that right?"

"Certainly that is right. They have nothing but a few thousand deluded followers and some troublemakers as leaders. That is all there is. Virtually nothing!"

"In that case, since the CPP is so strong and the United Party is so weak—why is it necessary to arrest their leaders and to ban their meetings? Why not allow them to hold their meetings? If they are so feeble, surely no harm can come of it?"

"Ha! I see you don't know Ghana! I see you don't know our country or our position here. This is what everyone says who does not understand the true position. Let me tell you this—our people are simple. They understand power; they are impressed by power. They do not understand weakness, and they are not impressed by weakness—above all in their own government. The CPP, under our Kwame Nkrumah, has been elected to govern Ghana, to rule the country. We shall govern, and we shall rule the country! These meetings that you speak of—what are they? They were intended to preach sedition, nothing else! Therefore we ban the meetings, and we arrest the leaders. That is government!"

"If sedition *were* preached," I agreed, "you have ample remedy in the law. You have very strong laws, designed for exactly this possibility. Cases could be brought in the courts against those responsible; they would then have been convicted by the courts, and not simply sentenced by the government."

"Better to prevent"—he shook a forceful finger at me—"better to prevent than cure. That is a principle of good government."

All this, I thought, would go down extremely well with Dr. Verwoerd, but if we are to get anywhere in this discussion, it is essential that I find some common ground between us.

"I think it's a mistake," I began, "to prevent the opposite view from being even *heard*. Truth never was entirely with one party—it's always somewhere between the two. Take the conflict between East and West, which you in Ghana are struggling to keep yourselves from being involved in. Being impartial, you can see that each side has a powerful argument. The West says that the individual can only make his fullest contribution under freedom; the East argues that the liberty of the individual requires to be controlled in the interests of all. As propositions, both equally are true."

"The East," declared Krobo, banging his fist down on his desk, "have been very good friends of Ghana. *Very* good friends! I tell you what—I wanted to buy twelve armoured cars to keep order among these trouble-makers for whom you speak. I ask the British. Their price, I am told, is one hundred and thirteen thousand pounds. One hundred and thirteen thousand pounds!"—he glared at me as if I had personally fixed the sum. "So what do I do? I talk to my friend Nasser, and Nasser tells me he can get for me twelve Russian armoured cars for only forty-eight thousand pounds. Less than half what the British are asking!" He flashed me another accusing glance, before adding in a quieter tone—"*and* with full sets of spares!"

"Look," I said, the idea of finding common ground having somehow faded from my mind. "As an old imperialist oppressor, let me tell you something useful."

"What is that?"

"You cannot get good armoured cars at four thousand pounds a time—it's just not possible. Why, you could hardly buy the engine at that price; that is, if they're new ones. Those Russian cars will have had hell knocked out of them, suppressing the Hungarians in Budapest, the Poles in Warsaw and the East Germans in Berlin—that's why they're offering you them so cheap. And if Nasser has been putting down *his* troublemakers with them for a year or two as well, then they certainly won't give you much service on the roads of Ghana. . . . I should think twice before you accept that offer."

This was so likely to be true, that it annoyed our host considerably.

"The Russians cars are good—much better than the British! I know that. And the Russians are good too—shall I tell you why? Once they have done a job, they go away. They stay here two-three months, they teach our men what they must know. And then they go. But the British—you never get rid of them. Never! Always having some excuse to stay."

"All the same," I said, "you got something better from the British than armoured cars."

"What is that? What do we *ever* get from the British?"

"Independence."

The Minister's voice shot up into a squeak: "You think the British *give* us our independence? Not at all! We fight for independence. We struggle. We shed our blood. We win our independence by fighting for it in the streets. The British do not give it to us—the British would *never* give us independence. Only we take it from them by fighting."

"I did not say the British *gave* it you; I said you got it from them. Do you suppose you would ever have got it from the Russians? To whom have the Russians ever allowed independence—whether they fought for it or not?"

"Of course they give it to us! Certainly they do! When we deserve our independence—then the Russians give it to us."

"Tell that to the Hungarians, the Poles . . ."

Luckily at that moment the phone rang again. It was the inspector reporting that he had now got all the men behind bars. When the call was over, I said:

"I appreciate that you had to struggle for the independence of Ghana, and I'm very glad you got it. But the British and Americans know something about fighting for independence too. We've had to fight for ours twice in this century already. For ours, and for other people's."

"What? The oppressors do not have to fight for freedom. They have their freedom already. *We* know what freedom and independence is—because we fight for it and win it. But the oppressor does not know."

*   *   *   *   *

Over supper that evening, I said to Ian: "I've talked to a fair number of African leaders now, but so far I think I've only met one—Luthuli—who doesn't think that Africans invented freedom, "uhuru", "kwacha", or whatever it's called, in the course of the last thirty years. Some seem to have no idea that freedom isn't a pound of apples—something you either have or else you haven't. It's an unattainable ideal which has had to be fought for, inch by inch, since the beginning of time—and will have to go on being fought for, inch by inch, until the end. The fact is that the very idea of freedom, as something man cannot live without, was brought into Africa from the western world. A lot of things were here in Africa already—but the need to live in freedom wasn't one of them. Europeans brought this idea, although it carried the seed of their own expulsion. . . . But to most African politicians freedom is something Westerners just happen to have *got*—like a wet climate. The idea that men fought, and were murdered and tortured by one another for centuries, in order to keep freedom alive, is something they simply brush aside."

"Historically, I suppose," said Ian, "the Africans have fought, like everyone else, for little bits of freedom and degrees of independence."

"Yes—kings and chiefs will have fought to overthrow other kings and chiefs, and to that extent both sides could say they were fighting 'for independence'. But when the battle was over, the subjects were still subjects—the only question was, who was to be their ruler? In a sense, therefore, they colonised and enslaved each other. However, the colonisation was temporary because the balance of power soon shifted."

"White colonisation has been only temporary too."

"Yes, and now the African—quite rightly—has seized on the idea of freedom from colonial rule. He may not always be ready for it, but the process is inevitable and has to be completed."

"Then what are you worrying about?" Ian asked.

"Because they're going to be disappointed."

"Why?"

"They expect 'freedom and independence' to be permanent possessions. They won them; they've got them; now they'll always have them. But freedom isn't something like a cup you won; it's more like a seed you have to tend into a plant—and which can easily die before it grows up. No one is 'free' because a black Minister now orders him around instead of a white one. He's a little less unfree if he helped to elect, or can throw out, the black Minister. If he's got less right of appeal against his own black ruler than he had formerly against the white one, then he's got so much less freedom than before. And if that particular black Minister abuses the power he's been given, then he's not a liberator at all—he's an oppressor. He's got himself over on to the wrong side—and he isn't a bit less wrong for being black, though he may possibly be less disliked."

"And liberators turn into oppressors quite easily in Africa—as they have done elsewhere."

"Not just easily, perhaps inevitably."

"Why do they *have* to?"

"Because when a people starts wanting to become free, it has to find men of drive, ambition, superior ability to lead it. But the same qualities of superiority which make men leaders of their fellows, tend also to make them despise the others as inferiors. We know best—so we must do all the deciding. Everyone else can shut up—or be shut up. Chaos would follow if we were to 'leave our task of liberation in-complete'—that's to say allow anyone else to do any ruling. So in no time at all the new boss is firmly in the saddle, and the whip cracking."

"Round the same poor old backsides as before . . . By the way, Henry told me about your interview with Krobo."

"Oh, what did he say?"

"He said: 'It's really *hell* these people coming up here from the South. I wish to God they'd stay away. They never understand how things are in this country. What's the point of arguing with a Minister? I *ask* you—Ministers aren't people you can argue with! And it makes all our lives far more difficult after they've gone back.' "

"Well," I said, "they'll have to start arguing with their Ministers some time, if they want to keep any 'uhuru'."

"Did you fix up all right with Krobo about running his life-story?"

"No," I answered, "I forgot all about it."

CHAPTER XIII

RELIGIOUS DISCUSSION

ONE DAY TOWARDS the year's end Nat Nakasa suggested I might like to come along with him one evening and meet some Afrikaner theological students. It was an extraordinary invitation to come from an African—almost as if he'd asked me to come along and have a few drinks with Dr. Verwoerd in a shebeen—and I looked at him with surprise.

"Oh, that's all right," Nat answered. "They're quite nice fellows really. Bit fixed in their ideas, of course; you must allow for that. But I thought if you hadn't had a chance of meeting any of them yet, you might find it interesting."

It was typical of Nat—a short, round-headed, bright-eyed reporter of about 23, very lively and alert, always coming up with new ideas and suggestions—to have made contact at all with the students. He had been preparing a feature for *Drum* on "Do Whites Hate Blacks?" This was an idea of his own which he had carried out ably, and which—with its fellow-article, "Do Blacks Hate Whites?"—had attracted a lot of attention in what we called "the white press". In the course of building up his collection of opinions, Nat had come across a theological student at Pretoria University, whom we will name van Tonder, and whom he had asked for his views on the subject.

Van Tonder at first agreed, but had obviously had second thoughts and discussed the matter with his tutor, his professors, the chaplain and numbers of his friends—all of whom had evidently warned him to be very careful what he said. From the two or three hundred words he finally gave Nat, it was quite impossible to make out whether whites have any feelings about blacks at all—or whether they are even aware of their existence. Naturally we did not use his "statement", but wrote him a letter of thanks and enclosed a few photographs of himself which Peter Magubane had taken while Nat was interviewing him.

This rather unpromising situation—in which one would have expected both sides to prefer never to see each other again—had been used by Nat in exactly the opposite way. He was on excellent terms with van Tonder, knew a number of his fellow-students, and had no proposed this meeting. We agreed on an evening, and Nat made the arrangements. A couple of days before the event I asked Nat whether he and Can, who was to come along as well, would have supper with us at the flat before driving out to Jim Bailey's farm where the meeting was to take place. I suggested half-past six.

"Oh, but we have to be in Pretoria by seven," Nat objected.

"Why at Pretoria?"

"To pick up the students."

"So we're to fetch the students from Pretoria. . . . Then we'd better have supper at six, and you'd better tell the students it'll be half-past seven, not seven. But how are the students going to get back to Pretoria afterwards?"

A suspicion had crossed my mind as to the role for which I was being cast; I'd been caught for all-night chauffeur once or twice already by my staff.

"Oh, don't let that worry you," Nat assured me cheerfully. "Lewis, or one of the other chaps from *Golden City Post*, will run them back. There's sure to be a number of cars going."

There was a blinding downpour as we set out, the height of a rainstorm in which $2\frac{1}{2}$ inches of rain fell in twenty-four hours. At the foot of every hill deep pools lay across the road, occasionally we splashed our way through a small brook, and here and there big boughs had been torn off trees.

"Don't go too fast," Nat urged as we drove into Pretoria.

"Why not?"

"I'm not too clear exactly where these guys live. I guess we'd better just stop at a garage and ask."

Towards nine o'clock, after enquiries, delays, misdirections, two calls from phone-boxes and one from a private house, we fetched up at the students' hostel. I was just getting out to go and look for them, thinking it might be awkward for the Africans, but Nat was already in the road and in a moment was hammering on the hostel door.

"We've been expecting you for hours. Is this trip still on?"

"Of course it is," Nat answered. "You live in such an awkward part of the town—that's why it's taken us so long to pitch up here. Pile in now, and we'll be off. Oh, by the way, this is our editor, Mr. Hopkinson, and that's Can Themba, the assistant editor."

There were two students coming with us; van Tonder himself, tall, stooping, fair-haired and bespectacled, looked the type of all students everywhere who prefer their books to games, and are automatically left out, much to their relief, from all arrangements of an unlawful nature. He had just finished his exams in theology and philosophy, he told us, and after further study would be going into the ministry of the Dutch Reformed Church. The second student, whom I have called Schoeman, seemed at first glance the embodiment of jolly athleticism. He was a huge man who looked as though, if I drove the car off the road, he could lift it back with all of us inside; his manner was hearty and his handshake powerful. But his eyes were pale and his lips—which he licked from time to time as policemen do when they are taking down particulars—were thin and tight. I noticed, too, that he and van Tonder did not speak to each other with any cordiality, and it appeared from Nat's questions that Schoeman had come along because someone else, whom Nat had expected, "couldn't get away", and "it had been suggested" that Schoeman "might be the best person" to come along instead. Who had done the suggesting was not clear.

When I asked him about his work, he said he was reading sociology, and later intended to take a government post and "do administrative work among the Bantu". Can gave a sharp snort at the word "Bantu", but no one made any comment, they were all too busy trying to tell me how to find the way to Bailey's farm. I had been there several times from Johannesburg, but never from Pretoria. Thanks to the flow of contradictory advice, we were knocking on Jim's door—having floundered down the grooved watercourse which served as road between his house and the entrance to his land some couple of miles back—at not much after ten o'clock.

Jim was in pyjamas, and his wife had gone to bed. He welcomed us, however, with a wry and patient smile—"I thought you were coming at eight o'clock"—and we all went through into his lounge, where we sprawled on low settees like Romans at a banquet, and drank white wine mixed with soda-water, with pieces of apple and cucumber floating in it.

For a time the talk was rambling; van Tonder spoke of studying philosophy, and Can asked what the hell the use of philosophy was anyway? Jim said it was "a discipline", and the study of a discipline enabled the mind to take shape and form. Van Tonder replied that a knowledge of philosophy helped one to recognise and comprehend the intellectual basis of religion, and so to confirm one's faith in God. Schoeman said that that undoubtedly was so. I said that philosophy began where other disciplines left off—at the point of asking what they were "in aid of". The aim of philosophy was to explore and define the purpose of life.

"Hell!" Can exclaimed. "We've no time for purposes. If you're forced to spend half your time dodging the cops, you can't hang around looking for abstractions. The activities of life supply their own purposes."

"Which are?" Jim asked.

"Whatever you're wanting to do at any given moment. Each activity has its own particular purpose tied on to it. There's no need to look for any other. The purpose of drinking is to get drunk." He looked sadly at the watery liquid in his glass.

"God," said van Tonder, "has supplied the purpose of life. We don't need to go wandering around looking for it. He's given it to us in the Bible."

"You're okay there, man," declared Schoeman. "That's what the professors tell us. There's everything you want in the Bible."

"But look here," objected Nat, "every religion has its own sacred book—and they all say something different. How's a chap to be certain which is right?"

Van Tonder was about to answer, but Schoeman got in first: "Only one of all the lot is right," he said flatly, "that's the Bible. Those others may have little bits of truth stuck in them here and there like walnuts in a cake, but in general they're misleading. Take my advice and steer clear of the lot."

I'd noticed Jim beginning to look interested, and now suddenly he lifted himself half up on the settee, and said directly to van Tonder: "Do you believe in predestination?"

"Well, yes, we do believe that."

"You believe that millions and millions of human beings are doomed to burn eternally in hell—and millions of others are destined to live eternally in heaven? And this is all fixed from the beginning of time?"

"Well—if you like to put it that way. . . . But of course that isn't the whole picture."

"I'm not trying to include the whole picture at this moment," said Jim. "I'm trying to sort out a few main points. What about yourself personally—and Schoeman here? Are you doomed to burn perpetually in hell, or will you two be rejoicing eternally in heaven?"

"H'm, well," van Tonder replied, with the smile, kindly but pitying, of the man who understands the answer well enough himself but is not sure of being able to express it so that his listeners can follow. ". . . it isn't all quite so simple. However, I *do* believe I am destined to be saved, and that, provided I continue to walk in the presence of God, I *shall* be saved."

"You've hit it, man," Schoeman assented. "We're saved all right— *provided* . . ."

"I see that you're neither of you Calvinists," Jim remarked, folding his hands behind his head and preparing to settle down again.

"Not Calvinists?" exclaimed Schoeman in shocked tones. "Why, man . . ."

"How d'you make that out?" asked van Tonder, equally taken aback.

"Because what Calvin said was not, 'If you live a godly life you may be saved, but if you live an ungodly life you won't.' That's the general Christian view, which is precisely what Calvin was opposing. He said something totally different—that your fate has been sealed from the beginning of time by your 'election' to salvation, or the opposite, and nothing you can do will avert it. If Can here is doomed to damnation, no amount of prayer and no amount of virtuous action on Can's part can affect his future in the slightest. And if you and Schoeman here are 'elected' to be saved, the way you and he may carry on in this life cannot possibly prevent your inheriting everlasting bliss. That *is* what Calvin said—isn't it?"

Van Tonder hesitated: "Well, yes, in a sense it is. But you've missed out the most important thing."

"Which is?"

"If I am destined to be saved, it's because God has given me the gift of faith. God knows what he's doing. He would never have given me that faith if I were the kind of person to misuse it. The fact that God has given it to *me*, means that I've been chosen, and now I have to show myself worthy of that choice."

"What our Professor says," Schoeman put in, "is this. No amount of reasoning ever leads to faith. In fact human reason is just about the biggest obstacle to faith there is in this world. That's why we've got always to look on reason with suspicion, and why—when it conflicts with faith, we know for certain that it's wrong." He looked round for our agreement.

"To get back to reason for a minute," said Jim, addressing himself to van Tonder, "you say that you have to show yourself worthy of God's choice?"

"Yes."

"How do you show yourself worthy? By choosing the good course and refraining from the evil?"

"By resisting temptation, avoiding sin, and holding fast to faith."

"So you *can* choose the evil course? It is possible for you to do what is wrong—even though you've been chosen? Or isn't it?"

"Theoretically it is. But in fact what happens is that faith brings repentance. Through repentance the elect make contact with God, and from that time those to whom faith has once been given are held fast in sanctity and holiness until the end."

"But when you talk of 'resisting temptation' you imply that you *can* yield to it."

"I don't see what you're getting at."

"This—if you do yield to temptation, which you imply is possible, are you still one of God's chosen and still saved, or do you then become one of the outcast and rejected?"

"Well, we know, of course, that we shall still be saved—by faith. 'By faith ye shall be saved.' Not by good works."

"I'm not talking about good works—I'm talking about *bad* works."

"That's where the love of God comes in. He exercises his love towards me and forgives me. But I ought not to try God's patience, just because I know for certain that it's there."

"God exercises his love towards you and Schoeman, then," said Jim, "whatever you do. But he isn't going to exercise any of that love towards Can. Can may spend his whole life resisting temptation and avoiding sin—but it isn't going to make a pennyworth of difference so far as his salvation is concerned, because Can wasn't 'elected'."

Van Tonder peered mildly at Can over his lenses, as though wondering how to express his fate in some not too unpalatable way. Can, however, was prowling around looking for something to pour into his long since emptied glass. "Don't mind me," he called over his shoulder. "I'm just seeking the wherewithal to cool my tongue."

"To be good," explained van Tonder, "may make Can's life here happier, because the wickeder his actions, the more miserable his time on earth is bound to be. That's God's law, and there's no getting away from it. But it isn't only a question of our happiness. It's the duty of all of us to lead good lives, regardless of anything we may get out of it."

"That's fine," said Jim drily, "when you feel quite sure of what you will get out of it. Otherwise it's like telling a man who's got no dinner to fill himself up with gratitude instead. But it's Can I'm concerned with now, and I mean to get this absolutely clear. If Can is *not* due to be saved from the beginning, then he cannot possibly be saved—regardless of how he may spend his time on earth?"

"No. Not if he were not destined to be saved from the beginning."

"And if you yourself *are* destined to be saved from the beginning, then it doesn't matter—strictly from the point of your salvation—how you live? You might—for the sake of argument—torture Can, or fifty Cans, to death. I'm not saying you would do it, I'm simply asking whether by doing such things you would deprive yourself of salvation *if you were already destined to be saved?*"

"Well, no. I shouldn't. But then God would never have drawn me to himself through faith if I were the kind of person who would torture others to death."

"*No?* But Calvin had his religious opponent condemned and burned to death—and presumably Calvin had the gift of faith, and had been chosen?"

"Well, but that was in the sixteenth century. . . ."

Jim leaned back as though satisfied and all further discussion must be a waste of time. The rest of us, however, were anxious to get our oars in.

"The point you none of you understand, man," Schoeman declared, "is that to be saved a man must have faith. For you to go around looking for faith is just a big waste of time. Faith is a gift of God. Either he's given it to you, or he hasn't. *See?*"

No one made any answer, and Nat picked up the discussion. "What d'you have all these missions for, and go telling everybody how they're to behave—if in the end it makes no difference to them?"

"But it *does* make a difference," van Tonder answered, blinking painfully. "It makes a difference to the happiness of their lives on earth. Don't you understand? You can't possibly be happy if you're sinful."

"*I* can," declared Can. "That's about the only time I can be happy."

"Look here," persisted Nat, "do you tell all these people you're missionising to that they're going to be damned just the same, whether they take any notice of you or not? Or d'you hide that side of things out of the way and make them believe it's all worth while being good, and they've got some chance of getting salvation in the end—even though you know quite well they haven't?"

"But it *is* worth their while being good," Schoeman objected. "If they're not good they'll only be unhappy here on earth as well."

"That's for them to choose?" I said. "If it's just a question of whether a good earthly life is going to make their time here pleasanter or more miserable, they have a right to a free choice with the issue plainly stated. If I'm due to be damned for ever, I may very well prefer to cause a bit of hell here before I get there."

"It's not just a question of what's going to happen to you person ally," van Tonder rebuked me. "You have to look at these things from a wider standpoint. It's a question of us, who have the light, and of ou duty. It's our duty to spread the word of God on earth, and we have to do that, even if it makes no difference to the fate of a single soul. Even if not one man in this whole world listens to us, we still have to spread the truth . . . and there's *another* thing you're forgetting. Some of those we are bringing the word to may possibly receive the gift of faith—they may be among the chosen. We know that there will be *some* saved from all races. These people can't have faith in the word unless the word has been brought to them. That's why we've been told we're to 'carry the Gospel into every land'."

"But what about all those chaps," Nat asked, "—let's say they're in the middle of China or somewhere, where you haven't got any of your mission places—who are all dying off without your ever having given them this word? Those chaps *can't* have faith, can they? Do the whole lot of these Chinese get damned and burned for ever?"

"They're not our responsibility," van Tonder answered. "After all we're only a small nation. We can only do so much."

"This gift of faith, then," I asked, "is something God reserves for Calvinists? He doesn't give it to Catholics or Buddhists or Moslems or Confucians?"

"Calvinists *have* faith," van Tonder replied. "That's why they're Calvinists. God *could* give faith to others, but if he does so they become Calvinists. Those who respond to his gift of faith naturally join up with those who have already responded through his Church. To have held another religion at some time—even Catholicism—is not necessarily a final barrier to salvation, though of course to make a deliberate choice of such a false religion must be."

"Why?"

"Because it means rejecting the gift of the true faith when God offered it. Even God can't help those who turn away from him!"

"Then for all those," I said, "who are not due to be saved, the only reason for accepting religion is to get through our earthly lives respectably."

"No, indeed, man," van Tonder replied. "There's a much stronger reason than that."

"What is it?"

"*Fear!* Fear that you yourself may be among those to whom the gift of faith was offered—but who spurned it. Theirs will be the greater damnation."

"It certainly will, man," Schoeman agreed with satisfaction. "Theirs will be the greater damnation all right—we have God's word for that."

"Greater or lesser," Can said, "I can't see it makes much odds. If you burn in hell eternally, you burn. The actual way I was burning wouldn't make a lot of difference to me, I don't think."

"It's the remorse," said van Tonder. "The knowledge that you'd rejected God's gift when it was offered."

It was getting on for midnight, and there were welcome sounds of disturbance from the kitchen. After a while Jim's wife, Gil, came in with hot sausages and rolls which we all took gratefully. While Gil stayed, an attempt was made to keep conversation general, but as soon as she'd gone with a tray of coffee-cups, the discussion started afresh.

"Doesn't it worry you chaps," Nat asked in a puzzled voice, "I mean as Christians and as human beings—because even with apartheid and so on, I suppose you *do* consider us more or less as human—to think that millions of your fellow human beings are sure to burn in fire for all eternity? . . . A good many whites among them too, I dare say," he added slyly.

"No," Schoeman replied. "Why should it? Some people on earth are happy. Some are miserable. That's the way it is on earth—and that's just the way it's going to be hereafter. Only more so, naturally."

"Their destiny," van Tonder explained, trying to mollify Schoeman's bluntness, "is not our responsibility. It's not something *we* can help. It's due to the depravity and corruption of man's nature—for which all are deservedly condemned, but some are saved by faith and the mercy of God."

"But does God himself *like* the idea?" I asked. "I mean the idea of a few chosen and a lot destined, not just to destruction, but to eternal suffering?"

"Those sort of questions," said van Tonder, gesturing with the half sausage he was holding, "are all meaningless. Questions about what God thinks, and so on. Utterly meaningless! God's mind is utterly different from our little human minds. More capacious for one thing—*and* on a quite different plane. God's *here*," raising the half sausage "and we're *there*." He lowered his piece of bread. "We simply can begin to understand the manner in which God thinks and feels. It presumptuous." He blinked at me reprovingly.

Schoeman punched a powerful fist into his open hand. "You've h it, man! That's the way it is! It's simply a waste of time trying understand God by earthly reason. That's where all these liberals ar humanitarians and the rest of them go so flaming wrong—trying understand God with half-baked earthly reason."

"All the same," I said, "you think you understand God's mind well enough to know that he means you two to be saved, while millions and millions of your fellow human-beings are eternally damned. So *you* aren't really in any doubt about what God thinks and feels. This is simply an argument you employ when you're disputing with people who're not Calvinists."

"But we know that by faith!" Schoeman replied. "We don't know that by reason. That's how we can be so certain."

"There's one thing I'd like to know more about," Nat began.

"What's that?"

"Well, you have this apartheid of yours here on earth—we all know that. You say it's in accordance with God's law, and he wants things that way. Am I right?"

The others nodded.

"Okay, then. Now let's suppose yourself and Schoeman are among the elect, and let's suppose for the sake of argument I'm going to be saved as well. You say some black men can be saved, don't you? Not very many, perhaps, but just a few here and there. Well, let's suppose I'm going to be one of those black men that get saved—through being given the gift of faith and so on. Do you follow?"

"Yes."

"Well, do I go to the same heaven as you lot—or to a different one?"

"It's the same heaven, man," Schoeman declared with assurance. "You can count on that. There's only the one heaven, same as there's only the one earth. We know that. But naturally the races will be separated off up there, just the same as they are down here."

"Why?" asked Nat. "I understood that the races were separated off on earth so that each race could reach its own fullest development, and this could only be done by itself in separation. Also any contact between different races was bound to lead to 'friction'. That's what Dr. Verwoerd and people of that sort are always telling us. But when we're in heaven, then we aren't developing any longer, I suppose, and obviously there can't be any friction. So what's the point of having Bantustans and separate places for the Coloureds and Chinese and all the rest of them, up there as well?"

"Not everyone agrees . . ." van Tonder began, but Schoeman silenced him with a gesture.

"God created the differences between the races," he asserted. "We know that. It's not a matter of opinion, it's a matter of fact, on record in God's book. After the Tower of Babel, where all the peoples of the earth tried to come together, he created the differences in language and the other differences too. He did that definitely so as to keep people apart. If God made these differences, then you can be sure they're not just temporary, they're eternal. That means they'll continue, and they'll be recognised, in Heaven too."

Nat scratched his head. I looked at my watch. It was after one, the students had to be returned to their hostel, a good hour's drive away. Nat and Can had to be taken to Sophiatown, in whose rapidly diminishing ruins each of them still had some sort of nest. It was going to be a good three hours before I got back to my flat.

"I think our guests should be taken home," I said. "They've probably got more theology lectures to attend tomorrow morning."

CHAPTER XIV

CHRISTMAS IN THE GOLDEN CITY

A COUPLE OF weeks before Christmas, Dorothy said to our servant, Martha:

"Mart, I want you to send this skirt to the cleaners."

"But you mustn't send nothing to the cleaners before Christmas, madam!" Martha answered with astonishment.

"Why ever not, Mart?"

"It'll only get stole."

Christmas in South Africa releases an annual wave of crime and accident. For days beforehand the papers are full of pleas—"white" papers with their white readers, "black" papers with the black—for a bit more of the genuine spirit of Christmas this year, for careful driving, a go-slow on the bottle, and respect for law and order. It makes no difference. Christmas means drink and parties; parties mean smart clothes. If you haven't got them, you must steal them. So dry-cleaners suffer an annual series of raids; hospitals prepare themselves for a flood of casualties; and the traffic police expect their usual spate of crashes.

Driving home from a day out in the country, two burdened figures by the roadside beckon to us for a lift. They prove to be a Portuguese market-gardener and his wife; a number of Portuguese have settled in the outskirts of Johannesburg to grow vegetables and fruit for the city market.

"We've been waiting here an hour," they say patiently. "We thought we were going to be here all night. Nobody would stop for us."

"Why ever not?"

"Because it's so near Christmas. Everyone's afraid of being robbed."

Around Christmas our thirsty staff become thirstier than usual. I am woken one night by the phone ringing.

"Is that Mr. Hopkinson?"

"Yes. Who's that?"

"It's me—Can," says a thin faraway voice.

"Where are you, Can?"

"In the office."

"God Almighty—what are you doing there?"

"I'm locked in. I think I must have gone to sleep."

It isn't hard to guess what's happened. Can has gone out for a few drinks at Whitey's, Under the Heavens, or one of the other shebeens near by. He's had the few drinks and not felt quite up to going home. So he has come back to the office, sat down automatically at his desk, and fallen fast asleep. In locking up the place, the attendants haven't noticed him, and now he can't get out.

I go downstairs and get the car. The streets are empty; it's been raining and a fresh breeze is blowing. It's only blowing off the wet asphalt and the puddles, but I feel as if it were blowing off a lake. Near the office the town seems deserted. I run the car up on to the pavement so that the headlights shine against the gates; the outer gates open without much difficulty, they are fastened with a combination lock whose formula I happen to remember. But our *Drum* offices are on the first floor, up a separate staircase to the side of the main one, and this staircase is secured with wood and plate-glass doors for which I have no key. I can see Can's shadowy form gesticulating on the other side.

"Can't you get it open?" His moan comes faintly through the panes, as though he were drowning in a glassy pool.

"The hell I can—I haven't any key!"

"Can't you go and get one?"

"Where from?"

"I don't know," despairingly.

"Would Paulson have it?"

"He might."

"D'you know where he lives?"

"No."

We are stuck. I go outside and take a look up at the windows; suddenly I notice that from the General Manager's office one could jump out on to the flat porch which overhangs the main doorway. I go back and slowly shout the plan through the closed door to Can. In a minute, he's capering about on the porch above my head.

"Now—lower yourself down! Hang on by your hands, and then let go. I'll catch you."

Can starts to lower himself over, but the distance evidently looks more frightening from above. "Hell no, man! I'll never make it. It's too far. Can't you get a ladder or something?"

Round at the back of the building, up a narrow yard, I find the night-watchman; he is carefully roasting potatoes on a bucket full of holes, quite unaware that his building is being broken into by the main entrance. He is a Zulu, as almost all night-watchmen are, with a fierce-looking moustache, pierced lobes into which bits of wood the size of dollars are inserted, and a collection of warlike sticks. It's plain that if anyone attacked him, he would be seized and trussed up on the ground before he could decide which of his knobkieries was right for the occasion. The night-watchman searches about the yard, finds a ladder and brings it round to the front door; when he sees Can hopping about up there on the porch he nearly falls into the road with laughing, but we get the ladder up and Can down, and Can manages to pick up a late-running taxi, which saves me the run-out to his home.

Not many days later my phone rings again; this time it's around midnight.

"Is that Mr. Hopkinson?"

"Yes."

"Who is that speaking?"

"It's me—Hopkinson."

"Then why can't you say so when I ask?"

"Who's that?"

"I'm trying to tell you . . ." A long pause. Then, faintly: "It's me—Casey."

"Where are you, Casey?"

"In Marshall Square."

"Good God! What's happened? Are you in trouble?"

"Trouble? Who's talking about trouble? The thing is this, Mr. Hopkinson—" another long pause, then, "they won't put me in the cells. This cop here won't put me in the cells. He just keeps telling me to go away."

"Casey—you're pissed!"

"No—no! It's like this, Mr. Hopkinson, I've had a drink. I will say that I've had a drink. Not a lot—just a drink or two . . . Are you there? I'm *talking* to you."

"Yes. I'm listening, Casey. You've had a drink."

"Just one or two little drinks. I don't want to go home when I'm like this—only cause trouble. Cause trouble . . . with my wife. So I've come along to Marshall Square. I said to the cops here—'Put me in the cells'. That's what they're supposed to be for, isn't it? And these cops won't put me in the cells—I've argued with them, but they won't."

"What do you want, Casey?"

"To go home," irritably. "That's what I want—to go *home*."

"Okay. I'll be with you in twenty minutes."

Twenty minutes later, when I arrive at Marshall Square and go in by the "Non-European" entrance, I see Casey sitting on a bench in a dimly-lit corridor. Never large, Casey—when he's cold, miserable and in a bad temper—huddles into himself and looks like a sick child. A white policeman is watching him in a bewildered way, as if he knows he ought to fling Casey out on to his ear, but somehow lacks the heart to perform his obvious duty.

"Come on, Casey—let's go." To the cop—"It's okay for him to come with me, isn't it?"

The cop shrugs and turns away. "We didn't pull him in," he says. "I don't know what the hell he's up to."

Casey climbs into the car. It's quite a long drive out to the township, and I am in no mood for light chat. Casey appears to have fallen asleep, which seems about the best thing he can do, but now after half-an hour's driving I can feel one eye fixed on me in the darkness. I take no notice and hope before long it will close.

"Mr. Hopkinson."

"Yes."

"D'you know what that cop said to me? That cop you were speaking to at Marshall Square?"

"No, of course I don't. How the hell should I know?"

"Well, he said—'If your boss comes out here at this time of night and drives you home, then he's a bigger bloody fool than I think he is'."

*   *   *   *   *

Christmas drinking is democratic. It goes on at all levels. Dorothy keeps a bottle of methylated spirits in the cleaning cupboard. Just lately she noticed it was getting less.

"Mart—what are you doing with the methylated spirits?" she asks the girl.

"*Me*, madam? Nothing."

"Well, it's going."

" 'Tisn't me takes it, madam. It's Abraham. He takes it away in his little tin."

Abraham is our "flat-boy". Blocks of flats provide certain services for tenants, such as polishing the parquet floors which are universal in Johannesburg, washing out the bathrooms, and cleaning the "stoeps", or balconies. Abraham—a lean, bearded African of about thirty, with a handsome face, a humorous eye and an agreeably deep voice—is the cleaner for our own and three or four other flats on the same floor. We had often noticed his little boot-polish tin, but without appreciating its purpose. I had foolishly supposed it held some special cleaning preparation of his own, of which we—or our floors—were being given the benefit.

Now Abraham is missing for two days, so I go up on to the roof where the Africans have their quarters, and make enquiries. Abraham, I learn, has been taken off to hospital with bad pains in his stomach. If he isn't at work by Saturday, we decide, I will go and visit him in hospital. On Friday morning, however, he is back again, his face a mauvish grey. Dorothy gives him some warm milk and a good talking-to. At first he denies everything, but when she tells him not to be so silly, she knows all about it and that he must have suffered agonies with his stomach, Abraham hangs his head and says he's sorry. Dorothy says that she doesn't mind about the methylated, but has he learned his lesson and will he lay off drinking poison in the future? Otherwise he'll rot his insides and suffer very much worse. Abraham says he *thinks* he'll know better in future and the methylated stops disappearing.

A day or two later Martha says:

"Madam, the boys upstairs are different now."

"How are they different, Mart?"

"Abraham's told them what madam said. They don't drink that methylated any more. They know it isn't good for their insides."

"Oh," says Dorothy, "*that's* a good thing."

"What they're drinking now," Martha tells her, "is benzine with little milk."

*   *   *   *   *

Christmas is over, but there is still the New Year to face. On New Year's Eve, feeling tired, Dorothy and I agree to go to bed early and forget about seeing the New Year in. But towards midnight we are woken by a deep vibrating hum. The whole city is humming like a hive of angry bees, the humming punctuated by shouts, fragments of singing and the continuous hooting of car-horns. We go out on to the balcony. It's a brilliant starry night, with the moon lighting up the silvery and brassy edges of the clouds, but out of sight itself behind one of the towering blocks of flats. All lights are on in all the blocks, and many people are either out on their balconies or at their windows. The whole city seems to be one gigantic party.

From our seventh floor we look down into the street. Up and down it range bands of Africans, many of them flat-boys and girls, but others who have come in from the townships. Quite a lot of them are dressed up, and some of the men are dressed as women. They roam up and down, shouting, rushing in front of cars, forming into knots and then separating again aimlessly. They are in a special African state, not exactly drunk or drugged but far from sober, a state of doped well-being, tranced elation, in which each one is lost in a private world of hazy satisfaction, but yet—like fishes—they must shoal together.

At cross-roads, street-corners or wherever there is a small open space, they jive, but pointlessly and without their usual rhythm—or rather each has his own different rhythm, and the musicians who wander in and out are all playing for themselves without co-ordination. A few guitarists lean strumming against lamp standards or in doorways, squeeze-box players thread a determined way in stride to their own music; one African is carrying a brand-new blue and white record-player on his head. But the deafening sound, which deepens as we get nearer midnight, comes from more primitive instruments. Dozens of small boys dodge up and down, rattling tin-cans full of pebbles, blowing piercingly on whistles. One youth carries a sheet of metal the size of a large book with which he repeatedly scrapes the hard surface of the road, sending up showers of sparks and producing a penetrating screech, like the death-cry of a tormented tram.

White motorists, no soberer than the Africans, force their way through the throng with horns continuously blaring. Some try to steer clear, others press as close as they can to the jiving groups or wandering couples, hooting to try and make them leap out of the way. Immediately below us a car slews to a stop in a wild skid; an African gazes up at it astonished, scrambles to his feet almost from beneath the bumpers, and vanishes into the crowd. The dancers in return rush after and surround the hooting cars, roaring "Happy Ha—Ha—Happy! Happy!" at the drivers, clinging to doors and bumpers, and racing alongside until the cars accelerate away out of their grasp.

Opposite our block is an old iron-roofed bungalow of a type that was built thirty or forty years ago, and is now fast disappearing to make room for still more skyscrapers, full of tinier and tinier flats. Four ducktails (teddy-boys or toughies) drive up to the gate in an old American car with the horn blaring. They fling themselves out and race after one another into the house, leaving all doors open behind them. The lights go up in all the rooms. Five minutes later they come pouring out—leaving all lights on and all doors open—pile back into the car, set the horn blasting even before they've left the kerb, and swing wildly off into the multitude.

And now suddenly from a vacant piece of ground are fired the maroons; it is either midnight or upon it. At this an uproar bursts out which makes everything hitherto seem like a whisper. Its undercurrent is a tremendous drumming, which seems to rise up out of the ground and go humming through the streets above the people's heads; it brings echoes of the drums of Congo and Nigeria, but this is harsh and clanging instead of threatening and sullen, a noise of metal not of wood and skin. It is the women, a few men too, but mainly women. They have gathered round the lamp standards and are hammering on them with stones and bits of iron.

The hammering rises to a throbbing peak, the youth with the scraper scours the roadway madly, the children rattle their tins and whistle, voices scream "Happy! Happy! Ha—Ha—Happy!", and the cars all sound their horns in one uplifted wail. It is as though the city were simultaneously being sacked and celebrating some stupendous victory.

At last the noise weakens and dies down. And now, rapidly as it poured in, the tide flows out. The whites on the balconies have gone inside to drink champagne or brandy and hope for still more prosperity next year. Curtains are drawn giving the feeling that the show is over. The streets begin to thin; the hooting cars have disappeared or lost their voices. A police-van drives up, and half-a-dozen African cops come spilling out. They take their stand on the corner of the crossroads, leaving their van—it's a pick-up cage or "kwela-kwela"—unattended in mid-street, its heavy metal doors swung loosely open. The cops make no arrests. On the contrary. One of them is soon drinking brandy from a bottle somebody has passed him. Another scrambles up into the back of the kwela-kwela with a house-girl. But their mere presence with the hated van conveys a warning, and the crowd melts rapidly away.

After ten minutes the cop lowers the giggling woman to the ground, the other police signal one another to climb in. After noisy attempts to start the engine, it coughs suddenly to life, and the kwela-kwela rocks off up the street, the doors, still open, clashing as it rounds the corner. The deserted streets are scattered with bottles, newspapers and rubbish, as though a fair has been taking place, and the whole uneasy city hums and mutters, as if the fiery lava were ready to burst through the surface of its streets at any moment.

*　　*　　*　　*　　*

Next morning among the letters on my desk is one from an African author who has asked me to read and criticise his work.

Dear Sir,

Please give bearer my MS. Thanks for having had a look at it.

I was hit with a hammer behind the ear Christmas Eve, that's why I can't come personally.

Yours,

D.B.

CHAPTER XV

END OF A PARTNERSHIP

AT THE BEGINNING of February, I sacked Can Themba. This was for me a real disaster, not only from the loss of an assistant editor, on whose knowledge of the South African background, quick wit, and what was quite often his cool judgement, I had depended very much for the past year—but as a sign of my own failure. I had taken more trouble to try and work successfully with Can than I had ever taken with anyone, with the possible exception of a brilliant and difficult German photographer at *Picture Post*. In the end, however, it had all proved to be a waste of time. Other people, I knew, had been able to work with Can to their joint satisfaction—some had even written tributes to him. Why couldn't I?

The occasion was a simple one. During a week when our South African edition was being put to press—the hardest week of the month—Can was absent for five days. He was also due to turn in two articles and a column, for which in his absence I was obliged to find the best alternatives I could. I was angrier than I should otherwise have been, because for two of the five days I was ill, and would gladly have worked shorter hours. On the Thursday morning, when the worst of the battle with the printers was over, I saw Can already sitting at his desk as I came in; he got up and followed me into my office.

"Hope it all went off okay, chief. Too bad I was away—" he hesitated, "our car broke down in Basutoland, so I couldn't get back sooner. We only got it on the road again last night . . . I suppose I could have somehow let you know."

"It's no good, Can," I said. "We can't go on like this, and I shan't try. This has been press week. You've been missing, and the whole staff knows it. You left us right up the pole and didn't even trouble to ring up. But in fact you couldn't ring up, could you, because I'd never even agreed to your going off to Basutoland in the first place."

"But you *did*, chief," Can pointed to the calendar hanging on my wall. "Don't you remember my coming in here a couple of weeks back and telling you I wanted to take a week-end off before long?"

"Well, yes—I do remember that."

"Well, then—that was for going to Basutoland, and this was the week-end I wanted off."

"Hell, Can!" I said, resenting being put in the wrong like this. "I remember your saying you'd want a week-end off soon, and I remember my saying you could have one. But not that you could just take it when you pleased and be gone a whole week—or damn nearly—just when we're going to press. You must have known what it meant to us in extra work. And what about your own articles—you knew I'd got to have those? Damn it, man, you're the assistant editor."

Can laughed. "I *was* . . . But look here, chief, I'm sorry there's been this mix-up, and it's true I ought not to have been away just now. I meant to ring you—but you know how it is . . ."

"Well?"

"Well, won't you forget all this and give me one more chance?"

I felt myself weakening. I liked Can; he had real ability; his going would shake the whole office. Who could tell? Perhaps this would be a warning and, if we tried again, we could make a success of our joint enterprise in *Drum*. But something inside myself remained detached from this imagined reconciliation; it said coldly: "You must have an assistant you can rely on. You're caught between several fires in this job; times aren't going to get easier. On the contrary they're going to get much worse. This arrangement isn't working never mind now whose fault it is—it isn't working. End it now."

I repeated the words aloud with extra emphasis to cover my own hesitation: "No! There are no more chances. We are going to end this now. I must have somebody I can rely on. You'd better finish right away—pack up now and go."

Can walked out of my room with dignity and good temper, said nothing to the others who were by now collecting in the office, but at once went over to his desk and started putting together his books and papers, and throwing away the accumulated rubbish of several years. I went immediately to see the management. I explained what I had done and insisted that, in view of his long service and senior position, Can must be given at least three months' pay. The answer was that this would be unnecessary: a month's salary plus any holiday money he might have owing to him would be sufficient. The argument proved lengthy and severe. Finally, I said that Can was about the most senior African in the firm and had been in a high position on *Drum* for years; a great deal of odium would attach to my getting rid of him in any case. As editor I was prepared to carry this odium, but only if Can was properly treated over money.

When the discussion had ended inconclusively, I looked in on the General Manager, who had gone back by now to his own room: "I want Can to leave to-day," I said. "It's fatal having people about the place once they're known to be going. I want a cheque for three months' salary made out to him which I can give him this morning before lunch."

"I don't think you'll get that. After all, the Chairman hasn't agreed yet."

"If I don't get that cheque, I shan't sack Can."

"What d'you mean? You *have* sacked him. You told me you had."

"Yes—but I shall weaken and take him back on to the staff. It won't be the first time I've changed my mind. I'm prepared to carry the responsibility of firing a man, but I won't carry the firm's responsibility if you refuse to give him the money his service here entitles him to."

The General Manager looked at me dubiously, as though wondering whether I meant what I was saying. "Okay," he said, after a pause. "I suppose I can fix things up. Look back again in an hour's time."

Back in my office I pulled out some photographs and began to try to plan some pages for the next Nigerian edition. But I was too worked up to apply myself to anything. In the course of the morning Can, who had now finished clearing out his desk, looked in on me.

"By the way, chief, what about my pay instead of notice? Have you fixed anything up? Perhaps you'd like to show this to the management." He fished a crumpled letter out of an inside pocket and handed it across. It was dated the previous year, typed on the firm's note-paper, and signed. It said that, in view of Can Themba's having agreed to give the firm three months' notice if ever he wished to leave, the firm on their side undertook to give him three months' notice in the event of his dismissal. I passed the letter back, and later the same morning received and handed over to him the salary cheque I had asked for. The whole heated argument had been a waste of time.

The same evening I was sitting at my desk after everybody had gone home. I had stayed behind to try to catch up on the day's work, but at this moment I was not working. I heard someone walking along the corridor and through the office, and then Can's head came round the door.

"Good night, chief," he said, "and thanks for everything."

If I hadn't known it to be hopeless, I should have run after him and called him back.

*   *   *   *   *

At this moment when times were bad, something agreeable and exciting happened. A few months previously I had been asked to write an article for the American magazine *Holiday* on *The African as Journalist*. It had formed part of a special issue about Africa. Now out of the blue came a cable from *Holiday* asking whether I would fly over to Washington late in March at their expense, and take part in a seminar on Africa to be held in the University of Georgetown. I rang Dorothy, who said immediately, "Of course you'll go." When I called in at the United States offices in Johannesburg to see about a visa, a friendly official said: "And we hope you'll stay on an extra week or two as guest of the State Department. We can work out a programme for you later on."

If I was going to the United States in six weeks' time, it was essential to secure an assistant editor before I left, and I was delighted when I found I could persuade Humphrey Tyler, my predecessor, to come back and take on the job. He would give notice to his paper straight away, and would be able to work with me for a couple of weeks before I left.

*   *   *   *   *

Meantime we had to get busy on the next issue, which we should have put to press before Humphrey was able to join us. As we were now a man short, I arranged to go out myself on some of the stories to help fill the gap. One of the stories we had agreed in conference to work on was "A Night with the Ambulance Men"—the week-end round-up of injuries and stabbings which kept the so-called "non-white" ambulances on the go from Friday night to Monday morning.

Drum's car was, as usual, out of action. This time it was not a break-down, but a first-rate smash. Peter had driven it head-on into the back of a stationary van in a Sophiatown street one morning. This was quite unlike Peter, who was an excellent driver, but the circumstances were exceptional. There had been talk of a "new deal" in regard to pass arrests; the police were going, it was said, to be more lenient in future, and anyone who had simply left his pass at home would be given a chance to collect it and report later—just as a white man is allowed to do with a driving licence. Peter and Nat were out early one morning checking up on this story to see how much truth there was in it, and found themselves in the middle of the early morning round-up of people sleeping in Sophiatown who had no permits to be there. At this time there were many people whose homes had been demolished, but who had as yet nowhere else to go. Some of them dodged around all day and came back at night to sleep in doorways and odd corners; others slept in hollows out on the open veld; all who could would beg some shelter with friends. All these activities were illegal, and there would be late night and early morning raids by the police to pull in as many law-breakers as they could. It was such a dismal collection of hand-cuffed victims, being marched off under escort, that Peter was now photographing.

He had already taken a number of pictures when an officer shouted at him to clear off. Peter got back into the car with Nat, but continued to take pictures out of the window whenever he got a chance. Suddenly a sergeant in a doorway—a Coloured—saw what he was doing, snatched out his revolver and came running towards the car. Peter stopped to take one more shot of the charging sergeant, and then— convinced that the man was about to open fire on them—ducked right down towards the floorboards, stamped on the accelerator—the engine of course had been kept running—and drove off. Unluckily for them, a small van had just pulled in in front of a shop a few yards up the street. They drove slap into the back of it, and the nose of our Volkswagen folded up like a concertina. Peter and Nat were at once hauled off by the police, and it took me the best part of a morning— plus the good luck of finding a friendly officer—to get them back.

Drum's car was therefore out of action. Peter never liked to take his own car, a big yellow convertible, out at night, since showy cars driven by Africans were invariably stopped and searched by the police—and his yellow car was, in fact, a car with a criminal record, formerly the property of a well-known gangster. So I agreed to use my car and act as driver; we arranged to join up with the ambulance men around seven-thirty on a Friday evening, and to follow along with them for the next two nights.

Our first evening proved a quiet one, but the Saturday was more lively. Our first casualty was a cyclist. He had been riding home to the township from the city when two men jumped out on him from behind a tree. One cracked him over the head with an iron bar, and the other went quickly through his pockets. Though his head was badly split, he wasn't out, and didn't at all want to come to hospital. He thought he had recognised one of his attackers, and wanted to go out to a police station in hopes of recovering his money. However, the ambulance men thought he might have delayed concussion, and insisted he should come along and be patched up first.

Our second victim was a drunk. He had come out of the huge beer-hall known as "Mai-Mai", got into a fight and been beaten up, stabbed and flung down in a shop doorway. The shop-owner, irritated by his groans or distressed by the thought of his sufferings, had called the ambulance. Once again I was astonished at how much the African can take; when I looked at this man he seemed to be a moaning mass of blood and injury. We rushed him back to the hospital, and he was carried inside on a stretcher. Doctors worked on him for an hour or more, cleaning, disinfecting, stitching. He was then given a sedative and put to lie down under a blanket. It was assumed he would stay all night and be re-examined in the morning. But when, after our night's work ended, I came back to learn how he was getting on— the man was nowhere to be seen. I asked a nurse what could have happened, and she made enquiries. After a couple of minutes she came back. "He's gone," she said. "One of the other patients saw him. He just got up and walked off home—they're always doing that. If his head doesn't get better, he'll probably look in again in a day or two —but it's ten to one we shan't see any more of him. Till the next time, that is!"

In between handing the drunk over for treatment and calling back at the end of the evening, a strange little incident happened, which increased my already high esteem for Peter. Our ambulance wa summoned urgently to one of the compounds in which the mine-workers—imported from many parts of Southern Africa—live their lives of hard work, rough play, and compulsory celibacy. As soon as I saw the casualty to which we had been called, I doubted if w should get him to the hospital alive. While the ambulance men wer arguing the easiest way of stretchering him, the mineworkers tol us what had happened.

This man, they said, was unknown to them. Half-a-dozen of ther had been quietly playing cards out in the open, when suddenly the heard a shout. Someone was scrambling over the high fence—a thi wall of corrugated iron—which surrounds the compound. They hear the sound of a fall, then this stranger came rushing into the middle them—and collapsed. When they picked him up, they saw that had a bullet-hole over his right eye, so at once they telephoned f an ambulance. That was all they knew. Had any of them heard shot? No. From which direction had the man come? From up t hill. Hadn't any of them any idea who this man could be? They sho their heads; he was a stranger. Had they sent for the police? No. T management did not like their bringing police into the compour and they knew that the hospital would get in touch with the pol when he arrived there.

As we were getting back into the car to follow the ambulance

Peter Magubane being taken inside the Magistrates' Court Building. Later he
s removed to a small room from which a major released him.

hospital, Peter said to me: "Sir, the story these men tell us is not true."

The moment he said this, I knew that he was right. No man could possibly have scrambled over the high compound wall and arrived running with a wound like that; it was doubtful if he could even have stood upright.

"What d'you think happened, Peter?"

"I can tell you, sir, what happened. This is now the end of the month. All these men have just been paid. They have been having drinks together, and they have been gambling."

"Well," I asked, "what then?"

"This man they call a stranger—he is not one of themselves. Certainly they know who he is, very likely he comes from another compound. To-night when they are all gambling together, this man wins. It's midnight now—let's say he was shot nearly one hour ago—so they have been gambling all evening and this man has won all their pay from them. Then one of the men who has lost his pay says: 'We've sweated away a whole month to earn six quid—why should this stranger take it all away? He hasn't sweated for it. He is not even one of us.' So either by agreement or perhaps just suddenly in a rage, one of them pulls a gun, and shoots him. I think that he shot him sitting down, just putting the gun up against his head; you can't shoot a man over the eye like that unless he's very close, and unless he's lower down than you are. This man who has been shot can't speak, or perhaps they would have shot him some more times; they will not fire more shots than they need because the sound might bring the overseer. Then every man takes back what he has lost, and they all make this story up together."

"Will the police find out what happened?"

"I don't think so, sir. The gun will be no longer in the compound. It will be buried somewhere outside. The men will all keep to their story—there is only one way the police can get to know what was done here to-night."

"What's that?"

"If one of those man has a grudge against that man who fired the shot, and he tells the police the whole story. But even if a man wished to tell the police, he would be afraid of what would happen to him if he did."

* * * * *

For the past few months *Drum* staff had led a more than usually harassed life. As the government pressed on with still more of its apartheid legislation, there were rumblings of trouble throughout the land. Particularly there had been storms over the government's insistence that now all African women, as well as men, should carry passes; the women were angry and resentful, and had made a number of determined demonstrations, in the Cape, in Durban, and in Johannesburg. Whenever trouble threatened, *Drum* staff were expected to be on the spot; particularly in the Johannesburg area, it was the job of Peter to be there, since our magazine lived by pictures. But whenever there was a disturbance in the streets, tempers mounted rapidly, and picture-snatching became a risky business.

Nowadays, whenever any of our staff were called out to any incident, I would follow a routine. I made sure my car was easily accessible, that I had all the identification I needed in the pockets of my coat, enough money for fines, all likely phone numbers including those of our lawyers, and a permit to go into all the townships at any time. Whenever the phone rang, I expected a summons and was ready to hand all the work over and be off. I was particularly concerned for Peter; first because he would always take risks to get his picture; second because—though a journalist can get his story without making himself conspicuous at the scene of action—a cameraman can hardly escape notice as he pushes his way close in to get his shots. Also, being preoccupied with his work, he has little chance to keep a look-out on his own behalf.

Twice recently I had had to go and recover Peter from the hands of the police when he had been, not "arrested" which involves the formulation of a charge, but picked up and taken inside. Usually, if I could find an officer, it was not too difficult to get him released; but at times when they were hard-pressed or ill-feelings had been aroused it was not always possible to get attention. Once he had been seized by four young policemen and taken inside the Magistrate's Court—a huge building on several floors with long corridors and dozens of smaller rooms, offices and so on, in addition to the courts. While I, having been summoned to the spot by Jurgen, was searching for him everywhere and getting no reply from anyone I questioned, the four had hauled Peter into a small room and locked themselves in with him. Happily, before anything could happen, a major, who had seen what was going on, hammered on the door, pushed his way inside, and ordered them to let Peter go at once. . . .

However, when the expected blow did fall, it was not on Peter that it fell.

CHAPTER XVI

"THE COPS HAVE GOT SIDNEY"

I WAS DUE to leave Johannesburg for the United States on a Saturday. On the Friday evening I had got most of my things sorted out for packing, we had finished dinner, and I was just saying to Dorothy that I would be glad to go to bed early, seeing I should have to spend the next two nights in the plane, when the phone went. It was Casey.

"Sidney Andrews has been pinched. The cops have got him."

"Where are you speaking from, Casey?"

"A call-box not far from Marshall Square. Sidney's inside. I've seen him. He's been beaten up."

"What happened?"

"Sidney and I and Matthew Nkoana—he's here in the box with me now—were walking across town towards the bus terminus. It must have been around half-past seven. There was another fellow from the office with us—Johnson his name is. We had some trouble with a cop out of uniform, and while Matthew was trying to calm him down, a squad car came along, the cops all seized Sidney and bundled him inside. I don't know why they picked on Sidney and not us. We guessed they'd be taking him to Marshall Square, so Matthew and I decided to follow along and see what we could do."

"Good for you. And then what?"

"Well, we couldn't see or hear anything of Sidney, so after a while I managed to slip in through a side doorway. I wandered around a bit, and then I saw Sidney. His head was bleeding and his face was all swelled up. He's still inside there now."

"Okay, Casey. I'll be with you right away. Where are you exactly?"

"Marshall Square, the Marshall Street side, round near the ' Non-Europeans' entrance."

"Can you hang on there with Matthew till I come?"

"Yes, sir, we'll stick here. They came out and tried to chase us away once, but if we have to move we'll hide in a doorway. We know your car and we'll be on the look-out."

"In ten minutes then."

I told Dorothy and got the car out. When I reached Marshall Square the two were standing on the pavement in the darkness. I made them go over the whole story quickly so that I could get it clear in case any argument arose over getting Sidney out.

Casey, Sidney and Matthew had been walking along the pavement in Commissioner Street. Johnson, the fourth man with them, I hardly knew; he worked in the Circulation Department. They were making for the bus terminus, from which, if they couldn't get a bus, they would share a taxi out to the locations; there would be plenty of taxis around then. As they got near the centre of the town, they saw a tall white man coming towards them on the inside of the pavement. As they passed him, he swerved and elbowed into Johnson. Johnson, they thought, had not realised till after this chap knocked into him that he was a cop; but Matthew spotted he was a cop because, though he had no tunic, he was wearing uniform trousers and a khaki shirt. Johnson then said something like, "That fellow must be drunk." He had not meant the cop to hear him, but obviously he did, because he swung round and made a grab at Johnson, tearing off the pocket of his jacket. Johnson dodged, slipped away—and ran out into the traffic.

"He was hopping in and out among the cars," Matthew explained. "It was just before theatre time and the streets were full. I shouted to him, 'Come back! Come back!' and waved my arms at him. But Johnson just ran dodging off—and that's the last we saw of him. So then the big cop turned on Sidney."

"And then what?"

"He slammed at Sidney once or twice, but he couldn't do him much harm because Sidney kept on twisting and turning about and covering his head with his arms. I saw this cop was getting mad, and I kept trying to catch hold of his arm and saying 'Don't do that! Don't do that!' I still thought we could calm things down."

"But while Matthew was trying to pacify this cop," Casey broke in, "a squad car drew into the side of the road just by us. There were a couple of white cops in the front—they didn't look much more than boys. This big fellow shouted to them in Afrikaans, and they all three grabbed Sidney by his arms and legs and flung him down into the back. This cop we'd been arguing with jumped in beside Sidney or on top of him—and off they all went."

"We knew they'd take him to Marshall Square," said Matthew, "so Casey and I came along here—we hoped they'd allow us to pay fine and take him home. But after a while when we saw nothing, and the cops had chased us away from the office where we were trying to find out what was going on, Casey slipped in through a side-door. An African cop spotted him, but he didn't give him away, so Casey went on down a passage—and there suddenly he caught sight of Sidney sitting on a bench . . ."

"I didn't know it was Sidney," Casey took up the story. "I just thought 'who the hell's this poor bugger they've been beating up?' Then he looked up at me, and I looked back at him—and then I saw from his eyes that it was Sidney."

"How long ago was this?"

"P'raps three-quarters of an hour now, sir. It was just a little while before we rang you."

"And as far as you know they've still got Sidney inside there?"

"He *must* still be inside there. They certainly haven't brought him out."

All the time we were standing talking on the broad pavement, pick-up vans were driving up to the kerb with their engines racing. White policemen, chatting and shouting to each other, were leading files of handcuffed blacks into the building. Then the whites would come out without the blacks, pile into the cars, and go roaring off again into the night. Once a door in the wall just beside us was flung open and a white-faced policeman, wild-eyed and handsome in a heavy way, stared out at us. He had no tunic and no shirt; just khaki trousers and a vest. He stared at me and at the others, seemed about to speak, then suddenly drew back and slammed the door.

"That's him! That's the one! Now he'll have gone back to report."

"Let him report!" I said, feeling myself growing angrier with every minute. "You two stick around here. If you're chased away, stay where you can see my car. I'll try not to be long."

Inside the charge office there were a number of police behind a grille. Some were entering up particulars in books; two or three were talking in the background. There was a general sense of bustle. The only one who appeared not to be occupied was a pale, uncertain-looking youth.

"I want to find a boy called Sidney Andrews who was picked up and brought in here about an hour and a half ago. Can you tell me anything about him?"

The youth I was speaking to said nothing, but the one beside him who was filling in a form, held the form up: "Sidney Andrews? This is him."

"Where is he?"

"He's gone to hospital."

"Gone to hospital? What's he gone to hospital for? There was nothing wrong with him two hours ago."

"It's his mouth."

"His *mouth*? What's happened to his mouth? I want to see him."

At this a sergeant, a short man with red moustache and reddish hair who had been listening to the talk, stepped in: "He's not in hospital. He's in the cells."

"Can I see him?"

"Who are you? Are you a lawyer?"

"No—I'm his employer. I can give you all particulars if you want them."

He looked me up and down. "No—you can go in and see him if you want to."

The sergeant lifted a big key down off a hook and led me across the office and down a short passage to a heavy metal door, which he un-locked. Beyond this door was a kind of small office or guard-room in which a young policeman was leaning back with his feet on a desk, reading a coloured comic. There were empty Coca-Cola bottles on the floor, and grape-stalks and a screwed-up paper bag on the desk in front of him. The policeman's gold hair and chubby face gave him a sort of schoolboy jollity. I said nothing to him, as I thought he might have had a hand in what had been happening to Sidney.

Meantime the sergeant had unlocked an iron grille to one side, and disappeared. After perhaps a minute he came back; he was leading a shambling figure by the arm. I wondered why he was bringing this with him; then, looking closer, I saw it was a kind of fearful parody of Sidney, who seemed to have become nothing but an enormous mouth. His lips always protruded; now they stuck out like those of a plate-lipped woman in a circus side-show. They were so swollen and heavy that the facial muscles could no longer hold them up. His whole jaw sagged loosely down—there seemed to be teeth missing—and blood was soaking down his shirt and dripping directly out of his mouth on to the floor. I could see the trail running away behind him. His eyes were full of blood, and his head rolled loosely on his neck. He was barefoot.

"Good God! Sidney—what's happened?"

He didn't speak. He mewed. For a minute I couldn't make out what he was trying to say. "Go away, sir. Go away. Don't stay here. Leave me alone"—and then with a pitiful attempt at threatening his captors, I caught the words "in court".

I wanted to stop Sidney threatening: I wanted to register my horror in a way that might be remembered: I wanted above all to get Sidney out of here. I turned to the sergeant. "This is a shameful and disgraceful sight."

"I quite agree, sir."

I remember putting my hand over my eyes.

"What's been done to this man makes one sick."

"I quite agree, sir," the sergeant said again.

I put a hand on Sidney's shoulder; it was damp and trembling. "I'll be back before long, Sidney. We shall get you out of here."

We went out, and Sidney was taken back into a large cell, on the floor of which I caught sight of what appeared to be half-a-dozen or more black bundles lying.

"What d'you intend doing with this man?" I asked.

"We are sending him to hospital."

"How soon?"

"As soon as we can obtain an ambulance."

"Can I go with him?"

"I'm afraid not, sir."

"What *can* I do? How shall I be sure he really *gets* to hospital."

"You can ring me at ten o'clock."

I looked at my watch: "All right. I shall do that. But how do I get hold of you. What's your name?"

"Just ask for the Charge Office Sergeant. Oh—and the case against Andrews will come on in Court B at nine-thirty to-morrow morning."

"Case *against* him? Good God—whatever for?"

"He is being charged with assault."

"Assault? But you couldn't even bring him into court in this condition." At the same moment the thought flashed through my mind that perhaps the best thing for Sidney would be to be brought into court in that condition, and charged with "assaulting" his powerfully-built captor. "He's going to be in bed for days."

"Possibly," said the sergeant. "In that case there will have to be a remand."

In the street Casey and Matthew were waiting for me. I had hardly begun talking to them when a thought struck me, and I went back to the sergeant.

"Look," I demanded, "do you know the name of the man responsible for bringing Sidney Andrews in here to-night?"

"I do."

"I'm not asking you to give me his name now. I'm asking you to be sure you can identify the man concerned when you are required to do so."

"I know the man."

Back again with Casey and Matthew, I told them the position. I was sorry I couldn't drive them home to the townships, but there was a lot to do, and I must be around to make sure Sidney really got to hospital. That was okay, they said, and they would make their own way home. I asked if they had money for a taxi, and they said they had. We shook hands, and I told them to be sure and be in the office by half-past eight next morning, in case the lawyers wanted statements from them.

*　　*　　*　　*　　*

As soon as I got home I rang the firm's attorney. I had taken the precaution of learning his home number some time back. Unfortunately he was out, and our General Manager proved to be out as well. Around ten I rang the Charge Office Sergeant, but was told he was "going round the cells", and I must ring back in half an hour. At ten-thirty I rang again, and he told me Sidney Andrews was now in the General Hospital; I thanked him.

A moment later our attorney, for whom I had left a message, rang through, and I told him briefly what had happened. Our attorney was a young man, Kelsey Stuart, whom I had got to know well during previous difficulties in the harassed lives of *Drum* staff. I knew him to be shrewd as well as sympathetic. After listening carefully to the whole story, he said:

"You've got your three witnesses, and you've seen Sidney in the cells. But it's terribly important to get the fullest record of the case you can. There's sure to be a remand to-morrow—they won't dare bring Sidney in the box in the condition he's in. But these sort of surface wounds can heal up very quickly. . . . See the doctor at the hospital and warn him to keep all particulars. Say you'll be needing them in court. Is there anything else you can do?"

"What about a photograph? Would that help?"

"That's the very thing! If you can get one of your photographers to go along to the hospital and take a picture of him as he is now—can you do that?"

"Yes. I'll fix it right away. Is there anything else?"

"No—I don't think so. You'll want Sidney defended on this assault charge?"

"Certainly. I can't get through to the General Manager, but I answer for that myself."

"Then I'll be down at the court first thing in the morning. Even if the magistrate remands the case, it's just as well to put in an appearance. And, by the way . . ."

"What?"

"If this proves to be what it looks like—an absolutely clear case of beating-up with no justification—it could be just what you need to stop this happening to your fellows in the future. We've had them taken inside and threatened, and we've had them knocked around and their cameras pinched, and so on, but there's never been an actual assault as clear as this one. If we can pull it off, it might be a turning-point for all of them."

I thanked Kelsey, and said I would get my own record of the night's events typed out and handed in at his office next day before I left; I also told him I had arranged with Casey and Matthew to be available in the office from half-past eight, so that their affidavits could be taken. I then went off to get hold of Ian Berry. Peter, I knew, would be out in the locations and it would be hard to find him and ring him back into town at this hour of the night, but Ian—whom I had now taken on to our staff whole-time—had a flat not far away. He was not at home, but I guessed he would be coming back before long, so I pushed a note under his door, telling him to go round and photograph Sidney in the casualty ward of the General Hospital, either when he got back to-night or first thing in the morning.

At the Casualty Ward for Non-Europeans a clerk greeted me immediately.

"You are from *Drum*? He said you would be coming," and took me over to the nurse in charge, who led me through to Sidney. He was lying in an alcove on a bunk with a blanket over him. He had been given sedatives, but the doctor had decided it would be better to wait a few hours for some of the swelling to subside before bandaging his face. I noticed now for the first time that he had a wound also on top of his head. A heavy smell of sweat came from the bunk and from Sidney's soaking shirt; I knew it was not the sweat of heat or of exertion, but the bitter, acrid sweat of pain and terror. I chatted to Sidney for a minute or two, assuring him that he was now safe, that nobody could pull him out of here, that I would come and see him in the morning and that the firm would back him in any case that might come on. I said that Casey and Matthew would explain things to his wife, and say that he was being looked after; then I went to find the doctor. She proved to be a friendly, competent, white-haired woman who—when I spoke about keeping a record—replied at once: "I always keep careful notes of these police assault cases. You can be sure I shall keep a record of this one."

Everyone about the place already knew, I found, that Sidney had been beaten up, first in the squad car and then again in the cell at the police station. The reception clerk to whom I spoke gave me his name without hesitation and said he was perfectly willing to be called into court to testify to Sidney's condition when brought in. On leaving the hospital I had a second thought and drove to Ian Berry's flat, where I pushed a further note under his door: "Don't leave it till to-morrow. Make sure you get round there to-night."

After that I went home and started to tell Dorothy what had happened.

"You look green, Hoppy," she said, and went to fetch a drink. I was too disturbed to go to bed, and kept going over the events of the last three or four hours, fearing I might have failed to take some step which could make all the difference when we came to court.

"There's nothing else you can do to-night," Dorothy assured me. "Go and see Sidney in the morning. If you want your notes typed out for the lawyers, I can easily do them for you. . . . What else is there you could possibly have done?" she asked, seeing me still undecided.

"I'm wondering if Ian will get back to his flat to-night. Supposing he stays with his family and only comes into the office in the morning. Perhaps I should try to dig out Jurgen or Peter, if I can find either of them so late."

However, at one o'clock when we got up to go to bed, I noticed a piece of loose paper on the hall floor. I picked it up and read: "Picture taken. Ian."

CHAPTER XVII

SIDNEY FIGHTS BACK

I WAS AWAY in the U.S. for between two and three weeks. I enjoyed my visit enormously and would gladly have stayed on for much longer; this is not the place, however, to record my impressions of America.

While I was away Sidney was brought to court by the police on a charge of assault. In the course of the hearing it came out that the policeman who claimed to have been assaulted was 6 ft. tall and weighed 175 lbs. he had learned boxing and wrestling at the police training college. Sidney—known as "Baby" to his colleagues—weighed 124 lbs. and was only 5 ft. 4 in. tall. Finally, after a two-day hearing, the case against Sidney was dismissed. The photograph Ian had taken was handed into court as evidence of Sidney's condition when he reached hospital, and it was as well it had been taken, since by now—more than a fortnight later—the only outward sign of Sidney's night of pain and terror was a missing tooth.

One thing happened in connection with this photograph which caused me some annoyance, though happily it did not prejudice the case. While the prints were washing in the dark room the next morning, a white journalist from *Golden City Post* happened to come in and notice them. He had heard of Sidney's arrest, and—without any discussion with Humphrey Tyler, Ian, or anyone else on *Drum*—he took one of the prints, dried it, and sent it off to the London daily for which he worked also as a "stringer". It appeared there with the caption: "The face that should shock the world." I certainly found Sidney's treatment and appearance shocking, but I had no wish for the picture to be published anywhere until it had been produced in court; my motive in having it taken was to help in securing justice for Sidney, and I was afraid that any previous publication might tell against its value in court, or even conceivably rule it out as evidence. In this I was mistaken.

Now that Sidney had been acquitted of assaulting the powerfully-built constable, the way was open for him to bring an action for damages. However, while the matter was still under discussion with our attorney, we were informed that the Crown intended to bring its own case against Sidney's attacker, thus taking the matter out of our hands. After a number of postponements, this came on towards the end of May, by which time I was back from abroad and able to attend the hearing. Sidney was the first person on our side to be called, and though cross-examined by an able and persistent attorney with a high local reputation, Sidney had all his wits about him and answered for himself with spirit.

"Andrews said under cross-examination that he knew his attacker was a policeman.

(*Attorney*) Even though you knew he was a policeman, you still interfered?—Yes.

Did it occur to you that he might have been doing his duty and that he was arresting Johnson?—No.

Did he appear drunk?—Yes.

Did it occur to you that here was a European interfering with a Native purely on racial grounds, and that therefore you should go to your friend's aid?—I am sorry but I am not a racialist, and that did not occur to me."*

Two points came up in the course of Sidney's evidence which were new to me, and which gave an even grimmer aspect to the case. According to his statement, after he had been bundled into the squad car, the car continued to drive around the city for something more than an hour, instead of taking him directly to be charged.

("It is possible that it took forty-five minutes," the constable who attacked Sidney had admitted at the earlier hearing, though the distance could easily have been covered in five.) Throughout the journey the constable in the back, Sidney said, kept hitting him—among other things he kicked off both Sidney's shoes, which were lost and not seen again. When they finally reached the police station his assailant and several other policemen seized him and rushed him straight through to the cells, without stopping at the charge office and here fell on him and knocked him about once more. Later when he was taken into the charge office—Sidney declared—all doors were closed so that no one could see the condition he was in.

The second point was that, after I had left the police station and while Sidney was on his way to hospital, he was assaulted yet again inside the ambulance. There were two white police in front, and Sidney and an African cop were sitting in the back. Halfway there one of the white police stopped the van, came round to the back, and

* From *The Star*, Johannesburg's evening newspaper in the English language, [...] 22, 1959.

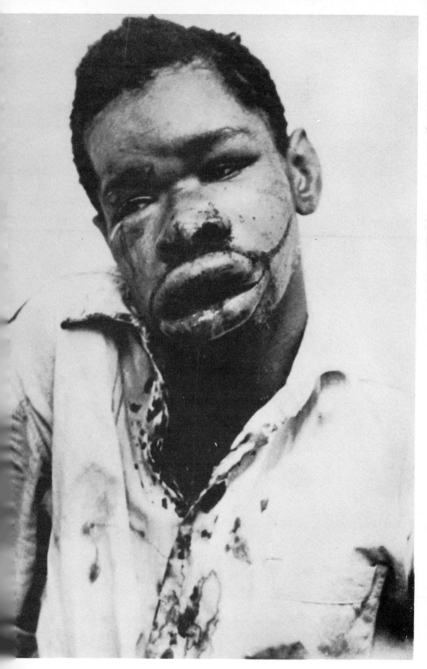

"The Face That Should Shock the World"—Sidney Andrews in Hospital
after being beaten up.

started laying into Sidney all over again—though he was in a condition when even an animal, I should have thought, might have refrained from touching him out of pity. The cop who did it saw the expression on the African policeman's face, and said: "You've seen nothing! Remember that—*nothing*!" The only explanation I have been able to find for what would otherwise be—and perhaps was—an act of senseless brutality, is that the policeman concerned was trying to obscure the evidence against Sidney's original attacker by adding further injuries for which he was not responsible. The explanation, however, seems far-fetched, and I doubt if it makes the incident any less detestable.

After Ian Berry and I had given our evidence, Casey was called into the witness-box. Casey happened at this time to have his head almost completely swathed in bandages, from which, however, his eyes peered out as sharp as ever, if slightly bloodshot. The defence attorney, who had made little headway hitherto, looked up with obvious interest.

"Hullo, Casey—what's been happening to you?" Casey, who resented being familiarly called "Casey" as much as any European in the box would have resented being called "Billy" or "Jimmy", replied:

"How d'you mean—what's been happening to me?"

"What's been happening to your head? How have you got that injury?"

"I walked into the wall," said Casey blankly—then feeling perhaps that this sounded lame, as God knows it did!—he added: "I was out walking with a friend. I missed my step and knocked my head against the wall."

After a few similar exchanges, the attorney suddenly burst out: "Come on now, Casey! Don't trifle with me! We're not children in this court."

Threatening, however, was not the way to deal with Casey; it both stimulated his intelligence and made him bloody-minded. A tiny figure, with not much more than his heavily bandaged head visible above the witness-box, he replied wearily: "I'm not saying you are children in this court." He paused and looked round for the implication to sink in. "I'm simply explaining to you how I got my head injuries. I knocked it against the wall."

As Casey said this, I caught his eye. He knew, and I knew, the wall against which he had knocked his head and the circumstances under which he had knocked it—however he was under no obligation to

answer questions he had not been asked. The attorney then turned to
details in the affidavits, and amongst other things picked on the
distance between the four Africans involved as they walked along the
pavement in two couples. How far apart had they really been? Three
out of four, it appeared, had used the phrase that they were "within
shouting distance". A very odd phrase, the attorney thought; very
surprising they should all have picked on this unusual phrase; how
had it come about?

"Have you four been talking this case over between yourselves?"
he demanded sternly.

"Yes," said Casey—to which the attorney could only answer that
it was "at least honest", and now pressed Casey to explain exactly
what he meant by this admittedly curious phrase "within shouting
distance". Casey, by now thoroughly at home, replied that in using
the phrase he had meant to convey "rather more than speaking
distance". It could in fact be understood to mean "about as far as a
man can shout and still be heard". When the attorney remarked that
the phrase still had a very unusual ring, Casey offered "screaming
distance" as an alternative. Nothing else the attorney started led to
more practical results; Casey just stood there, bowed, bloody, but in
full possession of his faculties, deploying a kind of unapprehendable
defiance, through which all enquiries and demands petered out to
nothing.

If Casey's was a negative and subtle insolence, that of Matthew
Nkoana was direct and positive. He had not been in the witness-box
three minutes before he was protesting: "Your worship, I *object* to
that question!" He never got the slightest change out of his worship,
who simply told him to answer what he was asked. Once, when
ordered to "answer properly", Matthew replied in an aggrieved tone
"But I did answer the question"—and then repeated the involved
explanation with which he had just evaded it. The attorney pressed
his questions, but Matthew—with his frayed collar floating around
his ears, his double-thickness spectacles, his long angular figure, and
his high-pitched intellectual's voice—dominated the scene. His defect
as a witness was that he too obviously considered all the implications
of each question before replying to it—and then talked his way through
or round or under all of them. Whenever the attorney tried to draw
any conclusions, or base any argument on anything he had said,
Matthew immediately interrupted him, always addressing himself to
the magistrate:

"But, your worship, I did *not* say that while we were at the restaurant none of us had a meal. I said that while we were at the restaurant I did not *see* any of us having a meal."

"And how long were you in the restaurant?"

"That would be difficult to say—very difficult. Time, you see, passes at different speeds on different occasions. No . . . I really couldn't say how long."

"Was it more than ten minutes?"

"Oh yes—it would have been more than ten minutes."

"And less than an hour?"

"Well . . . yes . . . it was probably less than an hour."

"So it was between one hour and ten minutes?"

"Possibly . . . but then as I explained just now"—and so on. Quite often he asked questions back, so that at last the attorney cut him short. "When you, Matthew, are standing here where I am standing, and I am standing there in your place, you may put questions to me—but till that happy day comes, *be good enough to answer my question*!"

For three-quarters of an hour, unaffected by rebuke or sarcasm, and quite unawed by authority, Matthew talked on, adding nothing to anyone's knowledge on any point at issue, exasperating everyone in court—including myself—but giving an astonishing display of voluble evasiveness. "I think," said our attorney when we got outside, "the cross-examiner this morning went through a good deal more cross-examination than he got the opportunity to do himself."

The most telling point made by the prosecutor during his cross-examination of Sidney's attacker, had been to enquire whether he had not been taught at training college that the most effective way to bring a man under control is to handcuff him, and added:

"It would have been quite easy for you to get handcuffs?"

"Yes—but I did not think it would be necessary."

He had not, he admitted, asked the two policemen in the front of the car either for assistance in subduing his prisoner, or to lend him their handcuffs. He could not remember how many times he had hit Andrews.

The magistrate then wished to hear evidence from the two policemen who had been in charge of the squad car—but they could not be found. They could not be found next morning, either, when the case came on again. They could not be found until the afternoon; they then testified that all Sidney's attacker had given him were "five or six slaps" which were necessary to bring him under control.

In his final argument, the defence attorney said that a photograph handed into court "shows that Andrews suffered the most horrible injuries. But the photographer has said that the only actual injuries were on the lips. I feel that because of Andrews' facial make-up, the swelling of the lips could have been caused by a few slaps".

The magistrate, summing-up, said that although an assault definitely took place, he could not say how bad the assault was. Addressing the prisoner, he observed: "It is probable that you were not completely responsible for the injuries to Andrews' face, since Andrews himself has said that another policeman had struck him a tremendous blow across the lips before he was taken to hospital. But I am satisfied that the five or six blows which you struck him in the back of the squad car constituted common assault. It was not necessary for you to hit him. There is no evidence that you asked your colleagues for assistance . . ."

"The photograph shows that Andrews could have been badly injured, but it is not entirely reliable. It is not clear whether the marks on the face are bruises or merely made by blood."*

Passing sentence, the magistrate said that the constable would be penalised, not for the violence with which he hit or did not hit Sidney Andrews, but for having hit him at all.

He fined him £25, or two months' imprisonment.

The fine was paid.

        *   *   *   *   *

Sidney's attacker had now been convicted. His sentence, in my opinion, was a remarkably light one—amounting perhaps to a fortnight's pay. But at least he had not been acquitted, and his conviction meant that it would now be possible for Sidney to bring a civil action for damages against the constable with every prospect of success. For a prosperous client, the natural way of proceeding would have been in the Supreme Court; but here, though the damages to be obtained would be much higher, the costs would also be much heavier—far more than Sidney could afford to risk. It was decided therefore to proceed by way of the Magistrate's Court. Here the maximum jurisdiction would be limited to £200; but our advisers considered that by claiming £200 for wrongful arrest; £200 for malicious prosecution; plus £200 for assault and injuries suffered, a maximum £600 might be obtainable.

Accordingly a summons was issued on Sidney's behalf against the constable concerned and against the Minister of Justice. Before long approaches were made from the other side with a view to settling the case out of court; after some negotiation, a figure of £250 was arrived

* From accounts in *The Star*, May 26, 1959, and the *Rand Daily Mail*, May 27, 1959.

at, and this Sidney, on advice, agreed to accept. Notification of acceptance was sent on September 1st, but it was only after letters, telephone calls and, finally, the threat of a further summons unless the agreed sum was immediately paid over, that it was received towards mid-November, and Kelsey Stuart rang me at the office to let me know that the long battle had been won.

At this point, however, a further difficulty arose. I had been to see Jim Bailey at various times to report the progress of the case; I now told him that the cheque had reached our lawyers, and suggested that he himself should hand it over to Sidney at an informal presentation in the office.

"But I don't think the money *should* be given to Sidney," Jim objected. "It's not his. Some part might be given him later on—we should need to think that over—but the money itself isn't his at all. It belongs to this firm."

"How is that?" I asked.

"Because we are paying for his legal proceedings—Sidney wasn't. As a matter of fact I think the best way to use the money is to set up a fund for defending cases of this kind in future. They're constantly cropping up, and it will give our chaps encouragement to know that the fund is there to help them."

I was so taken aback by this view of the matter that I could think of nothing, at the moment, to reply. I could only repeat that I thought Sidney had earned the money, and went out, worried and upset. As soon as I got home, I told Dorothy of the discussion. "What? Not give Sidney the money for which he was bashed around, had his teeth knocked out—and has now had to endure weeks of worry over the cases? Over your dead body—Hoppy! I *mean* that. Over your dead body! Sidney earned that money with blood and terror. Two hundred and fifty pounds could make all the difference to his life—what's an odd couple of hundred to the firm? A couple of pages of advertising more or less. . . . Of *course* there ought to be a fund to support people who get beaten up or land in trouble. That's obvious! But it's not going to be founded at Sidney's expense."

Dorothy, as many times before, had made a situation over which I was hesitating and confused as clear as day. But also, while she was talking, something else came back into my mind; it was a memorandum which had been shown to me weeks before, but which in the rush of later events, I had entirely forgotten. Next day therefore I brought the matter up afresh, saying I felt Sidney should be given the money he had paid for so heavily, which was after all an award of

damages for injuries which he and nobody else had suffered, and that
I hoped Jim would reconsider the matter and present him with the
cheque.

"No—I'm sure that would be wrong," Jim said. "I've thought this
over thoroughly. The right thing to do is to start an office fund for
defending our people when they need it."

"If Sidney *wants* to use the money in that way," I replied, "then of
course he can. But if he doesn't choose to, the firm can't make him.
It was Sidney who instructed the lawyers to bring a case for damages,
not '*Drum* Publications'."

"That's a mere technicality. The firm was paying for it all—how
could Sidney possibly have paid for his own case?"

"I don't know how he could," I said, "but he was going to have
to. I was shown a memorandum from the General Manager to the
accounts department, giving instructions that the costs of defending
Sidney were to be deducted from his pay at so much a month. That
will still be somewhere on the files. Sidney wasn't only bringing the
case, he was going to have to find the costs of it out of his own pocket."

"If that is true," said Jim after a moment's thought, "then there's
no more to be said. All the legal expenses must be deducted. You
can get a cheque for the rest from the accounts department and hand
it over to Sidney yourself."

The lawyers had kept their charges all through down to a minimum,
but there had been a lot of work involved, and in the end Sidney
received a little over £170. It was hardly a fortune, but it would be
enough, if he wished, to buy a small house in one of the locations or,
invested, would make something to fall back on in the many hazards
of African journalistic life. I thought it some of the hardest-earned
money I had ever heard of, but I think several members of our staff
would have accepted a night of beating-up, if they could be guaranteed
to come out of it with no lasting injury and the same financial return.

Sidney grinned a gap-toothed and grateful smile when I passed the
money over, and—calling in Casey and Matthew—said that he ought
to thank them for having stood by him that evening eight months
before, instead of melting away safely into the crowd.

*   *   *   *   *

South Africa is often accused of being "a police state". Certainly
the police in South Africa have many powers which they do not have
in more settled countries, and some which I think they ought not to
have even in our unsettled one. But that does not make a country

into a police state.* In this case it was shown to be possible for a white policeman to be punished, and for his black victim to obtain damages, for a piece of brutality which would be a daily occurrence in a police state, and for which there would there be no redress.

The same point would be made—much more publicly and forcefully—a year or so later, when the Government's case against the Treason Trialists would be thrown out, and all of the accused acquitted.

In addition, either because of Sidney's case and the wide publicity it was given in South Africa, or else because of changes in the higher levels of the police and the issuing of stricter orders, this was to be the last incident during my time at *Drum* in which any member of our staff suffered ill-treatment or injury at the hands of the police. The lack of tension which resulted made a real difference to our lives, and even later on at the time of Sharpeville, our reporters and cameramen were able to do their work unmolested. I hope therefore that Sidney's case may have marked the end of a spell of bad relations between African journalists and the police, and that a new period of more humane and tolerant ones has been begun.

*This was written before the introduction of the so-called "Sabotage Bill" in May 1962. This Bill alters the whole relationship between the individual and the state, gravely to the disadvantage of the individual.

CHAPTER XVIII

CONVERSATIONS IN A PLANE

In the middle of the year—this was after Sidney's two cases had been heard, but before we had succeeded in securing damages—I go a chance to go up to West Africa again. This was now my third visi to Nigeria and Ghana. As a rule I would read or doze the whole wa up in the plane, recovering slowly from the tensions of the office an the strain of its endless personal conflicts. This time, however, I foun myself quickly involved in talk.

Sitting next to me was a young South African of Jewish origin Lively and forthcoming, he told me he was in his early twenties, bor in Johannesburg, setting out for a three-month tour of Europe—"It the first time I've been further than Lourenço Marques." He had bee there a fortnight previously, he confided, "to get an idea of wh Europe will be like". About himself and his work he chatted wit freedom. "You think I'm a student? I'm not. I'm a commerci traveller. I'm not proud of it—in fact I'm ashamed of myself, becau I know I ought to be doing something better. . . . All the same, isn't as easy as you think to be a first-rate salesman. Good salesm are born." He shook a warning finger at me. "If you can't sell som thing, you *can't*, and there's an end of it! Five years ago I wanted go to university and study medicine—that was *my* big idea. But d said 'No!'; he wanted me to read engineering."

"And who won?"

"Oh, I studied engineering just to please him. I could *do* it all rig —I even got through a couple of exams—but I knew it was no go My hands are softer than a woman's"—he held them up and looked them with appreciation—"and I've no idea what's under the bon of my car. Haven't a clue!"

"How did you come to take this holiday?"

"I've always wanted to go to Europe—always. But I wanted to properly—for at least three months, when I went. In the end I w and told my Dad what I was thinking. 'It'll kill your mother,' he s 'You go away for three months and you might as well shoot her sto dead. She could never get over it. *Never!*' So I said nothing, and week or two he'd taken the whole thing over and was planning trip for me! Said he'd pay for it all on condition I go to Tel-Aviv."

"Why Tel-Aviv?"

"He doesn't think so much of Jerusalem—and then, I suppose, he's got friends in Tel-Aviv, or some of the family he wants me to visit. Of course, I'll never hear the last of it if he pays for me—never! Him and my uncle—what a pair! There's a real businessman for you—my Uncle Ben. He's not like us—city folk. He does all his business out in the platteland, travels around month after month, calling on all the big farmers. Selling's his business too, fertilisers and that stuff. I said to him once: 'Uncle Ben, how d'you manage doing business all the time with these Afrikaners? Don't they only want to do business with other Afrikaners? Aren't they against Jews on the whole?' And d'you know what my uncle Ben did? He fished in his pocket and pulled out a Nationalist Party card. 'There,' he said, 'that's my secret! So long as I carry that, pay my subscriptions, and go to three or four Nationalist meetings every year—I'm okay! I can have their business—and what's more I get it. Three-quarters of what's going in my territory.'"

The young man looked at me and smiled. "I can see the advantage of your uncle's plan," I said. "But how does he feel when some Nationalist Senator gets up and makes an anti-Semitic speech—or when one of your own people—such as Helen Suzman—has to fight in Parliament almost single-handed against some oppressive new Bill?"

"Oh," he answered, "my Uncle Ben isn't interested in politics. None of us is. Politics aren't our line at all."

The young man got on very easily with the few girls in the plane, his friendly approach—and his obvious interest and admiration—awakening an immediate response. He stood chatting for half an hour with the two air-hostesses, but when he moved further up the plane to attach himself to a drinking session, I could see that he was brushed off by the men—too voluble, I wondered, or too friendly? In spite of this, however, he hung on to the fringes of their party for some minutes, evidently passing on what he had learned from direct enquiries about myself and my own work, because after a few minutes a tall, powerfully-built, grey-haired man came down the plane—two glasses and whisky-bottle in hand—and sat down in the next seat to mine. He and his colleagues looked to me like a group of wealthy farmers from Natal off on a hunting-expedition. They might, I thought, be getting out in the Congo, and perhaps driving through to Kenya and Tanganyika.

"I should think you're pretty well a prohibited immigrant," he began, tipping me out half a glassful. "Don't you ever have trouble travelling up and down?"

"None at all. I've never had the least difficulty."

"What about your work in South Africa—editing this magazine of yours? Isn't that difficult? They don't like people doing your sort of work with the natives—giving them ideas above themselves and so on. It's not liked."

"I don't suppose it is liked. But personally I've never been hampered in any way," I answered. "I don't get any favours, of course. I've just been refused a shot-gun licence—I suppose because some official thinks I might start an armed insurrection with a twelve-bore—but then I never expected any favours when I came here, so it doesn't worry me that I'm given none."

"If they refused *me* a gun licence, I *would* start an armed insurrection," said my new acquaintance. "But tell me, coming out here afresh, what do you think of the position?"

"I think we're postponing the evil day," I answered. "I think evil days get worse from being postponed—but a lot of people would rather have their grandchildren's house burn down than have the trouble of cleaning their own chimneys. Specially the older people—and above all politicians."

"I'll tell you what the trouble is—far too many of us take no interest in politics, that's our trouble. We're not interested in politics, and we don't really do anything for the native. We farmers know that our labour's grossly underpaid—but we do nothing about it because the next man does nothing. All over the world at one time the farmer had virtually free labour—he looked upon it as a right. Said he couldn't possibly manage without it, he'd go bankrupt in a year if he had to pay his people properly. Now all over the world the farmers have been obliged to pay their workers decent wages—because otherwise they'd all have cleared off into industry—and now they find they've actually benefited by doing so. They all make a better living than they did before. It's only here in South Africa—and of course in the Portuguese territories—that we still expect to get our labour free, or bloody near it. We know in our hearts it's wrong, just as we know it's bad economics. But it's official policy to keep the native from pushing up too fast, and we all fall in line with the policy because it's always a damn sight easier *not* to pay out money than it is to pay it."

"What d'you think might bring about a change?"

"Well, one thing which could do it would be a real step-up in mine wages. The mines are in much the same position we are—they get their labour bloody cheap, on the argument that so many mines would fold up if they had to pay decently—so everything must necessarily keep pace with the oldest and most inefficient. It's the classic argument which trade unions have been fighting for a hundred years all over the world—but in South Africa, of course, the Africans can't join the white trade unions and it's illegal for them to strike. If the mines were to pay proper wages, then many more farm-workers would want to go and work there—and we'd be forced to raise our wages to keep pace. But that, of course, is another thing the government doesn't want. It would rather import mineworkers from other territories, knowing it can ship them all home again at the end of six months, and keep any cheap local labour on the farms."

"Is there anything else that could do the trick?"

"Yes. A government order calling for a substantial increase in farm wages—an order which is a long way overdue. Even a strong statement would be something. . . . Mind you, there's another side to it as well. Every big farm carries a good few hangers-on who do damn-all. I've got ten or a dozen on my own place—chaps who are past work or not really fit to work, and so on. If wages go up—out go all those hangers-on, and God knows what happens to them! They don't do a decent week's work between the lot."

"All the same, it would surely be better to shake out the idlers and pay the good ones decently. But is there any chance of your getting such an order?"

"Not a hope in hell! Half the government supporters in the platteland would blow their tops at the mere suggestion. . . . That's been our biggest mistake in this country—letting politics get into the wrong hands. And it's all through sheer damned laziness; we've no one but ourselves to thank. My family's been living here since van Riebeeck's time—three hundred years. Not one of us has ever bothered himself with politics—not one! I never bothered with them myself—not till I found I had a family to think of. That makes things look different. Three religions I've always had—my farm, my home life, and golf. I've had no time for anything else. Same's true of the lot of us." He pointed along the plane with his glass. "We're all alike—good, prosperous, hard-working South Africans. But a bloody sight too easy-going! And the Nationalist hasn't got three religions, he's only one—domination for his own people. And his method of achieving it is politics. Even his church is incidentally a branch of politics, and his business is only a means for building up political power—something else to be cornered for the advantage of the 'volk'. Result is they're a solid united mass—and we're just a lot of isolated individuals." He paused to fill both our glasses. "Wasn't there some chap in antiquity who invented a military formation where everybody packed in tight and they just marched along, flattening all opposition?"

"Yes," I said, "the phalanx. Philip of Macedon is supposed to have invented it."

"Well, that's just what they've got here now—a phalanx. There are members of my family who can't speak a word of English—not a single bloody word. There are others who can speak it just as well as you and me—but they'd pretend not to understand if you spoke to them in English. That's the phalanx!"

"What's your remedy?" I asked. "What would *you* like to see established here?"

"A Republic—they're entitled to that if they want it—but inside the Commonwealth, and with English as the official language. That would be a commonsense arrangement, fair to everybody. But we won't see it—not a hope! The minute they've got their republic, they'll set to work to have this country leave the Commonwealth. And they'll do it. I give us eighteen months from the day a republic is declared before this country is right out on its own. On a limb. And when that day comes it's the writing on the wall. One country can't fight the world—not nowadays. Even a united country couldn't do it. Five years after that, and the rest of the world will have us cornered—probably over South-West Africa—and you can't fight oil sanctions with skiet-commandos."

"But you're staying on yourself?"

"I don't know . . . I *think* I am. Sometimes I'm damned if I know what to do. Those who leave at the right moment sell at a good price and can take their belongings with them. Those who hang on are forced before long to hang on longer, because if they leave now they'll have lost too much. So they stay—and in the end maybe they lose the lot. . . . How about you? Do you mean to stay on?"

"Certainly. My wife and I were over fifty when we left England. We like the country and the people. We came out to stay—and so we shall."

"If they'll let you, my friend, if they'll let you. Don't you be too sure. As for me, I can tell you what will be the sign for me to start doing my packing."

"What's that?"

"If the Nats take action against the private schools—then that will be the finish. The private schools have been the backbone of this country —just as the public schools have in England. I've got a boy at a private school now. They're the last place in South Africa where people are still taught to think for themselves; to learn to live as independent beings, not as sheep. If they try to crush those, I'm getting out."

"Will they try to crush them?"

"Not yet, I shouldn't think. Not yet. Too many of the leading Nats send their own sons to them. Of course, the Dutch Reformed Church doesn't like them; it would like to see its own Calvinistic pattern enforced throughout the country—first in the universities, then in the private schools. There could come a situation in which the government badly needs the church's backing for its policy, and does a deal to give them control over the private schools, in return for their support on some aspect of apartheid."

The young Jew had finished his long chat with the blonde air-hostess and came back at this moment to his seat. Overhearing the last remark, he chipped in irrepressibly: "Oh, the DRC's got a big grip on this country. There's no doubt about that—a very big grip."

"Let's leave religion out of it, shall we?" said my new acquaintance roughly—and in view of our conversation, I thought, rather inconsequently—as he got up to rejoin his companions with the empty bottle.

*   *   *   *   *

Both in Ghana and Nigeria everything was outwardly going well for *Drum*. Since my last visit, we had successfully negotiated a price increase from 6d. to 9d. without more than a temporary loss in sales, so that the whole West African enterprise now rested for the first time on a paying basis—an asset to the firm in place of a heavy liability.

The few days I spent in Accra, however, were far from reassuring. It seemed likely before long that we should have to face both increasing competition from other magazines—which would be unlikely to leave this tempting market empty for long—and increasing pressure from a government which was becoming less and less willing to tolerate any form of criticism. The gap between the assembling of our material and its going on sale in the magazine was dangerously long. This had mattered less when the going was good, but as conditions grew harder, it would matter more and more. It left us wide open to the competition of any paper which could contrive to be printed on the spot, and it meant that we could easily be caught out by shifts in government policy and favour. We needed new printing arrangements that would permit of much greater topicality, and we needed a very much stronger board of directors, capable of giving us practical advice and guidance in the preparation of material, and of offering some solid support when difficulties blew up.

After talking these matters over with Ian Pritchard, who was well aware of our dangers, I put my opinions down in the form of memoranda to the management. They received theoretical agreement, but the question of printing locally was postponed in the hope that one day the firm would install its own printing machinery in Lagos, and the necessity for strengthening the board put off on the ground, first, that any serviceable new directors might expect to be paid more highly than the sum allowed for this purpose; and secondly that, in the ever-changing conditions of Ghanaian political life, it was impossible to decide with certainty whose guidance and support would be most worth having.

Having done what I could in Accra, I went over to Lagos, and this time I was determined to get outside that pulsating, vivacious—but damp and rather smelly—city, and to see something of the country. Nelson Ottah, having just cleared one month's edition out of the way, agreed to come with me for a short tour into the Eastern Region; Matthew Faji, the cameraman, was to come along too. We would take Nelson's Volkswagen and the personal chauffeur whom he now employed.

They called for me early, and we drove out to Ibadan, said to be the hugest black city in Africa, with a famous university and a medical school that turns out fifty qualified doctors and eighty midwives every year—a fact which meant little to me at the time, but was to come back to me vividly just a year later in the Congo when we learned, while attending the Independence Celebrations, that there was not a single Congolese doctor, lawyer or qualified accountant in the country, nor any officer in the army of commissioned rank. From Ibadan we drove, by way of Ife, to Akure, where there was a Rest House in which we could spend the night. These Rest Houses were originally built by the government for officials, district commissioners, doctors, engineers and others journeying around in a country where there are very few hotels outside the main cities. Today they are used by many of those who travel and, being situated outside the towns and sometimes in beautiful positions, they form an agreeable feature of the country's life. They have as a rule a central block with an office where one books in, a bar, restaurant and lounge. Scattered among lawns and flower-beds are bungalows, which one can reserve to oneself if there is plenty of accommodation, or share with a friend or a chance traveller.

Next morning we were up early for breakfast, but already the dining-room was full, both of Nigerians and whites. Nigerians who are prosperous tend to increase in size to match their importance. Their loose robes prevent them from seeming fat, and they carry their great bulk as a rule with dignity. At the table next to ours there were two such figures; we exchanged a few friendly words, and I watched their meal with fascination. Both took porridge, two platefuls each of poached eggs and beans, toast, marmalade and coffee, followed by a double brandy with ginger ale. Nigerians of position seem often to travel with a body-servant, as both these two were doing, and I was reminded again of the comparison—which often struck me in West Africa—with the life of eighteenth-century England. Prosperous Nigerians may require to learn, I thought, as English squires were forced to, not to do more than a limited amount of eating and drinking in a day, and to find some form of violent exercise to take the place of fox-hunting.

Neither Nelson nor Matthew looked likely to become fat, but then Nelson was consumed by his own inner fire—in which ambition, I fancied, played a large part, and irascibility a medium-sized one—both of which I take to be reducing rather than fattening qualities. And Matthew wore that particular aura—invisible to men but apparent immediately to women—which caused them to look at him, from the first glance, with a mixture of approval and speculation, suggesting that they believed him to be possessed of unusual and interesting talents, but would prefer to have these demonstrated rather than just taken on trust . . . Matthew, I guessed, kept slim on the arduous battlefields of love.

*   *   *   *   *

Having started early, we reached the banks of the Niger by mid-morning, and reached them just as the ferry was starting out, so left the car to reserve its own place in the queue and went off to drink "cold beer". The normal time for the double crossing is about two hours, but when after that period we wandered back, it was to see the ferry adrift in midstream, and then stuck fast on a sandbank. It worked itself free at last, but when it pulled in, the cars and lorries in their eagerness to get off jammed fast on the loading ramp—so, having reached the shore at ten-thirty, it was three o'clock before we got on board.

The Niger, however, made up for everything. A vast coffee-coloured flood, sweeping turbulently down towards the sea, rolling along tree-trunks, great masses of weed like floating islands and—it appeared to me—half the soil of the country as it flowed. Hawks and fish-eagles soared and screamed over it; along its borders lived crocodiles, small deer, snakes and all the creatures of the marshes. A whole river-population—amounting to hundreds of thousands—made their living on, around, in or out of its muddy waters. They lived in canoes, punts, dug-outs, broken-down launches, superannuated river steamers, tugs, lighters and barges of every shape and size; many were permanently moored to trees or piles; many were covered with crazy habitations of wattle, wood or tarpaulin; there were wattle-huts built on stilts over the water; and scattered over the sandy isles and beaches were countless villages of thatched dwellings and colonies of leafy tents.

Sheer size gives the Niger its nobility. It does not thunder through gorges like the Yangtse-Kiang, or ravel out into innumerable torrents and waterfalls lacing down over rocky places like the Congo river as it nears the ocean. It is not liquid history like the Nile. It is just there, immense, swift-rolling, irresistible. Like the gods of the Hindus, it i at the same time menacing and benign; carrying, supporting, cleansing providing food, drink and livelihood for its swarming subjects—bu also opposing, tormenting, befouling; destroying their children and their animals by hundreds; drowning them; killing them by water-borne diseases or the rank fevers arising from its swamps; often in th end burying them as well—or at least bearing them away out of sigh of those who knew them.

As the ferry slid sideways over the churning current, we talked o drowning. Matthew told me that as a baby, following the custom c the Warri tribe into which he had been born, he was thrown into th river which ran past his village. If the child comes up again, h is accepted thenceforth as a member of the tribe; but if he sinks, th family walk unconcernedly away—such a child would have come t no good in any case.

"If you float," I asked, "does that mean you can't drown ev afterwards?"

Matthew nodded and said "Yes," but whether because it was s or because he imagined his saying so would please me, I could not te As we crossed, I noted down some of the mottoes painted bold —as trade or owners' names would be with us—on the sides of t mammy-wagons crossing too; these were an unfailing source of interest to me in West Africa. "Trust in the Lord." "Trust the Lord Only." "Remember—All is Not As it Seems." (These last two I thought rather discouraging to prospective travellers.) "Trust No Woman." "Man of War"—and, most mysterious of all, "Man of Peace", under which was painted in smaller letters, "The Wizard of the Holy See."

CHAPTER XIX

BEYOND THE NIGER

WESTERN NIGERIA, THOUGH prosperous and fertile, is like Ghana, disappointing scenically, and in travelling one sees little beyond the forest fringe which hems one in. The main road is a narrow strip of tarmac, one and a half cars wide, which the heaviest lorry or the worst driver holds against all comers. At either side is a broad belt of red sand, which in dry weather blows away as dust and in wet weather washes off as silt. Armies of labourers continually rake and pat it back into position, and hoe off the vegetation which encroaches on it almost overnight. They also slash with their pangas or machetes the mass of trailing creepers, shrubs, rank weeds and overhanging boughs which depend or sprout up along all the verges, and which—in two or three years of neglect—would enshroud the road completely.

To carry off the deluges of rainy seasons, channels are cut every ten yards or so into the grass verges, channels as much as 3–4 feet wide by $2\frac{1}{2}$ feet deep, down which the stormwater sluices off into the forest. These channels, too, are ceaselessly being cleaned out and deepened; on bends, or at tricky points in the road, they are linked together to form what looks like a complicated system of defences and entrenchments to be manned by pigmies. Beyond the red sand and the grass verge hangs—mile after endless mile—the green curtain of West Africa, a wall of palms, cocoa, rubber and banana trees, cassavas, and what looks like a kind of flat acacia with enormous leaves and masses of pinky-orange blossoms hanging down in grape-bunches. Through the rare openings one can see, rising up out of the backlands, those "giants of the forest" whose silvery trunks of close-knit wood, soaring to cathedral height, terminate in a small umbrella of boughs and leafage. About twelve or fifteen feet from the ground, the trunk folds out into bastions and buttresses suggesting the gateway of a mediaeval fortress. With their slight tops, strong boles, and massive bases, these trees belong to that group who do not bow before the wind but stand like steeples, relying on their own strength.

Even in country districts the roads, in the southern regions of Nigeria, seem never to be empty. Towns are far apart, and the main road seldom passes directly through a village. Yet everywhere there are people trudging, raising the red dust from the roadside, women with bundles on their heads going to market, women with baskets, hoes and machetes balanced on their heads, off for a day's work on their farms—which are in fact not farms but vegetable gardens—men swooping by on bicycles, or standing arguing in groups. Nelson waved his arm contemptuously: "All Nigerians talk too much—and always about nothing." I was thinking to myself: "At the next turn we shall see a stretch of road with no one on it. We shall have got away from human habitations. We shall really be in 'the jungle'." But the next turn brought always a fresh chain of walkers, carriers, cyclists, mammy-wagons forcing us off into the dust and the long American cars of rich businessmen or government officials.

To accommodate and find work for all these humans, it is clear that the forest beside the road can be no forest at all; it is a mass of small gardens and cultivated plots scattered among the trees and scrub; and those numberless tracks which slide off from the main road, looking like hunters' trails or the paths to isolated dwellings, run in fact to thousands of busy villages.

Once over the Niger, the forest curtain opened and drew back and through the gaps one caught sight of ranges of blue hills; the nearer landscape had turned into savannah, rolling plains covered with stones and bushy scrub. In a few hours we reached Enugu, our destination and the capital of the Eastern Region. Lying in a bowl with hills all round—nothing so imposing as mountains, just green and pleasant hills—Enugu is a small but handsome city, with blocks of offices and flats, car-showrooms, banks, a hospital, and with its new government buildings placed at wide intervals apart, so that they seem to be standing in their own parks.

Here I had various people I must see, among them Ephraim, in charge of *Drum* sales throughout the Eastern Region, a big man wearing loose patterned robes and a round cap. Sales were going well—yes, very well—but his own problems were not going well. He badly needed a new car—otherwise how could he cover his huge territory properly? He had spoken several times about the need for his new car, but he had still not received it. Now if I were to speak about it for him, no doubt this failure on the part of the management would quickly be put right. Then there was the absurd anomaly of his pay. Others with far less than his experience were earning as much as he was every month, or even more. Clearly this must be due to an oversight, which only needed to be pointed out to the management with enough vigour and directness by myself for it to be rectified.

One cannot do one's best work hampered by lack of appreciation, or disturbed by what one feels to be injustice. Since I had the reputation of being concerned with justice and injustice, this was obviously a matter in which I should be bound to interest myself actively. . . .

He entertained us handsomely in his house, and we discussed what —if anything—could be done about his various difficulties.

*   *   *   *   *

Now that the paper was becoming more prosperous, *Drum* had also, as part of a modest plan of development, stationed a cameraman in Enugu to cover events in the Eastern Region. At such a distance from Lagos, he was operating very much on his own, and one purpose of my visit had been to see him, find out how he was settling into his new territory, and form some estimate of his capabilities. His name was Solomon Manquah. I asked Solomon what stories he was working on at present, and he told me he had two in mind. The first was a story about a big village some eighty or ninety miles away in the bush, in which there lived a race of dwarfs (or "dw-a-a-a-arfs" as he pronounced them) who were "King Makers". They lived under the protection of the chief, fulfilled many of the functions of Court Jesters—their impertinence, like that of the jester, being privileged— and were said to possess the right of deciding the succession. However, it was the second story about which Solomon was excited and on which he was longing to be at work.

"Not more than a hundred miles from here," he said, "there are some caves. In these caves are places so low, sir, that you would be obliged to travel on your belly. There are other rooms inside these caves in which"—and the tone of his voice showed he had little hope of being believed—"it is always raining, day and night, and other places where there are pillars, whitish pillars, which . . ."—he faltered at the coming tax on our credulity—"which . . ."

"You mean which grow up from the floor and down from the ceiling till they meet?"

"Yes—that is it, sir! You had heard of these pillars overseas? Perhaps even there are similar ones in other countries, which grow of their own accord like vegetation. But in these caves you have also to be careful," he went on in a matter-of-fact tone, now that the worst was over.

"Why?"

"Because in a certain part of the caves live leopards. In another part live lions. In a third part of the cave live crocodiles. People—a whole party of students from the university, not only men but girls as well—went into these caves and were never seen again! They had been devoured by the wild beasts! So you too, sir, would require to be careful."

"What story were you planning to do inside the caves, Solomon?" I asked.

"Oh, sir, just to take a pretty girl and picture her against the various surroundings."

"Look, Solomon," said the sophisticated Ottah, "these caves are no good. It is a lot of nonsense. There cannot possibly be leopards, lions and crocodiles inside—what would they live on? They would all have eaten each other long ago—but the King-Makers is perhaps a story. We shall go there to-morrow—and you, Faji, will come too. What about you, sir, shall you be coming with us?"

"No. Not to-morrow. I shall stay here. I want to walk around and get the feel of the place. I shall find plenty to keep me interested."

*   *   *   *   *

What I found to interest me in Enugu, however, was not any story for *Drum*, but my companion in the Rest House bungalow. His name was Forrest—"two R's if you *don't* mind"—Edgar Forrest. He had a ruddy moon-shaped face and a small blue eye pressed sorely into its red rim. A crest of pale fluff, like the comb of a dispirited but angry bird, rose along the top of his pink head. His huge frame was designed or had been adjusted by imperceptible changes of alignment over the years, to support an enormous—as it were floating—stomach. He contrived his life so that he was seldom obliged to stand upright, but when compelled to get up from his bed or chair, or to slip down off his high stool at the bar, he unconsciously braced his whole frame, leaning slightly backwards from legs planted well out to each side. A small moustache, precisely clipped, gave a martial touch to the general disintegration of his looks.

I had caught sight of him for the first time on the evening of my arrival, when I walked over from the office carrying my bag. It had been raining heavily for some hours but had now stopped, and shafts of brightness shone from the overclouded sky. Birds were—if not singing—at least calling, and coloured lizards darted in and out of the wet sparkling grass and the rows of snapdragons, sodden with rain, planted up against the walls of every bungalow. The track was mud, and I had all I could do to keep my feet, so was watching my steps closely when I was suddenly aware of an expanse of whiteness on a bush beside me. I looked up; it was the most enormous pair of pants I had ever seen, spread out, presumably to dry, though they were now as wet as the bush on which they lay; through holes and rents in the seat, big enough for the legs of any ordinary man, twigs and occasional flowers protruded gaily.

I glanced up from the bush to the verandah. Being slightly below its level, I could see nothing but the soles of two feet on the railing, some stretches of pink leg covered with blonde hairs, and a mound of stomach swathed in checks of green and white, which I later found to be our bungalow table-cloth.

"Are you looking for number seventeen?" asked a fruity, rather high-pitched, voice. The voice, I thought, sounded less than enthusiastic over my arrival.

"Yes. Hope you don't mind sharing. It's inconvenient, I know, if you were expecting to have the place to yourself—but there wasn't a whole bungalow left."

"Not at all. Not at all"—with a kind of eager, compensating welcome. "You shouldn't have carried your own bag. Why didn't you tell the boy to bring it over? He's got nothing to do—at least he does absolutely nothing."

"On the contrary. He was trying to distribute six people's luggage at once."

I came round by the steps and up on to the verandah so that we could see each other for the first time. We introduced ourselves, and Forrest—holding the tablecloth swathed round him like an elephant's sarong—did the honours. I asked him which part of the bungalow was his; he showed me the chest of drawers which belonged to my half and warned me that there was an ants' nest just behind the lavatory. Then he went back on to the verandah while I put out a fresh shirt and had a wash. When I joined him we sat silent for a while, contemplating our own and one another's feet on the rail, then he began.

"Bin out here long?"

"No. I don't live here. I'm just an occasional migrant—come up to the West Coast every six months or so."

"Ha! And what d'you do when you come here?"

I told him, and began asking the same questions in return.

"Three years," he said. "Three awful, interminable, soul-destroying years."

"Then you don't like it here?"

"*Like* it?" The mountain heaved volcanically, and the head rolled over to focus an irate blue eye above an enormous arm and shoulder

"*Like* it? My dear fellow, what *can* you mean? Like it—I loathe it, every single minute, as any reasonable, properly brought-up person would. I loathe the climate. I loathe the look of the country. I loathe my fellow-whites—none except absolute fourth-raters come out here any more. I loathe working for my horrible employers—they're a Continental firm drilling bore-holes for something or other which we never find. Most of all I loathe having to share my bungalow with black men because my firm's too bloody mean to pay for my having one to myself."

"I understand you wanting your own living quarters," I said. "In general I should feel the same. But at this time of day I think it's absurd to mind whether you're forced to share with black or white. The country will be independent in a year or two—then they can push the whole lot of us out if they want to. Anyway, what have you got against Nigerians?"

"Nothing against Nigerians—*as* Nigerians. I just don't like having them around me day and night. That's reasonable, isn't it?"

"Well, you couldn't suppose they'd all vanish after a certain hour to avoid giving you offence. You must have known they'd be here— didn't you—when you came out?"

"I knew they'd *exist*." He spoke in a hoarse, indignant rumble, as if life had disappointed him in his quite modest and reasonable expectations. "But I didn't expect them to exist inside my bedroom. What about yourself? Do *you* like it out here?"

"Very much. I'd be happy, I think, to live here if I had the chance."

"Ha!" A huge snort shook the tablecloth. "You've made terms, I see. You're heading for survival. Well—good luck to you if that's the way you think. Personally I refuse to compromise. I shall go on being exactly what I am, until I go under with all hands."

"And what exactly is that?"

"You mean you haven't noticed? Or perhaps you think I'll hesitate to put it into words? I'll tell you what I am. I'm the last surviving specimen of the ordinary decent English middle-class, who gave the modern world what little order and stability it's ever had. A class to which by all appearances"—he cocked an accusing eye at me—"you belong yourself, or used to. I went to a Public School, and I'm proud of it. I served in a famous regiment, and I glory in it. I'm a lifelong Conservative—and shall never be anything else. I'm a practising member of the Anglican Church . . . At home my wife and I maintain a comfortable middle-class English home—which is about as rare nowadays as living like a mediaeval baron . . . I'm aware that all this sounds funny, but it's the way of life we happen to admire and believe in."

"It doesn't sound funny at all," I said. "What *is* funny is that, if you really like that kind of life, you don't live it—instead of sitting here in a Rest House in Enugu complaining that West Africans aren't living a decent middle-class English life as well. Perhaps they just don't want to. Perhaps they prefer their own way of going on."

My companion hesitated, reaching down to scratch himself thoughtfully and intimately through the tablecloth. "You've rather got me there, old boy," he said at last. "I suppose the simple fact is that I'm an old fool. I hadn't got the money to live in England the way I want to live, and I haven't enough brains to earn the money without going abroad to do it." He paused, the moment of truth passed, and he went on: "I'm not one of your slick operators, thank God! I've precious little to offer except absolute honesty, normal intelligence—and a certain whatever-you-call-it manner, good breeding, background . . . I can order the right food and wine, wear the right clothes and so on."

The only clothes of my friend's I had yet seen were the pants on the bush in front of us and the checked tablecloth, but I grunted sympathetically . . . "Not that anybody bothers with all that nowadays," he added. "To-day everyone just mucks in anyhow, and Jack's as good as his master . . . I suppose that's the way you like it."

He appeared to be waiting for some comment. "I appreciate your feelings," I said. "And it must be hell living in any country to which you've taken a dislike. But it seems to me you've only got two choices: to live in England which you're fond of, for less money, or to live out here and put up with it for the sake of the extra dough. Instead of which . . ."

"Instead what?"

"Well, instead you're in a state of moral indignation because you can't live where you prefer and be paid the extra salary for doing it. You want it both ways."

"But that's my position in a nutshell, old boy," he declared, half sitting up as if to see me more clearly. "I couldn't have put it better, though I've been thinking about it for three years."

"Well then?"

"Well *what*? You think because you've stated two obvious alternatives, that all I've got to do is to pick one or other, and sit down and be happy with it. But why *should* I? Neither alternative is agreeable to me—living on too little or living where I don't like—and I'm damned if I'm going to pretend. Ah—I know what you're going to say! I'm unadaptable." He wagged a thick finger at me. "Of course I'm un-adaptable—and if that dooms me to extinction, I shall become extinct. The ichthyosaurus perished because it wanted to go on eating fish and wouldn't adapt itself to browse on weeds. Well, I'm a lot worse off than the ichthyosaurus—I require soup and fish and meat, all decently cooked and properly served, followed by a piece of ripe Stilton, some strong coffee and a glass of port. . . ."

His voice rumbled away down into his inner caverns. The last gleams of light were fading from the sky. The electric bulb, crawled and danced over by swarms of insects, had been on over our heads for the last half-hour. The air was heavy with rain that had still to fall, and seemed to be only waiting for night-time to slip down unnoticed. A small green praying mantis, seeking victims for dismemberment, levered itself along the verandah rail with the measured angularity of some self-propelling earth machine. As we reposed there, side-by-side and sweating, brushing our heads from time to time as insects dropped down off the light into our hair, my friend seemed to me to resemble, not the prehistoric creature of his fancy, but rather some elderly bull-hippo, ponderous but powerless, sinking slowly into his last swamp, grunting and belching defiance in tones which grew fainter and more querulous. The impression may have transferred itself to him, because he added: "I suppose I'm the last specimen of my type alive to-day—or very nearly. It can't be long now before some kindly Welfare State Official or United Nations euthanasia specialist comes along with his licensed hypodermic, and has me quietly put down as an anachronism . . . existing out of my proper epoch . . . un-authorised survival . . . the end of an old fool . . . Did you *say* some-thing?"

"Yes," I said. "I think we ought to bring in your pants. The rain's just started to come down again."

CHAPTER XX

AFRICAN OR COMMUNIST?

OVER THE PAST months quite a number of changes had taken place in our original staff. Jurgen Schadeberg had left, his post as the magazine's white cameraman being filled by Ian Berry. Joe Blumberg had moved to daily newspapers—a change I much regretted, since I enjoyed his lugubrious wit as much as I valued his hard work—and his job had been taken over by Bob Hitchcock from *Golden City Post*, who had come down to join that paper from Rhodesia. Hitchcock was a reporter rather than a sub-editor; he preferred to be out getting stories rather than knocking them into shape inside the office, so that I was doubtful if he would really settle down; however he agreed to give it a trial, and took Joe's chair beside Casey at the sub's table.

And now there occurred another change—at no very high level since it concerned our office-boy, Joshua—but it was one I was particularly sorry to see happen. Indeed there are few things which, a editor, upset me more than losing, or above all sacking, any member of the staff, once he had settled in and become a partner in our curious community. Joshua, though one could not call him a valued worker gave a certain colour and jauntiness to the dusty corner where h stamped letters, poured tea, and hammered out endless works of his own on any typewriter he could find for the moment not being used Just what he typed I never knew, whether love-letters, stories, article he hoped to get into our paper or another—or whether perhaps h just *typed*, in the way an old lady I knew used to knit, not with a view to producing anything definite, but as a form of general relaxation.

Joshua was young, not more than twenty, slight, good-looking. H favourite dress was a flowery Palm-Beach shirt worn outside h trousers, incandescent green socks, old gumshoes and a little roun straw hat with a piece of tattered chiffon tied round the tall crow. The hat attracted a good deal of ridicule in the office, but Joshu smiling and good-natured, was also obstinate. He wore the hat to car messages; he wore it round the office distributing the orange-colour tea with four heaped spoonfuls of sugar in each cup which was brew in the corner of a passage by the lavatory, and passed round twi a day; above all he wore his hat for the lunch-hour games of footba

This was a game played with such extraordinary skill and grace that whenever I could manage to watch it without being noticed, I would do so. Half-a-dozen of the Africans from our own office, with friends from other firms in the same building, would gather on the pavement outside the front door, or on a patch of waste ground a hundred yards away. They did not pick sides and oppose each other as whites would have done; their game was not a contest for victory so much as a mutual display, juggling an old tennis ball about among themselves with marvellous adroitness. One would bounce it with the sole of his foot, like a girl patting her ball in the roadway with her hand; then balance it on top of his instep, hopping in and out among the rest; roll it along his thigh and down again; deftly flick it up on to a pepper-corned crown, where it would be caught with a shout and the jerk of an extended neck, held, and then flicked accurately on to another head five yards away. In these games Joshua was the acknowledged master, playing with mingled control and dash, snatching his hat off to catch the ball on crown or forehead, perching it jauntily back the moment the ball was gone.

I had known for some time that we ought not to keep Joshua. Since we were allowed no trainees on *Drum*, the only place where I could employ someone who was not a trained journalist already was either in the dark-room or as office-boy; it was proper, therefore, to keep these posts for those who might have some future on the magazine. Joshua could not hope ever to become a journalist; he had no background of education; even his knowledge of English was rudimentary, and he had little application or capacity to learn. He got through his day's work in a kind of way, however, and he showed natural good manners, coupled with charm, which made the place more agreeable when he was around. He had a way of sweeping off his hat with one hand when he came into my office, while balancing a tray of slopping tea-cups in the other, which I always enjoyed; and, on the occasions when I sent him out to do something for me, as distinct from his office work, he would put his two hands together to receive whatever I gave him with a peculiar grace, making at the same time a sort of odd half-curtsey.

These were not very solid reasons for keeping Joshua as our office-boy, but then it wasn't a very solid job, and we all knew that if he were to lose it, such as it was, he would probably not find another and would simply become a "tsotsi", or small-time gangster; so he stayed on, and if he were missing for a day or two we took care not to report it. Everyone realised, however, that it was only a matter of time before Joshua crossed his own name off the list in some way which would make it impossible for the rest of us to save him.

A tiny incident which I had seen made me still more reluctant to get rid of Joshua. Coming back to the office in the middle of a lunch-hour, when most of the staff were playing cards in groups, Peter was cleaning his cameras, and Edna, the secretary, fast asleep with her head laid flat beside the typewriter as if expecting to be beheaded, I saw Joshua at his desk with a younger boy sitting by his side. When this boy looked up, I saw that he had one of the most beautiful and gentle faces I had ever seen; I took him to be about twelve years old. They were sitting like schoolchildren with their arms around each other. In front of them was an open book—I could see as I passed that it was a children's reading primer—from which Joshua, pointing out the coloured letters with his forefinger, was slowly teaching the younger boy to read. Later when he brought me tea, I asked who this younger boy was.

"My brother, sir."

"How old is he, Joshua?"

"Seventeen, sir."

"What does he do?"

"Nothing, sir. He's hoping to find a job."

But now Joshua was in trouble. He had been to the Post Office as usual with our afternoon's mail. While there he had—he said—found an envelope lying on the floor, and picked it up. According to the officials he had, while handing our post over to be weighed and stamped, abstracted this letter from the counter. Whether he had found or stolen it, however, mattered little, because the rest of the story was not in dispute. He had taken the letter home, opened it, found a number of postal orders inside, clumsily rubbed out the names to which they were made out, substituted his own—and then tried to cash the lot together at the very Post Office from which he had originally taken them. Naturally he was caught, and the firm had to pay for the destroyed postal orders.

Naturally, also, Joshua had to go. After being dismissed, he sat in his corner all afternoon with his head in his hands; and he turned up in the office as usual next morning—except that he was more punctual than usual—obviously unwilling to face the world outside, and hoping that if he sat there, his trouble might somehow be forgotten and everything be as it had been before. Weakly I told Edna to explain to Joshua that he must go away. And that was the last we saw of him.

*   *   *   *   *

At *Drum* months would go by without our having any sense of official surveillance, and then some incident would happen to show how closely and carefully in fact the paper was always being watched. All our post from West Africa would fail to arrive for a couple of weeks. There would be enquiries, followed by frantic cables yielding no results. Then the whole lot would be delivered at once, some with obvious signs of having been opened. Once, when the Nigerian edition was being packed at the printers, Special Branch police arrived and started leafing through thousands of copies—some story having been spread of "Communist Leaflets" being inserted into the magazine. Few papers have ever been less Communist than *Drum*, but since it is official policy in South Africa to regard all African nationalist movements as Communist-inspired—and since we frequently published articles by or in support of African leaders—the mistake was an inevitable consequence of the policy.

Incidentally, this identification of African nationalism with Communism is, I believe, not merely an ideological illusion but a grave error of tactics; it is an error which American policy has now abandoned, but which still exercises a tight hold on British policy in Africa, particularly as a result of influence from the Federation.

At about this time I had a visit from a British official who had lately come out to take up a post in Africa. I imagined from his paying a friendly call that he wanted to talk over the position in the country, to meet African members of the staff, and possibly be taken to see some African leaders. He proved to have no interest at all in what Africans were thinking, and no wish to meet anyone. All he was eager to know was whether there were "many Communists" among the Africans in South Africa, and did I think it likely that "Communist agents" were being landed and making their way into Basutoland from submarines.

The fact is that African nationalism is not in its nature or its origins Communist at all; it is, if anything, anti-Communist. This is, first, because the African is not interested in, and does not want, a closed system of thought, prescribing his whole way of life and governing his whole outlook on the world—such as Communism (like Calvinism or Catholicism) prescribes for and insists on in its followers. What attracts Africans about the Western way of life is precisely its looseness of structure; its many compartments and wide fields of interest; the possibility of living in different ways and exploring diverse fields of activity—of being at the same time, businessman, politician, poet, athlete, student of religion and good-time man-about-town. Not only does the African not want a closed system of thought, he does not even want what "Communism" is vaguely taken to mean among those who, claiming to discover it everywhere, have never troubled to learn anything about it—that is, some sort of general sharing-out of all belongings, and the abolition of degrees and grades. The African who has come into contact with Western civilisation has taken very quickly to the ideas and standards of the acquisitive society; he is by no means in favour of a general share-out; and he is, like his cousin in tribal areas, a profound respecter of degree and rank. If ever any identification does take place between the aims of African nationalism and those of Communism, it will not be because of any natural affinity, but because white governments in Africa and outside insisted, in what they took to be their own interest, on bringing this identification about.

African nationalism leaders are united, logical and persistent about one point—their absolute determination to see the end of white domination over the whole of Africa. It suits, or is presumed to suit the policy of certain white governments to represent this as the determination to see the end of white existence in Africa, coupled with the determination to hand the whole continent over to Communist enslavement. Every truculent or hostile statement by any black politician is therefore seized on and given wide publicity, while every moderate, friendly or appeasing statement is dismissed as eyewash. The purpose of this misrepresentation is to try and ensure that, in face of so dreadful a "black menace", all whites in Southern Africa march into the laager of resistance, and that white races outside regard this resistance with sympathy, instead of with abhorrence, and lend their practical support. An imagined "granite menace" is thus employed to justify a "granite policy".

But in fact it is plain to anyone who has talked to them with an open mind—and has also studied their speeches to their followers— that African leaders as a whole are not struggling to free themselves from one set of masters, in order to import another, and much tougher set; and secondly that they are far too well aware of the advantages white co-operation to desire a general expulsion of all whites. "For God's sake," said a Congolese Minister to whom I was talking recently, "persuade some of your white industrialists to come and set factories in our country. They are our biggest need. We'll give them all the help we can, and all the guarantees they want."

On this one point—of no more white domination—every African leader, probably not even excepting Tshombe, is united. But everything else their policies vary enormously, being for the most part idealistic and impractical until they attain power, when—like those of Western statesmen in a similar position—they become opportunist and eclectic, the leaders now being primarily occupied (just as are their white counterparts) with the maintenance of their own position, and the extension of their own influence and prestige. Some, for example Nyerere in Tanganyika and Luthuli in South Africa, are profoundly Christian, moderate and humanitarian—though it is the moderation arising from conviction not from softness. Others, like Lumumba, are—or were—unstable enthusiasts, highly egotistic, constantly torn between the possibilities of rival systems and the promises of rival spokesmen, lacking the background to formulate a coherent body of convictions, or the patience—such as Kasavubu has—to allow problems to provide their own solutions. They want it all, on a plate, now. What Krushchev said of Lumumba at the time when Russia was sending aid to him in the Congo (and the world therefore concluded that Lumumba must be a convinced Marxist) was not a stupid attempt to mislead, but a penetrating comment on the Congolese prime minister and his brilliant, though ill-organised, mentality: "If Lumumba is a Communist, then I am a Roman Catholic!"

One or two other leaders—Tshombe in the Katanga is an obvious but not unique example—have hoped to ride simultaneously the horses of local nationalism and of international capitalism, so making themselves popular heroes and wealthy tycoons at the same time. Others, among them certain leaders in Northern Nigeria, are men of vast hereditary wealth and position, acute enough to perceive that the hereditary system is doomed by the forces of the modern world. They have therefore made use of their wealth and prestige, while they still enjoy both, to place themselves at the head of those same democratic forces which would otherwise carry them away.

To sweep this whole medley of African nationalist aims and aspirations into one heap, and label it "Communist-inspired", is simply to assure that Communism gets credit for the successes nationalism is bound to win—and gets it without making the required effort or providing any solid support. It is partly this misguided attitude on the part of certain white governments which makes the newly-liberated African territories reluctant to criticise the Eastern bloc, even when they do something so brutal and so opposed to all their policies and leadings, as to launch a prolonged and dangerous new series of atomic tests. Those white governments having insisted, through this false identification, that "Communism" and "Communists" are in some undefined way behind every African nationalist movement, nationalists are reluctant to denounce their reputed allies.

In South Africa, not content with a loose general identification, the Government has adopted as its main weapon against African nationalism what it calls "the Suppression of Communism Act". This further fixes in the mind of African politicians the belief that Communism is "on the same side" as they are (even though they see little to attract them in its creed), and that Communists, with whom they may have had little or no contact, are the enemies of their suppressors and must in consequence be allies of their own. It is therefore not surprising to find that, according to newspaper reports, Communism is now beginning to make some degree of headway among politically-minded Africans, whose own political movements have been ruthlessly suppressed partly on this very ground of a supposed Communist influence and direction. "Give a dog a bad name long enough, and in time you compel it to become a wolf."

This, however, is a digression, arising from the search of our Nigerian edition by Special Branch police, acting on an official presumption that a belief in Nigerian independence is evidence of the opposite belief—that the world, and South Africa with it, ought to be dominated in the interests of the Soviet Union.

$$* \quad * \quad * \quad * \quad *$$

Just at this moment, as it happened, I was given another proof of the combined suspicion and interest with which our efforts at an independent African journalism were officially regarded.

Among the changes made when Jurgen Schadeberg left was to bring out of the dark-room a young assistant, whom I will call Robert Ndledle; his ambition was to become a photographer, and he had already shown signs of talent, but there was clearly no room on the staff for another cameraman in addition to Ian and Peter, so I told him that, if he would help me with the donkey-work of laying-out the magazine, ordering up the blocks and so on, I would give him what chances of photographic work I could. Meantime he would at least be working with pictures, and learning something of journalism through day-to-day contact with the staff. Robert took the job on, but asked me to write to the police and get him a press pass, so that if chances of taking pictures occurred, he would at least have the necessary papers.

I duly wrote the letter—it was one of the absurdities of my position that, having been refused a press pass myself, I had to make applications for them on behalf of members of my staff—and forgot all about it. As a result of the application, however, a Special Branch policeman called at Robert's home (he lived in one of the townships out eastwards of Johannesburg along the Reef) and, finding him away at work, left word that he should report at the Police Station the following Saturday. Robert said nothing to me about this interview beforehand, but on the Monday he at once came into my room and began telling me what had happened.

"When I got to the station, they seemed as if they were expecting me, sir. I just gave my name and one of the cops led me straight through into an inside room. There was a very tall thin chap there—I think he was a major. He was smoking a cigarette. He told me to sit down, and he even offered me a cigarette, too. I didn't know what to do. You know I never smoke, but I could see he meant it as a favour and I thought he'd be angry with me if I refused—so I took it and let it go out, and then put it in my pocket.

" 'Well,' he said, 'so you're Robert Ndledle, are you?'

" 'Yes, sir.'

" 'And you're working for *Drum* magazine—are you? Is that right? How long have you been there?'

" 'About a year, I think, sir.'

" 'What d'you want to go on working in that place for, Robert, eh? Why d'you do it, now?'

" 'Well, sir, I'm very interested in photography, and in journalism. I want to learn to become a photographer, and I think this work is giving me a start.'

" 'But don't you know this *Drum* is a political magazine, Robert? Don't you know that it's Communist, Robert—eh? Surely you know that it's run by the African National Congress, Robert, and that it's against the Government? Hasn't anyone told you that—eh? Don't you realise that?'

" 'I don't think it's Communist at all, sir,' Robert replied. 'I know that it doesn't support the Government.'

" 'Who's this Tom Hopkinson they call the editor? Who is he, Robert, eh? Tell me now, man, who is he?'

" 'He's the editor, sir,' Robert answered feebly. ('Well—I didn't know what else to say to him,' he explained.)

" 'And Peter Magubane—what about him? Who's he? Who's this other—eh?'

" 'He's one of the photographers, sir.'

" 'Is he the chap who was beaten up by the police? Is that the same chap—eh, Robert?'

" 'Well—he *has* been beaten up once or twice by the police, sir, but he isn't the one who has just been beaten up lately. That's Sidney . . .'

" 'Oh, we know all about Sidney Andrews,' said the officer. 'Now look here, Robert, just you listen carefully to what I'm going to say to you. Have you ever been interested in detective work, eh? Have you ever thought of becoming a detective yourself—now?'

" 'I did when I was a little boy,' Robert replied, with an unconscious irony which happily passed unnoticed.

" 'Well, then, Robert, since you're interested in being a detective . . .' "

At this moment, Robert said, two other policemen came into the room. He had the feeling that the first officer was anxious to go on talking to him, but didn't like to do so while the others were in the room, so cut things short: "See here, Robert, does your office make you work Saturdays, eh? Are you free sometimes on a Saturday, now?"

"Sometimes I'm free, sir, and sometimes I have to work."

"Well, then, Robert, the next Saturday you're free, just come along here and ask for me, and we'll have a little chat together, see? We'll try if we can't arrange something that will be good for you and a help to us as well. Have you got that now? Eh? Well, don't forget!"

As he finished the story, Robert began to laugh. "What the hell are you laughing at, Robert?" I asked. "D'you think all this is funny?"

"I'm laughing to think about this important cop offering me a cigarette—and his thinking I shall come in every week or two and make a report about everybody here."

"Well—what's so funny about that? It sounds like a damn good offer to me. You do one job—and you get paid twice. What more can you ask?"

Robert chuckled. "I mean—he's a detective, isn't he, sir, this officer I talked to?"

"Of course he is—and a very big and important one. So what?"

"Well—couldn't he detect that he'd come to the wrong shop? Couldn't he even detect that I don't smoke? I thought they could spot all these sort of things about you right away."

"Evidently not . . . So what shall you do now?"

"Nothing, sir," said Robert with surprise. "If he sends for me, I have to go and listen to him again. But it's ten to one he'll expect me to call for a week or two, and then when I don't, he'll just forget about me."

Which was exactly what did happen.

CHAPTER XXI

"IMMIGRANT RACES, DO NOT FEAR"

IN THE COURSE of my visits to the West Coast I had made contact with some of the leaders there. In South Africa I had met and talked to Luthuli, Robert Sobukwe, leader of the recently-formed Pan-African Congress, Duma Nokwe, Robert Rhesha, Nelson Mandela, Oliver Tambo and others of the African politicians. But I had for a long time been eager to meet the leaders in East Africa, in particular Julius Nyerere and Tom Mboya. Towards the end of 1959, I got the opportunity.

One of the successes we had enjoyed on *Drum*, second only to our success on the West Coast, had been to build up a considerable sale for the magazine in East Africa. This was largely due to the energy and enthusiasm of the man on the spot, a young journalist called Alan Rake. On taking over the paper, I found the files full of stories he had sent in, also of letters pleading for these stories to be printed. The theory was that a certain number of pages of the normal South African edition were changed in each issue after the supplies for South Africa had been run off, material sent down from East Africa replacing whatever in the South African edition might be supposed to have least appeal for the eastern territories—Kenya, Uganda and Tanganyika. But in the rush of work and general short-handedness it had, it seemed, not been possible to do this regularly. I was impressed by Rake's obvious eagerness to develop the magazine in his territory, as shown by the angry expostulations in some of his past letters, and at once arranged to change eight pages for him every month. In conjunction with him a plan was worked out whereby we tried to include some material from each of his three territories in these eight pages; after a while we also arranged to have the covers specially overprinted with the words EAST AFRICA EDITION, and the price marked on them in local currency.

The arrangement worked, and as sales moved rapidly ahead, Alan who had begun by doing everything himself, from writing the articles and taking the photographs, to typing the correspondence, licking on the stamps, checking the accounts, persuading shops to sell the magazine and putting up the posters in their windows—acquired an office-boy, some office furniture, a second telephone, a few mainly unreliable contributors, and finally a whole-time cameraman. We imagined a future in which he, from Nairobi, would control small local staffs operating in Kampala and Dar-es-Salaam, with African or Asian "stringers" at two or three other key points in his vast territory.

Though it was pleasant to be building a success, Alan's life was a harassing one. The local offices and the stringers were in the future; meantime he chased around Kenya in an open M.G. doing nine-tenths of the work himself, besides paying frequent dusty visits to Uganda and Tanganyika. In addition he had a recurring worry every month over whether supplies of the magazine would arrive in time. Copies for East Africa, printed in Johannesburg, were railed 400 miles to Durban, and then shipped up coast to the ports of Dar-es-Salaam and Mombasa. Our method of dispatch was through the post in bulk, and copies caught whatever vessel happened to be sailing. By ceaseless nagging at my end it was usually possible to make sure that the circulation department got the copies away in time to be on sale by the due date, but occasionally they would be late, and once a whole month's issue was completely lost by the postal authorities. No one could tell us where it had got to; it was believed to have been put by accident on to a boat going to Japan, but was discovered, after a fortnight's search, in some wagons in a Durban siding. Desperate efforts were then needed on Alan's part to get it on sale for at least ten days or a fortnight before being overtaken by the following month's issue.

Sometimes, too, our Johannesburg accounts department—in the anxiety to produce what they called "a good figure" at the month end—would omit to send any money to East Africa. When I complained bitterly about this, they would assure me that the matter had "already been dealt with", and I had once as many as three telegrams from Alan on my desk at the same time, imploring me to get the staff's salaries and petty cash sent up before they all starved or were arrested for debt. Despite these difficulties, the circulation in East Africa had been built up in two years from under ten to well over twenty thousand, and the moment had now come for a dramatic change. Instead of our merely altering a few pages from our own edition, East Africa was to follow the example of West Africa, hive off and become a separate paper on its own, with its own small editorial staff controlled by Alan, and with separate advertising pages publicising the goods locally available. For the time being the material Alan prepared would still be sent down to me in Johannesburg to be made up, but the only things the new edition would have in common with others would be the general policy, the style of make-up and planning, and the coloured cover which we should continue, for economy, to run off for all our editions at the same time.

I imagined this new step as being followed in two or three years by a separate edition for the Federation (Nyasaland and the two Rhodesias) which we would build up in exactly the same way, starting by changing a small number of pages and establishing a capable all-round journalist on the spot to supply material and get sales moving. In the further future I foresaw—or thought I foresaw—still other *Drums* in other parts of Africa, possibly including one or two editions in French which we would print in conjunction with one of the big French publishing houses, with whom I was already beginning to cultivate friendly contact through the exchange of pictures.

The East Africa project had been discussed over and over again in letters and memoranda between Alan and myself, and between Alan and Jim Bailey. It had been threshed out in Johannesburg in discussions with Jim Bailey and the General Manager; argued out, and finally accepted, over the Board Room table. Bailey had also been up to Nairobi a number of times to see the position for himself; an advertising representative had been sent out from *Drum's* London office to sound out the interest of the big firms and advertising agencies. And now I had got the chance to go up there as well and put the final touches to our editorial arrangements.

* * * * *

Alan Rake—whom I had never met, though we had corresponded closely, appreciatively, and sometimes with mutual exasperation—proved to be an unusually tall young man in his twenties with a mop of dark hair, a slight hesitation in his voice, large feet and hands, and prodigious interest in Africa. One of the aspects of his work in which he had been most successful was in making contact with, and gaining the confidence of, the African and Asian leaders in his territory. He had achieved this at the cost of friendly contacts with the whites, which someone more detached and less exuberant might possibly have managed to retain, but from the magazine's point of view the goodwill of the non-whites was much the more important of the two. After a few days of office work, Alan took me round to meet Tom Mboya and his close associate, Dr. Kiano, as well as a number of the African Leaders. In the course of my stay, I met Tom Mboya several times, at a lively party for all races as well as for serious discussions. Mboya is as handsome as his photographs; young, but already of great

political experience; equally adept at handling a local trade union
squabble or a "summit conference" of African leaders; and with the
powerful build a politician needs if he is to stand up to the racket of
international life. For it is perhaps not generally realised that the strain
on a present-day politician is many times greater than it used to be in
the days when a man was politically active almost entirely within the
borders of his own country. Today, as soon as he attains any degree
of leadership in his own land, he is obliged to become an international
figure with worldwide obligations; attending conferences and discussions in other continents; giving television, radio and newspaper
interviews which can be crucial to his reputation, in what were once
his spare half-hours. As recently as the Versailles Conference, eminent
politicians found time to make notes for future books, carry on ardent
love-affairs, make use of their inside knowledge to amass large personal
fortunes, pursue one another with bitter vendettas, and lead a rich and
enjoyable life as social lions; it is doubtful if their counterparts get
much time for on-the-side activities today.

For the old-timer—operating abroad mainly through the post, or
if he were prime minister, through ambassadors, in those days a
dignified and unhurried body of men—it might take a month to put
a foot wrong, and two or three more to climb, almost unnoticed, out
of the mess. Today he can put both feet wrong in front of fifty million
onlookers in two minutes, and the bill comes in immediately by telephone, cable, and in next morning's papers. It can be observed that
those who stand up to this strain best are the heavily-built, deep-
chested bears—the Churchills, Stalins, Khrushchevs, Azikiwes, and
that the load weighs crushingly on the more slightly-built Edens,
Crippses, Eisenhowers and Lumumbas.

In all physical respects Tom Mboya is outstandingly equipped for
political success; in addition he has charm, though at present it turns
on and off too visibly; and he is also an orator of power and subtlety
who can play on his audience like an organ—pulling out the stops
when he wants them to shout back enthusiastically "Uhuru! Uhuru!"
calming them in a moment when he wants their quiet attention for a
point to be remembered. Either his particular experience of life,
however, or the cageyness of one born to politics, has formed his
handsome face into a mask. It is impossible to tell (I should say that I
found it impossible to tell) when he is talking to a brief and when, if
ever in our talks, he spoke directly out of feeling and conviction. Like
so many Western politicians, perhaps, he has already learned the game
too well. In contrast to Julius Nyerere, whom I saw shortly afterwards

it seemed that Nyerere is the father of his country, with a father's detachment and authority—just as ready, if the occasion calls for it, to rebuke and instruct his followers as to call for their support; whereas Mboya is still the politician with his way to make, mindful that his first need is to extend and develop his own personal position.

*   *   *   *   *

From Nairobi we flew down to Dar-es-Salaam. Most cities fall short of the magic of their names, but there are a handful—Galway, Edinburgh, Lisbon, Cape Town and Marseilles are among the few I have seen—which surpass it, and Dar-es-Salaam is one of them. With its natural harbour, not large but neat, in which dhows as well as liners ride; its sea as blue as a child's painting, fringed with a powder of sparkling sand; with its tall, feathery palms which toss even when no breath of wind seems to be stirring; with the mosques, minarets and bustling activity of its Asian quarter, it looks more like a city of the East than the capital of a modern African state. It is one of the cities I feel happy to be in, and I have sat at my window, and sweated and looked at the sea, and looked at the sea and sweated, too hot to stir, but breathing the tepid air with deep enjoyment.

On our first evening, after finding somewhere to stay, Alan and I set out to visit the African quarter of the city. One of the things which had happened to me, after eighteen months in Africa (it had happened long since to Alan, but I noticed that it never happened at all to most of my white colleagues), was that in any new place I now went first to blacks for information rather than to whites. This was not from any hostility on the part of whites—on the contrary, most white officials seemed perfectly willing to help despite any feeling they might have had about *Drum*; it was rather that I felt I knew what they would have to say, but what the African said would often be new and unexpected. This evening we intended to call on three or four local newspapermen: we also wanted to visit the headquarters of TANU (Tanganyika African National Union), talk to the officials, and make arrangements to see the party's leader, Julius Nyerere.

The day had been stunningly hot, and the tarmac road was bubbling like a pond full of frogs in spring, but it was now a little cooler, and we agreed to walk. Facing the harbour, into which sailing-boats were just being run down by white men for their evening's sport, stand the government buildings. Since Independence, imposing new government offices have gone up, but the old ones, dating back to the German occupation of sixty and more years ago, have the charm of the totally unexpected. These are roomy, two-storied buildings painted in stripes of black and white like the warehouses of Hanseatic ports; the offices inside are spacious, and lofty enough to remain fairly cool; but the broad balconies of wooden planks supported on struts—up and down which officials in tightly-buttoned duck suits must once have paced, argued, and stamped their booted heels in salute—have long been too rotten to walk on safely. The German regime has left its mark on the capital—and also on some of its people, for one can still find old men here and there who served in the army or police, and who show with pride a back deeply scarred from the days when discipline was as sharp as the crack of a whip, and lashes a normal punishment for trifling misdemeanours.

We passed through the European shopping centre, little more than a few smart streets which might have been in Durban, and on into the Asian quarter. Here life swirls faster and more noisily, for if the Europeans are still the country's bankers, merchants, shippers and business managers, the Asians are the shopkeepers and traders; they meet the customers, draw in the crowds, and take the cash. Shops and stores stay open till all hours. In the upper stories of business blocks families swarm in packed contentment; washing droops listless from the balconies, and children shout to one another over the thronged street. Through the air heavy with talk and heat, big American cars of junk-heap antiquity roll, hooting to clear themselves a passage, like steamers in a crowded estuary.

Further on where the crowds have thinned, a shrill jabbering makes me look up. The street is already in shadow, but around the little pink dome of an Ismaili mosque a swarm of thousands of swallows dart twittering and screaming in and out through a stucco lattice, making their last flight of the evening in a kind of frenzy, as if the sun were about to go down for ever. Past the Asian commercial quarter lies a number of ornamental villas for the wealthy; with their decorated balconies and porches, flat roofs, tiled verandahs, and their Indian or Persian names, they suggest the suburbs of Calcutta or Bombay. Through this narrow belt of prosperity we push on into the sprawling city of the Africans.

Here all is bare utility. Houses of plastered mud, roofed with rusty corrugated iron, open straight on to the unpaved road, in which goats and babies nuzzle each other aside for anything worth chewing. The shops are mere piles of goods heaped in a window, on a table, or stacked on a verandah; an office involves no more than a painted sign over a room with the street door left open; the vehicle here is bicycle, swerving in and out among the sprawling children and the heaps of rubbish. An occasional venerable car creaks by, raising a dust-cloud, but such cars as there are have mostly sunk down long since upon their weary haunches. With split tyres, blind eyes and metal skeletons picked clean, they crouch in the gaps between the houses, never to rise again, their carcases serving as refuge for a few scrawny hens.

A sound of singing leads us up the street to a one-storey building, which might be a large bicycle shed or the canteen of some unprosperous business. A notice shows this to be the headquarters of TANU, probably the strongest and best organised political party in any African territory; TANU was at this time only five years old, but had already built up a membership of over half a million, with 70 district headquarters, nearly 1,000 paid party officials, and a branch office in every chiefdom. A year later at the general election TANU would win 70 out of the 71 seats in the legislature, and already those working late in this tumble-down headquarters were in virtual control of the whole vast territory of Tanganyika, with its nine million Africans—many of them among the most backward and poverty-stricken in all Africa—seventy-five thousand Asians and Arabs, and twenty-five thousand Europeans.

Drawn by the singing we pushed through the half-dozen small offices—little more than horse-box divisions cut out of the main room, in most of which party officials were still at work—and came out at the back into a narrow yard surrounded by sheds. Here, seated in splintery wooden benches, was a group of perhaps forty Africans, ranging in age from four to seventy. They were gazing with concentration at a blackboard—on which a teacher was pointing out words and syllables to them with a cue—and singing as they read.

To one side, watching the singers with an air of humorous benignity, was a slight dapper man in his middle thirties. He had a cheerful, unlined face, a toothbrush moustache, and his curly hair sprouted far back on his high forehead. He wore sandals, a freshly-ironed dark green shirt (the TANU uniform) outside his trousers, and carried—rather as if it were a wand of office—a black walking-stick with an ivory handle. A number of African leaders—Nkrumah and Kenyatta among others—never appear without their special walking-sticks; Nyerere follows the pattern, but his stick is much the slightest, and has the unusual feature of being both black and white; an ivory handle on an ebony shaft.

"What is it they are learning to sing?" I asked, when Alan, who knew Nyerere well, had introduced us.

"They form part of the choir which attends all our big meetings; we have a mass meeting on Sunday at the airport at which twenty thousand people will be present. These people learn the party songs— but mainly they just enjoy singing, so we teach them. We have a backward country, and we have to teach everyone everything we can. We teach all kinds of things here in this building"—he waved an arm towards a row of treadle machines. "We teach our women to sew and to make clothes, that's a very important part of TANU work."

"What's the meaning of this song they're learning?" Alan asked.

Nyerere's quick smile showed startlingly white, filed teeth. "I begins—'Immigrant races, do not fear' "—he told us.

*   *   *   *   *

We went next morning to visit Nyerere in his office. Instead of th endless form-filling and waiting which makes some African politician far more difficult of access than the Pope, a secretary rang through t ask if he were free, and we were taken straight into a cool study Nyerere, as usual in a TANU shirt, sat at a big desk on which in glass of water stood a head of frangipani blossom, a cluster of five petalled white trumpets unfolding into stars, and revealing, as the open, their buttercup-yellow lining. The frangipani carries a stron delicious scent, and from time to time he sniffed the blossom as w talked.

Nyerere came directly to the point: "It is essential for us to be giv Independence quickly. Instead of the present government—which a government of civil servants with a few elected ministers—we mu have an elected government in which a few civil servants still parti pate. It is essential that we have this soon, and the first reason is th we want to maintain goodwill and a harmonious relationship wi Britain. I want the people of Tanganyika to understand that the Briti are their friends, not their oppressors; and I want to demonstrate the people of Britain that the white man who comes here in the rig spirit will be *more* welcome when we have our Independence than was before. We must demonstrate the true position to both sides. T frightened Europeans must be shown that they can stay and wo with us on just and proper terms. And those Africans who want sit on the heads of the white men—because their own black he have been sat upon so long—must give up ideas of 'getting their o back'. Both sides, you see, have got to give up something. We wan make this country an example of races working together; we want world to say, 'Look at Tanganyika! If they can do it, why can't we

He turned to me. "You," he said, "come from South Africa; a white minority dominates your country. They do this because they have come to believe that their only security lies in domination; they equate domination by their minority with safety—so they are terrified of even the hint of change, and cling to power like limpets because they dare not share, and they dare not relax. But we mean to prove to these tight clingers-on to power that the truth is the opposite of what they think. We want to show that in Tanganyika lives a white minority which is *more* secure—as well as much happier and more free—than the white minority in South Africa, Kenya or elsewhere. Once we have shown that this is true, then the question is bound to be raised in all men's minds—is domination by a minority the best way of achieving peace for ourselves, and for our children and grandchildren?"

He paused, as if for us to answer, but seeing our close attention, went on again: "I got this letter a few days ago"—he held it up—"it comes from a retired civil servant who worked all his life in Southern Rhodesia, but who came not long ago to settle down in Tanganyika. He tells me that he has been very happy living here, but now he has received a letter from an old colleague in Southern Rhodesia asking if he should come and settle down near his friend. Would he like it here? Will there be terrible changes after Independence? Will his wife be safe when he is away—and so on. So now the first man has written to me to ask what answer he should send the second one . . ." As he finished the story Nyerere began to laugh: he laughed freely and delightedly, surrendering himself to laughter.

"What answer shall you send him?" Alan asked seriously, but the only answer Nyerere gave was to go on laughing. After a minute he began to talk again. Alan had asked him what he thought of the situation in Kenya, saying he was afraid "Tom"—that is Tom Mboya—was beginning to think racially and becoming less ready to co-operate with Asians or Europeans. Immediately the practical politician in Nyerere came out, and the doubts I was feeling as to whether his astuteness and firmness would be equal to his goodwill were lightened.

"You must understand Tom's position," he explained. "The position here and the position in Kenya are quite different. There Tom is between two fires. He has the settlers on the one hand, who are fighting for their livelihood and their privileged position, and he has the masses of the people on the other, who have had little political education and veer naturally towards extremes. Tom has to steer a middle course, but each time he accepts an approach from one side, the other accuses him of selling out. A politician can easily destroy his whole career in a position of that sort, by doing something from goodwill which his enemies seize on and misinterpret. Tom has to go very carefully—the people who ought to be making the gesture in Kenya are the Europeans."

"How d'you mean?" Alan asked. "What gesture should they make?"

"The gesture that will give assurance and peace of mind to the other side, and at the same time assist Tom in maintaining his moderate position. Here in Tanganyika we Africans are the more powerful—we hope that Independence is coming next year, or at latest in 1961 but we *know* for a fact that it is coming. There are nine million of us and the power is already in our hands—so it is for us to reassure the white man and the Asian, and that is just what we are deliberately doing. Any white man or Asian who accepts loyalty to Tanganyika can come and live among us and get on with his lawful business." He turned to me. "Your Dr. Verwoerd can come here, if he likes! Provided he accepts loyalty to Tanganyika, and doesn't expect to boss people around because they're black, he can come and live here just like anybody else. But in Kenya it's the European who has still got power—so it's for him to come forward with the offer to the other the offer which will enable Tom to live on his future political dividends"—when he saw how I chuckled over this phrase, he repeated it smiling—"to live on his future political dividends. Tom knows perfectly well that in the end there has to be a compromise in Kenya, but that compromise must emerge *out of the situation*. If he tries to force a particular compromise before the country is ready to accept it, Tom will simply destroy his own position and the possibility of achieving something really important in the future. . . ."

Alan, who was building up material for a life-story of Nyerere, began to question him about his childhood.

"There was nothing special about it. . . . I was one of 26 children . . . I was sent to a Catholic school while I was still quite young . . . wasn't keen on sport, as most of the boys were, and I hated injustice . . . So I was always getting into trouble through speaking out. . . In the end the headmaster made me a prefect to keep me quiet. . . The prefects had great power at my school. . . ."

"Did the headmaster's plan work out?"

"Not very well. I had the idea that a particular boy, one of my fellow-prefects, was ill-treating one of the juniors—so I went to the headmaster and told him what I felt. The headmaster sent for the th-of us and went into the matter; then he decided in favour of the other prefect. He told me I was in the wrong, and insisted I should myself punish the boy for whom I had spoken, by giving him six cuts with the cane. I fought hard against this—but in the end I had to submit. I hated it, but I had to do it." He paused, and repeated, ". . . the prefects had great power at my school."

"Yes," I said, "it's the English way of teaching tyranny," at which he laughed delightedly, and went on . . . "Near the end of my time at school, it was suggested that I should be made the head prefect. 'No,' said the headmaster, 'I won't make that boy head prefect.' . . . He was quite right, of course. . . . He knew my defects. I should have been too lax. I was not interested in discipline."

He told us how, after coming back from taking his degree in Britain, he had met his old headmaster again, and the headmaster had congratulated him on being the first university graduate from Tanganyika, telling him he ought to be proud of this great honour.

"No," said Nyerere. "I don't think that's any cause for congratulation—for me or anyone else. I think it's shameful there should never before have been a university graduate from this country—we ought by now to have had hundreds of them."

We ended up by talking about our plans for the East African edition. "You can do a first-rate work with it," he said. "You can help to explain the races to each other. You can help us to make people understand what we are trying to do, and why we can't always go as fast as they would like. You can inform our people about what's happening in other parts of Africa, and in your other editions you can tell them what we're doing here. And then with your pictures—which attract people's eyes and minds—you make people *want* to read, and in this way you help us to spread literacy. Make your paper in two languages, English and Swahili, using both languages together in the same paper —then those who speak only one of our languages will get to know something of the other. Your magazine can be of real value to us in what we are trying to do here, and I shall see that you are given all the help we can."

CHAPTER XXII

"WE JUST CAN'T DO IT"

ON THE MONDAY morning after my return I went into the office with a new excitement. In West Africa the paper was expanding fast, so that there it was mainly a matter of keeping the ball rolling; in South Africa we seemed to be doing little more than holding our position; but in East Africa we had opened up a new field in which it should be possible both to develop the magazine rapidly, and also to have some real effect on the movement of events. I was particularly pleased and elated by the encouragement of Julius Nyerere.

Our new edition was due to come out in February 1960; there were only a couple more issues to be published before then, and I had spent some time on the way back working out how to use them to the best advantage. The way to do this, I decided, was to change a greater number of pages, so as to get in more local interest; to print the largest number of copies we could hope to sell, in order to build sales up before the change-over; and to announce as dramatically as we could all the new magazine would be offering. Working on a shoestring as we always did, these announcements in our own paper would have to take the place of general advertising. Jim Bailey was not yet in, so I called in on the General Manager to get agreement for the extra expense involved. When he heard my request, he laughed: "You haven't a hope in hell! I can tell you that right away. It's out!"

"Why?"

"He won't want it."

"What d'you mean—'he won't want it'? You haven't even heard what things are like up there, or what the prospects are."

"No—and I don't need to hear. Nor anyone else either. I know what I'm talking about; I tell you Jim Bailey won't want it. Here." He passed me across a memo. "Your print order for East Africa has been stabilised for the next six months at 20,000. And you can forget the idea of any more change pages, you'll be lucky if you can keep the ones you've got."

"But look here," I said, "I've just been up there to investigate the prospects. Now I've come back to say what they are. All these things can't be settled before we've even talked them over."

"Oh, can't they!" said Weatherstone. "You'll see. Oh, and by the way, there's to be an all-round reduction in expenses. I'll see you about that later in the morning."

"God damn it!" I said. "What the hell's the point of sending me up to East Africa for three weeks if the whole matter is decided before I get back?"

"Don't ask me!" Weatherstone replied. "But I'm through with all these arguments anyway. I've arranged to leave in a few days' time."

It was clearly no good talking any more under such conditions, and I should have to wait until I could speak to Jim Bailey himself. Meantime, my desk was covered with unanswered letters, and there was a new South African edition to be laid out, so that it was Wednesday before our meeting took place. Jim asked me briefly how the trip had gone, and then we settled down to our discussion.

"About your memo," I began, "saying that we must cut back circulation in East Africa. Before deciding what you want to do, would you like to hear what the position is up there?"

Jim nodded, putting on his "double focus" look, which meant there was a question of finance at stake and I should need careful watching, and leaned back in his chair with his feet on the blotting-pad.

"The idea of a magazine specially for East Africa got a great welcome. Both Nyerere and Tom Mboya promised it their support, and are going to write something for us. The Government people I talked to weren't at all unfriendly. The advertising agents say it will certainly catch on, but some of their clients want to see a few issues first to make sure this isn't just a flash in the pan. Alan and I went very carefully into the sales position—we're pretty sure he can sell 26-27,000 copies a month, for the next two months. That means we should have our 5,000 readers all lined up for the new paper in February."

"I'm afraid that's quite out of the question."

"Why?"

"Postage is far too high; we're losing money on every copy we end up there. We can't possibly send an extra 13,000 copies over these next two months—it's simply giving circulation away."

"But we have to aim a bit high to be sure of having our guaranteed 5,000 readers by February. If we're only selling 20,000 copies in December and January—we may not get the 25,000 in February when we need them."

"In that case we shall just have to build up more slowly," Jim replied.

"But we've *guaranteed* a sale of 25,000 to the advertiser. We must keep to what we've said."

"The *facts*," said Jim, "are just the other way about. It's the advertiser who's not keeping faith with us. This is November now—we come out with the February issue at the end of January. So far we've only got eight pages of advertising booked. Eight pages! It's just not good enough. We need at least twenty to break even."

"Eight is rather miserable," I admitted. "However, we can't expect advertisers to rush to buy space in a paper before it exists. Give them a few issues to look at, and they'll come along. All the agents agree that a new magazine is badly wanted up there."

"That's very nice of them! But it would be still nicer if they'd do something to help us in starting it. How are we going to pay for those few months when there isn't any advertising—or very little?"

"No magazine," I urged, "has ever yet made money from its first issues. The cost of producing the first few is our investment in the territory. It'll all come back—just as it's coming back to us in West Africa. After all, if we were launching a new magazine in Europe we'd have to face an advertising campaign costing at least £100,000, and the certainty of losing money heavily for two years."

This was a grave mistake in tactics, as I saw the moment I'd said it; Jim smiled patiently. "But Africa is *not* Europe, and if you're to operate successfully in Africa it's necessary for you to adapt yourself to African standards and African methods. Here we have to finance our own efforts as we go along. With printing and postage costs as high as they are, we simply can't throw money around. I've had to tell Weatherstone that pretty sharply, and I'm having to call for economy right through the firm. Copies of *Drum* printed at an uneconomic price and shipped to East Africa at present postage rates are simply so many shillings down the drain. If the advertisers aren't prepared to support us when we're launching something of value to them—then they can't expect us to spend money building extra circulation for their benefit."

I paused. "I'm really puzzled," I said, seeing the whole picture falling to pieces.

"Puzzled? What about?"

"Well, if things are so difficult, and every penny must be counted twice—why have I been up to East Africa at all? What was the point of the exercise, if you've got the whole thing cut and dried down here? The last thing you gave me before leaving was a memo suggesting that an edition partly in Swahili could sell 30,000 copies in Tanganyika alone, plus another 30,000 in Kenya—'provided Rake and I play properly'. One of the things I was told to arrange was for putting part of the text into Swahili, with a view to getting these high sales. B if we aren't going to print more than 20,000 copies until May, all that's a waste of time and money. We can sell far more than 20,000 just in English."

Jim put his head in his hands, like a schoolmaster faced with an impossibly dense pupil. "It's simply a matter of finance! Since you haven't got the South African edition on to a paying basis yet, we just haven't the money available to push ahead in East Africa as fast as we might like. Believe me—I should be just as happy as you to print thirty, forty or fifty thousand copies of the East African edition—provided they were all bringing in money. But as the one who pays the bill, I'm not prepared to do it at a loss."

"But the financial position has been with us all along," I argued. "We've been planning this undertaking now for a good six months. We've had Board Meetings on it. You've been up there to make plans. How is it, after all this, we now suddenly find we can't afford what we were all agreed on doing?"

There was a knock at the door, and Cecil Eprile—who had looked in several times during the last twenty minutes and gone away again—asked: "May I come in, Jim? It's really important."

"Yes, Cecil. What is it?"

"Something I badly need your advice on. Would you say it's all right to use the word bloody in a tabloid?"

"Yes."

"Thanks, Jim. That's all I wanted to know."

Jim turned back to me. "You can see the facts and figures if you want to, Tom. I don't think there's much point in your doing so because you never really pay any attention to the business side of the magazine. You simply will not realise that we have to pay our way, and in order to pay our way we may have to give up or postpone certain things we should all very much enjoy doing."

"I realise," I said, "that you've got a small potential gold-mine in East Africa—but you have to put down the machinery to work it. You expect the mine to pay while the machinery is going in."

There was a silence, then I asked: "If you find it difficult to develop the edition at this moment on your own—would you consider taking someone in as a partner from outside, and running it as a joint venture?"

"Certainly—provided it's someone reasonably in sympathy with our ideas. If you know somebody who will come in and carry part of the burden, I shall be only too happy to let him do it."

"I think it's possible I might."

"Good—and meantime there's just one thing more."

"What's that?"

"It would help a lot in this situation if you would agree to put the price in West Africa up from ninepence to a shilling. It will make the balance sheet look a lot healthier, and could help to finance our going ahead in the East."

I hesitated. This was a matter on which we had had some discussion already, and about which I had always argued that it was too soon after the last increase, and we should be bound to lose circulation if we now imposed another rise in price. It was tempting to agree to anything which brought the East Africa edition nearer, but I felt these were issues which ought to be decided separately on their merits, and so answered that I would like to think it over. Before I left we agreed that we would print 25,000 copies from February onwards, that the print order for the next two issues should be left over for the moment, and that I would see if I could find a suitable partner, with resources, who might come in on our project for East Africa.

*   *   *   *   *

Now, in speaking of a possible partner, I was not just talking idly; a definite possibility had come into my mind. While in Nairobi I had been to see Michael Curtis. Michael was an able and experienced journalist under whom I had worked for a couple of years in London, when he was editor of the *News Chronicle* and I was its features editor. Like myself, he had left the *News Chronicle* when he saw that it was determined to sail itself into a watery grave rather than change course in a more promising direction. Besides having edited a Fleet Street daily while still in his middle thirties, Michael had other qualities not common among newspaper men; he was an extremely capable organiser and business executive; he was also of a sanguine go-ahead temperament and, having once worked a project out thoroughly would carry it through and not baulk half-way.

Just recently he had set up a printing and publishing house in Nairobi with the backing of the young Aga Khan, and was now only awaiting the arrival of the newest litho machinery to go into the newspaper and magazine field in East Africa on a big scale. People from the rival organisation—the old-established *East African Standard* firm—with whom I talked, had told me so decidedly that Curtis's new undertaking was doomed to early bankruptcy and ruin, that I could see they were frightened of it. I thought they had good reason. In a general way I had discussed with Curtis the possibility of his firm printing *East Africa Drum*, once his machinery had bedded down and was running satisfactorily, and had reported this conversation after I got back. Accordingly I now wrote to Curtis, asking whether the possibility of a joint venture would appeal to him, and saying that if he liked the general idea, I would arrange for him to meet Jim Bailey, and see if the two of them could reach agreement. He replied at once, saying the proposal interested him very much; would Jim Bailey come up to Nairobi, or should he fly down over Christmas—which was the earliest he could get away—and hold the meeting in Johannesburg?

* * * * *

While these negotiations were going on, two things happened in connection with our South African *Drum* which gave impetus to the staff and satisfaction to myself. The first was that our cameraman, Ian Berry, won the *Encyclopaedia Britannica* award for the best sequence of pictures taken during 1959 by any cameraman in the Commonwealth. This is the most prized award open to any magazine photographer outside the United States, and had been won a number of times in earlier days by our cameramen on *Picture Post*—but this was the first time it had ever been won by anyone outside Fleet Street. Ian won with a set of pictures of a witchdoctor at work which we had used over four pages in *Drum*, but which I had difficulty in persuading him to send in at all. "I suppose the subject's quite interesting—but they're not really up to much as pictures." Since the pictures had had to be taken in a small unlighted room, he had for once been obliged to use flash—a practice he detested; I think he would almost have preferred not to win the award, rather than to win with a set of flashed pictures.

At the same time Peter Magubane won a South African competition open to all non-white photographers. For a magazine employing only two cameramen, it was possibly unique that each in a single month should have won about the highest award open to him.

Our second success caused a much wider stir. A little while before, an African woman named Mrs. Mafekeng, living in Cape Province, had been served with an order of banishment on the instructions of Mr. de Wet Nel, the Minister of Bantu Administration and Development. Mrs. Mafekeng, mother of eleven children and a determined trade union leader, did not like the idea of being banished to some remote part of the country with the prospect of lingering there for years, away from her family and friends—as happened to more than 100 other Africans who incurred the Government's displeasure. So, without waiting to be transported, she disappeared. A large part of the world's Press was now looking for her—and nobody could find out where she was.

At the height of the excitement, we received on *Drum* an indication that Mrs. Mafekeng was in Basutoland. Like much else that we got on *Drum*, this was not a clear statement from a recognised source, but a not very audible telephone tip-off from someone who immediately rang off. If we acted on every such tip-off, we should spend our time rushing wildly round the country; if we acted on none, we should have missed several of our best stories. Were we to take this one seriously or not? Humphrey Tyler and I, with our political reporter Benson Dyantyi, talked the matter over, finally agreeing that to find Mrs. Mafekeng would be such a notable scoop—above all for a monthly magazine—that we ought to take a chance.

One difficulty we did not have on *Drum* was jealousy over assignments between black and white; the only question asked was who could do a given job best. In this case we agreed that, for a variety of reasons, a white team would have the better chance. So, while I briefed Ian Berry and Bob Hitchcock, Benson went off to contact African leaders in Johannesburg and secure letters of introduction showing that our two men were to be trusted. This was one of the moments when the fact that *Drum* had the confidence of African political movements proved invaluable; Benson brought back just what we required—but the introductions, of course, could only be effective once Mrs. Mafekeng was found, since those who wrote them knew no more than we did just where they should be addressed.

With Bob and Ian I arranged, first, that they should have an alternative story to work on in Basutoland, and secondly an easy system of reference for telephone or telegram. They must have a "cover" story because, in drawing money for the trip, they had to give some explanation to the management, and if they gave the true one it could soon be all over the office, and *Golden City Post* might get there first. In addition, we might easily *not* find her, and then—unless we had some other justification for the trip—there would be an inquest over the expense. Third, it would be a help to have a job they could talk about openly, while casting round for a lead. As for the code, it would clearly be unwise for them to refer to Mrs. Mafekeng, "Mrs. M.", or anything of the sort, yet I knew from experience that any code which at all complicated only causes confusion. So it was agreed that in any communication they would refer to Mrs. Mafekeng as "auntie".

The team set off in the old Volkswagen with our driver, John Taukbong, and on the way they worked out their plan of action. It wou be fatal to make direct enquiries, that would get them marked down at once. If Mrs. Mafekeng was in hiding, she was in hiding from whites, and particularly from whites coming from South Africa. It was no more practicable to conceal their Johannesburg number plates than it was to conceal their white skins. The only person who might pick up useful information casually was the driver, John: the only way he might get it would be if no one suspected he was looking for it. John was instructed therefore to chat freely about their "cover" story and about themselves; on no account to ask directly for Mrs. Mafekeng; but casually, when the opportunity offered, to slip in that the crazy people in Johannesburg were all steamed up about this woman who had lately come into the country. What woman? Why, this Mrs. Mafekeng, the trade union leader with all those children. . . . After a fruitless day or two, at a certain point, chatting to a bus conductor, the man replied: "Why, she's staying just at the end of my run—near where the bus turns round."

"Yes, of course," John replied, "and she's staying with that Mrs. . . ."

"You mean Mrs. XYZ," said the conductor, supplying the name, "in the house half-way up the hill."

Next day our team drove out there; they left the car and walked up towards the house. One of the qualities of a good cameraman is that he instantly recognises a face from photographs, and on the way up to the house Ian spotted Mrs. Mafekeng in some trees beside the path. As they walked they held a whispered consultation: should he steal a picture now and make sure of something in the bag, at the risk of annoying her and her hosts and perhaps being refused further pictures? They decided to go on and ask permission. When they reached the house they were at first under suspicion—Bob Hitchcock's moustache could be that of a cop, and a beard such as Ian wore is often a badge of Afrikanerdom. However, the letters soon put matters right, and they got all the pictures and information they wanted.

That evening Bob rang me at home from his hotel in Maseru. After one or two commonplace remarks he added—"and you might like to know that auntie's in the bag."

Restraining myself from shouting, but anxious at once to know what the pictures were like, I answered—"Good. But I hope Ian was pleased with his auntie too."

"Yes. We are both of us quite satisfied."

Two days later they got back—and now our real anxiety began. We had the pictures and the story everyone was looking for, but we had no issue of our magazine coming out for more than two weeks. What we had particularly to fear was our fellow-paper *Golden City Post*, who shared the same office, the same darkrooms, the same picture library—and who published every weekend, instead of once a month as we did. The fact that we had got our story was bound to get round among our own staff; the only course was to explain the whole situation to them all and ask them to keep quiet. I therefore called them all into my room, including our new office-boy, Joshua's successor, Victor. I told them just what we had got, and what it would mean to us if we could keep the story safe until our next issue, the one for January which would go on sale before Christmas. I told them that the least hint or casual remark to anyone outside our own small circle could be fatal, and so could a word within our circle which happened to be overheard. I said that they were now all fully in the secret, and should all do what I intended to do, forget the whole matter for a fortnight. With Ian I arranged that he should print his pictures at night when everyone had gone home, and that, once printed, I would hold them under lock and key.

The whole staff kept the secret—just as everyone kept the secret a year later when we secured the only picture interview with the missing Cape Town political leader, Philip Kgosana, and held it back for even longer. Two Sundays before we came out, we had the satisfaction of reading in *Golden City Post* that Mrs. Mafekeng was not in Basutoland at all; she was hundreds of miles away in Bechuanaland. One Sunday later the same paper asked: "Where is Mrs. Mafekeng? No one knows. She may be in Basutoland. She may be in Bechuanaland. No one knows." Even in face of this provocation, nobody let on, and when our story at last appeared, the *Rand Daily Mail* gave half a column to *Drum's* success in finding Mrs. Mafekeng, and the *Daily Mail* in London paid us £50, with an acknowledgement, to use a couple of Ian's pictures of her with her newest baby.

*   *   *   *   *

Over Christmas Michael Curtis flew down from Nairobi. He had some talks with Jim Bailey at which I was present, and others on their own. On his return, he wrote accepting the draft heads of an agreement proposed to him by Jim, and suggested what he thought would be the most practical method of working together.

I was delighted that, after our initial difficulties, everything now seemed to be working out so well.

CHAPTER XXIII

TO GO OR STAY?

WE SPENT CHRISTMAS with some friends in great comfort at their home. It was a welcome respite and the only break in our few days' peace was agreeably ridiculous. In the issue of our paper which had just come out there had appeared a little story about a Beauty Contest in Durban; in this our Durban editor, G. R. Naidoo, happened to mention that two or three likely candidates who had promised to take part never showed up, "among them Belina Manners, the famous belly-dancer". Casey, who was given the story for "subbing", added: "She was widely rumoured to be detained in court. The charge was selling gavini*—a brew strong enough to knock the tusks off an elephant."

I queried this addition with Casey, who at once said that he had been down in Durban at the time, that the story of Belina's arrest was all over the town, and he actually gave me the date on which she had appeared in court and been remanded. "All the chaps on *Post* were talking about it," he declared. It was obvious that Casey had gone into the matter carefully, and I was naturally anxious not to lose that phrase, "strong enough to knock the tusks off an elephant", so I let it stay. No sooner was the paper on sale, however, than I got an urgent call to come into the office and speak to G.R. on the telex. When I got through to him, G.R.—usually the politest of men—began tapping out straight away: "Who the hell's been messing about with my Beauty Contest story. . . ." As he continued to tap, the full horror of what had happened became clear. There *had* been excitement in Durban over the story of Belina Manners' arrest, and Casey—who was on holiday in Durban and by chance had called in at the office —had overheard the talk. What he did not know was that, soon after he left, it had come out that this was not the famous Belina at all, but another girl with the same name.

Result, an infuriated belly-dancer storming into G.R.'s office, threatening him and the paper and saying she was on her way to her attorneys now. To me it appeared that she had such a cast-iron case she need hardly bother to ask their help. Clearly the only person who

* Illicit home-brewed liquor, particularly popular in the Durban area.

could relieve the situation was G.R., and the first thing to do was to mollify him. I told him therefore that the whole thing was our fault —as indeed it was—and that we were extremely sorry to have landed him in the mess, but the question now was one of protecting the magazine. Would he use all his charm and well-known appeal to soothe Belina down; we would publish an apology "ample but not crawling"; and we would be glad to do a picture feature on her justly renowned dancing in a couple of months' time.

A day or two later, G.R. telexed me through again. Belina had been into the office, they had had a most friendly interview; she was not any longer thinking of bringing an action, and didn't mind whether we put in an apology or not. Besides being a tribute to G.R.'s tact, I thought the little incident a striking example of African tolerance and good humour. Ninety-nine out of a hundred whites would not have been concerned with whether what had appeared was due to a mistake or not; it would have been an opportunity to make money which they would think it foolish to let slip. They would have pressed the case and got damages. Belina, once her temper had died down and her vanity been soothed, was content to let it go at that.

*   *   *   *   *

I had been back at work only a few days in the New Year when I got a call to come through into Jim Bailey's office. Weatherstone had gone, and Ian Pritchard had been brought down from West Africa to take charge. He and Roy Paulson, now head of the accounts department in Johannesburg and company secretary, had evidently been out to lunch with Jim and were already sitting with him when I came in. Ian, I thought, looked white and strained.

"We've called you in, Tom," Jim began, "to give you the position with regard to East Africa. I know you claim that you're never consulted on reaching important decisions, so I want you in this case to have all the facts and figures straight away. Launching the East African edition would mean a loss of £1,000 a month for several months followed by a loss of around £500 a month till the end of the year. After that it might begin to break even, and in eighteen months' time it could be paying—that is if everything goes well. But I don't need to tell you that our general experience is that everything does *not* go well; there are always unexpected setbacks and unforeseen expenses."

I nodded. "Is this thousand a month your estimate of the whole loss or is it the firm's share of a loss which would be shared with Curtis?

"It's the whole loss. But I want to tell you that we have all been very fully into the firm's financial position, and we simply must not incur a further monthly loss of a thousand or anything like it, on top of all the other difficulties we've been experiencing."

"A thousand a month for six months, followed by £500 a month for six months, is a very modest cost for starting a new magazine. Divide that in half, as being our share, and deduct what we shall gain by increasing the price in West Africa to a shilling—and the amount's tiny, compared to what's at stake."

"I don't think I need tell you," Jim went on, "that we are all just as keen to launch the new magazine in East Africa as you are"—"Certainly," agreed Roy and Ian—"but *we* are the ones who have to deal with practical realities, and for the present it is quite impossible even to think of going ahead."

"A month ago," I said, "we were not merely thinking of it, we were all agreed to go ahead. What's changed the position so much since then?"

"That's just the point. The position *has* changed. We've been going into the books. There have been losses, not concerned with our normal trading, which completely upset our balance sheet. I won't go into them in detail now—but I can assure you we have no choice in this matter at all."

"So what have you decided to do about the East African edition?"

"Cocoon it," Jim replied. "We have all agreed to cocoon it for a year. In twelve months' time when we have built up our reserves—which I must ask you to help us to do—we shall be able to return to the territory and push right ahead. But now it's right out."

"Quite out of the question," said Ian.

Roy nodded agreement. "Not a hope."

"Well, Jim," I said, "it's your money, not mine. If you don't want to spend it on promoting an East African edition, I can't make you. You have the right to decide. But don't let's deceive ourselves over the facts."

"In what way?"

"Don't imagine you *can* 'cocoon' the edition and go back in a year. can't work, and you won't do it. We are disappointing everyone 've encouraged to become enthusiastic over the new paper—staff, dvertisers, distributors, circulation workers, the public. They've all en told we're going to do something big. Now we suddenly find e can't afford to do what we undertook—so we're backing out. kay—we're free to do so. But how are they all going to receive us if

we go back in a year's time and say—'Now we're ready to get started'?
How would you receive it if you were them?"

"We can't do what we can't do. It's far better to go back in twelve
months' time with a real prospect of success than to launch the thing
too soon and be a flop. There's no gratitude in business—but there's
no resentment either. If we make a go of it in 1961, no one's going to
complain that we didn't launch it in 1960."

"I don't think we will launch the thing in 1961," I said, "or in 1962.
But there's something more important still."

"Which is?"

"It's the next few years—1960 to 1965—that are going to matter
most in East Africa. That's why we got so much support from the
serious politicians—they see we can affect the big issues at a crucial
time. To tell them we're sorry we have to abdicate for a few years"—
"Just for twelve months, Tom, only for twelve months"—"but we'll be
back again in due course, just isn't on. To them it's like saying we're
afraid we can't send any troops for the battle, but they can keep us a
seat for the victory celebrations."

"Is that all you have to say?"

"Not quite. I presume this means that we don't do any deal with
Curtis. . . ."

"We *postpone* doing any deal with him. We postpone it for twelve
months."

"I doubt that," I said. "Curtis isn't the kind of person to sit around
waiting for us for twelve months. Besides being the critical time for
politics, the next five years will be the golden time for publishing.
Other papers are going ahead fast. One magazine has gone from
25 to 40,000 in six months. In a year or two's time there may be a lot
less room for us to fill—apart from whether people want us to fill it
or not."

"There I agree with you," said Jim. "Now is undoubtedly the ideal
time to go ahead in East Africa. That's obvious enough"—"Quite
obvious," agreed the other two—"But in view of the setbacks we've
just experienced, our own firm can't do it. Our top priority must be
to cut costs and avoid all unnecessary expense; that will be top priority
for the whole of this year. Get all the papers up on to a thoroughly
paying basis—we must put through the price increase for West Africa
at the earliest possible moment—and consolidate our financial position.
Then in a year's time, provided all goes well in the meantime, we can
think about East Africa again."

"What becomes of the staff?" I asked.

"The staff will be well looked after," declared Ian.

"I shall hold you to that."

"You won't need to."

"Look, Tom," said Jim, "it's no good your being angry or upset over this. I've been concerned with East Africa a lot longer than you have, and I know many more people up there. I assure you I feel all this quite as much as you do, if not more. It's just a matter of simple business necessity, which is something we all have to accept."

*　　*　　*　　*　　*

When I got home that night I said to Dorothy: "I think it's time I finished up with *Drum*."

"I thought you were beginning to feel that," she said, "but why just now in particular?"

"We've killed the East African edition. We're saying it's 'cocooned' —but I think it's dead."

"I know you'd set your heart on that—but is it fatal if it has to be given up?"

"Not fatal to the firm at all, though I think it's a golden opportunity let slip. But it means a lot to me."

"What does it really mean to you?"

"If we're trying to do something on this continent—then East Africa is the test. The need for a magazine there is obvious, and everyone admits it. And the door's wide open."

"Then why aren't you going ahead?"

"Because the firm isn't willing to lose a quite modest sum of money there for one year, or possibly for two—but only a fraction of what we're cheerfully talking about spending on a printing press."

"Well, wouldn't a printing press be useful?"

"It might—or it might not. My own feeling is that it wouldn't. But in any case it would still be available in twelve months' time, whereas the need for this paper is now. It isn't 'publishing' to buy machinery and miss opportunities."

"Are you sure you're not just thinking this new paper would be profitable because you're so anxious to see it started?"

"I'm not the only one. Michael Curtis is as sure as I am. . . . But that's what makes publishing a funny business."

"What does?"

"That if you fill a genuine need in publishing, you make dough out of it. It isn't just a straight commercial transaction like selling bars of soap. It involves a special relationship with the public. You have to put something in, in order to get something back—and you can't start by getting back before you've done the putting in."

"How does that apply in this case?"

"That I think we should go ahead now in East Africa even if we had to borrow the money to do it with. . . . But we shan't. We aren't responding to a need, and we aren't recognising an opportunity. If we can't do one or other, then we shall never really grow. The future isn't ours. . . . I don't know what the hell we're in this for."

Dorothy came over and sat down. "I know how much you've put into all this, Hoppy, and I understand your disappointment. But aren't you making exactly the same mistake you made at *Picture Post*?"

"What mistake is that?"

"Not recognising that the one who pays the piper calls the tune? You think that because you've put all your vision and a terrific amount of work into something, that gives you the right to decide how that thing is to be handled."

"Well?"

"Ideally, it should—but in fact, as you very well know, it doesn't. The decisions belong to the one who supplies the money. You may not like it, but that's the way things are."

"Of course I know that . . ."

"But you don't *act* as if you knew it. If your employer chooses to do something you think is wrong, you can't stop him. After all, it's his property, and what he does with it is his own affair. There's a further thing."

"What's that?"

"Working too hard and too long hours makes the person you're working for suspicious."

"Suspicious of what?"

"Suspicious that the man who's giving up all his time and energy in this way is not merely doing so for a salary, but has plans of his own. In this case—you must admit—your employer would be right you have got ideas of your own, and you *are* constantly trying to put them into effect."

"But I wouldn't be much use to anyone if I didn't."

"Not if you didn't try at all, of course. But from an employer point of view you'd be more 'use' to him personally if you tried le —because he'd be getting more of his own way. Can't you unde stand? You give your loyalty and effort to what you feel the particul project ought to be. In this instance, a wonderful picture magazin raising the cultural standard, increasing knowledge, and providing training ground for writers, photographers and so on. But an employer doesn't want you giving loyalty and effort to realising *your* visions—having supplied the cash, he expects loyalty and effort in his interests, in the form in which he sees them."

"But when the visions are realised, they're to his advantage. He gets the profits. All I ask for is a reasonable salary."

"Yes. But you made masses of money for Edward Hulton with *Picture Post*, but in the end he wasn't content with profits, was he?"

"You mean that an employer isn't content just to make money, he wants to feel he's exercising power as well? He wants it *both* ways?"

"Exactly."

I snorted, but before I could say anything Dorothy put her hand on my arm and looked at me intently. "Men with capital to invest in schemes are rare enough. Visionaries, with the drive to make their schemes reality, are rarer still. If the two could come together and each be content with a fair return, there's nothing they couldn't do. It's the possession of cash that's fatal. The owner naturally thinks it entitles him to the lot—cash, power and credit. You're a visionary, Hoppy, but you've also got the drive to put your visions into effect. Employers want men of vision and drive, but equally they want them to keep their place. . . ."

"Which is?"

"To be a submissive employee."

"But look here. I'm a professional. I know my job, and I have to do it properly. You can't expect the captain to sail the ship on to the rocks just because the owner likes to hear the sound of bumping."

"No. But if a professional captain hires himself out, he must expect to sail where the owner chooses—even if he personally thinks they'd do much better sailing somewhere else. Also . . ."

"Also what?"

"A tactful captain would spend some time asking the opinions of the owner, even if he knew all the answers a lot better than the owner did—and was privately determined to do what he knew to be the right thing, despite the owner."

"Oh God," I said. "I have to admit all this is true—and I feel a bloody fool for not seeing it myself. . . . However, it's silly to work where I can't be effective and shall always be over-ruled. Once I was sure the *News Chronicle* was sailing in the wrong direction, I jumped overboard. I think the time has come to jump again. *Drum* is a fraction of what it ought to be and could be—and what the opportunities call for it to be—a chain of magazines all over the continent.

It needs a big injection of money, courage and faith, and a great drive to expand."

"Whereas?"

"Whereas our policy is always to cut down and contract. So we live in an endless series of economy campaigns—scraping away at our own bones for enough sustenance to march another mile, discharging the soldiers because uniforms cost so much, and eating the horses because otherwise they would want hay."

"I understand, Hoppy, how frustrated you feel and if you can't stand it any longer I agree that you should leave. But *can* you? What's your position?"

"I signed on for two years. My time's up next month."

"Think it over for a week then. Remember, you'll miss your friends on the staff and the bustle of the life—just as you missed it when you left *Picture Post*. But if you want to get out—*do*."

"You haven't asked," I said, "how we shall manage if I leave."

Dorothy patted my arm. "That's one thing I never worry about with Hoppy. If you make less, we shall live on less. But I've never any doubts as to whether you can make a living. All ducks know how to swim."

*   *   *   *   *

When the end of the month came, I wrote to Jim Bailey, as proprietor, saying I would like to finish up at the end of my two years, and that I had no doubt my leaving would be in accordance with his own preference. He wrote back saying that he did not want me to leave and hoped I would remain with the firm for a long time. Would I reconsider the position and stay on?

This made me hesitate. I had become very attached to the staff, and particularly to the half-dozen members—in West Africa as well as in the South—who I felt were both developing on their own lines and getting some benefit out of my long experience in journalism. Secondly—even though I seemed to myself to be making very little headway—I was reluctant to write off finally an attempt in which I had invested so much energy, which had brought me half across the world, and on which I had set out with such high hopes. Moreover—in the course of the last week, and probably because of a remark Dorothy had let fall—I had got the idea that it might be possible to give our firm some of the financial weight and consistency of policy it seemed to me to lack, by forming an alliance or partnership with one of the big newspaper organisations, either South African or British. When I put this possibility directly to Jim Bailey, he said that he would be only too happy to join forces with such an organisation, provided it could be done on reasonable terms.

So in the end, after talking it all over with Dorothy once more, I decided to stay on at *Drum* for at least another year. My salary was improved, and in return I agreed that, if I should later decide to leave, I would work out a full six months' notice.

CHAPTER XXIV

THE WIND OF CHANGE

FROM THE BEGINNING of 1960 we had all known that this was to be a critical year for Africa, and therefore for the paper and ourselves; the number and vast area of the territories which would achieve independence during 1960 alone made that certain, including as they did the Congo, Nigeria and Somaliland. But none of us had imagined the extent of the shocks which this year would impose; shocks which were not only tremendous, but decisive, opening the eyes of all but the most resolutely blind to the certainty that there were much worse shocks to come. They were therefore both an end and a beginning. The continent we lived in was on fire, and a whole era in history—the Colonial Era, with all its considerable achievements and its lamentable shortcomings—was going up in flames. The New Africa would require to be created quite afresh.

There was a period during 1960, from late January to August, when events happened so fast, and were at times so horrifying, that one came to live in constant expectation of renewed disaster and to feel something had gone wrong when the newspapers or radio reflected an apparently calm day. To this, as to everything else, there was a credit side; South Africans who, with many virtues, are perhaps the world's most complaisant people, were shaken to their mental core. Following Sharpeville, came a month or two when, had there been any opposition leadership at all, changes might have been set on foot which would have brought South Africa into line with—instead of directly in opposition to—the course of twentieth-century history. The chance was missed, or rather it was deliberately by-passed, since what the bulk of the United Party want and wanted is not change, but to be able to blame others for maintaining an obsolete and detested order which they merely wish should be continued. The country's nineteenth-century rulers—to whom their bitterest opponents must allow consistency and courage on their backward course—caught up the fallen reins, and gave their followers stern orders. There was to be no change of direction and no change of pace. Instead there was to be "order" and "security" in the present—and not far away in the future that head-on collision which people of all races and colours increasingly now believe to be inevitable.

*   *   *   *   *

The first shock the year brought us was a physical one. Late one afternoon towards the end of January, Ian Berry put his head round my door and said: "There's been a terrific mine accident. Hundreds of people cut off underground. It's in the Free State. I'm off there now."

Ian stayed out all that night and most of the next day. Tired and filthy, he looked into the office late the next afternoon, and from then on we had someone down at Coalbrook, fifty miles away from Johannesburg, almost all round the clock. The cameramen were waiting chiefly for that dramatic and sometimes appalling moment in a mine accident when those from below would be brought, alive or dead, up to the surface. None of us yet imagined that no one of the 434 Africans or six white men who were down there would ever come up into the light of day again.

On the Sunday when Ian was due for another long spell of waiting, I drove him out there. The news had filled the papers since Friday morning, and every road leading to Coalbrook was thronged with sightseers. They had come from all over the country, bringing wives and children, making a day out and picnicking by the roadside in the clouds of dust raised by other scores of sightseers. It was a rowdy crowd of some 10,000 people. Forced to abandon their cars a mile from the mine, they trudged up the road and past the pithead, staring at the nothing there was to see, and milling around the black mine-workers' compound and the trim villas of the whites. As all cars were being stopped, we had difficulty in getting by, but Ian waved a variety of documents and called out explanations with such insistence that for a time we were allowed through. At last we came to a policeman who was letting no one past, whatever their business, and I was just planning to drive into a field used as a car park and come out at the top end, when a small car he had ordered to go back stuck in the road. The cop was obliged to go over and sort things out, dozens of cars were now piling up behind, so he wearily waved us through.

As soon as we got to the mine, Ian vanished. He knew all the other journalists and cameramen, so that two minutes with them would bring him up-to-date on all that had happened since last night. If any of the "regulars" were missing, he would nose around until he found out where they were, and made sure no one had stumbled on something important without his knowledge.

All efforts to break directly through to the entombed men were proving hopeless; some miners said there was as much as a mile of fallen rock between them and the rescue parties and that it would "take months" to reach them. A special drill with a crack team had been brought from two hundred miles away with which it was hoped to cut down into the workings where the men were presumed to be, lowering them food, water and medical necessities; later perhaps enlarging the hole so as to bring men up one at a time. But as no one knew in what part of the mine the men might have taken refuge (if any of them were now still alive) the drill seemed a slender hope. Moreover, for technical reasons, it was not managing to cut at anything like the speed expected, despite day and night-long efforts by the drillers.

Over the whole sun-baked stretch of veld lay a feeling of despondency and horror, made worse by the picnickers with their radios and Coca-Cola, and the shouts of their holiday children. I wandered off over the countryside. This is a district of flattish uplands where three-quarters of the view is in the sky; against the deep blue, puffy white clouds were massing for the regular thunderstorm of a summer afternoon. Looking away from the pithead and the cluster of nearby buildings, one could see this as open farming country; most of it was growing mealies, now five or six feet tall. On the edge of one huge field a strange, long-legged bird with a crest looked out from between the rows, and hawks sat on the gateposts watching for mice. Only the huge cracks in the surface of the tarmac road—some of them six inches across—were evidence of the upheavals underneath; I found myself peering down as if expecting to see something far below.

I had parked my car next to one with a Natal number-plate, in which three heavily built men were lounging. Despite the heat they sat all together in the back with their feet on the front seats, drinking canned beer, reading the Sunday newspapers, playing the radio and chatting. After reading in my own car for a while, I noticed they had gone, and looked round to see where they were. They were talking to a man I knew, a reporter on the *Rand Daily Mail*, who was standing with a black cameraman from *The New Age*, whom I knew as Joe and to whom I had been talking only a few minutes before. I got out of the car and went over to join them, but as I approached the three men were already moving off.

"What did they want?"

"Oh—the usual thing. 'You better stop talking to that black boy there—see? We don't like it. We're three miners—and we'll lay in any man we see chattering with blacks. What's he doing with a camera anyway—eh?' "

I experienced the feeling of rage which threats of violence always produce in me, so stayed chatting with the two of them. We were near a shed which had been turned into an unofficial Press Room, so that if we proved unequal to the trouble it would not be difficult to call up one or two allies. However, the miners had now settled back to their canned beer and radio, and no more was said. I thought it a strange comment on our unhappy country: I have little doubt that if the same miners had been underground, and the African had been entombed, they would have risked their lives to save him; but once he was above ground and safe they were ready to bash anyone who spoke to him like a fellow human-being. Even in the heat of the catastrophe, when services of prayer had been held for the buried miners, there had been one service for the friends and relatives of the six whites, and a separate one for those of the four hundred-odd blacks. . . . Did they suppose God listened to each through a different ear?

Later on in the afternoon there was a Press Conference. For a couple of days following the accident, mine officials had been openly hostile to the Press, taking the line that all attempts to find out what was being done in the way of rescue were intrusions into their private accident. There had been angry scenes between reporters anxious to establish the facts and check on the many rumours which were flying round, and officials refusing to confirm or deny almost anything except the date. It had taken nearly two days to find out how many Africans were underground, though the presence of the six whites was admitted at once. Now, evidently on orders from high up, this attitude had changed, and the Press were being treated as though they also had a serious job to do.

At the conference we pressed our questions on a few specific points. First, the proportion of white to black—6 to 434. Was this normal, or were there fewer whites than usual—and did this mean that there was any less supervision? The answer we got was that they could not say. They did not know what a normal proportion would be. They would have to think it over. . . .

Secondly, questions were asked about the mine's modernity. There had been a number of pit ponies brought up and seventy were reported to be trapped underground. Did this mean that the mine was old-fashioned and less mechanised than others? The official replied that in his opinion more ponies were used in other Free State mines than in this one, and that this mine in general was "the most highly mechanised".

Thirdly, we were anxious to know who the missing Africans were and where they came from. Twelve hours after the accident there were said to be "approximately five hundred" of them; by the Saturday this had become 400, now it appeared that there were 434. Why did it take so long to find out the correct number? And now that it had been ascertained, surely we could have their names. The names of the whites had been quickly released, partly at least to reassure the families of all those who were safe: equally there must be thousands of friends and relatives in a state of desperate anxiety over the missing Africans. Could not the anxiety of some of these be set at rest—after all, it was now three full days since the accident had happened?

The surprising answer given to us was that they did not know who was down the mine and who was not. Why didn't they know? Because they only knew who was missing from the compound, but not all those missing were necessarily down the mine. Would they be issuing a list? At some time. When? They couldn't say. Finally we were handed a slip stating that of the entombed men 230 were Basutos and 196 came from Portuguese East Africa. In fact, it later appeared that these figures were far from correct, 125 came from Portuguese territory, and the other 300 odd from Basutoland. A possible explanation of the difficulty of knowing who was trapped appeared in the Press by degrees. It was said that for some while before the accident there had been ominous noises and creakings in the mine, that these had been particularly strong on the Thursday when the cave-in took place. A miner coming up while the afternoon shift was waiting to go down had, it was said, given a warning to the waiting men. A number of the Africans had then rushed away across the veld to avoid going underground: some had later been induced to go down, and were now missing; others had simply vanished, and nobody knew where they were.

*   *   *   *   *

The English-speaking Press is under incessant attack in South Africa on the ground that it is "unpatriotic", "anti-South African", "despicable", "politically brutal", "the enemy at our throats", "completely irresponsible", "prints nothing but lies" and should therefore "be destroyed immediately and mercilessly".* From my everyday reading I had long since formed the judgement that the English-language Press in South Africa is, for the present day, unusually moderate and restrained. Despite certain weaknesses, I would much rather have

---

*All these are statements which have appeared in print; a few examples out of very many of the attacks made by Nationalist politicians or their followers.

defend its integrity and sense of responsibility, than that of either the British Press, or the newspapers and magazines published in South Africa in Afrikaans. But though I had always read the English language papers critically, I had so far seen little of their reporters at work. Now that I did, I was impressed. They picked on the essential points, and put their questions good-naturedly and firmly; perhaps, in fact, with rather too much good nature. Questioning under similar circumstances would have been a great deal tougher in England or the U.S.

In the course of the day there was shown one difference between the English and Afrikaans language papers, which may account for some of the constant ill-will between the two. The incident was tiny but revealing. Late in the afternoon, Jan de Klerk, Minister of Mines and one of the most powerful figures in the Nationalist hierarchy, arrived to visit Coalbrook. He had come from the Cape, and no doubt was tired. But to the English language Press his visit only meant one thing —a chance to add to the little we already knew. The Minister, if anyone, would have been given the facts; we were anxious to question him; not to do so would seem unpardonable.

To the mine officials, the Minister's visit was an act of sympathy and recognition. He must be piloted round, protected from all intrusion, and enabled to get away as conveniently as possible. Their view—if of little help to us—was understandable. But it was the action of a journalist from an Afrikaans newspaper which pointed the difference in our outlooks. He put no questions to de Klerk, but as he was leaving ran after his car holding out his hand and shouting "Oom* Jan! Oom Jan! Ek is van die ——"—giving the name of his newspaper. What he chiefly wanted to do was to shake the Minister's hand and thank him for being there at all.

It is difficult, but important, for the English-speaking person to realise that, to the Afrikaner, members of his own government appear in a quite special light. They are not looked upon as ambitious men who have chosen politics as their career partly, if not largely, for the considerable rewards it offers—in return for which rewards, granted by the community, the Minister is the servant of the people, any one of whom has the right to ask information or assistance within the limits of a given situation. To the Afrikaner his politicians are revered figures, the leaders and fathers of the "volk", whose attitude towards them is

*"Oom" is untranslateable. Literally it would mean "uncle", but is used simply as an address of friendly respect to an older or more important man. If you imagine a reporter running after the Chancellor of the Exchequer calling out: "Uncle Selwyn! Uncle Selwyn! I'm from the *Daily Mirror!*" you get some impression of the enormous difference in outlook and custom between the two white sections in South Africa.

summed up by the phrase with which a parliamentary back-bencher almost automatically begins a speech following any ministerial statement: "Ons dank die Minister . . .", "we thank the Minister. . . ."

To the immigrant from a European country, accustomed to regard his own political figures with anything but reverence, and to judge them not on their office but on their performance, there seems no reason to view Ministers of the Nationalist Government in any different light. Such a detached and casual attitude, however—often interpreted as hostility and contempt—is one of the biggest obstacles to mutual understanding. It is also, I believe, at least partly responsible for those hysterical accusations of "treason", "betrayal", "anti-whiteness", "political brutality" and so on, continually levelled at the English Press, and which the ordinary reader finds either ludicrous or incomprehensible.

There was a final touch to this day's outing. As the Minister drove away in the direction of the "white" villas, we asked where he was going. He was going, we were told, to visit the families of the six white miners who were underground, and the Press were particularly asked not to follow, since both sides—it was said—would wish to express their emotions freely. Everyone agreed to this restriction—which I thought generous of the cameramen, seeing that they had been hanging around for the best part of three days for nothing, and the meeting would certainly have given them pictures.

Was the Minister, I asked, going also to speak to the relatives of the African miners underground? No. He would not be doing that. Why not? Because they had no relatives here. Then what, I asked, were the photographs which had been printed everywhere of African women weeping at the pit-head, the women among whom a special service had been held two days before? Oh, those were just friends or girl friends who had "been upset by the disaster". Since all the black miners came from far away, none of them clearly could have official families on the spot. There was therefore no occasion for the Minister to see and talk to them.

*   *   *   *   *

The Coalbrook disaster took place on a Thursday, and the rescue attempt was not abandoned for more than two weeks. By the Monday however, it had been elbowed off the front pages by an outbreak of violence at Cato Manor, a tumble-down hillside location outside Durban, in which nine police—five Africans and four whites—were battered to death by an infuriated mob. The incident was horrible in itself, but made far more ominous by the thought that, in the rising temper of both sides, a few such incidents might set light to a general flare-up.

There was a curious financial aspect to this mass-murder, and a touching social one as well. The financial aspect was that the killings were consequent on a long series of liquor raids by the police. These raids were designed to destroy the home-brew produced in many of the yards and sheds on the Cato Manor hillsides; the reason being not only that home-brewing was illegal, but also that, if the men stayed at home to drink, they did not frequent the beerhalls run by the city authorities. The social aspect was that, if the men did go off to the beerhalls to drink, they left their wives behind, women not being admitted to African beerhalls any more than white women are admitted to a white bar in South Africa. The wives, whose husbands worked exceedingly long hours throughout the week, naturally did not like their men-folk being away from them at the weekends as well. It is also a Zulu custom for the women to brew liquor for their men and serve it to them, and they resented bitterly not being allowed to make drink, and the repeated raids in which their carefully prepared stocks were dug up out of the ground and poured away before their eyes. The women stirred up their men to action. They also took to carrying sticks themselves, and when police officials and others reproached them, saying, "It is not the custom for Zulu women to carry sticks," they answered, "No—and it is not the custom for Zulu women to carry passes. But the Government has forced us to do both these things."

These two tragedies were still fresh in all minds when, at the beginning of February, came the third profoundly stirring event of the year, the speech of the British Prime Minister, Harold Macmillan. I had heard Macmillan make a short speech at a garden party in Johannesburg, which contained nothing but the customary mouthings. His speech in Cape Town, however, was a very different matter. Except for the 230 listeners from the two houses of the Union Parliament—who got it, so to speak, full in the face—it had rather a delayed effect. I listened to it in the offices of *Golden City Post*, with Can Themba, now back there as a reporter, Ronnie Manyosi, *Post's* news editor, and three or four other Africans from our two staffs. They listened with mounting disappointment. The formal phrases and urbane delivery made this sound like just another politician's talk; the implied rebuke, the careful dissociation from Nationalist policy and its inevitable consequences, passed for the moment unnoticed.

'It is our aim, in the countries for which we bear responsibility, not only to raise the material standards of living, but to create a society which respects the rights of individuals—a society in which men are given the right to grow to their full stature.

"And that must, in our view, include the opportunity to have an increasing share in political power and responsibility; a society finally in which individual merit—and individual merit alone—is the criterion for a man's advancement, whether political or economic."

The most striking of all the impressions he had formed during his tour of Africa was of the strength of African national consciousness. "In different places it takes different forms. But it is happening everywhere. The wind of change is blowing throughout the continent. . . .

"The British Foreign Secretary, Mr. Selwyn Lloyd, has summed up the British attitude thus:

" 'In those territories where different races or tribes live side-by-side the task is to ensure that all the people may enjoy security and freedom and the chance to contribute as individuals to the progress and wellbeing of these countries. We reject the idea of any inherent superiority of one race over another. Our policy, therefore, is non-racial.

" 'It offers a future in which Africans, Europeans, Asians, the people of the Pacific and others with whom we are concerned, will play their full part as citizens in the countries where they live, and in which feelings of race will be submerged in loyalty to new nations.' "

Smoothly, effortlessly, the polished—somewhat platitudinous—phrases rolled out of the office radio. When the British Prime Minister had finished, Can shrugged, and Ronnie turned away. Nor did it seem to me sitting there beside them that anything remarkable had been said. It was only when Dr. Verwoerd began his reply, hesitating and audibly searching for his words, that I realised something dramatic had been happening nearly a thousand miles away in Cape Town. The *Rand Daily Mail's* gallery correspondent described the scene next day:

"The face of the South African Prime Minister grew slowly more pale and tense. It stared stonily ahead as if listening to increasingly bad news. It gave the impression of a loose mask trying forcefully to keep itself in position.

"Mr. Macmillan gradually developed a faintly scientific manner, more and more like a family doctor offering a friendly solution to excessive indulgence. He understood what the situation was: the difficulties that drove us to do what we did. But then came the grave warning, retaining the friendship of Africa for the West meant more to the West than supporting the racial policies of a handful of white men in South Africa. . . .

"There was hardly any surprise among those watching that only half of the listeners applauded the speech. Minister Paul Sauer was so enthusiastic that he applauded more than anybody. But the rest looked fixedly at Dr. Verwoerd. The South African Prime Minister was obviously very angry indeed. He began to stumble through his impromptu opening sentences. Listeners stirred with enbarrassment. . . ."

*   *   *   *   *

The speech we hadn't thought much of was to play an important part in the year's events; it had already added a new, if not particularly striking, phrase to political and journalistic jargon. The "wind of change", usually in the plural, would blow through many editorial columns and whistle through many political speeches during 1960. In the townships copies of Macmillan's speech, cut from newspapers and pasted on to wood or cardboard so that they could be read without falling to pieces, had soon become treasured possessions. Read, re-read and passed from hand to hand, they were familiar even in shebeens. And within a couple of months Nationalist M.P.s would be blaming Macmillan's words for the new spirit of defiance which had been shown, they said, at Sharpeville, and which looked for a week or two as if it might break down the whole artificial structure of apartheid, and bring a new order into being in South Africa.

CHAPTER XXV

PAN-AFRICA AND SHARPEVILLE

Early in March Dorothy and I moved home. We wanted more space and we wanted to be nearer to the country, and so rented a flat in a new block two or three miles out, with a garden on one side and some school playing-fields on the other. I took two weeks out of the holiday owing to me to help Dorothy—who redecorated the whole flat herself—over the move. During the fortnight I was away Humphrey Tyler had already done most of the work of preparing the new issue, and when I got back we were faced with a peculiarly difficult decision.

For years African politics in South Africa had been dominated by the A.N.C.—the African National Congress. "Congress" was run on conventional party lines, or as though it were a white trade union—with an annual subscription, elected officials, lists of members, party cards, branch offices, roneo'd circulars, office rent, telephone accounts and all the rest. It claimed a paid-up membership of 120,000, but probably there were not more than two or three thousand who were in any way active, and the organisation was only kept from falling apart at the seams by the personal nobility and leadership of "Chief" Luthuli, and the devoted work of some few dozen leaders who were continually harried by the police and constantly in and out of prison. On the other hand, though few were willing to exert themselves for "Congress", most Africans gave it their sympathy, as did a small number of liberal whites, and it stood to the world outside as the main expression of African political consciousness inside the Union. There was one paradox about the A.N.C.; for years its leadership had been moderate—"feeble" was the word used by its opponents—but it had also for some time been much under the influence of a body called "The Congress of Democrats". This was a body with a mainly white leadership, some Asian support, and a strong Communist influence.

On these two points—of a supposed Communist trend and an excessive influence from whites and Indians—there had lately grown up inside Congress a challenge from a loosely knit group known as "The Africanists". The Africanists, though they were not always candid about stating it, wanted an almost completely African state—to which only Africans and Coloured would belong by right, but to which, they sometimes said, whites and Asians who accepted African authority would be admitted as citizens. Though they were little known to the country at large, we had already published two or three articles in *Drum* about them. They had attempted to carry the day at Congress meetings in Durban and elsewhere, but had been defeated, and during 1959 they began to organise a separate political movement under the letters P.A.C.—Pan-African Congress—and to build up connections with other "Pan-Africanist" movements in different parts of Africa. When, following later successes, the movement became popular, it was generally known not, like the A.N.C., by its initials, but by the initials spoken as a word—"Pac": "Oh, he's a 'Pac' man", or "There are a lot of 'Pac' supporters in East London".

Gradually during the past year a leadership had emerged for the new movement with at its head a remarkable young man, Robert Mangaliso ("Wonderful") Sobukwe, a lecturer in Bantu Studies at the University of the Witwatersrand. I had several times met and talked with Sobukwe and with some of his associates, such as Peter Raboroko. I found him an unusual mixture; he had a handsome person and agreeable presence; he gave the impression of thinking a good deal more than he was prepared to say; his rather quiet, polished manner suggested the educated negro more than the African politician. But when he wrote *Drum* an article outlining his views—which included a united continent ruled by a single central parliament—I found it strangely naïve; I felt we could not even publish it without listing some of the obvious objections, which, by agreement with him, we did; and one or two African political figures in other parts of the continent to whom I later showed the piece dismissed it as utterly unpractical.

Sobukwe and his associates had spent the last months of 1959 and the early days of 1960 travelling around the country in a Volkswagen bus given them by sympathisers, building up support for P.A.C. Their efforts and eloquence had some effect, particularly among the younger people, but this was largely confined to a few cities, among them Cape Town and Port Elizabeth. One of those they had influenced most strongly in the Cape was a young student, Philip Kgosana, who led the renowned march on Cape Town after Sharpeville. P.A.C. did not believe in an elaborate organisation, and thought there was no time for it in any case: their aim was to exploit deep-seated African grievances by a series of dramatic gestures. Of A.N.C. leadership they were strongly critical, arguing that Luthuli ought to have disregarded the government ban confining him to his home town, gone openly about the country speaking, and been arrested and imprisoned. When their time came, they declared, they would be the first to accept imprisonment. "We will send our leaders to jail first. That is where our leaders belong—in front." Being so loosely organised, they had no chain of command through whom activities could be set in motion, but had made instead a curious arrangement, entrusting to their president, Sobukwe, the right to call upon his followers to take action in accordance with the spirit of their joint undertaking, at any time at three days' notice.

During early March it had become known that Sobukwe would call a Press conference on Friday, March 18th, at which he would instruct his followers what they were to do on the following Monday, March 21st, and it was this piece of timing which set us our complicated journalistic problem. The normal day for the April issue of *Drum* to go on sale was Wednesday, March 23rd, and the whole of the contents had to be passed for press nearly a week earlier, on Thursday, March 17th, well before Sobukwe's announcement would have been made.

What had happened during my two weeks' absence was that Humphrey Tyler and Benson Dyantyi had been seeing a good deal of the Africanists, attending their meetings and conferences in the townships, and had come to the conclusion that Sobukwe's statement on the Friday was going to include a dramatic call for action—and that this call would meet with a much greater response than was anticipated. They wanted us to play the story big in our April issue. This would give us the chance of a quite extraordinary scoop, since no other paper was paying serious attention to the movement. Against this was the likelihood that Sobukwe's call—like so many calls for action in South Africa before and since—would go unanswered. Our article would then be a flop; in addition, publicity for the break-away movement would get us in bad with the A.N.C.—and worse than we were already with the Special Branch and the authorities. We should be in hot water from both sides.

Humphrey and Benson suggested that I should see the Africanist leaders, attend one or two meetings, and form my own impression of how the African public was reacting to their efforts. My view was the opposite. "You've done all that already, and I'm sure your impressions are genuine. You've formed a picture of how the followers are preparing; I'll try and get the feeling of the opposition and the inert mass. I'll start by seeing the leaders of the A.N.C., and then we can put our two impressions together."

Cecil Eprile kept, I knew, fairly close contact with the A.N.C., so I went over to his office, told him I was thinking of playing up the P.A.C. in *Drum*, and asked his advice.

"There's absolutely nothing to these P.A.C. boys," he said in effect. "They're only trying to cash in on all the work done by the A.N.C. The call for action will be a complete fiasco—but why not come along and hear what the A.N.C. chaps have to say themselves? It may save you sticking your neck out. I've arranged to meet a few of them next Sunday evening."

At the Sunday meeting the A.N.C. leadership was fully represented, with half-a-dozen of the top figures. After supper we got down to talk, and I soon raised the question of the Africanists, and what was likely to happen in a week's time when the call for action came.

"Absolutely nothing," was the unanimous opinion.

I waited till all the leaders had spoken and then said: "I want to put another point of view. You're all dismissing this crowd of break-aways because they haven't got the things you have got. They've got no typed lists of members, no offices with telephones, no real national organisation. But the point is—they don't want these things. They aren't trying to get them. They argue that typed membership lists only get your supporters arrested, and that telephones are only good for being tapped. They're trying to make a new kind of organi-sation, which will operate in a quite different way."

"What way?" someone asked. "It can't operate at all. How can you have a movement without organisation? Anyone of us can give a 'call to action'. The problem is to get anyone to act. We know from our own experience that unless you've got your followers all lined up, knowing exactly what to do, and trained leaders there to make sure they do it, the whole thing is bound to be a flop. We've proved that, time and again."

"But what we're dealing with here," I said, "is a quite different analysis of the situation. What these people argue is that the country to-day is like the veld in dry weather—all ready for a blaze. They say the people are angry and fed-up, waiting for a lead. They believe they can cut out all the machinery and laborious organisation—and get through to people, not by talk but by example. They argue that if they choose the right issue—and the right issue, they believe, is the pass laws—and if the leaders are prepared to go the whole way them-selves, including prison sentences, then they will set off a chain reaction. The fuel will be the people's grievances, and the spark their personal example."

There was silence for a moment, then one of those present said: "It *can't* work! You can't get action that way. It will fail, and the few who take any notice of it will be rounded up and penalised as they always are. Sobukwe is leading the people into trouble with no real chance of success. His plan is completely irresponsible."

Among those who had assembled was a lawyer-politician, and it was his remarks which—as events later proved—went directly to the point. "Looked at in the way you've put it, the scheme just *might* come off. Odds are against it—but it might. But there's one thing these people are overlooking."

"What's that?"

"Their policy, as no doubt you know, is to go along to the police stations in masses on the appointed day, say they have given up carrying passes, and demand to be arrested. They intend to flood the police stations, cram the law-courts, fill all the prisons, making it impossible to go on arresting people—and leading finally to a breakdown of the whole pass system. They criticise us for having spent thousands on legal defence—for instance over the Treason Trial. For themselves, they say, there will be none of that. They have a slogan: 'No bail. No defence. No fine.' The aim won't be to keep out of prison, but to get in. As soon as they're released, they'll all refuse to carry passes and get themselves arrested and imprisoned all over again . . . It sounds good—but the plan's got one fatal weakness."

"Which is?"

"They're expecting to be sent to prison for three weeks for not carrying a pass, come out, hold a few meetings, then get re-arrested and go back inside. That may happen to a few harmless followers— but when it comes to the point the leaders won't be sent to jail for three weeks for not carrying passes—they'll be sent to jail for three years for conspiracy or sedition. And what will happen to the movement when anyone who tries to give an active lead is certain to get three years?"

*   *   *   *   *

I reported back to Humphrey; we called a meeting of the staff, and argued the question out among ourselves. Finally, we agreed that we would lead the paper with an article "Who are the Africanists?" In it we would tell the story of their movement's growth, leading up to the present attempt. We would illustrate it with action pictures of the leaders talking or addressing meetings, with a short biography in place of caption under each, and we would put a catch-line on the cover calling attention to the story inside. But we would make the pages of it instead of five, and though we would give the facts, we would not take sides or advocate any action; the readers would simply be given the fullest information on the personalities and issues.

As soon as our first copies came off the machine, I realised that the crucial day for sales would be the Monday—on which there would at least be the expectation of action; if nothing were to happen for two days, our story would be dead. I therefore went to the circulation department and arranged with them to speed things up and put the paper on sale two days early, on the very day the call for action was due to take effect.

Sobukwe duly held his press conference on the Friday, outlining his plans and calling on all his followers to assemble first thing on the Monday morning at their nearest police station. They were to court arrest deliberately. He and the other leaders would be there as well; he had already resigned his university post so as to apply himself full-time to the work of leadership. The announcement received only a moderate amount of notice in the press, and the white public regarded the threat as negligible. Most whites had heard vaguely of the A.N.C. and regarded its activities as a joke—black men trying to play politics. But this P.A.C. they had never even heard of. On the Sunday I rang the editor of a "white" newspaper and asked him what he thought of the position and whether his staff were expecting anything to happen; he said that all was quiet and they fully expected it to remain so. Cecil Eprile, as a final check before deciding to play the whole thing down in his week-end editions, had rung up the police. They told him they were not taking the threat seriously and did not think anyone else need do so either.

And so we came to the Monday of Sharpeville.

*   *   *   *   *

We had made our plans on Saturday, disposing our tiny staff to what seemed the best advantage. Benson and Peter, with our only car, were going to meet at daybreak in Orlando and keep close to Sobukwe from then on. He was visited very early by the Special Branch, and Peter got pictures of him talking to his followers and surrendering himself, with a few companions, at the police station. They were told to wait and a good deal of discussion went on inside as to what to do with them. A phone call from Alexandra told us that there a mere dozen "Pac" men had turned up to claim arrest. In Durban a total of thirteen had done the same; elsewhere in the country everything seemed normal. We had all been in the office since the very early morning, and by about ten the feeling had spread that nothing was going to happen, and those who sympathised with "Pac" were looking very despondent. Suddenly the phone went. It was one of Ian Berry's contacts saying that the police had opened fire in Evaton, a location near Vereeniging, thirty miles or so away, and that the people were in a state of excitement and had started cutting the telephone wires. Soon afterwards came another call saying that trouble was boiling up at Sharpeville. None of us knew exactly where Sharpeville was, but we soon found it was another location outside Vereeniging, comparatively new, with an adult population of about fifteen thousand. Ian was raring to be off, but our only car was still in Orlando.

"What about your own?"

"Laid up."

"Oh—hell. Take mine. Try and not get it shot up," and I threw him the keys.

"Can I go too?" called Humphrey. He looked so eager that, though I would have been glad to have him around in case one of us had to rush out and bail members of our staff, I could not refuse, and in a minute they were both out of the building. On such a day I did not dare leave the office, and was just having a sandwich sometime after two o'clock when Humphrey rang through.

"There's been one hell of a mess-up here. Masses of people shot—it was just like a bloody battlefield."

"Where at?"

"Sharpeville."

"Where are you calling from?"

"A café near Vanderbijl Park. We're wondering whether to go back and look for more, or come on home."

"Did Ian get pictures?"

"Yes."

"Are they safe? Has he had his films pinched?"

"Not so far."

"Then for God's sake don't stick around. Come on in with what you've got."

By three-thirty, dusty and excited, they were back in the building. Ian sat checking his cameras over and counting his rolls of film while Humphrey talked. They had had a close-up of the whole incident which was even now hitting the world's press like a bomb and making the name of Sharpeville both odious and renowned. They were the only two journalists—the only two whites—who had been there among the crowd or close to it when the firing started. One other cameraman—Warwick Robinson of the *Rand Daily Mail* with the Mail's crime reporter, Harold Sacks—had been inside with the police. The rest were nowhere.

"Hell!" Humphrey kept saying. "They were just mowing the people down, kids and all. And Ian was dodging in and out among the bloody bullets taking his little pictures! He just ran out into the middle and knelt down. Hell! What a cameraman. He's nuts, of course. Completely nuts! He just ran out into the middle and knelt down . . . Hell! And then half-way through he just thought he'd try the other camera and switched over."

When he'd finished his story, I asked: "What about my car?"

"Hell!" exclaimed Humphrey, fishing in his pocket for the keys. "*Is* yours a lucky car! Not a bloody scratch! and the *Mail* car which went in just behind us has got two bullets in the back and the windscreen shattered by a stone."

Ian printed up his pictures. He had got the crowd running towards him, many of them children, many of them still laughing, thinking it was all a game, thinking the police were firing blanks to scare them. He had got a woman lying dead and the man beside her staring stupefied at his blood-stained hand. But he had got something more—a picture that was going to be produced dramatically later on at the Sharpeville Enquiry when police officers denied there had been any firing from the Saracens. It showed two policemen—one with a revolver and one with a Sten gun—firing into the fleeing crowd, and the policeman with the revolver reloading when he had emptied his magazine. In the course of a couple of minutes, and at the risk of his life, he had taken a handful of pictures that were to be historic. At the Sharpeville Enquiry later on he was to say, in his diffident and hesitating way, a sentence that would do more to destroy the official picture of a savage horde baying for the lives of a hundred and fifty policemen than a volume of argument. He was asked if, while he was walking about—alone and unarmed—among the crowd some minutes before the shooting, he had experienced any difficulty or sense of danger. Ian thought for a moment, then replied: "I had to say 'Excuse me' once or twice in order to get past."

When the two of them had had a cup of tea, Humphrey went off to write his story while it was still fresh. We were all in a strange state of mind; horrified by the tragedy; excited and disturbed as to what would be its consequences; amazed at the strange way our gamble on the Africanists had succeeded; elated that *Drum* should be the only paper in the world to have got pictures and an eye-witness account of what had happened; perplexed as to what to do with this precious material now we had it. Our April issue had been published only that morning—how could we wait a month till May?

"Don't worry," I said. "Get it all written down and get all the pictures printed. Maybe we can produce a special issue of everything that happens during this week. Have it on sale in a fortnight's time."

We did not guess at that moment that it would be six months before—under the Emergency Regulations soon to be brought in—we should be able to print Ian's pictures in South Africa at all; and that by the time it was possible to print Humphrey's article, Sharpeville would have become ancient history. Here, however, is what he wrote. It appeared in London in *The Observer*, and in South Africa in Patrick Duncan's courageous and independent magazine, *Contact*; as well as in the United States.

"We went into Sharpeville the back way, behind a grey police car, and three Saracens. As we drove through fringes of the township many people shouted the Pan-Africanist slogan, 'Izwe Lethu', which means 'Our Land', or gave the thumbs up freedom salute and shouted 'Afrika!'

"They were grinning, cheerful and nobody seemed to be afraid. Some kids waved to policemen who were sitting on Saracens, and two policemen on one of the Saracens waved back. It was like a Sunday outing, except that we knew that Major Att. Spengler, head of the Rand Security Branch, was in the front car, and that there were bullets in the Saracens' guns.

"Spengler led the convoy towards Sharpeville police station, and policemen on Saracens obligingly signalled left and right turns in the road to us, and when they were slowing down. Perhaps they thought we were members of the Security Branch. Then we caught a glimpse of a crowd around the police station at the top of a long rise ahead. Abruptly Spengler turned his car around and the Saracens followed.

"We followed the convoy to the main gates of the township where policemen were stopping all cars from town. We stayed on the township side of the barricade. Then Spengler was off again, and his Saracens. We were going back to the police station, but this time there was a difference.

"The policemen were all inside their Saracens and the hatches were battened down. The police were looking at Sharpeville through

chinks in their armour plating. But the residents did not regard the
tanks with concern; they were interested, and some of them grinned.
There were crowds in the streets as we approached the police station.
There were plenty of police, too, wearing more guns and ammunition
than uniforms.

"Major Spengler and his Saracens drove through the policemen
around the police station and we hesitated. Then we parked our car
and Berry went to see what he could photograph. Every time a policeman looked at him he whisked into the crowds. Then an African
approached him and said he was the local Pan-Africanist leader. He
told Berry his organisation was against violence and that the crowd
was there for a peaceful demonstration.

"The crowd swelled around Berry, listening to what their leader
said. But Berry thought the police would come too, so he said: 'For
goodness' sake, get these people to move.' The leader spoke to the
people around him and they dispersed immediately.

"In the meantime I decided to drive through the police cordon and
find Berry. I hooted and some policemen moved away but others
looked more closely at me. Then a constable shoved the butt of his
rifle against my car's windscreen and another pointed his rifle at my
chest. A policeman in a tunic leant into the car, red in the face and
explosive.

"He shouted: 'Have you got a permit to be in this location? Have
you got a permit?' I said no. He shouted: 'Get out! Get out! Get out
or I'll arrest you on the spot, do you understand?' He had his police
gun in his holster and a black pistol tucked into the top of his pants.
He seemed almost hysterical. I backed down about twenty yards and
waited for Berry where I had left him.

"Then Berry came back and we decided to go around to the other
side of the police station. This was about seven minutes before the
police opened fire and the crowd seemed perfectly amiable. It certainly never crossed our minds that they would attack us or anybody.

"We drove around to the other side of the police station and we
parked in a big field. We could see a couple of Saracens sticking above
the heads of the crowd ahead of us, just more than one hundred yards
away. The crowd seemed loosely gathered around them and on the
fringes people were walking in and out and some kids playing. I
certainly could not see more than about 3,000.

"I said to Berry: 'This is going to go on all day.' And he replied,
'Let's hang on for a bit anyway.' Then there was a report, over to
the right it seemed, away from the police station.

" 'That's a shot,' said Berry.

"I was still wondering if it was, when there were sudden shrill cries of 'Izwe Lethu'—women's voices it sounded—from near the police, and I could see a small section of the crowd swirl around the Saracens and hands went up in the Africanist salute.

"Then the shooting started. A gun opened up toc-toc-toc-toc and another and another. The shots had a deep sound.

" 'Here it comes,' said Berry, and he leapt out of the car with two cameras. He crouched in the grass taking pictures. The first rush was on us, and then past. There were hundreds of women. Some of these people were laughing, probably thinking the police were firing blanks. But they were not.

"Bodies were falling behind them and among them. One woman was hit about ten yards from our car. Her companion, a young man, went back when she fell. He thought she had stumbled. He turned her over in the grass. Then he saw that her chest was shot away. He looked at his hand. There was blood on it. He said: 'My God, she's gone.'

"There were hundreds of kids running too. One had on an old black coat and he held it behind his head as he ran, to save his head from bullets, I suppose. Some of the children were leaping like rabbits, hardly as tall as the grass. Some of them were hit too.

"Still there was shooting. One policeman was standing on top of a Saracen and it looked as if he was firing his Sten gun into the fleeing crowd. He was moving slowly from side to side. It looked as if he were panning a movie camera—from the hip. Two other policemen were on the Saracens with him. It looked as if they were firing pistols, but I could not hear pistol shots separate from the toc-toc-toc of the automatic guns.

"Most of the bodies were strewn in the road which runs alongside the field we were in. I saw one man who had been lying still get up, dazed, and walk a few paces. Then he fell in a heap. A woman sat with her head cupped in her hands. One by one the guns stopped shooting. There was nobody moving in our field except Berry. The rest were wounded or dead. There was no crowd any more. It was very quiet.

"Berry ran back to the car with his cameras and he said, 'Let's go before they get my film.'

"We tried to find a way out of the township that did not lead past the police on the main road. Nobody molested us as we drove around the township looking for the back way. We could not find it so w

6] Sharpeville, March 21, 1960. The crowd starts to run, still thinking it's a joke or that blanks are being fired.

7] "My God, She's Gone." One f the historic pictures of the harpeville shootings taken by n Berry at the risk of his life, larch 21, 1960.

went out on the main road, looking straight ahead. Nobody stopped us.

"I heard no warning to the crowd to disperse before the shooting started. Yet the police had had all morning to rig up a public address system which they could have used and I understand that police Saracens carry loudspeakers. Nor was there a warning volley. When the shooting started it did not stop until there was no moving thing in the huge open space in front of the police.

"I have heard that the police claim that they were in desperate danger because the mob was stoning them. But only three policemen were reported to have been hit by stones and more than 200 Africans were mowed down. So there seems to be some disparity here. I have also heard that the crowd shot at police. But before the police opened fire I heard only one shot, and that seemed to come from a long way away.

"I was told that the crowd around the police were armed with ferocious weapons, and that these littered the area around the police station after the crowd fled. But I did not see them, although I have looked very carefully at pictures of the death scene. And when I was there I saw only shoes and hats and a few bicycles left behind among the bodies.

"It is also extraordinary that the police did not use the leaders of the crowd to keep order. This had been done earlier that morning at Bophelong township, Vanderbijl Park. A mild-mannered and calm White, Mr. Knoetze, township manager, and the local Pan-Africanist leader kept everything there completely under control. Only one person was killed in Bophelong. He was Steven Mathe, nineteen years old. A policeman shot him because he was throwing stones. Tough stuff!

"And it seems to me that tough stuff was behind the killing at Sharpeville. The crowd gave me no reason to feel scared, though I moved among them without any distinguishing mark to protect me, quite obvious in my white skin.

"I think the police were scared though. And I think the crowd knew it.

"That final shrill cry by the women before the shooting started certainly sounded much more like a jeer than a battle-cry. It did not sound like a battle-cry at all. And while the policeman who told me to get out of Sharpeville was red in the face and almost hysterical, the first wave of the crowd that ran past me when the shooting began was still laughing.

"A sad postscript to the Sharpeville shooting was written for me at a small café in Vanderbijl Park. Vanderbijl Park was pretty close, I imagine, to Dr. Verwoerd's apartheid ideal that day. There were no Africans there. Whites were working the petrol bowsers in the garages and pumping up tyres. Other White workmen were just standing around because the factories were closed for lack of Africans. The place was pure White.

"No bread was delivered to the little café that morning; no milk, no other foods either; nor any minerals.

" 'It looks pretty bad,' I said to the White woman behind the counter.

" 'Yes,' she said. 'They should shoot all these bloody kaffirs dead, and they'll all come back to work to-morrow,' she said."

*   *   *   *   *

When the death roll of Sharpeville was completed, there were 69 dead and 180 wounded. Before the figures had been received, a Nationalist M.P., Mr. Carel de Wet, said in the House of Assembly: "It is a matter of concern to me that only one person was killed." When a United Party member, Major van der Byl, declared that this was "a terrible remark to make", Dr. Verwoerd intervened to say that Mr. de Wet's remark had been completely misinterpreted. All he had done was to plead for order. It was shocking that one Christian should attach such a meaning to the words of another Christian.

At the end of the week the Government, faced with a mounting clamour in the country and throughout the world, issued its own statement. It said:

"According to factual information now available, the disturbances resulted from a planned demonstration of about 20,000 Natives in which demonstrators attacked the police with assorted weapons, including firearms. . . .

"The demonstrators shot first, and the police were forced to fire in self-defence to avoid even more tragic results. . . .

"The allegation . . . that the demonstrators were unarmed and peaceful is, therefore, completely untrue."

CHAPTER XXVI

THE WORLD PRESS DESCENDS

THE NEWS THAT *Drum* had got pictures of the shootings seemed to go round the world almost as fast as the story of Sharpeville itself. Within a few hours I received five cables from overseas papers asking for photographs. As no one else had the full facts and contrary to our usual custom, we decided to sell the story. Late at night I was also rung up at home by the *Daily Mirror* from London; I told them I could do nothing till next morning, but would then have five pictures printed up and radioed through. The pictures consisted of four of the actual shooting—three of the crowd running away and one of a woman victim lying on the ground—and one picture giving the general scene before shooting started; all were handed in for transmission in good time on the Tuesday morning, and we concluded they had been sent.

On the Wednesday we were rung up by the post office authorities who said that "owing to unfavourable atmosphere conditions" only one of the five pictures accepted had actually been radioed. They had been in touch—on our behalf—with the *Daily Mirror* in London, who had told them that, as the pictures had been delayed so long, there was now no point in their transmitting the other four. Would we therefore kindly collect the prints and pay £1 for their trouble. Humphrey, who was handling the matter, said: "I must have an explanation of this in writing."

"What do you want that for?" the official asked. "I'm telling you now."

"Because we made an agreement with the *Daily Mirror* which we have not been able to keep. We insist on your sending us a written explanation which we can pass on to our client."

"Oh very well . . ."

"We needn't wonder which picture got through despite 'unfavourable atmosphere conditions'," I said to Humphrey.

"No," he said. "The one with no shooting in it."

And so it proved.

In the course of the morning, as we were all talking things over, Nat Nakasa remarked: "You know we can't just leave it like this—two hundred and fifty Africans dead and wounded, and the rest of us do absolutely nothing—as though it were just some kind of a little mistake."

"What do you suggest?"

"Chief Luthuli ought to declare a 'Day of Mourning', and the whole country should stay away from work as a sign of respect."

Luthuli was at this time in Pretoria, giving evidence almost daily at the Treason Trial, which was still wearily dragging on. I was sure Cecil Eprile would be in contact with him, so went over to his office.

"People on *Drum* are suggesting that 'Chief' ought to declare a national Day of Mourning for the Sharpeville victims. Do you know how to get hold of him?"

"Yes. Dennis Kiley is going out there this evening. He can pass the idea on."

Next morning I asked Cecil what had been decided. "Chief" had told Dennis that he could not make any move without consulting his principal supporters. He would do this as soon as he could, and let Dennis know the result.

However, in Thursday's *Rand Daily Mail* I read that Luthuli had announced the next Monday, March 28th, as a Day of Mourning, when everybody throughout the country should stay away from work.

On the Friday afternoon I went along with Cecil Eprile to meet some of the A.N.C. leaders. I was anxious to learn how they were reacting to the P.A.C.'s sudden success—for the P.A.C. leaders had become heroes overnight, and children in the townships were cutting pictures of Sobukwe out of newspapers and magazines, pasting them on to cardboard, and wearing them as medals. Present were Duma Nokwe, Nelson Mandela and Robert Rhesha. Though their policies were unchanged, their attitude was very different from when I had last met them only a few days before. In particular they shied away from the description of themselves as "moderate", as though it had suddenly become a dirty word: the most they would claim was that they were—not more moderate—but more "responsible", the leader of P.A.C. being irresponsible by implication. They expected more trouble in the next few weeks, and said the Government would make use of this opportunity to ban all political activity of any kind, classing everyone together as "revolutionaries" and "extremists". It had, only the day before, banned all public meetings over large parts of the country, including the chief cities.

Dr. Verwoerd had set out the Nationalist line in a speech in the House of Assembly immediately after Sharpeville in which he declared that the shootings were the result of "attempts to organise massive revolt"; said that the way in which the police handled the situation had "earned the gratitude of everyone"; "congratulated them on the way they had controlled themselves"; and added that the pass laws were not to blame. Instead he blamed "the newspapers" which, by expressing disrespect towards authority, had brought about a spirit of resistance among the Bantu, adding that the A.N.C. was "no less culpable" than the Pan-Africanists for what was happening.

He thus paved the way, as the A.N.C. leaders had foreseen, for legislation in which the A.N.C.—who had opposed the pass demonstrations and been derided by Africans for their moderation—would be banned equally with the P.A.C., who had organised those demonstrations.

Monday, March 28th, the Day of Mourning, was by far the most impressive African demonstration I have seen in South Africa. But it did not depend on organisation for its success. It was an emotional response to a widely publicised appeal, following a disaster which shocked the whole country, white and black alike. Thus on the black side there was no need for close organisation, and on the white side no real attempt to prevent the Day of Mourning being held, most white employers co-operating with their workers to make it easy for them to stay away. Along the Reef and in the Cape the stay-away was practically complete. During the day the townships were mainly quiet, but towards evening there was some violence, mainly stone-throwing and burning of buildings. Mobs began to gather around the stations towards nightfall, lying in wait for those who had been to work, chasing them and beating them up.

During the morning I drove out with Ian Berry and three or four visiting journalists and cameramen on a tour of the townships. Orlando was quiet, so we drove on to Moroka. The streets were deserted, except here and there a woman or child hurrying along with food or milk. We stopped at a house known to our driver, and knocked. Like almost all township houses, it was a tiny dwelling—not much more than a garage divided into rooms. For a moment there was silence, then someone from inside recognised the driver through the window, and in a moment a dozen or fifteen men had come pouring out. They told us they had organised a pass-burning which was just about to start. We had hardly begun talking to them before other doors opened all up the street, and in no time there was a crowd of sixty or seventy people.

"Look," I said to a man who was clearly in authority—he proved to be an A.N.C. official. "If the cops turn up suddenly, we shall all be pinched for holding an illegal assembly. Send away all those who have nothing to do with this, and let the others collect on some open ground with a view in all directions."

The official shouted a few words; the women and children, and most of the men, vanished as rapidly as they had appeared. Then he and about ten or a dozen others led the way to a patch of waste ground. They were carrying a quarter-filled sack and what appeared to be a bottle of gin, but which was actually paraffin. When they reached their chosen spot, the leader shook out the contents of the sack, poured the paraffin over, and began burning about seventy of the precious and detested documents. Though there was no kind of ceremony, he managed to give dignity and an air of ritual to the occasion. As the passes—cloth-bound books with a large number of stiff pages—caught fire, men seized one in each hand and began to dance and shout, waving the blazing passes in the air. I was surprised by their readiness to be photographed in this highly illegal activity; when a Fleet Street cameraman who was with us wanted them to pose grinning over the bonfire into his camera, even those who had been doing no burning hitherto rushed to get into the picture.

Ian's quickness and resource astonished me, as they had done before and were to do many times again under more difficult circumstances. I was still wondering how he could get anything usable from the artificial arrangement organised by the Fleet Street man, when I saw he had already darted off ten yards or more to one side. From there no one was looking into the lens, they were all gazing intently away, and the scene as the men pranced and waved their unfolded passes over the little fire looked like some strange tribal ceremony. Next day when we printed up the pictures, he had got three or four vivid shots in which half-burned passes, with the flames curling up from the opening pages, looked like fiery flowers dangling in front of the exultant faces; and he had one close-up of a kneeling man, his face intent and brooding as at an incantation, pressing his charred pass into the flames.

As the week went by, excitement mounted. Three Africans working for the South African Broadcasting Corporation were sacked: one had put on a record of a song which had strong patriotic association for his African listeners. Two had stayed away from work on the Day of Mourning; as marked men, they or their families would certainly have been attacked if they had not. Their sacking led to a campaign in the townships, where gangs of youths went round the house pulling out all the rediffusion sets. Many were thrown out into th streets and burned. They also cut down the poles carrying the wires, and—when these were re-erected during the week—went all round and cut them down again.

"I was listening to a lovely jazz programme last night," said Can, "when a lot of young chaps came in. They just tore the machine right out with the wires, and flung it all into the street. It was no good arguing. Then late at night I was in someone's home when we heard someone scrambling about on the roof. I wondered what the hell was up, and should I go out to look or not, when a voice called out: 'Don't worry down there in the house. There's no danger to you people there. We're only tearing the radio wires off all the houses'."

And now the big waves of arrests were starting. On Tuesday, March 29th, more than 200 blacks and whites. Early in April, hundreds more. Emergency Regulations brought in on March 30th, and made retrospective for four days, virtually put the country under martial law. The government could arrest and imprison anyone they pleased for 30 days, without giving any reason, bringing any charge, or making the fact of the arrest public. After the 30 days, notice of detention had to be tabled before both Houses of Parliament within 14 days. This meant that anyone could be imprisoned without charge—or without even the intention of bringing any charge—for longer than six weeks. Many in fact were imprisoned for the whole period of the Emergency, late March to the end of August, without having any idea why they had been arrested—some of them had not been active in politics for years—the Government indemnifying itself by special legislation against any legal actions which might otherwise be brought.

Moreover, in terms of the Public Safety Act, it was forbidden to publish—or even to pass on to another person—the names of people arrested under the regulations. Strict new laws controlled all newspapers and magazines, indeed every form of publication, including gramophone records and tape recordings. Before these Emergency Regulations were withdrawn, it was generally estimated that about twenty-three thousand persons were imprisoned throughout the Union; the vast majority of these were Africans, described in official pronouncements as "tsotsis", "idlers", "workless", "troublemakers" and so on. It was forbidden to print any description—much less any photograph—showing the conditions under which they were held.

In addition, the Minister of Justice, Mr. Erasmus, announced that "in order to halt the reign of terror", penalties for intimidation and victimisation would be increased tenfold. "And if necessary the

Government will not hesitate for one moment to come with even more severe sentences." On April 8th, following another series of dawn arrests, the Minister announced the Unlawful Organisations Act, banning the A.N.C., P.A.C., and "certain other organisations". They are still banned.

The United Party in an involved but typical manoeuvre, voted for this Bill, but "made it clear that by doing this the party was not in any way endorsing the Government's racial legislation".

*   *   *   *   *

The Sharpeville shootings brought the press of half the world pouring in on Johannesburg—and pouring into *Drum* offices as well. At times it was difficult to get any work done. Visitors all, naturally, wanted something. One wanted a desk and a telephone—and stayed using them for a whole week. Most people wanted to look round the townships and meet a few African politicians—and for days Benson was so busy as escort that I seldom saw him. Almost everyone wanted "to have a quick look through your files and take away just a couple of pictures".

Of all our visitors, two of those who applied themselves most seriously to trying to find out what the trouble was about were Canadians, Norman Phillips of the *Toronto Star*, and Gerald Clark of the *Montreal Star*. Norman Phillips later went down to Durban, where he was arrested and imprisoned for $3\frac{1}{2}$ days for sending a cable giving the story of the police attack on Nyanga, one of the two big African locations outside Cape Town. Of this attack, Peter Younghusband—who had succeeded Ken Mackenzie* as *Drum's* Cape Town editor—a tough and courageous journalist now working for the London *Daily Mail*, and himself a South African, wrote: "For two days this place has been the scene of a relentless and violent campaign of terror. If I had been told a fortnight ago that this would have happened in this country, and perpetrated by my fellow-countrymen, I would never have believed it."

Not all visitors, however, were anxious to go into things as thoroughly as Clark and Phillips. In the course of a few days I had visits from a television producer, a man from the B.B.C. in London, and "an expert on international affairs". What the television man wanted was a string of appointments laying on, ranging from Nationali

---

* Mackenzie's wife, Myrna Blumberg, was one of those arrested under the Emergency Regulations, held in prison for months, and then released without ever being charged. She has told the story in her very successful book *White Madam*.

spokesmen—"but *moderate*, if you know what I mean"—to Africans who had taken part in the recent disturbances. I warned him that this last might be difficult, unless he was content to show only the backs of the speakers' heads. He thought this wouldn't really matter, but added—"only get safe ones, please."

"What d'you mean 'safe'? Any of them is liable to be arrested if they're spotted on the screen."

"No, no. I don't mean that . . . But you know what it is on television. We don't want any *left wing* characters."

After he'd gone, Humphrey and I talked it over together—what constitutes a "left wing" character in South African politics? Was Bishop Reeves a "left wing" character? Or Japie Basson, former Nationalist M.P., who had broken away to found his own independent movement? Was Helen Suzman (now the only Progressive M.P.) "left wing"? Or Chief Luthuli? Is a man who is prepared to take a hammering and go to prison for three years because he thinks the Pass Laws an affront to human dignity, a "left wing" character, from whose reckless persuasions the British viewer ought to be protected? And if the answer in all cases is "yes", whom could we find for our television friend's programme except his "moderate Nationalist spokesman" and some police colonels?

The man from the B.B.C. had different requirements. He asked to be given rapidly the story of the last ten days—plus some introductions and telephone numbers—then he started.

"But what are these African leaders doing that's *constructive*?"

I explained that, as all the leaders had been arrested and virtually all the second-rank leaders too, there was very little leadership left, constructive or otherwise. In fact, in the absence of the politicians, there was a grave risk of control in the townships slipping into the hands of gangsters and tsotsis—and this situation was already being used in turn to justify further police raids, and further series of arrests.

"All that's no good to me," he said. "I can't tell my listeners *that*. But what are the Africans really aiming at? What concrete proposals have they? What's their programme?"

"A hole has been punched in a solid white wall. It's been half patched-up. Maybe it will be all patched up and made stronger than before, or maybe they'll punch a new hole somewhere else. Their hope is that, if only they can loosen things up a little, change will come. They feel in their hearts like men in prison—'only let us get out, and we'll decide what to do when we're free'."

"Good God!" he said, horrified. "Is *that* all? You mean they're just trying to bust things up without having anything prepared to put in its place?"

"From the Africans' point of view," I answered, "white supremacy is the enemy who has to be knocked down. Knocking him down is bound to cause confusion for a time, but out of that confusion, they believe, will come a fairer deal and a new order. Only you can't arrive at the new order without first facing the confusion."

"Well, it's not a bit of good telling my listeners *that*! I've got five million listeners next Tuesday evening who are interested in hearing something *constructive*."

"There is one thing you might tell them."

"What's that?"

"In these last two weeks there have been signs of a change in the attitude of Afrikaners. They aren't very strong signs yet—but they're enough to give some hope. You might tell your listeners something about that. I can put you in touch with a few people."

"I've seen no sign of it at all," he answered. "None! And none of the people I've talked to have seen any sign of it either."

"When did you get here?" I asked, a little nettled that my efforts to help should meet such a flat rejection.

"Three o'clock yesterday afternoon."

Nat Nakasa seemed to me the most patient and good-tempered member of our staff, so I passed this visitor on to him. Nat had just got back from taking him around when, in the middle of the afternoon, the expert on international affairs was brought in. I had been warned of his coming, as someone of particular importance, anxious to make contact with urban Africans who could give him the latest on current feeling in the townships. All the general information, background of the country and so on, he was said to have already—no doubt from his study of international affairs. As our own African staff consisted of no more than three (Peter not being much of a political theoriser), I had asked Can, Lewis Nkosi and one or two others from *Golden City Post* to help us fill the room. I introduced our guest as impressively as I could, then turned to him and asked if he would like to start the discussion. He looked round, and began:

"What d'you all think about apartheid?" There was a painful silence. This was, I thought, the very worst opening remark I had ever heard —like asking a set of Calvinist ministers whether they agreed with the practice of confession, or a Mother's Union meeting whether they were in favour of prostitution. I looked quickly round at the faces and thought it best to step into the gap.

"I think what our friend has in mind is really—what would you think of partitioning the country up on an equal basis? Not the usual 13% of the land for 70% of the population—but a reasonable division. It might be partly proportionate to population, partly related to historical ties and how particular areas came to be settled in the past. But with each section getting some ports, some cities, a proportion of mineral wealth, a share of good farming land, and so on." I was filling the outline in as best I could.

"You mean," Can demanded, "more or less *equal*? Based on a *fair* division?"

"Well, yes. I suppose so," replied the expert on to whom this new conception of apartheid had been fathered.

Can looked round at the others with a quick, delighted smile: "Cripes, boys—let's jump at it!"

"Why?" asked the astonished visitor. "I thought you were all of you *against* apartheid?" Can hesitated a moment, then burst out: "Because the only way we can treat with the white man is to have him clean out of the way. Separate—on his own! If we're both supposed to be sharing the same thing, he'll always find a way to do us down."

When the visitor had gone and the office was empty, I started to go through my post. Among the pile was a cable from a New York paper asking me for a survey of the current situation in South Africa to arrive next day certain. It was to "take in chief conflicting viewpoints, give backgrounds to important personalities, take account implications Commonwealth cum United Nations"—and the length was to be two hundred words, about half the amount of reading matter on this page. I thought of cabling back to ask if they wouldn't like to have it engraved on a pin-head as well, but finally threw it back into the basket. By to-morrow the deadline would be up and I could forget all about it anyway.

* * * * *

Meantime, the general unrest among the African population had had its effect on members of our staff. During the early days of the excitement, they worked like beavers. Literally at times through day and night, without appearing to think about food or sleep. Now, in a brief lull at the end of March, they presented a long document setting out their demands. The first I knew of it was when Cecil Eprile came into my office, closed the door carefully, and said:

"Do you know what's going on?"

"No. What is?"

"All the staff are demanding at least fifty pounds a month—otherwise they'll all walk out!"

"Well, I suppose either they'll get their fifty pounds, or we shan't see them any more."

"It isn't only my staff—it's *yours* as well."

"Then they'll all walk out together."

"But what about the management's reaction? If they see this notice, they'll go up in smoke! We've just *got* to keep it from them. Get the chaps to modify it considerably. Take out the demands. Make it reasonable requests. What's Jim Bailey going to think about it all when he gets back from the U.S.? Have you thought of that?"

"But the demands sound reasonable enough. Our staffs ought to be paid far more. I know mine ought."

"Yes, I've got a great deal of sympathy with the *demands*: it's the way they're expressed that's so absolutely impossible. It'll only put the management's backs up."

"But if it's meant for the management, the management will have to see it. After all, it's they who'll have to deal with it. *We* can't give wholesale wage increases—it's hard enough to get someone an extra fiver. So if the chaps want to show it to the management, they'd better."

In the end Cecil thought it wisest to take the document himself to Ian Pritchard. By next day the management had a copy in any case, as I had myself. To Ian I said that I thought the demands were justified, and to the staff that I thought they were damnably expressed and contained insinuations which I thought unjust. Jim Bailey, when he got back from a long tour abroad, said the final word. He rejected the memorandum completely, but authorised Ian Pritchard to deal with the demands contained in it. He added that, if the editors had maintained any contact with their staffs at all, they would have prevented such a memorandum from ever being presented.

"The only thing that matters," I said to Ian, when he told me of these comments, "is—can you give the staffs the sort of increase they're asking for? They're long overdue, and we shall have no peace unless you can arrange it."

"Certainly," Ian answered. "And what's more, I intend to work on annual wage scales, so that a chap will know that, if he stays with the firm and does his job properly, he can count on moving steadily up."

I felt better after this short talk than I had for a long time, but was not to last. A couple of days later, as I was writing at home one Sunday morning, Cecil Eprile looked in to see me.

"What are you going to do?"

"What about?"

"Haven't you heard? *Drum's* just been banned in Ghana. It's said to be under the direct or indirect influence of the South African government. I heard it on the radio."

"Oh."

"I think you should at least issue a statement to the Press. They'll be expecting it."

We issued no statement, but a few days later Ian Pritchard and I were up, once again, in Ghana.

★   ★   ★   ★   ★

Ian and I were obliged to leave with the issue of the ban still undecided. Listening to the radio one evening I had heard news of the shooting of Dr. Verwoerd. It was evident that all our difficulties in South Africa would now be much intensified. Jim Bailey stayed on for a time to continue negotiations before flying over to England. Four months, however, would drag by, and yet another visit to the West Coast would be required, before we should get the welcome news that the ban on *Drum* in Ghana had at last been lifted.

CHAPTER XXVII

A RAID BY THE SPECIAL BRANCH

On the day Dr. Verwoerd was shot, and while I was still in Ghana, Dorothy happened to be at a garden-party given by some Afrikaner friends. We did not know many Afrikaans-speaking South Africans, but we did our best to keep in touch with those we did know. On this occasion Dorothy had been asked to go along early and help with the party arrangements, and had agreed to do so. Late in the afternoon she was standing by a table with two or three other women, when the news of the shooting came suddenly over the radio. Everyone looked at each other with surprise or consternation. An African servant who was carrying round drinks banged his tray down on the nearest table, let out a piercing yell, leaped high into the air, rushed for the house—and was not seen again all afternoon. Dorothy was watching this little scene when a heavily built woman came up to her and demanded:

"You're English, aren't you?"

"Yes."

Wham! The woman gave her a stinging slap on the face. "You English have shot our Dr. Verwoerd!"

As she walked away the woman muttered: "The English! I've always hated them."

"Are you hurt?" the woman near by asked Dorothy, adding, "She's not one of us, that woman. She's a Hollander."

"Not at all," said Dorothy. "She was naturally excited, and took it out on me. For goodness' sake don't tell our hostess. I don't want her to be upset."

In the townships the news caused wild excitement. Coming so soon after Sharpeville, it was felt that the whole machine of oppression had begun to rock. Where would the next blow fall? Youths danced around singing: "He will die! He will die! The bullets have killed him!"

Just a few of the older, politically minded men tried to calm the young ones down. "No! No! We don't want this man to die yet. It is too soon."

"Why not?"

"He's doing our work for us. He's teaching our people that nothing is worth while until we get the vote. He's giving our people their political education."

"How d'you mean?"

"Left to yourselves, lots of you would be happy if you got better pay; if the whites just treated you as human beings; if the police stopped harassing you, and the pass laws ended. But that way you would never grow up, and you would always be at the mercy of the whites."

"Well . . .?"

"This Verwoerd—with his passes for women, his more and more apartheid, his Bantu Education, his Job Reservations and the rest of it—he makes you face the facts. There can be no improvement in our lives until we've got the vote! The vote is the key—then we decide what improvements we want for ourselves. 'One man, one vote'— that's what Verwoerd is teaching our people. And till everybody learns the lesson, we still need this man around."

* * * * *

From the airport at Johannesburg, Ian Pritchard and I drove—after a quick visit home—to the printing works, where a new edition of *Drum* was being put to press. Under the Emergency Regulations we felt obliged to read every line and word and caption several times over; a lawyer was there to read it with us. I had already received a confidential message from an M.P., who had spent a morning with one of the Nationalist Ministers most concerned with implementing the new legislation.

"They mean to close you down," was the message, brought by a friend coming up from Cape Town where Parliament was in session, for in these days everyone was extremely careful of the post. "Give them the slightest excuse, and they'll be down on you at once."

We had scarcely settled to our task of going through the pages, when a call came from the office: "Come back now. There's a raid on by the Special Branch."

Ian and I ran down to my car and drove into town as quickly as we could. Three members of the Special Branch were in the office when we got back, two of them men I knew from previous visits. Cecil Eprile was chatting to them, but left when we arrived.

The lieutenant in charge held up a copy of our April issue which had carried the "Africanist" story.

"I must tell you that we are thinking of bringing a prosecution against you for this issue of *Drum*—and I want to ask you a number of questions in connection with it."

I felt an enormous relief; if all they had come about was the April issue, we must be in the clear. I had been afraid that some members of our staff might have been more involved in politics than I knew.

"May I ask you a question first?" I said.

"Yes."

"Is this prosecution to be brought under the Emergency Regulations?"

"Well, in fact it will be—yes."

"And do you know which day the Emergency Regulations came into force?"

They did not, and there was some discussion among themselves. In the end, however, they took our word for it that the regulations had been brought in on March 30th, and made retrospective by four days.

"Okay—but what's that got to do with this prosecution?"

"Do you know when this magazine went on sale?"

He held it up. "You can see. There's the date 'April' on it."

"It's dated 'April'," I said, "because ours is a monthly magazine, and we have to try to sell all through the month. But it was actually on sale on March 21st—nearly a full week before the Emergency Regulations took effect, and ten days before they were introduced."

Our police visitors looked dubious. Suddenly I remembered that the Afrikaans evening paper, *Die Vaderland*, had printed much of our article about the Africanists next day. This copy of *Die Vaderland* must be still in my office, and I went to fetch it. The Special Branch men turned the pages over. There it all was, quoted from the previous day's *Drum*, in a reliable Afrikaans newspaper which had been published on the 22nd. They handed me back the copy.

"But this issue of yours is still on sale? It's on sale now—although the Emergency Regulations have been in force now for two weeks?"

"Quite right," I said. "But nobody said it ought not to be on sale. This is the first time the question has even been discussed."

Our visitors left. Their stay had been short, and perfectly civil. Next day we learned that the distributing organisations had been ordered to call in and hand over all unsold copies of the April issue. It meant some loss to the firm; however, as the magazine had now been on sale for a clear three weeks, we felt we had little cause for complaint. Norman Phillips, the Canadian journalist, writing of the African article in his book *The Tragedy of Apartheid*—published in the United

Kingdom in 1961, but banned in South Africa—said: "This was a magazine scoop—as if the Democratic nomination for president had been won by an unknown and *The Saturday Evening Post*, planned, written, and edited weeks in advance, had appeared the same day with a profile of the dark-horse candidate."

The Special Branch, naturally enough, had been unable to believe that we had simply backed a hunch that the Africanists meant business; they suspected some sinister relation between us and them. However, they clearly could not prosecute us under the Emergency Regulations for an article published long before these came into force, and the scoop, engineered by Benson and Humphrey Tyler, had given a big stimulus to sales, so that there were now only a few thousand copies scattered about the country for the police to lay their hands on.

*   *   *   *   *

On April 7th there had been a second wave of pre-dawn arrests, and by now a large number of those, both white and black, who had been in any way associated with liberal or progressive politics, were in prison. Others, feeling the net about to close on them, had fled the country. Numbers more, including some who were probably in no danger, had taken to a kind of hide-and-seek life. They attended to their work and normal interests by day, but slept always away from home; since the arrests took place in the very early hours of the morning, they relied by this means on being given some warning by their families, and so perhaps being able to slip away and cross the borders into Basutoland or Swaziland. Respectable citizens who had avoided taking part in politics, but had worked in close contact with Africans and mixed with them on terms of friendship, lived this kind of life with a small hand-case always ready packed. One made a nest for himself in a loft in his own outhouse; it commanded a view of the front door, and had a back entrance by which he planned to creep quietly off through the bushes to a lane where his car stood all night, ready fuelled.

Since telephones were tapped, families worked out their own codes by which wives could let husbands know if the police had called for them: "The postman's been", "Your uncle was asking for you just now", "The man from the Prudential wants you", and so on. And as, under the special regulations now in force, it was illegal for a wife even to tell her friends that her husband was in prison, one got used to being given ambiguous messages in reply to phone calls: "John's away in Pretoria. We don't know when he'll be coming back." In a number of cases both husbands and wives were arrested, so that relatives or friends had to take charge of the children at a moment's notice.

On Saturday morning as we were going down in the lift, Dorothy said to me:

"When's your turn coming, Hoppy?"

"I don't know. How should I?"

"Would they imprison you, or deport you?"

"Deport me, I should think. But who can say?"

"Well, I've just about got our flat in perfect order—but if we have to pack up everything and leave, I'm quite prepared to. It's been well worth while."

"I don't think we shall have to go."

"Well—I don't *want* to go, because I'm happy here and I love this country. . . . You don't think you ought to take any precautions, do you, like X and Y?"

"Sleep somewhere else you mean? No. Why be harassed? Let's have all the normal life we can. We can start being harassed when I'm pinched. And I'll have to sleep away then anyway."

In the office Cecil Eprile called a meeting, himself and myself with Jim Bailey. He wanted to know whether, in view of all the arrests and the threats of prosecution that were flying about, the management would stand by us and look after our families if we were sent to prison.

"Certainly," said Jim. "If an editor is sent to prison in the execution of his duty, the firm will stand behind the editor and give him full support. But we don't want our editors in prison. The real question is not 'What does the firm do about editors who go to prison?', but 'What can we all do to ensure that none of them go there?' "

"I shouldn't mind a bit of prison," said Cecil. "It would be rest-cure."

"But we don't pay editors to have rest-cures," said Jim. "One way would be the system they had in nineteenth-century France."

"What was that?" I asked.

"Each paper had an editor specially to go to prison. He was imprisoned and well paid for it, and the real editor got on with the work."

"What d'you think about that idea?" Cecil asked me.

"Not much. I'd rather do my own going to prison. Anyway it could only work in a society which paid great respect to legalistic forms. Here, if editors took to sheltering behind dummies, the Government would just pass a law enabling them to disregard the dummies and pinch the people really responsible—and I must say I should think it justified. So all we'd do would be to discredit ourselves and get pinched just the same."

Jim smiled. "The main thing is for you both to exercise all possible care. Everything you print should be read by the lawyers first. If you see that's done, and if you are both thoroughly familiar with all the regulations, then it'll be your own fault if you get imprisoned."

* * * * *

During the last ten days of April the division in the Nationalist Party, which had started with Sharpeville and been strengthened by the attack on the Prime Minister, burst out into the open. For some days there had been talk, both in *Die Vaderland* and *Die Burger* (organ of the Cape Nationalists, who always tend to be more moderate than those of the Transvaal), about a better life for the African, and the necessity for a change in outlook on the part of the whites. Then, on April 19th, at the Union Festival Celebrations, Paul Sauer, Minister of Lands, made a dramatic speech. "The old book of South Africa was closed a month ago at Sharpeville," he declared. For the immediate future, South Africa "must reconsider in earnestness and honesty her whole approach to the Native question". "An important adjustment" would have to be made to the reference books system; the Native must be given hope for a happy existence; and he called also for higher wages in urban industries.

Since Mr. Sauer, besides being a Minister of long standing, was also chairman of the Cabinet and acted on the Prime Minister's behalf during his incapacitation, his speech seemed highly significant. A murmur of hope ran through the land. Was there going to be a change of heart—and policy—at last?

The answer was not long in coming. Next day Mr. Eric Louw, Minister of External Affairs and leader of the extremists in the absence of the Prime Minister, bluntly stated in the House of Assembly that no one but the Prime Minister was entitled to make any statement of basic policy. In other words, Mr. Sauer should shut up and toe the party line—or else! Next day another extremist, Mr. B. J. Vorster,* Deputy Minister of Education and Social Welfare, rubbed it in. He spoke to a meeting at Wellington, and *The Star* carried a report:

"Recently doubts have arisen even among Nationalists as to whether we are on the right road, but there is no reason for panic."

* Currently Minister of Justice and responsible for the recent "Death for Sabotage" Bill.

He believed that Providence was behind South Africa and could not leave her in the lurch.

Talk of coalition was idle as the United Party had never had a policy to offer.

There was no place in the United Party for an Afrikaner nor for any decent, well-meaning English-speaking citizen.

There was a better relationship between English and Afrikaans citizens today than ever before.

As he had said in Parliament, there was no emergency in South Africa. There were local disturbances because the Bantu had been incited to riot from the pulpit and by the overseas Press.

Political rights were demanded for urban Natives because they worked for the White man. But although he was dependent on the Bantu for his labour, the European was doing him a favour by providing him with work and a livelihood.

The campaign declaring, "We've done nothing wrong. There's nothing to be ashamed of, and no need for any change of policy," was accompanied by one of personal adulation for Dr. Verwoerd. There had always been some reservations in the minds of many Afrikaners, on the ground that Dr. Verwoerd was a Hollander and no one of themselves. This new publicity—which had the Prime Minister's undoubted personal courage to build on—aimed at making him a kind of honorary Afrikaner. He had shed his blood for the fatherland therefore he was mystically linked with the soil of South Africa; he was even more "our leader", and even more South Africa's Prime Minister, than his predecessors. In addition, a statement of his doctor that the bullets fired into him had missed killing him "by a hair's breadth" was made the basis of propaganda—sustained by newspaper writers, in pulpits and in public speeches—to the effect that only the direct intervention of God, diverting the bullets at the last smallest fraction of a second from the fatal spot, had saved Dr. Verwoerd's life. He was thus more than ever under the personal protection of the Deity, and the people he led could be surer than ever that they were God's chosen people, and that anyone who opposed their policies was trying to thwart the just purposes of the Almighty.

Why, if God had indeed intervened in this way, He should have allowed the assassin to approach so close, and the bullets to penetrate so far, was not explained. Indeed the question would seem never have been asked. It was enough that He should have stepped in at the precise moment when He did.

Meantime the leaders of what Mr. Erasmus, Minister of Justice, had called "the reign of terror" had still to be punished. On Wednesday, May 4th, Robert Sobukwe was sentenced to three years' imprisonment for "incitement to commit an offence as a protest against the Pass Laws"—very much as the A.N.C. leaders had forecast that he would be. His lieutenant, Potlako Leballo, fiery orator and the national secretary of the P.A.C., was sentenced to two years; other leaders who had either surrendered themselves or stayed to face the music received varying sentences. Among them was an engaging figure, Josias Madzunia, a black-bearded orator of biblical fervour who made his living by the sale of cardboard boxes and pieces of packing. Conspicuous in a long black overcoat—which he was never without even on the hottest day—he did all his business on a particular street corner in Johannesburg, where I would sometimes exchange a word or two with him on my way out to lunch. He was a warm-hearted, difficult man who believed—I think—that whites should be driven into the sea, or at least asked to go there quietly. He had not much use for many blacks either, and though he stood his trial as a P.A.C. member, retracting nothing, he had actually quarrelled with all the others and been expelled from the movement before he was even arrested.

Not all the leaders could be found. Peter Raboroko, Peter Molotsi and some others had fled the country, and showed up in Ghana before long. Matthew Nkoana, our former free-lance contributor, was sentenced to eighteen months. He appeared in the dock with 141 other Africans and acted as spokesman for them all, addressing the court almost without a pause for half a day, covering the whole field of present-day South African politics. Once again, as when he appeared to give evidence for Sidney, Matthew—who, as a boy, had wanted to become a lawyer, but whose parents could never find the money or the opening for him—succeeded in dominating a legal scene. When the magistrate, after hearing with exemplary patience what Matthew had to say, addressed the men in return to deliver sentence there was some shuffling and occasional interjections—natural enough when more than 140 men were standing shoulder to shoulder. At last the magistrate appealed to Matthew to secure him a quiet hearing. "Yes," said Matthew, "I spoke for more than three hours, and it is only fair that we should give you a chance to speak. But I would like to point out that a lot of the things you have said are very provocative." "You also," the magistrate replied, "said a lot of things which were very provocative."

A year later the staffs of *Drum* and *Post*, with some special assistance from Jim Bailey, would combine to raise the necessary amount to pay the fine which would absolve Matthew from finishing his prison sentence. He came out and was around Johannesburg and the locations for a few months, still looking like a black undergraduate, and arguing politics with anyone who would stop and listen. But besides arguing he returned to writing, producing a small paper called *Mafube*.

It was not long before charges under the Suppression of Communism Act were brought against this ardent African nationalist, and he was convicted in December 1961 of "wrongfully and unlawfully performing an act or acts calculated to further the achievements of the objects of Communism". This time his sentence was one of three years. Matthew appealed, but, by the time his case came on, he had left the country.

CHAPTER XXVIII

CAMERAMEN IN ACTION

IT WAS DULL work editing a magazine in which virtually nothing could be said, so I was glad when the chance came to visit a new part of Africa. This happened in a round-about way.

It had been suggested to me earlier in the year that I should fire Ian Berry, on the ground that there was only room in the magazine for two or three picture stories by him each month, and that if he were employed by someone else he could still do these few stories for *Drum*, but at less cost. I did not take any notice of this suggestion since, apart from the fact that I could not fire someone who was working excellently, I was not going to kick away one of the two pillars on which our magazine rested. Working in the peculiar conditions of South Africa, it was essential to have both a white and a black cameraman, since there were many situations in which the one could operate and not the other. Moreover I was convinced that, in Africa's "Independence Year" of 1960, the news which would mean most to our readers would come increasingly from other parts of Africa—in which Ian with a British passport could travel freely, and where Peter with no passport could not travel at all. In addition, as regards both Ian and Peter, I felt like a manager with two good fighters, or a producer with two stars—I would sooner lose one ear than lose either, and the pressing question for me at this moment was not whether I should get rid of Ian, but how I could possibly make it worth his while to stay.

His growing reputation in South Africa, plus his spectacular successes in the *Encyclopaedia Britannica* competition and at Sharpeville, had made him known in Britain and Europe as well as in America. He was being bombarded with offers from overseas, and was losing money by working for us at his existing salary—which obviously for a while I could not expect to get much increased. After some talk together we worked out a scheme whereby Ian, besides continuing as a cameraman for *Drum* on the same terms, could also free-lance for an agency in Paris, the money earned in this way going partly to himself and partly to the firm. It was the kind of complicated arrangement I dislike, but the advantages far outweighed the drawbacks since it meant, first, that we could keep Ian; second, that we should obtain picture stories from other parts of Africa where *Drum* would never itself send anyone on account of cost. Incidentally it had a third advantage, in that the money made through the sales of pictures and through "retainers" during this year much more than paid the whole cost of Ian's salary; this, however, was not my main concern, which was to keep hold of a man of outstanding talent.

This arrangement was worked out and agreed early in June, and the first assignment proposed by the Paris agency was due to take place towards the end of the same month—the Independence Celebrations of the former Belgian Congo. I had been in to see Ian Pritchard to make final arrangements when, as I was going out of his office, he called after me:

"Why don't you go up there with Ian yourself?"

"Can I?"

"Yes—why not? Arrange the work with Humphrey."

Humphrey was more than helpful. "I had my day out at Sharpeville—now you can have ten days out in the Congo. Anyway it's a story we simply must have in the paper, and this way we'll get it nearly free."

"I'm coming with you," I told Ian.

"Good—you can speak the bloody whatsit and carry my spare thingummies. It's hell trying to shoot in colour and black and white unless there's someone to give you a hand with all the doo-dahs."

*　　　*　　　*　　　*　　　*

In Leopoldville we were lucky to have a good friend already installed. Jim Bell, in charge of the *Time-Life* office in Johannesburg, was a thrusting, tireless bald-head who had been up to the Congo half-a-dozen times before Independence, was up there now, and would go back at least half-a-dozen times more in the course of the next twelve months. He lent me his notes on the political situation; extraordinarily detailed and complete, they supplied far more concentrated information than could ever find its way into his magazine, and he gave up the next morning to taking us a quick run-round the city. Our immediate need was to secure press passes; and here, in our first task on our first day, we came up against the barrier—that blank wall against which so many journalists would exhaust, and a few destroy, themselves in the next few months—of Congolese military stupidity or Congolese military bloody-mindedness; it was difficult to know one from the other.

The office issuing passes was inside the Palais de la Nation, an imposing building with a central dome and pillared portico, where the new-born Parliament would meet. But to get to this office it was necessary to go past the sentry on the gate—and he would let no one in who had not already got a pass to show. We argued with the sentry for a minute or two until I could see he was about to lose his temper —and he had a long thin bayonet and a loaded rifle—so we arranged for one of us who already had his pass to go through and speak to the Belgian official. The Belgian came out and shouted to the soldier to let us through, but he took not the least notice, and it was only when the official actually came and escorted us into the Palais, keeping between us and the sentry, that we were able to obtain our passes. Similar incidents would happen to me, and other journalists, in different parts of the Congo many times over later on, and it became quite commonplace to be summoned to a press conference by Lumumba—or equally by Tshombe—and then driven away by sentries on the door, despite the shouts and cries to let us in from Congolese officials.

Our first few days were spent in photographing official celebrations, openings of Parliament, ceremonial parades and banquets. But though these official occasions went off as a rule without visible hitch, there was a mounting undercurrent of excitement and distrust.

"Why do you wear this piece of foliage?" I asked some young men in the crowd, waiting apparently to cheer their new leaders.

The first two I asked would not reply. The third declared: "This is a sacred herb. It makes us fearless in battle. Nothing can harm us if we are wearing this." He fingered his green spray proudly—but whom, I wondered, did he and his friends mean to fight?

Gradually the tension mounted, despite a nightly curfew at eight o'clock, and the presence everywhere of Force Publique, the Congo's police-force army, officered by Belgians. A day or two before Independence, when there was some kind of big reception at the Palais, we arrived early to secure a good position. Crowds had already assembled, and more and more people came piling in, lining the streets and scrambling all over an ornamental fountain which provided a vantage-point. What everyone was waiting for was the procession of cars bringing the new President, Kasavubu, the new Prime Minister, Lumumba, and all the other twenty-odd Ministers, each in his new black shiny limousine.

However, an hour before the official party arrived, an old American car and a van drove into the open space between the Palais and the fountain. Three or four men scrambled out and rapidly set up a loudspeaker system, through which a small man—climbing up on to the roof of his stationary car—harangued the crowd. The small man had an unusual appearance; he combined the thrust-out chin and arrogant, ranging eye of a Mussolini with the small moustache, strutting walk and flow of angry eloquence made familiar by another dictator. For half-an-hour he talked on, denouncing the leaders in whose honour the crowd had supposedly assembled. Lumumba, he cried, had promised him a top job in his government; now Lumumba had gone back on his promise, and he had been squeezed out. His party, he declared, would not accept this. Nor would they accept the results of the recent elections—the first in the Congo's history—since they "do not truly reflect the importance of our party in the life of the Republic". Having finished his harangue, he climbed down from the car and began to walk up and down, inspecting the crowd, occasionally conceding a nod or accepting a handshake, and being received with a stir of excitement, especially among the women.

The small man, I soon learned, was Albert Kalonji, an important chief of the Baluba. A month or two later, following the secession of Katanga, he would seize the opportunity to declare independent his own "Diamond State" of South Kasai, with an army of a few hundred uniformed soldiers, plus a great many tribesmen armed as best they could. In place of a capital, he would have some fifty villas lent to him and his entourage by the Belgian company who owned the diamond mines and the town—it is really no more than a residential suburb set down on the bare veld—of Bakwanga, which was now his, as well as their, headquarters. Here he would be dependent on the company, not merely for revenue and accommodation, but for water, light, and also food—which had all at times to be flown in to the single landing-strip. Established here, Kalonji conferred on himself a new title—"The Mulopwe"—which, he explained, meant that he was not only a great tribal chief and the head of his own independent state, but also implied near-divinity and entitled him to semi-divine prestige. The title, though no doubt comforting to Kalonji, seemed to have little practical effect, since almost the only success achieved by the disintegrated and incompetent army of Lumumba would be to rout Kalonji's Balubas and kill about a thousand of them.

After strutting about for some minutes, Kalonji drove off, and almost at once the Ministers started to appear. Ian shot the necessary pictures, and then we set out to walk back to our hotel. The Palai was a couple of miles out of town, the other journalists had all left and there was not the least hope of getting a taxi. We had not gon far when we heard shouting and saw, coming along the road behind us, a hundred and fifty or more women, supporters of Kalonji. They had linked arms and were sweeping, thirty abreast, along the boule-vards. Many of them were big and powerfully-built, and they made a fine sight as they stormed along, turbanned, shouting, their loose robes swirling round them, and the dust of the boulevards rising up in clouds. Ian was soon running with them, or rather backwards in front of them, dropping on one knee every now and then to snatch a shot. For a few minutes we ran along beside the women, then they took a side-turning, broke up, and we were left standing at a cross-roads. We were still in the residential suburbs, a district of pleasant villas with wide gardens, well-watered, full of flowering shrubs and palms, and I was just looking for the road which should lead us back to town, when there came a shout from Ian—"Hell, what's this?"

Fifty yards away was a small square, into which armoured cars and lorries full of troops had suddenly begun to pour. We ran as quickly as we could to make out what was happening. Further on up the road leading back into the city was a small crowd, shouting and brandishing sticks—they proved to be some hundreds more of Kalonji's supporters trying to join up with the main body. This crowd was being held back by a thin line of Congolese soldiers under a Belgian officer, and the motorised troops filling the square were clearly the reinforcements they had sent for.

Suddenly a jeep in the square started to move. It ran rapidly up the road towards the crowd and a Congolese soldier standing up in it began to fire. He was not firing directly at the crowd, but lobbing canisters which turned over and over in the air and then fell, hissing, among the people. Small clouds of smoke fizzed out of every canister, and a pool of emptiness at once formed round it in the crowd. I did not understand what was going on, but Ian, who had more experience of riots, cried out delightedly—"They're using tear-gas"—thrust his leather case into my hands, tied his handkerchief round his nose, dodged past the soldiers in the square, and disappeared up the road towards the trouble.

I tried to follow, but as soon as I got into the tear-gas area I was driven back choking and with streaming eyes. Three times I tried, and each time turned away. After about five minutes, looking up the road, I could see that the crowd had been driven out from the con-finement of the houses to where the road ran between fields and the gas could get away. I put my handkerchief over my face and ran to overtake Ian, who was now hard at work.

Here, almost within arm's length of us, a strange, slow-motion struggle was going on. The crowd, packed tight, many wheeling bicycles and some women carrying babies, was being herded in reluctant flight along the tarmac. Deep ditches on either side stopped the people from breaking out into the fields. A section of eight Congolese soldiers under a Belgian officer was hounding them along; the eight wore steel helmets clamping down over their brows and ears and neck; they had goggles against the gas, and carried rifles with long thin bayonets fixed. The officer had a revolver, a stick and a whistle.

They did not fire any shots nor stab any vitals with the bayonets, though there were one or two men in the crowd with streaming head-wounds. They just herded the people before them up the road, bashing them on arms and shoulders with their rifle-butts, nipping in to crack heavily down with rubber truncheons, and kicking. Particularly they kicked the bicycles, their heavy boots crunching in the mudguards and the spokes. There was one tall young soldier who had inwardly gone mad. Sweat streamed down his harsh features with the effort not to run berserk. Only the presence of his officer kept him from killing.

His special victim was a small man in a yellow vest. Printed on the vest in big black letters were the words MANGEZ LE POISSON DU MARCO. Yellow Vest dived and turned and twisted, but he was always finding himself at the tail of the crowd, and the tall soldier would be after him with blows and eyes of murder. In and out of the batons, kicks and curses, Ian was dodging—dropping on one knee as a soldier brought the butt of his rifle down on a woman's back; standing on tiptoe to catch the angry scowl of a protester whose bicycle wheel had been kicked in. Hastily he swopped some of his gear with me, then slid back into the fight. Not only the soldiers were shouting at him. Some of the other cameramen—four had magically appeared like vultures—shouted at him too.

Soon, as suddenly as it had begun, the action ended. The road came out into the town, and the people scattered in all directions. The soldiers pushed back their helmets, and mopped their streaming brows. "Thank God for a bit of action!" Ian said. "I shouldn't be surprised if I haven't got a couple of decent pictures in that brouhaha. Did you see the way the tall thin guy was lamming into the little fellow with his yellow whatsit? And how that little officer at the same time both urged the soldiers on and held them back? Should have been a scene in a movie. . . ."

"I can see it did you good," I said. "You haven't been so lively since we got here."

"I didn't feel so lively when the trouble started. Did you see what happened?"

"No. I couldn't get through the gas."

"A bloody Congolese soldier knocked me down. Hit me with his rifle-butt. I was dodging round the back of one of those villas so as to catch up, and he came on me from behind. I think he really meant to clobber me—but just at that moment one of the officers bellowed at him like a bull, and he had to hop off back into the fight."

As we were sitting in the hotel for a drink half-an-hour later, a Frenchman who had consistently grabbed the best positions on all ceremonial occasions by private arrangement with the Belgians came up to Ian in shrill complaint: "You should not do such things! It will not be the fault of the police if you get hurt! It is not fair to the authorities. You should show more consideration!"

Ian, who did not know what the man was talking about, went on sipping his soft drink.

"Look," I said. "We work our way—you work yours. If you call *that* working."

I knew what was biting him. While Ian and two of the others were in the thick, he had been running along on a mound beside the road out of harm's way. All his pictures, if he got any, would have other cameramen in the foreground, much nearer to the scene than he was.

* * * * *

Ian, slight, blue-eyed, bearded, diffident, was in his element when there was trouble. He came to life, like a racing-man when he hears the shouting and sees the horses in the paddock, or an Italian at sight of a pretty woman. Normally he said little, and was inclined to say till less when bored or fed-up, as he always was in periods of inaction. When he *did* talk, it was in a language of Kafka vagueness, demanding crossword puzzle acuteness in the listener: "What about going round to the howsit and sending off the other thingummy?" In the hunt for pictures he was inexhaustible. Often, as I settled down to a half-hour's reading, I would hear the suggestion, soft but insistent as the voice of conscience: "Don't you think we ought just to slip up to the so-and-so, and try to grab a couple of shots of old who-ha? I'm sure the last ones I got were under-exposed."

With his toughness in action, he combined a feminine squeamishness away from it. The sight of an insufficiently cooked steak—he seemed to eat only steak, because it was easy to order, and he didn't like messy things—turned him pale.

"It's alive," he complained, prodding it with his fork disgustedly. "When did they catch that?" Then I would call the waiter and send it back, saying that this gentleman liked his meat much-cooked, too much cooked—"really black, like charcoal".

Through Ian I soon got to know others of the cameramen on this assignment. Barry von Below worked for an evening paper, the Johannesburg *Star*. He was out for single pictures; Ian and I were trying to build picture stories. Short, sturdy, a jockey in build, I would see him darting in and out of trouble in a well-cut suit with an inch of elegant shirt-cuff flapping around his wrist. Never satisfied with his own work; always sure someone else had done better than he did; off duty, Barry enjoyed talking about books. He had read and thought a lot.

"Have you read *Dr. Zhivago*? What do you think of it?"—but before I had started to reply, he had interrupted himself: "I say, Ernie's not here. I bet he's on to something. He was on the spot yesterday when that Belgian was arrested. Just half a shake while I see if he's in his room. Hang on to my drink, someone!"

Ceaselessly on the go, Barry's usual expression was tired, distracted —like the man in the advertisements who wants an Aspro. He *had* a headache, too. Trying to develop his films in washbasins, drying them in the Congo's Turkish Bath atmosphere, making his own prints— then rushing out to get them radioed to Jo'burg, a taxi journey of twenty minutes each way with the added difficulty of a strange language. And all the time the fear that in his absence he was being scooped. South African reporters have never been trained to help their cameramen, and the reporter with Barry seemed scarcely interested in what he did.

One day, when Ian and I and the reporter were having lunch in the hotel, I asked: "Where's Barry?"

"Oh, developing his films, as usual."

"Will he get anything to eat?"

"I don't suppose so. By the time he's been out to the airport and back, it'll be all over."

"Good God!" I said. "You ought to be standing outside his door with a plate of sandwiches and a bottle of beer—instead of sitting here over your second coffee."

The reporter laughed sarcastically. But a minute or two later, he got up: "I'll just go and see what Barry's up to."

*   *   *   *   *

Another South African was Ernie Christie. Alert, dapper, grinning —always on the ball. Knowing just what was due to happen every day. Knowing the times of planes and the situations of post offices; whom to approach for permits, passes, facilities, free cars. Slipping in everywhere with a Cockney smile and no French. "Just stand out of the light, mate, while I get my picture"—and the bewildered Belgian official or sweating Congolese sergeant, instead of thrusting him away, would hold his spare camera or push the crowd aside. Unlike Barry— who always thought his pictures ought to have been better—Ernie was constantly delighted with his own success. "Wonderful stuff this morning!" he would say as he joined us for a beer. "Cops pitching into the Congolese like mad. Only waited till I turned up to get started. Then as soon as the *Life* boys showed up, they packed it in. Couldn't have been better!" He rubbed his hands with satisfaction.

He seemed the 100 per cent happy extrovert. But Ernie really *did* have ulcers, so his drive and bustle took their toll. And when things failed to go well—as when someone pinched King Baudouin's sword at the other end of the town—his face wore an aggrieved expression, as if the least you'd expect was a telegram warning him to be on the spot.

* * * * *

Tall, lean, bespectacled Larry Burrows had worked for *Life* for seventeen years. English by birth, but indistinguishable from an American by now, except for a certain gentleness not usual with American newsmen. Working for *Life* meant all the newest equipment; cars at his service all day long, instead of struggling for taxis; a hired interpreter; now and then a charter plane or helicopter. Yet, with all the lavishness of *Life* and *Time*, it comes down in the end to the cameraman.

I was in the city one day. It must have been the day before Independence, and the King was due to give the whole place away tomorrow; I had walked to the boulevard to see his arrival, and was sitting at a table drinking, waiting.

A stir came in the crowd and a few motor cyclists hammered by. "This must be it," I thought, and got up on to a café chair. More motor-cyclists—and then, running like hares, but stopping every few moments to swing round and shoot, there tore past me Ernie and Barry, Ian and Larry Burrows. They had dropped their coats somewhere, and their damp shirts flapped against their backs. The sweat streamed down into their eyes. The crowd and police kept getting in their way. But they ran while I watched, for quarter of a mile, constantly turning to shoot at the slow-moving royal car. Ernie, once a well-known footballer, was the least in trouble—dodging and darting up the wing. Barry, more worried than ever, scudded on up the middle of the road. Ian, scarf flying, ran with a high loping trot. Larry, white and exhausted, seemed ready to drop, but held grimly on. He explained it afterwards in the hotel with his own particular mannerism of speech.

"We were in a lorry—an' that. The four of us. We were following the King—an' that—into the city. The Belgians, of course, had the first lorry. It was all fixed up with stands—an' that—so they could shoot down into his car. The French had the next best, just like they always do. . . . We were given the last lorry—right at the back. Well, we're just coming into the town—with all the people cheering an' that—when our lorry breaks down."

"Belgians fixed it," grunted Barry, nodding grimly.

"We think we've had it now, and we all hop down—cursing an' that. Ernie spots that the King's going all round two sides of a square, and if we cut across the middle we can get in front of him. But there's a line of troops in the way and the crowd an' that behind."

"Yes," said Ian, cutting in. "And Ernie just takes one look, shouts out 'Follow me'—and busts his way past the line of soldiers. One chap I saw would have struck him with his bayonet, only by then Ernie was half-way across the square."

"Well, then," Larry continued, "we have to dive through this crowd and the line of troops again over the other side—and we find we're in front of the King's car, an' that. We run like hell, an' that, and we shoot our pictures. Backwards."

He laid his hand on his silk shirt with its embroidered monogram.

"You know when that sod of a driver pulled up the lorry and stopped suddenly?"

"Yes," they agreed.

"I was flung up against the corner post. I think I've bust a rib, an' that." He had.

*   *   *   *   *

Lastly there was Rock—that wasn't his name, but it will serve—an Italian American working for one of the big television companies. Short, stocky almost to fatness, with a comb of grey hair, black eyebrows and a small moustache. He walked with the perky strut of a barnyard rooster, and when we first caught sight of him—it was in the struggle along the road—he was steaming into action with a big cigar, puffing away among the tear-gas, as he dodged blows here and there, switching from camera to camera as he caught sight of something that would make a bit of colour. Rock had the most limited vocabulary of anyone I've ever worked with; in fact one word served him for all occasions—with variations and additions.

"Taam," he called over to me as a big corporal followed him threateningly. "You know their f—ing language. Tell this sh—head to leave me alone. Tell him to get back to his f—ing sh—house. Oh sh—!"

"What you guys bumming around here for?" he sang out, puffing up to us one crowded afternoon, unhitching his camera for action as he puffed.

"Nothing's going to happen round this sh—house." His eyes darted over the scene, taking in the uneasy family pretending to be busy in the yard; the Congolese patrol nipping round the back; the bayonets thrust up into the thatch as the troops made their search.

"You sh—heads better all clear off back to your hotels. You don't win any f—ing Pulitzer prizes here. In fact this whole f—ing Congo's just one ruddy sh—house. There—what did I tell you?"

There was, it proved, nothing in the house. But we all knew this was just Rock's genial way of shovelling us all aside—if he could—while he cleaned up the incident.

I last saw him photographing belly-dancers on the Leopoldville sports ground. There had been a big football match; it was brilliant football—played with scrupulous attention to the rules and the referee's whistle. When it was over the teams shook hands and vanished, while 23 new black shiny Mercurys drove round the stadium, with 23 new Congolese Ministers inside. No sooner had they gone, than from every corner teams of dancers poured on to the ground—each with its own music of hollow logs, stringed instruments and whistles, each with its own little crowd of yelling followers. Many of the dancers were stripped to the waist—their bodies smeared with grease, with orange clay, or white, or dusty red. Some had pale blue and pink circles the size of pennies painted on their faces and their skins. Their hair was greased and plaited. Stirred by the throbbing rhythm, they flung themselves into the dance, pendulous breasts jerking, grass skirts waving. Women of enormous girth stamped and rotated with the agility of fighting dogs. Drummers and shouting bystanders provoked them on.

A little crowd surrounded a young girl, not more than fourteen.

She had just finished one dance and the sweat ran off her in rivers. Urged on by the other women she started a new dance; it was a kind of parody of soldiers drilling, very intricate and exacting. Twice at a certain point she stopped, exhausted, but the women would not let her rest. Savagely excited as if at some sexual rite, they whooped her back to a fresh effort. A third time the girl tried—and failed, giving up with a rueful, almost sophisticated smile as much as to say: "I can't do more than I *can* do. I've danced a lot for you. You might let me off the rest."

On the verge of tears, she raised a corner of her skirt to wipe her face. A little river of sweat poured down over one nipple.

Ecstatic from behind the crowding women, Rock emerged, patting his camera. "Great stuff!" he confided. "I got it all. An' that's not for my sh—ing corporation. That's for my own kids back home."

*   *   *   *   *

It was a long time since I'd been out on a job with cameramen. Dismissing from my mind two I met later on in Katanga, the cameramen I was with in the Congo were a bunch of genuine professionals; quick-witted as weasels, hard-boiled as jockeys; wary, astute, hardworking. Always alert to steal a march, but equally ready to share a chance, give a lift, or cover up for a man who had missed the boat.

Their company did me good. I kept wishing I had a paper that could hire the lot.

CHAPTER XXIX

WAITING FOR LUMUMBA

We had gone up to Leopoldville originally for ten days, and after about a week—which had been a strange mixture of the pompous and ferocious, the official and the disorderly—Ian was glossy with achievement, as near satisfied as I had ever seen him. But I still hankered after one thing; I wanted to interview Lumumba.

"Oh hell," said Ian. "Everyone's trying that one on. You'll never get hold of him, and if you do he won't say anything. Cut it out, and let's go round the townships again. Yesterday the Force Publique were simply carving one chap up—only I couldn't get close enough to catch the pieces."

I persisted; but Lumumba proved no easy prey. I began with his secretary, Mandolo, going up to him in the lounge of the Memling Hotel—the nerve centre of Leopoldville where all the strands of public and journalistic life cross and entangle.

"But certainly! An interview for your paper with the Prime Minister. Delighted! Where are you staying? The Stanley. I shall ring you there as soon as I have fixed up the appointment."

More cautiously I approached the mysterious Mme X, part Italian, part Creole—loaned as "adviser" to Lumumba, it was rumoured, by Sekou Touré of Guinea. Circuitously, with many compliments and tentative propitiatory phrases, I led up to the question of the interview—towards which I invited her to use some fragment of her enormous influence. For a moment I believed we were there; a decision in my favour was struggling across that large pallid countenance which seemed to have been built up—like composite photographs of Twentieth Century Man—by laying pictures of all nations over each other, and printing out the highest common factor. But just then a shadow fell. It was Jason Sendwe, Lumumba's choice to take charge of the province of Katanga as soon as ever the troublesome Moishe Tshombe should have been eliminated.

"Jason!" she exclaimed delightedly. "You will take me out to lunch! And as for your interview, Monsieur—you can depend on me. You can depend on me!" she assured me over her shoulder as she vanished.

Undeterred by these failures, I went next to the office of M. Lumumba's newspaper. On the first four visits the office was closed —a new experience for me in newspaper offices. On the fifth I found the door open and walked in; in one room was a young Congolese with his feet up on a desk, eating a potato. We conversed in a sort of pidgin French.

"M. Lumumba, he no come here longer. Why he want come here? M. Lumumba print this paper so he become Prime Minister of Congo. Now he Prime Minister—why he want come office any more?"

"But doesn't his paper still appear?"

"Sometimes yes. Sometimes no."

"What do you do here then?"

"Me Circulation Manager and Chief of Staff. Also Head Political Executive," he added as an afterthought. I took him for a caretaker or perhaps the man who passed the copies out to the street-sellers.

"Look," I said, "I have an urgent message for the Prime Minister. I expected to find him here. Can you give me his telephone number?" He shook his head—then, catching sight of the hundred-franc note, "Telephone number? To ring Prime Minister?" I nodded.

The Political Executive fished in a drawer, pulled out a scrap of paper and carefully printed out the number 81.82. We exchanged our scraps of paper. Two days and about fourteen telephone calls later, I learned that the number he had sold me was that of the night-watchman in the National Museum. It was time now for a front attack. On the evening of Independence Day, at the State Banquet for 1,000 guests, seeing that M. Lumumba had not spoken a word for ten minutes to the Belgian dignitaries on either side—and having noted that his bodyguard was securely drinking in the Press Bar—I went directly up to him.

"Mr. Prime Minister," I began, "I am in your country on behalf of one of the leading European picture magazines. In the past few days my cameraman and I have made a truly impressive record, both of the ceremonies surrounding Independence and also of popular reactions. One thing is still missing—a short interview with yourself on the future of the Congo."

M. Lumumba said nothing, but continued to listen politely with bent head.

"As Prime Minister—and as leader of one of the very few parties which has stood consistently for the unity of the Congo—your views are of intense interest to readers overseas."

Still no answer.

"There has also," I added, "been a good deal of criticism overseas about your speech this morning when you attacked the Belgians at the ceremony of the transfer of power. The speech is said to have been out of place. I should very much like the opportunity of sending a reply."

M. Lumumba looked up. He was a tall thin man, of considerable presence, wearing his evening clothes and his sash—some order, I imagined, recently conferred—with an air. He had a small goatee, not thick but wispy; as with many Africans, the hair on his face seemed to grow hesitantly, giving the impression that if once this soft beard were shaved away, it would be the work of months to grow another. About his mouth there was something sardonic and contemptuous, but his eyes—behind powerful lenses—had a formidable glow, seeming to look both outwards and inwards, as Nkrumah's do. He had large hands with twiggy fingers, which he clasped and unclasped as he spoke.

"Criticism of my speech? Surely it was plain enough. What could anyone find in that to criticise?"

"Your critics, M. Prime Minister, say that this was a formal occasion calling for a formal response—and that you made it the occasion for a polemic."

"Every occasion is a proper occasion for saying what is true. The Belgians have done next to nothing for my country. Am I expected to praise them for this remarkable achievement? What would my followers think of me if I did?"

M. Lumumba's Belgian neighbours were beginning to show interest. A waiter was hovering near with a fresh course.

"It is exactly these points which I am anxious to discuss, and on which my paper is hoping to obtain your views. If I may stay and discuss them now, I shall be happy to do so—but if you prefer me to call at some more convenient time . . ."

"Be at my house before eight o'clock to-morrow morning. You know my house? Well then—to-morrow morning. But be sure you are there by eight o'clock."

I found Ian. He had been photographing some painted belly-dancers in a tent, described as a "Grande Démonstration Folklorique".

"It's in the bag," I said.

*　　*　　*　　*　　*

The gate of M. Lumumba's modest villa on the main boulevard was guarded by a soldier. But a man in dirty white shorts and a torn vest—he might have been a gardener—was evidently in charge. There was a small crowd round the gate, including one or two whom I recognised as journalists.

"No good hanging around here." The gardener waved his arms. "Better you all go home. Prime Minister never see anyone till nine o'clock."

I waited till the others had drifted off.

"Look," I began. "M. Lumumba himself commanded me at the State Banquet last night to be here at eight for an interview. He insisted we were to come inside and talk to him."

"M. Lumumba not at home. He not yet got up. He still in bed after the banquet. He has gone to a Cabinet meeting."

Leaving us our choice of these explanations, he turned away to join three other odd-job men who were enjoying breakfast of tea and half-loaves, sitting on upturned packing-cases just inside the gate. Once he was started on his loaf, I turned to the soldier and told my story over again. The soldier proved sympathetic. M. Lumumba's secretary, he said—glancing apprehensively at the breakfast-eaters— was now inside the house. If I would write a message to the secretary, giving my name and explaining about the appointment, he would take it in to him. I wrote the note, and after five minutes received word from the secretary to come back in the middle of the morning.

At ten, I learned that the Prime Minister had already left to see M. Kasavubu, but the secretary explained that if we were back promptly at eight next morning he would personally take us for our interview. So we continued, from appointment to appointment. Two days later, however, when we were paying our fifth call, to our astonishment the garden gate opened—an official, a tall distinguished Belgian standing on the steps of the small porch, was waving a lordly arm for our admittance.

The official led us straight through into a typical suburban living-room. On one side it opened on to the corridor and staircase, on the other was a dining alcove with the remains of breakfast. The room contained a new suite of varnished furniture covered in green plastic, a large new radiogram, a reproduction of a Mary Cassatt painting of two little girls in a leafy garden, and six large photographs—several of them framed as pictures—of the Prime Minister. About half-a-dozen people were already present. My practised eye told me with relief that none were journalists. We had left our rivals far behind

In a mere hour or so, I thought, we shall be inside—then ten minutes without interruption will see us home and dry.

*　　*　　*　　*　　*

The Belgian diplomat was bowing courteously in front of us. "Which of you two gentlemen is Lord Dundee?" he asked.

It was tempting, but it clearly wouldn't work out. "Neither of us is Lord Dundee," I answered. "We are two English journalists whom M. Lumumba instructed to come here at eight o'clock for an interview."

His face fell—but clearly once in, you were elected. "I'm afraid you may have to wait some time," he said. "This is our morning for receiving state representatives." He looked round the room. "Those who will later become ambassadors."

I answered him that we were quite prepared to wait, and turned to consider my fellow diplomats. "Which country do you represent?" I asked a grey-haired, grey-moustached figure, sitting next to me. He hesitated, then replied not in French but English: "I am from Saudi-Arabia. That gentleman opposite is from Iraq. Next to him is the representative of Iran. The group in the corner is of Liberia."

"And the tall gentleman?" I asked, indicating a handsome Nordic figure whom he had not yet identified.

"He is the future ambassador from Nebbidge."

I racked my brains. Though my education was old-fashioned I doubted if there could be a whole country I had never heard of, especially a European country. Ian, opposite, was looking puzzled too.

"From *what* country did you say?" I asked again.

"From Nebbidge," the future ambassador repeated crossly.

At that moment a tall handsome presence with a square jaw, a clipped moustache and greying hair was shown into the room, accompanied by a man whom I knew to be the British consul.

"Bulldog Drummond," Ian whispered.

"Lord Dundee," I whispered back. At the same moment it suddenly struck me where to find "Nebbidge" on the map. My informant had lapsed into French—the language of diplomacy. It was Norvège, Norway, from which the handsome Nordic came. After a short wait a door into the passage by which we had come in was opened, and the secretary came out from what was clearly the Prime Minister's study. He shook hands cordially with Lord Dundee and led him and the consul inside. Five minutes later they were out, but two new arrivals

—they appeared to be Cabinet colleagues of the Prime Minister—were in.

During the next hour only one person among those waiting managed to gain admission. He was a dapper little man nobody had noticed. Seated unobtrusively behind the curtain, he was clearly nobody's ambassador, but might have been a small Levantine trader. However, when the secretary next came out, he caught his eye and smiled. The secretary nodded. The little man—now seen to be carrying a large silver tray wrapped in tissue paper—got up and vanished, bowing, into the interior. In ten minutes or so we could see him emerge into the passage and make his smiling way to the front door. He was no longer carrying his tray.

Our only alleviation for the next slow hour was the appearance of a small boy about nine years old, eldest of M. Lumumba's sons. He wore shorts, a little bow-tie and a blazer. His bare legs ended in white socks and sandals. Down one lapel of the blazer were school badges, for good conduct and the like; down the other were political badges, for Congolese Independence, the M.N.C., his father's party, and so on. Shyly, but with great dignity and charm, he went the round, shaking hands with each of us in turn. Wishing to prolong his stay, I asked if he had been to the big football match the day before.

"I couldn't go because of school, but my Pappy went," he answered proudly, adding after a moment: "My Pappy goes to everything."

He stayed with us a few minutes, but the arrival on hands and knees of a small brother gave him the excuse he wanted to escape. By now everyone was getting restive. One or two of the diplomats got up and walked about, shrugging their shoulders at each other. The hostile gardener came and stared at us through the window with contempt, before entering by way of the kitchen and carrying off a packet of corn flakes from the breakfast table.

"Let's pack it in," Ian whispered. "God knows what we may be missing in the streets."

"Give it half an hour," I hedged. It was now ten-thirty. Punctually at quarter to eleven the door of Lumumba's study opened, and he came through, followed by his secretary. We all stood up as he made the circuit, shaking every hand. I nudged Ian: "Get cracking. This is all we'll get." He followed the Prime Minister round the room, snapping away in the half-light.

When he came to the point at which he had come in, the Prime Minister turned and faced us: "Gentlemen, I am happy indeed to see you here. I welcome you personally, and I welcome you as the representatives of your different countries. We are glad to have had you with us for the celebration of our Independence. I give a particularly warm welcome to the representative of a fellow-African nation"—he looked across at the Liberian delegation—"whom we know we can number among our true friends. I should have liked," he continued, "to have talked to all you gentlemen individually; indeed it was for that purpose that I invited you here this morning. Unfortunately, however, I have received an urgent summons from the Head of State, M. Kasavubu, which I cannot refuse.

"Here, however, is my secretary"—pushing him forward. "M. Mandolo is an excellent secretary and I have the fullest confidence in him. He will be happy to see and converse with any of you. I hope you will stay and talk with him. M. Mandolo will write in his notebook whatever you wish to convey to me, and, when I get home this evening, I shall go through his notebook with him. It will be exactly as if we had conversed in person. And now, gentlemen, to my great regret, I must say goodbye."

He smiled, nodded—and was gone into his large black limousine.

Lumumba spoke fluently, with considerable charm. He used his hands in talking, making gestures as though he were squaring up a block, measuring gestures, such as a professor of mathematics might use. His short speech would have been admirable—if it had not been disastrous. The future ambassadors murmured a polite "Au revoir". As the Prime Minister left the room, they glanced meaningfully at each other, and strode out to their waiting cars. All passed the waiting secretary without a word.

*   *   *   *   *

That evening I jotted down in my notebook: "A rather weaselly face, screwed up towards his spectacles. At times has a fine, though also a distinctly nervous look. Excited at finding himself where he is, but unsure how he got there and doubtful whether it will last. Touchy, susceptible to flattery. Aggressive. Violently ambitious, but with tendencies to retire into his shell. Unable to endure delay, and without the capacity to organise. An astonishing mixture of the gifted and inexperienced; the impressive and the inept. Not a government in himself, but could be one ingredient in a government—if he would accept the need for fellow-ingredients.

"It is no kindness to a country when its independence comes too easily, since its leaders lack any chance of learning how to cope with the enormous difficulties of their task."

CHAPTER XXX

MAN ON THE RUN

W E W E R E D U E to fly back to Johannesburg on the Monday, and by the evening of Friday—it was July 1st and the day following Independence Day—we had finished most of our planned stories. I was hoping to keep either Saturday or Sunday for writing up my notes; however, on the Friday night there was trouble at a village out near the airport, several houses burned down in tribal-cum-party fighting, and about twenty people injured. We drove out there on the Saturday morning; the ruins were still smouldering and there were slogans daubed over the scorched walls, but there was little to photograph. In the afternoon Ian said he wanted to go out again, but I said I thought it was a dead duck and meant to have some sleep. They got nothing that afternoon, but the city was full of rumours, and in the evening someone handed us a slip of paper with the name DENDALA printed on it in capitals—I have the slip of paper by me as I write.

Dendala, or Dendale, is a suburb of Leopoldville, part of the African quarter and a stronghold of the Bakongo people; Kasavubu, the Congo's President and leader of the numerous Bakongo tribe, obtained his first electoral mandate as Burgomaster of Dendale. The slip had nothing on it except the name, but it seemed as good a lead as any, so Ian and I decided to get up early and go out there next morning, and Barry von Below said he'd like to come along with us. The first taxi we took wanted not only the usual hundred francs an hour, but to be filled up with petrol too, so we ditched him. We were lucky to find another quickly, and doubly lucky that the driver proved to be a tough fellow with a sharp eye, a sense of what journalists are after, and not over-cautious about his taxi or himself. He drove us to Dendale.

Wide tarmac roads; broad dusty fringes, almost the equivalent of another road on each side of the central one; behind that straggled a wall, usually yellowish and made of mud or stucco, occasionally dwindling to a fence, or merging into shops, a bar, a few houses. At right-angles led off dusty unmade tracks, too rough for anything but bicycles, on either side of which were dwellings—usually baked mud with roofs of corrugated iron, but sometimes huts of wattle roofed with matting. Their gardens—if you could call them such, strips of sand for scrawny hens to scratch in—were protected from passers-by with a lattice fence, home-made, or by criss-cross strips of metal looking like old bedsteads up-ended. Sometimes there would be an open court with half a dozen whitewashed houses grouped together, and a yard in which women were washing clothes among a horde of playing children.

Being Sunday, the streets were crowded, partly with women out shopping, partly with people going to church, but mainly with a throng of young men and boys in white shirts or vests with khaki shorts or long grey trousers. Other journalists, I find, have the same impression of the Congo, as peopled by hordes and droves of these white-shirted youths; to-day many of them were carrying sticks, and the air smelled of danger. I caught sight of a spiral of smoke ahead, and directed the driver towards it. It was coming from a brand-new bicycle, lying under a tree with its tyres burning. There was something oddly sinister about this sight—the bicycle burning quietly and the passers-by taking no notice—and I was sure now we should see trouble.

From time to time as we drove along we caught sight of a swirl of movement among the white-clad youth; tension seemed about to canalise into action, but by the time the car got through there was nothing to be seen—and through it all the people went on with their shopping and were flocking steadily into the open-walled churches where mass was being celebrated. A lovely girl, not more than fifteen or sixteen years old, was passing close beside us on the pavement. She wore a white dress and a round white hat, held her little head high and clasped a prayer-book beneath her arm against her tiny waist. I must have been gazing at her with obvious delight, because the driver, turning round from the wheel, called over his shoulder to me: "You want that girl? I get her for you to-night. You tell me where you stay —I go now. . . ."

"My God!" came a shout from Ian. "What's that over there? Quick! Tell him to drive across there—now!"

"Go on up the street and turn," I told the driver. "Then come slowly back down the far side. Keep right into the gutter."

"Quick! Quick! For Christ's sake, hurry!" Barry shouted.

It was a man-hunt.

A big, powerfully built fellow in a white sleeveless vest was running through the crowd, pounding along slowly but determinedly like a Rugby player going through a crowd of would-be tacklers. His pursuers dodged along after him, slashing and beating at him, some with sticks or strips of rubber cut from car tyres, one or two had short iron bars, and everyone, as they saw him coming, joined in with whatever was handy—some even slipping off their shoes to crack him. We were right into the gutter now, keeping slow pace with the runner, Ian and Barry shooting through the open windows. The man was tiring fast, but most of the blows fell glancingly and he kept going. Now he stumbled, coming heavily down on to one knee, but he forced himself up and held on, waving his arms before him like a swimmer. They were throwing stones at him too, not the pebbles boys chuck at one another's heads, but quite big stones, small boulders such as go into an English garden wall. Suddenly somebody ran up and threw a bicycle full in his path; the runner trod on it, slipped, and came crashing down immediately in front of us.

The taxi stopped, and the two cameramen worked feverishly sighting and snapping, then all at once the crowd closed round him. I saw one pursuer run up and kick the fallen man full in the face, another began systematically cutting into his back with a long rubber strip. I realised that they meant to go on hacking away at him till he no longer twitched. Beside myself with rage, I slipped out of the taxi, took two steps to the spot, and stood over the man. "Assez! Assez!" I shouted furiously. "Laissez-le!" I had no feeling at all that the crowd might attack me; on the contrary, I knew quite certainly they wouldn't. But I was afraid they might seize hold of the man, drag him away from me, and finish him off out of my reach. When two or three boys rushed in with their sticks and slashed again, I shouted at them so fiercely that they shrank away. Directly facing me, a yard away, was a Congolese in a blue shirt; I looked at him, he looked at me; I saw he was on my side, and he put up his arms to hold back those nearest to him.

I began to wonder what was to be done next. I could hear Ian and Barry shouting to me from the taxi: "Come back, you bloody fool. You can't do that! Come back!" I thought, we can shove this chap into the back between us and get him off to hospital. I called out something about this. "No! No!" they said. "Come back, for God's sake! The driver won't have him in." I caught sight of the driver: he was laughing heartily. Suddenly, as I hesitated, the hunted man got up; he staggered out into the road, crossed it unharmed, and began to trot, slowly and brokenly, up one of the side-turnings. A few boys followed, hitting at him in a desultory way as if their heart were no longer in it; I followed too for a moment till I felt that he would get away. It was amazing to me that he could still get up and run; his face was a pulpy

"The Man on the Run." Leopoldville, Sunday morning after Independence y, 1960.

mass, with his smashed lips hanging loose, like Sidney's when the cops had hammered him, and his back was striped as if he had been flogged, great dull red scores whose open lips were grey with dust. His blood was splashed over my trousers.

"God, Tom!" said Barry as I slipped back into the car. "You mustn't do that—you're a journalist."

"Well, thank God we're all safe," said Ian as the car slid off. The driver was still laughing.

*   *   *   *   *

We spent the rest of the morning in the African city; as tension heightened we didn't care to be on our own, so attached ourselves to a patrol of military police, four jeeps with about sixteen armed Congolese under control of a Belgian officer. His patrol ran up and down the streets continuously, whenever he saw a man being beaten up he would stop to rescue him, push him into a jeep to be taken to hospital, or, if he were not too badly hurt, tell him to point out his attackers. Several times we were led by such victims into one of the courtyards where half a dozen sullen men would be pointed out, manhandled into a prisoners' cage that followed with us, and hustled off to the police station. They may have been his attackers, or they may have been his father-in-law, or people he had never seen before. There was no time for strict enquiry. One or two of the captured men broke away and made off round corners or up side-streets, but most of them were soon recaptured. An injured man climbed into a jeep and sat down in the front seat, where his bleeding back was staining the upholstery; the officer made a sign to put him in the back seat where there was no upholstery for him to mark.

"How long have you been at this job?" I asked.

"I was called back from my holiday in January, 1959, when the first trouble started. I've hardly had a day off ever since," he said, wearily mopping his strained face.

Suddenly he let out a shout. Dave Snell, a *Time-Life* writer who had joined on to our convoy during the morning, was coming towards us, walking awkwardly, and constantly peering back over his shoulder. Dave was a big, heavily built man; he was wearing shorts and a coloured baseball cap; in one of his two shirt pockets was a row of ball-point pens, in the other a row of cigars. As he came nearer, we could see why he looked so anxiously around, for close behind him rod an evil-looking troll, his steel helmet jammed down over his eyes, his wickedly thin bayonet in the small of Dave Snell's back.

The officer roared a second time. Sullenly, reluctantly, as though robbed of his due booty, the troll slunk off. Dave passed the officer a cigar. "For God's sake," he said to us all, biting off the end, "keep close to me. With me and my men here, you'll be safe. Don't wander off! That little chap was from the Force Publique—their own officers can hardly handle them, and if you get into their hands, there's damn-all I can do for you."

"What's the real cause of the trouble?" I asked, as we rested for a moment by the jeeps. "Why are these particular chaps being hunted by the others?"

"Tribal hostility. . . . The fact is that we Belgians have rather played up tribal differences and encouraged tribal organisation. It makes things easier for the politicians—or they think it does—because they can keep people divided. But it makes life a bloody sight harder for us."

"Why?"

"Because it means that the people never really settle down together. Take this hole Cité Indigène, with its various suburbs such as this one —it's all part of the territory of the Bakongo tribe. It looks just like any African suburb anywhere to you and me, but to them it's their particular tribal land. Into this territory in the last years have been brought thousands of people from other tribes, brought here by the needs of industry. Fellows with some bit of skill—lorry-drivers, machine-operators, builders, or whatever it may be; they find themselves a lodging and settle down. . . . During the week, when everyone's at work, it's okay. But when there's a Sunday or a holiday, trouble starts."

"What usually starts it?"

"Well, you see these chaps we keep on picking up—chaps who've been knocked about, like this one crying now inside the jeep?"

I nodded.

"You notice they're a different type from the others? The Bakongo on the whole are small and slight. As individuals they're docile. When I go like this to a Bakongo"—and he thrust his helmeted face into mine with a grimace—"he's frightened, and gives back. If I'm questioning, he spills the beans. The Bakongo are only dangerous in a mass— these others are mainly Bayakas."

"What are they like?"

"As you see—physically different. Squat, heavily-built, often with a rather brutal expression. They're also individualists—much more courageous, and more arrogant, than the Bakongo. Trouble start because one of them behaves arrogantly or says something tactless; o

9] "The Man on the Run" comes close to our car.

9] The hunters close in for the kill.

else a number of the Bakongo get together into a pack and just turn on any Bayaka they happen to come across. That's where the Bayaka's physical difference is a handicap—they're so easily spotted."

"What d'you do with all the chaps you're pulling in?"

"Take the injured to hospital."

"And the others?"

"Give the trouble-makers a taste of their own medicine." He waved his arm and shouted to his men; we all piled into our vehicles and drove off. Later that morning, when we stopped at a police-station, we got a glimpse of the trouble-makers' "medicine". At the back of the station was a bare space with high walls all round. In the dust, some yard or two apart from one another, squatted perhaps fifty Congolese. Each held a paving-stone over his head. Walking among the ranks were half a dozen uniformed Congolese who delivered a sharp kick to any man who lowered his paving-stone; at the corners three or four more police kept guard with automatic weapons. It was a rough way of dispensing "justice", but it was clearly impossible to bring all these men to trial, or to obtain any evidence if they were tried, and after seeing what I had that morning I felt that at times justice needs to be rough. Most of the men, we were told, would be kept there for a few hours and then sent home. In all, according to the midday radio, some eighty to ninety people had been taken to hospital that morning injured, and some 150–200 arrested. Astonishingly, no one, it seemed, was killed.

As we paid our taxi-driver off and took down his name for future journeys, he shook his head sagely at us: "When things like this are going on continually, where will it all end?"

*　　*　　*　　*　　*

As we sat drinking in the Memling Hotel, where all the journalists met to exchange gossip and keep an eye on one another, Ian and Barry told the story of our morning's activity to one or two others who came up. I was pleased when Ian—who always himself showed complete disregard, almost indeed a total unawareness, of danger when he was working—said, "Craziest thing I've ever seen." This gave me pleasure because I know that one of the qualities most lacking in me is craziness, and that my actions in general are planned and cagey to excess.

However, at this moment of complacency, with my friends around me and a drink in my hand, another picture came into my mind which spoiled the smooth impression.

I was sitting in my car not far from the office; this must have been about a year previously, perhaps even it was exactly a year since anniversaries have a subtle way of forcing themselves on our attention. I had taken refuge in the car from a heavy downpour which was just starting as I walked back from lunch. As I sat there, idly watching the rain lashing against the screen and hearing it hammer down on to the roof, I was aware of a strange little scene. About ten yards from me, leaning against the side of a green bus, an African boy—he might have been nineteen or twenty—was standing, weeping bitterly. He was wearing a lumber jacket. He had a soft, loose-featured face, and he was crying—not just the occasional tear from a screwed-up face of the man in misery or pain—but crying as a child cries, abandoning itself to its own grief.

Occasionally he put his hand up and rubbed the back of his neck as though it hurt him, but I felt he was only doing this to justify his tears, since he was clearly not crying from pain, but from humiliation and despair.

I knew at once what I ought to do, which was to go up and speak to him, tell him to come and sit in the car out of the rain, allow him to recover from this storm of feeling—and then either do anything I could to help him or just let him go on his way. I waited, not quite able to act, but expecting to be able to act in a few moments.

And now I caught sight of the other half of the story, though it was impossible to make out how the two halves were related. Standing in the middle of the road was a little group—they must have been a repair gang dealing with water or electric installations. It consisted of a thin white man in khaki trousers and sports jacket, with three or four rather undersized Africans. They had a red flag on a thin cane and a bundle of tools; they were taking up the metal covers in the road and doing something to them—checking them over possibly. The white man was being jolly with the Africans, as if trying to get them on his side or perhaps to cover up something that had happened, and they were half-responding, half-withdrawn, as though not willing to commit themselves. From time to time the white man glanced not unkindly and not quite apprehensively—more as though he didn't know what to make of it—at the weeping boy. And all the time the rain came streaming down.

In one of his paroxysms, the sobbing boy rolled round so that I could see his back. His lumber jacket was torn from the neck down, but whether the tear were new or old, and whether it had anything to do with his hurt neck, I could not tell; most of the clothes worn by the group were torn and ragged anyway. After a time the white man spoke to one of the Africans, who came over wheeling a bicycle. It seemed to be an official bicycle, as it had two more red flags fastened to the cross-bar and a basket with a parcel in it. The African propped the bicycle against the bus, went up to the one who was crying and spoke to him, but got no answer. Then he noticed the boy's hat lying on the ground among the rain and mud; he picked it up for him and put it on his head, but it fell off. A second time he picked it up and put it on the boy's head, where it remained at an odd angle. The boy took no notice of the hat, no notice of his companion, no notice when the bicycle slipped and crashed over into a puddle. The second African shrugged, turned away, and went back to the others with the bicycle.

All the time I sat there like someone paralysed.

After perhaps ten minutes, as the rain continued to pour down, the little group from the road went over and sheltered with the bicycle, their bundle of tools and their red flag, under the overhanging eaves of a small warehouse. They waited there: I waited. Suddenly the boy jerked himself upright; put his hand once or twice up to his neck, staggered, his limbs loose like a puppet's, and began to run across the road. I expected to see him fall, but instead he gained momentum and ran on, still weeping, up the street and away out of my sight. The white man watched him, half-turned as if to follow him, stayed chatting with the others for a minute, then wheeled and ran off in the same direction—not exactly as if he were following the boy, but as though he had urgent business that way which demanded his attention. . . .

Whatever the little scene had meant, it was all over now.

At the thought of the paralysis which had prevented my breaking in on what was manifestly a complicated drama, too complicated perhaps to be resolved by those entangled in it, I could do nothing the whole afternoon. I sat there idle in my chair, or else walked up and down the room, self-reproaching and distracted.

After work I had a lesson in Afrikaans, which at that time I was trying to learn. Half-way through the lesson I found myself actually unable to speak; no words would come out of my mouth. I fumbled some excuse and went away.

*   *   *   *   *

That evening in Leopoldville, pondering these two incidents, I thought: we are each a confusion of courage and timidity. Even after one has begun to know oneself a little, it is still impossible to know under what circumstances we shall behave in one way or the other. Fortunate is the man to whom it happens that his positive acts are the ones which become public, and whose cowardice, blunders, cruelties and treacheries remain private to himself and to those on whom they were inflicted.

CHAPTER XXXI

TSHOMBE'S NEW STATE

TWO DAYS AFTER we got back to Johannesburg came the full-scale revolt of the Force Publique.

"That settles it," said Ian. "No one'll look at all the stuff we took three days ago. It'll have been knocked right out. Did you see Barry von Below's picture of the nuns crouched under the doodah at the Leopoldville airport? God Almighty—I knew we ought really to stay on."

"I couldn't stay on anyway," I said. "We shall only just get the next issue pushed through as it is. But what d'you want to do now?"

"Go back, of course. Soonest possible."

"Well, cable your agents and see if they can get backing for the costs. If they fix that up, we might get away next week."

Ian's series of pictures taken on the troubled Sunday morning had been the best-selling series of that week, and I was pretty sure Ian's agents would want him to return. I hesitated to suggest the idea to Dorothy; however, she said at once: "You do what you think best. I don't like your going, but it's entirely for you to decide."

By the time we were due to leave, Tshombe had declared the Katanga independent, there had been riots in the capital, Elisabethville, and the Belgians were now pouring out of there as confusedly as they had poured out of Leopoldville a week earlier. "Magnum", the agency for which Ian was working, cabled from Paris urging him to go this time to Katanga, offering substantial guarantees, and asking that if possible I should go with him again. *Drum's* South African edition for August had just been completed; by a lucky arrangement of timetables there was a ten-day gap before the printers would start needing copy for the two West African editions, and so, just before the middle of July, we were off again.

At Ndola, in Northern Rhodesia, the airport was flooded with refugees, mainly women and children on their way to Salisbury, from where they would be flown direct to Brussels. The Rhodesians had set up a system of emergency aid, and there were feeding arrangements for grown-ups and children, and rest-rooms with doctors and nurses in attendance. Ian took a number of shots as we hung around waiting for a plane to take us on, and I chatted with some of the people who were leaving. As is natural when people take the painful decision to abandon their homes, they were concerned to impress on us the dangers from which they were escaping. Two favourite stories were of a small boy who had been cut in half by a Force Publique soldier, and of "six Greek shopkeepers" who had been "hanged from lamp-posts" in a suburb of Elisabethville. I was never able to investigate the story of the small boy, but I learned the truth about the six Greek shopkeepers in a day or two.

At Elisabethville airport, which we reached in the late afternoon, there were again crowds of refugees. All customs and immigration services had broken down; arriving passengers collected their own luggage and looked around for some means of getting into town; would-be departing passengers—some of whom had driven in hundreds of miles with whatever possessions they could load into their cars—sat disconsolately about on suitcases waiting for planes or information. This breakdown of the usual formalities seemed a blessing at the time; later it would prove one among many factors that would land us in trouble.

A bus took us into town where we got a room at the Léo Deux; the hotel had been practically taken over by journalists and has remained a journalists' headquarters ever since. It was functioning quite well, but the town was practically empty. Shops were closed; there were guards on the post office and radio station; armed patrols moved continuously about the streets. There were no women to be seen, or so few that everyone turned and gazed at each one as she passed to see whether she were worth gazing at or not. An early curfew was in force, but hearing there was to be a meeting that night of the Provincial House of Assembly—a rumour which was quite untrue—Ian and I set out to walk there through the darkness. The streets were totally deserted and completely dark, so it was not long before we were rounded up and taken off to the police station. In the yard, as we were escorted inside, I caught a glimpse of a scene that would have made a most telling photograph—but it was far too dark to shoot, also we felt we were in enough difficulty for the moment without adding to it needlessly.

In the open courtyard, about seven yards away from us and shadowy as ghosts in the faint light reflected off the walls, four Africans were kneeling with their hands over their heads. As many black police kept watch over them with Sten-guns, their fingers on the triggers. All around were stacked piles of miscellaneous goods, furniture, kitchen

utensils, radios, a heap of bicycles—recovered loot with four appre-
hended looters. We were soon on easy terms with the four or five
sweaty-faced and exhausted Belgian officers, and I arranged with one
that he would take us on his midnight rounds of the Cité Indigène.
From Ian's point of view it was a wasted night. Rioting had been
checked, and in the whole city of darkness we saw not a gleam from
any door or window; the sole sign of movement picked up in our headlights were two gloomily copulating dogs. Outside numbers of the
houses stood piles of goods carefully stacked as if to be collected by
removal men. "Loot!" the officer told us. "Four days ago they sacked
those shops I showed you on the main road. We shot a few looters
and got things under control, and now people are frightened we shall
come round and search their homes. So they bring out their loot and
stack it at street corners, and we drive round with lorries and pick
it up."

I asked him about the six Greek shopowners.

"All nonsense!" he said. "No one has been hanged, and so far only
one white person has been killed inside E'ville. That was the Italian
consul. When the looting started, some Italians appealed to him over
the telephone for help. He went rushing out there in his car. The
rebels (Force Publique men who had revolted were generally referred
to by the Belgians as 'the rebels') had a post on the corner, they opened
fire on him with automatic weapons and practically cut the poor chap
in half. His car burst into flames. I'll show you the skid-marks and the
burns in the road on the way back."

I got an excellent impression of the Belgian officer, in all but one
respect—and in that one, I thought, might lie the explanation as to
how it was possible for the Force Publique, on whose loyalty the whole
security of the Congo had so obviously depended, to be in a state of
imminent revolt, while the officers remained quite unaware of the true
situation; and, on the very eve of the mutiny, at an American Fourth
of July party, its Commander, General Janssens, could make such a
fatuous statement as: "The Force Publique? It is my creation. It is
absolutely loyal. I have made my dispositions."* Three days after
making it, he had been dismissed and left the country, a bewildered
man.

Our officer was tough, fearless, systematic, even-tempered; an
admirable officer in all respects but one. He lacked contact with his
men, and quite clearly did not think it necessary, or perhaps even
proper, for him to have any. Part of his work that night as he drove

* Quoted by Frank Barker: *South Africa in Exile*, Vol. 5. No. 1.

us round was to call in on various sub-police stations and small outposts, to hear how things were going. In most of them there would
be perhaps a dozen Congolese soldier-police under a sergeant. We
would drive straight into the courtyard; a man on guard would turn
out and call the sergeant; a few routine questions would be asked, and
we would be on our way.

But at no point was there anything approaching human contact.
These men, after all, were alone in their small outpost, in a city which
had been torn with riots a few days before, and where at any time
fresh trouble might break out—trouble in which it was all-important
to the whites that these police should be on their side against natural
sympathy with their own countrymen. Yet never was there one
question which showed interest or concern for the men themselves—
as to whether they'd had their food, or were glad of a quiet night, or
any of the questions which a natural sympathy might suggest; nor
was there any sign of friendly recognition between man and man—
they might have been enemy outposts which he was inspecting. I was
to be struck by the same thing a year later when travelling round big
agricultural estates and factories in remote parts of the Congo where
two or three Belgians, unarmed, would have charge of an area containing tens of thousands of Congolese. A dozen times then I noticed
a Congolese—perhaps in charge of a machine being demonstrated to
me, or of some particular operation on an estate—waiting after doing
what he was asked, waiting and visibly hoping for a friendly word,
a nod or a smile from the Belgian showing me round; waiting, but
very rarely getting it. Yet the same Belgian manager would assure me:
"Our relations with our Congolese employees are excellent. They are
all delighted to have us back."

On the whole, I believe, the record has been unjust to the Belgians
in the Congo, who had done a lot more for the country in the way of
education, health services, agricultural development and so on, than
they were given credit for. But much of this practical work was under-
mined by a monumental tactlessness in human contacts, which extended right up from the poorest colon scratching a living on his plot
to the highest state officials.

*   *   *   *   *

At Jadotville, eighty miles away, there had been fighting and heavy
looting. Peter Younghusband, who had left *Drum* to take up an
excellent offer from the London *Daily Mail*, had been the first journalist to get into the town, having made his way in the same day we

arrived. After hearing his account, Ian and I decided to try to cadge a lift out there next day, and luckily in the morning we found a shop-keeper who was driving back. He had left during the looting four days earlier, but was returning now in a jeep with a couple of friends to salvage what he could. We were welcome, he told us, to the ride, but we must trust to luck as to how we should get back since he would be staying on in Jadotville.

It was a strange journey. Every now and then along the road we would pass a burned-out car or an abandoned jeep. "When the Force Publique revolted they seized all the transport they could get hold of, but a lot of them couldn't drive—or else they ran out of petrol, or there was no oil so the bearings seized. Then they just left it by the road-side." At Luisha, fifty kilometres from Jadotville, was a hospice out in the bush, to which the priests and monks from Jadotville retreated: "There is an old priest in charge there, a Biblical-looking old chap with a white beard who has been there fifty years. When trouble started the natives all came to him and asked what they were to do. He told them they were to be good and keep quiet. So they did. . . ."

Closer to Jadotville, the signs of trouble grew more frequent. A dead Alsatian was lying in the road. Patrols of paratroops in their dull red berets and camouflage jackets were searching all cars for arms.

"Why are they doing that?" I asked. "Surely one needs a weapon or two at a time like this?"

"Some of the people they are stopping are like myself—owning a home or a business in the town. One or two of the first people who went back and saw what had been done just ran wild; they wanted to kill every black man they saw. So now everyone going back has to be disarmed."

The Congolese we passed on the road seemed friendly enough, many of them stopped and waved. "Ah!" said our driver. "When we drove out on Monday, the natives were all shaking their fists at us and cursing. Now they have no money and no food, since they have already looted all the shops, so they start welcoming us back."

A few kilometres outside the town we passed a prison, the biggest prison in the Congo, our driver told us. "When the rioting started, all the prisoners were let out. They rushed off, but in two days most of them were back again—they wanted their three meals a day. . . . The Prime Minister, Lumumba, was imprisoned there. He was there for embezzlement. The Special Police used to talk to him and keep a record of his sayings; one of the things he said was: 'Either I shall swallow the whole of the Congo, or I shall destroy the whole of the Congo.'"

"What did he mean by that, d'you suppose?" I asked.

"Oh," answered our guide, "it was just his arrogance."

Inside the town a good many shops had been burned and looted; our guide—who had a stationer's and bookseller's shop—had suffered less than most. He had an excellent Congolese assistant, he said, who had stayed on the spot and saved everything he could; but he kept calling our attention to the fact that the looters had taken all the expensive fountain-pens and wrist-watches, while leaving him with the games of ludo and the rag-books for babies, as though, if they had had any sense of looting decency, they would have done the opposite.

We found one man, at a jeweller's shop, in tears. "Six million francs' worth of goods stolen—one million francs' worth of goods left. And what's left is grandfather clocks and fish-knives, which I can't sell any-way . . . and my boss says he will hold me responsible for the loss. . . ." He put his head against the battered lintel, and shook with sobs.

After a while we started looking for a lift home, and were lucky to find one. As we drove out, the tide had set the other way. Dozens of cars were coming in in convoys. The drivers had taken their wives and children to Ndola, and were coming back to protect their pro-perty. Beside the paratroops' searching points there were mounds of arms the size of hay-cocks.

*   *   *   *   *

We stayed on a few days in Elisabethville. Having found out that large numbers of the rebels were being held at two points, we managed to wangle our way in and get some pictures. Some hundreds, perhaps fifteen hundred or two thousand, were being held in the open on a sports ground. They made a strange impression, all in a uniform that looked like denim overalls, confined by a loose roll of barbed wire such as might be used to keep cows off a cricket-pitch. But outside the wire walked soldiers with automatic weapons, and machine-guns were sighted on them from scoreboards and press-boxes. The men had nothing to do but sit there in the sun; their hair was full of little bits of grass from lying down to rest. Though bored to desperation, they seemed on tolerable terms with their Belgian guards; there was a pipe of water continually flowing for anyone who wanted a drink, and one or two of the guards obligingly played it over the heads and shoulders of those who asked for cooling.

Ian, having taken all the close-ups he wanted, slipped up into the grandstand, and secured two or three of the finest pictures he took on this trip, showing the whole body of prisoners huddled together with bowed heads, and the dozen or so guards standing over them. Meantime, chatting around, I had heard that there was another mass of prisoners confined out at the airfield in an empty hangar, so we drove out there quickly. At first everyone denied that there were any prisoners on the airfield, and ordered us to clear off, but we chose a route for leaving which led us past the various hangars, and drove slowly.

"Stop a minute!" I told the driver, and when the engine was switched off we could hear it—the whole hangar seemed to be vibrating as if full of angry bees. We got out of the car and after a minute or two found an officer, showed him our permit to photograph the men on the sports ground, and managed to convince him that it applied to the men in the hangar too. It was packed to bursting; from time to time the sliding doors would be rolled back a couple of feet, and two or three men allowed out to the latrine or to get a drink of water, always under guard. These were more of "the rebels", who had turned on their officers a few days before, been got under control and disarmed, and were now waiting to be shipped off in trains to the country district from which they had originally been recruited. Later, when Tshombe issued a national call to arms to resist the United Nations, most of them would come flocking back—"rebels" no longer—to be issued with the same weapons which had been taken from them, and to resume their military careers where they had left off.

Every afternoon at about three we assembled at Tshombe's villa for his daily Press Conference. Usually he would be inside talking with some of his Ministers—of whom Munongo, the sleek, powerful Minister of the Interior, was always one—or else closeted with Colonel Weber, the Belgian parachute commander who was credited with having "put down the revolt". After hanging around for a while, one of us would put a head round the door to say we were ready now, or else Dicky Williams, the B.B.C. correspondent, would write a note on a card and send it in. Dicky had a kind of unofficial seniority among us, partly as representing the B.B.C., partly because he was known to be excellent at his job, and partly because he spoke better French.

Conferences were short and informal. Tshombe, smartly dressed and easy-mannered, would welcome us all, and then read—with manifest interest at times as to what was coming next—his own typewritten communiqué for the day. Then there would be questions, which he dealt with or diverted easily. He was loquacious, natural, charming—

his face full of expression when he talked or argued, but going quite
dead and empty in repose, as I have noticed many African faces do;
as if requiring a call to action in order to be reinhabited by its own
vitality. There was often a contradiction too between his features; he
would smile with lips or eyes while his forehead wrinkled in a frown.
Usually the figure of Munongo would be standing, silent and formidable, at his elbow.

One day we were let into the conference room before the President
arrived. On his desk was a huge piece of cardboard with thirty or so
small flags painted on it in colour. They were not the flags of existing
countries; clearly they must be suggestions—from whom or where?—
for the new flag of Katanga. A couple of days later we attended a brief
ceremony—the formal christening, if that is the right word, of the
new state. It took place in a military barracks just on the edge of the
city, its offices and buildings still scarred with bullet-holes and chippings
from the "revolt" a week before. Inside the barracks some fifty or so
Katangese soldiers were drawn up on three sides of a square. On the
other side stood Tshombe and the indispensable Munongo in formal
dress, with ourselves in a straggling row behind them. In the centre
was a flagstaff and attached to a rope was the chosen flag, an affair of
red, green and white with three copper-coloured crosses to represent
—we all immediately whispered to each other—"the controlling
interest of Union Minière". The flag had obviously been stitched
together the night before from patches of different coloured material.

At a signal from President Tshombe, the new flag was run up. Half
a dozen Katangese soldiers—they were the only ones allowed to carry
arms—fired a ragged volley into the air, closely watched by a dozen
Belgian officers with their hands on their revolvers. A Belgian radio-
man with a tape-recorder came up to Tshombe and asked him for a
speech: "This is a great, indeed a historic, occasion," said the President,
"marking the birth of our new state of Katanga. May it live long and
enjoy prosperity." Disappointed, the radio-man turned to Munongo
and asked him for a speech. "I can add little," said Munongo, "to
what our great President has said. This is a great, indeed a historic
occasion, witnessing the birth of our new state. May it live long and
enjoy prosperity." There was a watery cheer for Katanga and another
for Tshombe. A small military band struck up, and we drifted away
to our hotel. The new republic had been born.

*   *   *   *   *

At the next Press Conference somebody asked with concealed irony:
"Now that Katanga has a flag, will it also be getting its own coinage?"

It was Munongo who replied brusquely: "Coins, postage stamps— the lot!"

After the Conference was over, Ian and I decided to go in and see Colonel Weber. We felt we had got all that was likely to be going in Elisabethville for some weeks, and we didn't want to waste the few days we had left. If we could get Weber to talk, perhaps he would give us an idea of where trouble might still be found. The parachute colonel made an impressive figure, grey hair, grey eyes, tanned skin, a smooth face sloping forward to his powerful chin. He had the air of genial brutality common to many successful soldiers, making you feel that if he had to shoot you he would do it with a handshake and a smile. We started by asking him about his position in an independent Katanga. He had it all quite clear.

"I am not under the control of President Tshombe. I am under the control of my home government in Belgium. For the present my government has told me to obey whatever orders President Tshombe may give me, so I do so. If my government gives me different orders to-morrow, I shall obey those too. At this moment I wish to go to Brussels. I should like to see the King in order to explain my work here, and ask his permission to continue. . . ."

We asked about the military situation. "In Katanga all is quiet. My troops are going out from all centres. . . . The revolt is now under control. . . . The rebels are being disbanded. . . ."

"What do you believe was the cause of the revolt?" I enquired.

"It was Lumumba who inspired and fomented it," the colonel answered. "We have definite evidence in our hands. The revolt of the Force Publique was organised by Lumumba."

As the revolt had done more than any one thing to harm Lumumba's position, and as in its early days he had rushed desperately around with Kasavubu, trying at the risk of his life to calm it down, and insisting —until it became hopeless to do so any longer—on the appointment of Belgians to key defence posts, this seemed to me a most unlikely action for Lumumba to have taken. I did not, however, raise the question; instead I asked: "If all is now quiet in the Katanga, that implies there is trouble elsewhere. Where would you say is the most troubled spot at this moment?"

"At Luluabourg in the Kasai things are not too good," the colonel told us. Ian kicked my ankle; the kick meant—"Don't waste any more time being polite. We've got what we came for. The problem will be to find a plane going to Luluabourg. Pack all this in and let's get started."

It had been a pleasant interview. There are people who like the company of journalists and those who detest us. Both Weber and Tshombe in different ways, I felt, liked having journalists around. It gave them a pleasing sense of having a part to play, of being at the centre of world interest; and in return they treated pressmen with good temper and consideration. This may have influenced journalists more than it should to clothe the toy state of Katanga with an appearance of reality.

CHAPTER XXXII

"I THINK YOU ARE BELGIAN SPIES"

"PEOPLE AREN'T GOING to Luluabourg any more—they're getting out," the man in the Sabena office told us.

"Will there be a plane?"

"I don't know if there'll be a plane; but if there is, you won't have any trouble getting on it."

There was a plane. It flew the 700-odd miles to Luluabourg in a series of short hops. Two newsreel men had had the same idea and travelled with us. Nominally rivals, working for different Continental programmes, they had reached a friendly understanding; neither was to take any unnecessary risk, and they would work out their expenses together in case their bosses happened to know each other and check up. . . . "I say, have you had a man in the Congo, Frans?" "Yes, Hans." "Well, what has he charged you for the flight to Luluabourg?" . . . I don't know whether they imagined it just like that, but at least they thought it best to be on the safe side.

Of all the confused situations in the Congo, that at Luluabourg in mid-July was one of the most complicated and explosive. Luluabourg, a tiny modern city with a huge hut-town of Africans a mile away, is the capital of the Kasai, the most central of the six provinces making up the ex-Belgian Congo. Political control, following the May general election, was in the hands of the supporters of Lumumba, but the whole state was split by the great tribal feud—strong in several other provinces but dominating everything in the Kasai—between the Balubas and the Luluas. The Luluas, a proud but rather primitive people, had clung to their early way of life. When the Belgians came the Luluas wanted nothing to do with them, their organisation, or the religion they brought with them. The Balubas have been called "the Jews" of the Congo. Alert, intelligent, adaptable, they made friends with the invaders, learned all they could from them, and had soon become the clerks, foremen, telephone operators, machine minders—the holders of the best-paid jobs and the manipulators, under the Belgians, of much administrative power in a host of minor ways. This powerful position gained by the Balubas, partly through hard work and partly through their close cohesion and mutual support, had long been resented by the Luluas, who now—with the departure of the Belgians—feared they were going to be dominated by a people who had formerly been their slaves, and were determined to take action first.

The revolt of the Force Publique, running like wildfire across the Congo, broke out in Luluabourg as well. The rebels attacked the Europeans, who shut themselves into a big office building in the heart of the town and suffered for a day or two a kind of desultory siege. Then, a few days before Ian and I arrived, the Belgian paras had come in. They had dropped into the bush a few miles away and converged on the airport, which they seized. They had pushed on into the town, raised the "siege" of the Europeans, escorted all who wished to leave out to the airport—from which they were flown off by degrees—and then dug themselves in. The fact that the "siege" had not been wholly bloodthirsty was shown by the fact that some fifty men and two women had refused to be evacuated; they had made a hotel in the middle of the town their headquarters, and at this time seldom ventured out of it except in cars, several at a time, and armed.

There was extreme resentment in the town over the action of the paras, who—said the Congolese—had created a military operation where none was necessary, with a loss of Congolese life that could easily have been avoided. The paras in their pits and trenches had exactly the opposite opinion; they felt themselves to be the defenders of white civilisation against hordes of mutinous barbarians, and were only disappointed that the hordes seemed reluctant to fling themselves against their automatic weapons. That was the picture the men held; the officers, who had contact with Belgian officers of the Force Publique —a number of whom were courageously continuing to live in camp with their men, though not allowed to exercise command—had received from them a view of the situation which was more confused, and therefore closer to reality. Between the Belgians on the airfield and the Congolese five miles away in the city there was at this time virtually no contact except for the visits of these Force Publique officers; there was talk of running joint patrols of paratroops and Force Publique through the city for the sake of guaranteeing order, but as both sides distrusted each other profoundly these plans had so far come to nothing.

On our arrival we reported to the Commandant. He warned us strongly against going into the town, except possibly in a jeep with an escort of his men for a quick in-and-out glimpse, and hospitably said he would find us a blanket and probably something to eat later on.

We thanked him for his offer, which I had already made up my mind not to accept, for we should obviously get no pictures and little idea of what was going on by sitting on the airfield. We therefore started to look around.

On the airport's control tower a couple of machine-gun posts had been established, and from the top we saw an unexpected sight. Though there were only fifty Europeans left in the town, there were hundreds of cars lined up below us. We went down to examine them, and the cars told their own story. They were mainly new, for the owners had been prosperous; a number had only a few thousand miles on the speedometers. Some were not locked; a few had the ignition keys still in position. A number, dusty or spattered with mud, must have come hundreds of miles on their last drive; others looked as though they had been washed down that morning—and almost every one was full of luggage. Clearly the refugees had loaded all they could into their cars, only to find on reaching the airport that they could only take a small allowance on the planes.

Suitcases lay open on the back seats, the contents scattered all about in the search, perhaps, for some special possession; women's clothes and shoes; baskets of food; children's books and toys, a huge teddy bear; some had hopefully brought large trunks and packing-cases half across the province, only to abandon them here at the last minute. From the condition of the cars one could see something of their owners' state of mind. The majority had simply been parked and left there—"we shall never come back; someone might as well have our belongings". Others were locked and the windows wound up, as if the owner half expected to come back before long and drive away. A few had been deliberately driven into each other and remained, with shattered windscreens, clinging fast to each other's bumpers like boxers in a clinch. And just one or two drivers had evidently gone round with hammers or tyre-levers, doing all the wrecking they could before they left.

"What'll become of them all?" we asked a paratroop.

"God knows!" he said. "You can take one if you like, as far as I'm concerned. The only thing is you won't have any papers for it. You may get shot as a looter somewhere along the line—and suppose you get it to the border, you've *still* got no papers. They may haul you up there for having pinched it. Take a chance if you like, but I doubt if it's worth the risk."

Just on the edge of the airfield, at the farthest point reached by the paratroops' patrols, there was a small hotel in a clump of trees and bushes. It was called "The Oasis". Before the flight, it had evidently been the favourite place for Luluabourgers seeking a gay time; it had a restaurant with a dance floor; a cinema and a night-club; and there were chalets in the grounds for those who had reasons for not going home. I suggested to the others that we should all stay at "The Oasis" instead of dossing down in the airport building. We should have a bed and a bath, possibly a decent meal, and if we took two rooms next to one another between the four of us, we could probably look after ourselves; we had been warned that Congolese—as well as paratroop —patrols visited "The Oasis", and that a night or two before three Belgian civilians staying there had been dragged out of their rooms and beaten up.

We agreed to stay there and got a lift down in a jeep. The Greek proprietor welcomed us in. We noticed that the half-dozen cars parked outside his door had all had their tyres stabbed through with bayonets, and the proprietor told us that two evenings previously when the Congolese came round he had hidden in the loft and only been saved by the action of his Congolese steward, who called out to the soldiers to come and have a drink on the house, at the very moment when they were starting to go up into the loft with their bayonets. After a couple of drinks, happily, they had forgotten their intention of visiting the loft.

We enjoyed a bath, a meal and sleep with no interference from out-side, and when Ian and I appeared for breakfast next morning the two newsreel men were already hard at work.

"What are you charging for lunch on the way up?"

"It was free. They gave it to us on the plane."

"I know—but you've got to put down *something*."

"Say a hundred and fifty francs."

"Okay—plus fifty for drinks, eh? What are we paying at this place?"

"Two-fifty a night."

"Better make that five hundred, don't you think? Otherwise the balance of everything else gets upset. . . . Plus another fifty for phone calls, and fifty for odds-and-sods?"

"Now—hire of car for going into Luluabourg. . . . What are you putting down for that?"

"But we agreed last night that we wouldn't try to go into town. You haven't changed your mind, have you?"

"No, of course not—and there aren't any cars to hire anyway, if it comes to that. But it would look the natural thing to hire a car—and after all we didn't *ask* the ruddy companies to send us here."

Having had a Puritan upbringing, I find myself rather got down by the expenses racket, so I made a sign to Ian—who was just finishing his coffee—to slip away and join me outside.

"I can't take this any longer."

"What d'you think we should do?"

"Go on into town."

"But we've no transport."

"I can fix that. We'll stand by the roadside a couple of hundred yards up, where our friends here won't see us, and thumb a lift into Luluabourg. There are certain to be cars going in with people who have jobs, or lorries with vegetables—or something. The important thing is they must be Congolese, not whites, for getting us past the search-points."

"Okay," said Ian. "Just let me grab my cameras and I'm with you."

We hadn't long to wait. The first car we thumbed slowed down for us; it was full already, but the Congolese moved up to make room; I at once told them who we were and what we were doing, knowing that if we were questioned at the search-points it would all have to come out, and it would help them if they could declare that we'd told them the same story. Twice we were stopped by patrols, but each time the driver vouched for us and we got through. He put us down at the "white" hotel in the middle of Luluabourg, and, not for the first or last time from a Congolese, I was shown real kindness.

"I don't know how you're going to get back," he said. "How do you think you can manage it?"

"We don't. We're hoping for the best."

"Well—I'll be going out again around mid-day. You and your friend be here at half-past twelve, and I'll take you out with me."

I thanked him and shook hands. It was just nine o'clock. Half-past twelve seemed a very long way off.

*   *   *   *   *

Talking it over, Ian and I had made up our minds that the first thing we must do was to secure some kind of permit, which we would then pin on to our shirts. By looking preoccupied and walking quickly, as if late for an important appointment, a journalist can usually get by unnoticed, or at least unstopped. But taking pictures is a different matter; first, it's obvious, and, second, it's suspect. Walking up the street, Ian with his cameras under his jacket, every face stopped and turned; I could see them in the shop windows without looking round. But there were very few faces, and not many shop windows. No shop was open, and many had their windows either boarded up or broken. In a quarter of a mile of the main boulevard we didn't pass twenty people; all Congolese; all men; all in white shirts and shorts. Everyone stared at us, and no one smiled.

At the first military post we stopped to tell our story. Here there were a dozen soldiers with two jeeps and some automatic rifles. We asked for "Monsieur le Capitaine", who proved to be a sergeant-major, bespectacled, with a small Hitler moustache, but friendly and glad to smoke a cigarette. All we want, we say, is a permit to walk quietly about the streets of this handsome city for an hour or two and take one or two photographs of the principal sights, in order to show the outside world that all is calm.

"Photographs? But this is certainly a matter for the colonel, and not one to be decided by a non-commissioned officer."

Taken to the colonel in a jeep, I show him the one copy of *Drum* I have brought with me, and explain what it is we want. The colonel asks if he may keep the magazine, to which I agree—an agreement we regret later in the day. He then tells us that permission to take photographs is not a military but a political decision, and can only be obtained at the main Government offices. There, after much argument, it is decided that we have to see M. le Ministre des Affaires Intérieures himself. After half an hour's wait, M. Luhata sees us. We are now in a much colder climate. M. Luhata is a highly intelligent and capable young man. But he is also suspicious. He takes down all particulars, asks us to hand over our passports, and says he will consult the President and let us know. May we take a picture of the Minister? No. If any pictures are to be taken, it will be proper to begin by taking the President first.

We wait an hour, an hour and a half. The sky has become overcast, and suddenly there is a crack of thunder overhead, followed by another, and a heavy downpour. Now from the gardens outside the Government buildings comes the echo of a shot. Then half a dozen more. We make an excuse and go to the windows; a few dozen white-shirted Congolese are rushing up the street, away towards the country, out of town. Two jeeps race by with automatic weapons ready.

"Hell!" says Ian. "They're starting a bloody war out there. Let's go down and see what's happening."

"Better not move just yet. We're being looked at with suspicion."

Another quarter of an hour's wait, and we are sent for. M. Mukenge, President of the Kasai, a slightly-built young man with a sardonic face, sits at a big desk at the end of a long room. The Minister of the Interior sits at a corner of the desk facing him. Between the two is a young man whom I take to be a clerk, but who is—it soon appears—a Security Officer. We are waved to seats, and told to tell our story. Everything I say the President notes down. It is not an encouraging beginning.

"You tell me," the President asks, "that you were in Leopoldville two weeks ago?" I nod. "But you have no stamp in your passport for Leopoldville. How is that?"

I am certain there must be a stamp, but this is a passport on which I have travelled constantly in Africa for the last two and a half years; it is full of stamps, and, not expecting to do much reading, I have left my glasses at the hotel. I can only gaze blankly at the pages. At last Ian finds the stamp, almost invisible against a whole page visa for the Congo obtained a month ago in Johannesburg.

"Ah!" says the President. "*Now* I begin to understand! You are really South Africans calling yourselves 'English'. What contacts have you been having with the Belgians?"

I explained that we arrived in Elisabethville five days ago and came up to the Kasai only last night.

"Then where are your stamps for entry at Elisabethville?"

Now we are getting really entangled. I explain that, when we landed at E'ville, there was such confusion owing to the departure of refugees, that no passports were being stamped: it sounds so thin, I almost wonder myself if it is true.

Now the President turns his attention to Ian Berry's passport. Ian— a handsome young man of twenty-six with a beard and wavy hair—is represented in his passport by a fat-cheeked, pop-eyed boy in his teens. The President tosses it down with a sarcastic laugh. "Why! It does not even begin to look like the same person. It is an insult to us to pretend that this is a genuine passport belonging to that man."

Once again, in the most fluent French I can manage, I make excuses. My friend is a young man. Until a year or two ago he was a student and found it convenient to travel as a student; this is a picture of him from those days. It's true, I concede, that it doesn't look much like him now, and we ought perhaps to have had it renewed—however, we were forced to leave in a hurry—and so on.

"And what paper do you say you represent?"

"The magazine *Drum*. It is published mainly in South Africa, with editions also in Ghana and Nigeria."

"There—I said you were South Africans! What kind of a magazine is this which is published in Johannesburg?"

Patiently I explain: *Drum* is a magazine mainly for Africans; though published in South Africa, it supports their interests and deals with their activities. I had a copy with me, but it was taken by a colonel at one of his military posts; if the President cares to send for it, he can prove what I am saying. Travelling for this magazine, I have met on friendly terms many of the present-day African leaders—M. Nyerere, M. Mboya, Chief Luthuli—only the other day my friend and I had the pleasure of meeting and photographing M. Lumumba.

"Again what you tell is absurd. There can be no magazine which supports the Africans published in Johannesburg. The South African government would not allow it—that is obvious to anyone. I believe you are Belgian spies. Where did you and your companion spend last night? With the Belgian soldiers on the airfield?"

"No. We stayed just outside the town, at the Oasis Hotel."

"Good. We shall check up."

I feel nothing but relief as the President himself dials the Oasis; now at last some part of our story is going to be confirmed. Exactly the opposite happens. The manager of the Oasis, scenting trouble, takes the safe course—and denies that we ever slept there.

"There were two English journalists here for dinner, but they went away afterwards and did not spend the night."

The President turns to us with scorn. Clearly, he thinks, we are not only spies but clumsy ones.

All I can do now is start talking. Let him send one of his men back to the hotel with us immediately. We will show him our room with our luggage still in it; our names must be in the hotel register. Then, feeling we are getting deeper and deeper into difficulties, I let fly.

Why are we being treated like this, I demand? Why, when we have taken the trouble to come and see the Congolese side of things, are we being persecuted? Nothing would be easier for us than to sit in the airport and write about murder and violence in Luluabourg. There are other journalists who never leave the airport; instead we have decided to come and find out for ourselves. Does the President really wish that all accounts of events in the Kasai should be written from the Belgian airport—if so, he need not be surprised if they take a Belgian point of view. We are two English journalists of good standing, living and working in South Africa. We have not come to the Congo out of hostility, but because we wish to know and tell the truth. If this is the reception to be expected, then I think other journalists will be wise to stay away and make up their stories at a safe distance. We acted in good faith in presenting ourselves to his military outpost. Now we ask for some good faith in return.

For the first time we feel a small response. The President says that he will give us one more chance; we have spoken of photographing M. Lumumba two weeks ago in Leopoldville. He will phone through to M. Lumumba and enquire. . . . We've had it now, I think. How can the Prime Minister of the Congo—who must have talked to 150 journalists at least during Independence week—possibly remember Ian Berry and myself, with whom he was present for perhaps ten minutes among a number of diplomats?

But our luck is turning. Somewhere along the line there is a strike of telephone operators, and the President cannot be put through. He himself is still suspicious, but the other two, the Security man and the Minister of the Interior, have come round invisibly, mysteriously, to our side. Neither of them says a word, but we all feel the division. Four people round the desk now think we are not spies: four to one, instead of three to two. The President says nothing. He rings a bell, and his *chef de cabinet* brings in a folder of official papers; ignoring the rest of us, he starts to sign. The telephone rings: "No!" he shouts. "All that *bagarre* this morning was nothing but a scare. No bombs were dropped —it was thunder. The Belgians remain quietly at the airport. There are some of our army who are soldiers—but there are *others* . . ." He leaves the rest unsaid and goes back to signing papers.

He signs the last one, then turns to his *chef de cabinet*. "These two English journalists may go round the town and take pictures in the streets. They will be accompanied by two soldiers to see that there are no incidents. But they are not to come back into the town once they have left. To-morrow they must leave the Kasai. You will be personally responsible. To-morrow!" A pause, and then he adds: "But first you are to give them something to eat." He holds out a hand. We see for the first time something like a smile, and we are dismissed.

*　　*　　*　　*　　*

For two or three hours we are driven around in a jeep. Apart from a few families of Balubas making their getaway with furniture piled high on to shaky lorries or the roofs of aged cars with boiling radiators, there is little to see and less to photograph. The railway station is thronged with Balubas too, most of whom seem to be making for the South Kasai, where Kalonji has set up his short-lived "Diamond State", to which refugees from other provinces are already pouring in. Long before six o'clock curfew we are set down by our guide at "The Oasis"—and here the grimmest joke of the day is still in store for us. We go to our room to wash; all our belongings have been

removed and there is no sign that we have ever stayed here. I go over
to the office and look in the register; if our names were ever entered
last night when we filled in various forms for the proprietor, they have
now been removed.

We ask for our two newsreel acquaintances. They left for the airport, we are told, having learned that we had been arrested. At the
proprietor's suggestion, they took all our things with them "for
safety". So, if we had come back to the hotel under escort, in order
to point out our luggage as proof of our stay, we should have found
a completely empty room.

★   ★   ★   ★   ★

We slept that night at the airport, Ian on the counter where they
normally issue tickets, I in two deck-chairs. Late in the afternoon we
cadged a lift in a paratroop plane to Kamina, the great military base,
where the Belgians put us up for the night and gave us food. During
the meal—which was in a huge mess seating hundreds—a Belgian Air
Force officer suddenly ran wild, and began hitting and kicking the
Congolese stewards. His friends soon sat him down again, and one of
them told us what had happened. A plane bringing in troops, and
piloted by one of his friends, had been shot down by chance rifle fire
up in the north of the province. This officer had been sent up with
others to bring in the bodies—which he found stripped and mutilated.
Now, in a delayed reaction, he attacked the first black man he saw. . . .

And so by troop and cargo-planes we got back to Elisabethville,
and then on more normally to Salisbury and Johannesburg.

CHAPTER XXXIII

TROUBLE IN PONDOLAND

Eᴀʀʟʏ ɪɴ Sᴇᴘᴛᴇᴍʙᴇʀ Humphrey Tyler, who had been our assistant editor for eighteen months, told me he wanted to leave. I was more than sorry to lose him, he was someone on whom I had always been able to depend, also I felt at once that this was the beginning of a crack-up. However, Humphrey was a person who liked to change jobs and places frequently; he had the offer of a job in Durban, which he much preferred to Johannesburg; his family wanted him to take it —in short, he'd already made up his mind to go.

"But when are you wanting to leave, Humf?"

"In four weeks' time, if you can manage to let me go."

"Well, you know I wouldn't hang on to you against your will— but aren't you on three months' notice anyway? Won't you have to work that out?"

"They changed that," said Humphrey with a grin.

"How d'you mean?"

"Didn't you know? At the beginning of this year the management revised all the contracts with the staff. They took me off three months' notice, which I was on before, and put me on to one month."

"But Good God, Humf, why didn't you tell me? I never knew your contract was being changed."

Humphrey grinned again. "I thought it would probably work out to my advantage to have it the way they wanted it—and you see it's going to."

So Humphrey was leaving; and there would be another big gap before long when Alan Rake, who had been acting as chief sub since the East Africa office was disbanded six months or so earlier, was appointed to take charge of the two West African offices.

Otherwise life seemed, on the surface, to be as it had always been. The African staff, in a fit of recklessness after a long session in a shebeen, fought a pitched battle with each other over, in, and around our one means of transport, the Volkswagen, knocking out a window, tearing off a door and bashing its roof in with rocks. Some of the rocks were still inside the car when I looked at it next morning. A day's enquiry yielded fascinating—but conflicting—reports, so I said that the car must be repaired and the cost split up among all those involved. The staff answered, in effect, that I seemed to be making a lot of fuss about a little high spirits, but that the arrangement about the bill was a fair one. On this perpetual, and by now rather tiring question of drink, the management had worked out new regulations of its own, which I was told to read out to my staff. Anyone drunk in the office or on a job would in future be fined—£5 the first time; £10 the second; £20 the third, and fourth time out! I saw Casey smile as these regulations were introduced, and he gave his answer in his next month's column "On the Beat".

"The Editor gives me an ultimatum. He says to me I've got to choose between boozing and working.

"Now you will agree that this is no easy proposition by any means seeing as boozing and working are bed-fellows. Look at it this way: I like to get boozed up and I hate to work. But to get boozed up you must have the necessary boodle to buy the booze. And to have the boodle you have to work to earn it.

"All the same, I decide to lay off the booze for a day and see how things will work out. That's why I'm sitting in this fly-ful hotela Bantu sipping some soda water and thinking what a terrible thing life can be when you're not supposed to pep it up with hooch.

"But I just have to lay off the stuff on account my Editor makes boozing a very expensive hobby for me by threatening all over the place that he will knock off five quid from my monthly allowance—which is what he calls my salary—if I come into the office smelling like an old empty vat of hooch.

"I am still racking my brainpan on the major problem of how the world can rid itself of Editors and still run smoothly when who should walk into this fly-ful hotela Bantu but this character called Kid Nice.

"Now the gang calls this character Kid Nice on account each time he wants to get drunk he says, 'I wanna get nice, man, nice.' Kid Nice spots me the same time as I spot him and he walks over to where I'm sitting and sipping soda water. He takes the bottle from me and downs what's left of the soda water, whereupon he makes such a face you'd think he had swallowed caustic soda. After regaining his normal features, he says he thought I was sipping gin.

"Before I can tell Kid Nice why for I'm committing the unpardonable sin drinking soda water while vines still grow, he says to me we should go and get nice seeing as his ship is in. Now Kid Nice is one tough character who never takes no for an answer.

"Jobs and fivers are tight these days, but I reckon I might as well go with Kid Nice on account a set of false teeth cost many times more than a fiver and I'll definitely need a set if I refuse to go with Kid Nice on account he'll ram my God-given set down my throat.

"That is why, in spite of my Editor's ultimatum, I find myself sitting in Aunt Peggy's joint and listening to Kid Nice ordering a straight of mahog, which is the sweetest music my soda-water-sodden soul ever hears in many hours.

"By the time the straight is polished off I'm feeling so at peace with the world and instead of going down to the courts to cover the case the Editor assigns me to, I zig-zag right down to Marshall Square Police Station singing: 'I wish I were a brewer's son-in-law,' which song I make up myself.

"Now the reason I'm going to Marshall Square is to beg these cops to arrest me on account the charge for 'dronkennoise' is just a quid—which is four quid less the price my Editor wants me to pay for being just human. But these cops refuse to arrest me on account of this Better Deal affair, which says they shouldn't arrest God's children for petty offences. I get a brainwave and tell them they should arrest me for not having squared up with my poll tax and they reckon that's no petty offence and throw me in.

"And what do you know. The Editor hears about it the following morning and he nearly breaks his neck running down to pay the necessary before the law ships me down to some farm or other.

"Just goes to show the wonderful miracles a little booze can work. . . ."

It had not taken Casey more than about quarter of a second to see that the best way of avoiding the new regulations was to stay away from the office whenever he'd drunk more than he could carry. But by an understanding which was never mentioned or discussed between us, he was always in the office when he was likely to be needed—during press weeks or in times of general upheaval, and if he disappeared for an afternoon when times were slack, I said nothing about it.

He and most of our two staffs had a narrow escape one evening when they were all drinking in their favourite shebeen a couple of streets away. This shebeen was disguised as a general store; customers known to the owner simply walked straight through to a yard at the back and sat around on benches. Some twenty or so happy customers were sitting around in this way when a white face topped by a uniform cap appeared over the wall. Soon it was followed by the rest of a cop, brandishing a gun and telling nobody to move. Nat—whose good angel usually warned him of approaching danger—and Peter, who genuinely didn't care for drink, had left in good time. But the rest, including Can and Casey, were soon handcuffed in pairs and being taken off to Marshall Square.

While they were still on their way to the police station, the shebeen-keeper—who had been away for an hour arranging about fresh supplies of liquor—came back and heard what had happened. He was a forceful, confident character and, seeing at once that it would be bad for trade to have all his customers spending their money on fines, jumped into his car, soon overtook the party, and asked the young cop in charge to have a word with him on one side.

"Look, baas," he said, "why you carrying all these people off like this? It isn't good. It won't be good for you, baas, either. The government says there's to be 'no more petty persecution of the African'. Haven't you heard that on the radio? Everybody knows they're planning for us to have liquor legally. Everywhere else they stopped these raids now, baas, why you come here now and pick on me?"

The cop, who seemed new to the job, began to explain, but before he could get out six words the shebeen-keeper interrupted: "Haven't you heard of this 'Better Deal' they're giving us, baas? Don't you know the rule is 'no liquor raids on inoffensive people'? Were these men making noise or giving trouble? Were they shouting around or fighting? Why, they aren't even drunk! You be careful, baas—there's going to be a big laugh on you when you get back to Marshall Square with a lot of peaceful, law-abiding men . . . Who are your officers, baas? D'you know Major X, or Captain Y? You *do*—well, they're both friends of mine. I tell you what to do, baas, you go speak to the Major—tell him you're planning to raid my place—see? If he says 'Okay, good idea, man!', you come back to-morrow. We'll still be there. If he says 'Ag! man, don't be a bleddy fool . . .' then you've saved yourself getting into a big lot of trouble, because the officers all know me."

Within a few minutes the handcuffs were off, and half an hour later the drinkers were all back in their places, happily drinking the fines from which they had been saved.

*   *   *   *   *

At the end of August the Emergency Regulations, which had lain like a gloomy fog over the country ever since Sharpeville, were lifted, and a great many people who had been missing for months came home to their wives and families. But there was one part of the country where an undeclared emergency was in force, in Pondoland down in the Transkei, where the people were in revolt against the government's attempt to impose the so-called "Bantu Authorities" system on them, with the equally-disliked "Bantu Education". The people complained bitterly about lack of hospitals, the enforced carrying of passes, the culling and inoculation of their cattle. They were in open revolt against many of their chiefs, who were paid by the Government and whom they regarded as "Government stooges"; there were killings and burning of huts, followed by mass arrests. The district was full of police with Saracens, armoured cars, planes and helicopters, and finally, at the end of November, an official State of Emergency was declared. The Minister of Bantu Administration and Development, announcing this, said that the trouble in Pondoland was not due to any opposition on the part of the people to the Bantu Authorities system, it was stirred up by "white agitators". "Communist agitators from outside the Transkei are doing all they can to wreck the positive political development of the Bantu Authorities in that area."

Since the police, despite all their armament, had failed to catch any of these supposed white agitators, the Minister announced that the Government had decided to give the chiefs—now in effect Government officials—"immediate powers to arrest and hand over to the police white Communist agitators at present operating in the Transkei". Though these special powers did not result in the capture of any white agitators, any more than the police operations had done, they were something entirely new in South African political life, and needed careful explaining to the Afrikaner, whose basic belief had always been that no black may under any circumstances lay hands on a white man—a belief carried to such extremes that Cape Town was having to cease recruiting Coloured traffic police rather than have Coloureds issuing orders to, and possibly even rebuking or criticising, whites. This, then, is how *Die Transvaler*, the Afrikaans morning newspaper which had once been edited by Dr. Verwoerd, explained the new situation to its readers:

"With a view to what has happened in South Africa in the past, this decision of the Minister may perhaps appear a little drastic to some people. Great feeling has always existed since the days of Slagtersnek and the Second War of Freedom about non-whites having the right to catch whites. Let those who think and feel that way about the situation, however, consider that what the Minister now intends to do cannot in the least be compared with the incidents of the past. Those who are now inviting trouble in the reserves are adherents of Communism and have only one aim. It is to cause the Natives to rebel against the legal Government of the Union. People inspired with such crimes do not deserve the least sympathy from other whites and therefore it will be quite permissible to allow them to be caught by the tribal chiefs so that they can be punished before a court."

In other words, whites who oppose Government policies in the reserves have ceased to be whites, and can be treated accordingly; just as, a year later, Afrikaans newspapers would have the task of explaining to their readers that Japanese who buy South African iron ore and wool are no longer Asiatics, but have acquired a new official status as honorary whites.

The daily and weekly papers had carried next to nothing in their news columns of what was going on in Pondoland, even before the declaration of an Emergency; from now on they would really publish nothing. It seemed therefore to be particularly a task for *Drum* to send in to the area and bring back both news and pictures. We discussed the proposal at a conference, and Benson—our political writer—and Peter Magubane both said they were prepared to go. It was a risky undertaking because the police, who were everywhere, would not welcome *Drum* journalists on the one hand, and on the other the Pondos—who had had a good many police spies planted among them—looked on everyone not personally known to them with hostility; in particular everyone travelling by car was likely to be an enemy.

Our two men succeeded, however, in living for ten days among the Pondos, and in bringing back the first real account of what was going on, together with a few good pictures. These included a photograph of a chief and his four henchmen addressing a crowd of his people shortly before they rose up against him and murdered him. Now came the problem of getting the story into the magazine. Having discussed the whole article with our lawyer, I took out three or four passages which he thought unsafe; the rest he approved. In the course of press day, Ian Pritchard pointed out a further passage which he considered dangerous, and Jim Bailey said we should also include a statement giving the Government's point of view. After some discussion, I agreed to both these alterations. But now, late in the afternoon, just as the pages were being finally okayed, we got word from the printers that they were extremely worried about the article, and that their lawyers had said it must either come out altogether or be drastically altered.

The firm which was printing *Drum* at this time was an Afrikaner-owned firm, publishing a pro-Government evening paper in Afrikaans, as well as a number of Afrikaans magazines and journals. Some of its directors held high positions in the Nationalist Party, and probably all were its supporters. We had, however, worked amicably together hitherto, and this was actually the first time there had been a real clash as to whether an article should or should not be printed.

In the Board Room when we arrived were the firm's Managing Director, the Works Manager, and the lawyer, a pale, round-faced young man. On our side there were Bailey, Pritchard and myself. The procedure agreed upon was that the lawyer should read the article through and raise each query as he came to it, and there should then be a general discussion. In this way he read all through Benson's article once and asked for a number of changes—nearly all of which were finally agreed to—and when he reached the end, I supposed that we had finished. However the lawyer said that he had hitherto been going through it in order to consider the detail, he intended now to go through it all again with an eye to policy; and now the argument was properly joined, and I got an idea of what it would be like if ever—as has been proposed more than once in Government Bills—an official censorship were introduced, for, contrary to general belief outside the country, there is not as yet any official censorship of newspapers or magazines.

"That reflects on the police; you can't say that . . . This criticises Government policy—anything that criticises Government policy is an offence under the Emergency Regulations."

"How is that?" I asked.

"Because you're 'setting one section of the population against another'—the people against the Government—which is expressly forbidden."

"But we're *not* setting them. We are saying that they've set themselves against the Government."

"Saying that they've set themselves is an encouragement to set themselves further. . . ." So it went on.

When this point had at last been argued out, the lawyer wanted all reference to a certain chief removed. This particular chief was accused by the Pondos of having tortured some of their number to death because they refused to tell him what went on at secret meetings of their illegal organisation, known as "The Hill".

"You can't print any criticism of this chief at all."

"Why not?"

"Because all chiefs are now Government servants. Criticism of a chief is criticism of the Government—and therefore ranks as a subversive statement."

"But the Government has itself admitted that certain criticisms made by the Pondos have been justified, and that some chiefs acted unwisely."

"The Government may say that if it chooses—but *you* are not permitted to print criticism. It's undermining confidence in the chief."

"Is that the real reason," I asked, "that criticism of this chief would undermine confidence in him?"

"Yes."

"But we can't undermine confidence in this chief whatever we say about him."

"Why not?"

"Because he's dead. The Pondos killed him." After insisting on a check-up of my statement he finally passed the passage, but returned with new vigour to the next one—"All this bit must come out."

"Why?"

"Undermining confidence in the chief. Same as before."

"But it isn't the chief the article is criticising—it's the chief's uncle."

He read the passage through again and saw that I was right. "Well—chief or uncle, the principle's the same."

At this I sat back. "Let's not spend our time going through this any more. We've already wasted two hours reading through it bit by bit. We've been all through it once; now we're going all through it again. When that's done, perhaps our friend here will want to go through everything a third time. We've shown—I think you will agree—that we were ready to compromise on points of detail. But it's impossible to transform an article which is essentially a criticism of government policy in Pondoland into one which praises government policy. We sent two very good men into Pondoland. *They* lived there—you didn't. They saw a great deal themselves and they talked to a great many people. They came back with a very decided impression that some chiefs have acted wrongly, and that some government policies are mistaken. We are now told that all criticism of either chiefs or government policy is illegal under the Emergency Regulations. I don't believe this is true, and our lawyer certainly didn't believe it's true. But that's what we're being told, and the article is being slowly twisted before our eyes to try to make it mean the exact opposite of what our two men reported."

"Well—what do you propose to do?"

"Leave it out. Our friends here say they won't print it as it is, and I won't have it distorted. The only thing to do then is to drop it."

"But what are you going to put in instead?" asked the Managing Director.

"I've no idea. How can I possibly tell you now? That's the main article in the issue. The whole magazine will obviously have to be rearranged."

"How long will all that take?"

"Well—we would try to give you something by Monday."

But at this, as I was expecting, the Works Manager blew up. "This is impossible! There's a whole staff standing by downstairs. I've had them there on overtime for the last three hours. We've *got* to run to-night. Who's going to pay for keeping the machines standing idle till Monday?"

"That's not our business," said Jim. "We've presented you with an article which has been carefully read and approved by our lawyers. You've called for further changes—and we've made a great many. We've gone a very long way to meet you. If you're now going to start calling for more, you must obviously be responsible for the consequences. This isn't the first time you've seen this article; it's been in your works for several days. It's you who've called for this last-minute conference, not us."

In the different atmosphere which now prevailed, the remaining difficulties were speedily overcome. The article, I thought, read like hell in its mutilated form, but the pictures were intact, and the two together formed the best impression anyone had yet given of what was really going on in Pondoland under the official cloud of silence.

* * * * *

Among the letters for me next morning was one which told me that Ian Berry had won the *Encyclopaedia Britannica* prize for the second year running—a unique achievement—and had won it with the pictures taken on our two visits to the Congo.

CHAPTER XXXIV

THE FINAL ARGUMENT

During October I had been told by the new Circulation Manager that it had been decided to double the price of *Drum* and sell it for a shilling instead of sixpence: "So will you please make all the necessary arrangements."

"What arrangements?"

"Arrangements for it to sell at the new price."

"But I think the idea's disastrous. We should lose a quarter of our sales at least."

The Circulation Manager shrugged his shoulders. "Those are the instructions anyway. I was told to tell you, and I have."

I went to see Ian Pritchard.

"Yes," he said. "It *has* been decided—tentatively."

"It'll be a fearful setback."

"I think it might be too . . . What d'you think about ninepence?"

"Better than a shilling. But how can something so important just be 'decided'? Surely we should all get together and argue the thing out. It affects everyone—the editorial most, but also circulation and advertising. I feel we should have a meeting on it and all say our piece."

"I don't think there's much point in having a meeting. But if you like to think over how you feel it will affect the paper and send a copy to Jim and one to me, that'll give us a basis for discussion."

During October, therefore, I worked out the arguments for and against a price increase, how much circulation we might expect to lose, what steps the magazine should take in the way of new features and increased value to offset the inevitable fall, and how the change should be timed in order to reduce its effects to a minimum. In November I learned from Ian that my memorandum had been "rejected" and that sometime in December the new price was to be $7\frac{1}{2}$ cents (or ninepence) instead of 10 cents (one shilling). Now, shortly after our Pondoland discussion, Jim Bailey called me into his office.

"I want to make plans for putting over the price increase, and I'd like to have your full agreement and support."

I hesitated. "I'd rather we began by discussing whether there should *be* a price increase. You know we've never really talked about it yet. It isn't that I'm absolutely opposed to the idea—if we can get nine-pence instead of sixpence for the same number of copies, it's obviously a good thing for the firm. But I'd like to think we'd gone into it all thoroughly and knew how every department would be affected."

"How would that be possible?"

"First, I'd like to have a whole afternoon for everyone to say their say. Then I suggest we have an investigation made by an outside firm to see if our readers can afford the increased price. I think many of them can't; but maybe I'm wrong. Why don't we find out? There are several firms who could tackle it."

"I don't think that's a good idea at all. An investigation would cost money, and it would waste a lot of time. We've made a managerial decision to increase the price of *Drum* to ninepence. All I want to do now is to discuss necessary changes in the contents and make-up of the paper resulting from the increased price. We must get this edition on to a paying basis straight away."

"Yes . . . But if our readers can't really afford ninepence, we don't get *Drum* on to a paying basis just by printing ninepence on the cover. We'd have to work out something on a different basis."

"What 'different basis' is there?"

"Making the magazine into a fortnightly would be one. Reduce the number of pages, so as to cut down printing costs and railage. Keep the selling price at sixpence. But speed up all the printing arrangements so as to be far more topical and newsy."

"I quite like the idea of making *Drum* a fortnightly," said Jim after a pause. "It's an obvious development, and later in the year it's a step we shall probably decide to take. But we've got to get this price increase through first."

I could see that we were getting bogged down in one of our slow-motion wrestling matches—however there seemed no way of avoiding this one: "I'm afraid it doesn't work that way. The two courses don't make a sequence; they're alternatives. If our idea is to put up the price, then we must make a lusher sort of magazine, use colour if we can get it, improve the covers, find a little money for new features, and so on. But if we decide on a fortnightly—which is what I think is wiser— then we want the opposite, the most rapid production. Provided we get speed, quality won't matter much. Going to a fortnightly would have another big advantage, too."

"What's that?"

"It's the best way of hitting our rivals. If we make a topical paper twice a month, people won't like to miss a copy. They'll buy two *Drums* a month, instead of *Drum* and something else. Whereas if we take the lead in putting up the price, the other papers may follow—but if they're clever they can do us a hell of a lot of harm before they do."

"Look, Tom," said Jim, "I'm not against the idea of a fortnightly—please understand that. It may very well come later on. But our position at this moment is that a managerial decision has been taken to increase the price of *Drum* to ninepence. That has to be done right away. All I want now is to make sure of your full support in the editorial changes which necessarily follow that decision."

"What changes are those?"

"The first essential is to bring the magazine more in line with its reading public. It must be styled much more to their requirements. I appreciate the care and craftsmanship which you have always put into the paper—but this concern for detail is wasted on our public. It's resulted in a London paper not a Johannesburg one. If we are not to lose circulation at the new price we shall require an entirely new outlook and approach."

"How will that be expressed?"

"In the first place we shall need much less serious and much less political stuff—certainly not more than one political article or picture-story every month. We must concentrate on tough, down-to-earth, hard-selling features from now on. Do you agree?"

"If," I said, "anyone knew with any certainty what stories sold papers or magazines, our task would be easy. We should only have to make up our minds whether we wanted to produce a magazine full of such stories—or not. If we did produce one, we should be certain it would sell. If we didn't, it would be because we didn't think it was worth doing. But in fact we don't *know* what sells a paper and what doesn't."

Jim laughed. "I don't think it's difficult to know what sells a paper to our readers."

"What?"

"It's the strong sensational stories such as we have in *Post*—'The Confessions of the Panga Man' and so on. That's what people really want—not highbrow stuff."

"But 'The Africanists' and our Pondoland story have been two of our best sellers. And if confessions of panga men and retellings of immorality cases really sold papers, why don't they sell *Post*? But *Post* is stuck where it's been for the last four years, despite all the panga men."

"I'm afraid, Tom, the fact is you put into the magazine the sort of stories you yourself like and think interesting. That may have worked all right in London, where you were in tune with your public because you were one of them yourself. But it doesn't work out here because you don't think like your readers do."

"That may be true. But if the opposite formula, the immorality cases and the panga men, really worked, why doesn't it work for *Post*?"

"Well, it doesn't do too badly . . . The paper more or less holds its own. But if it comes to that, what's your own formula for a big increase in sales?"

"I'd like to try a topical fortnightly—really up-to-date and based on news. . . . But in a long-term sense, my formula's a different one."

"What's that?"

"After three years of trying everything to make this edition really sell—and achieving what I agree is only very moderate progress—I'm beginning to wonder if the African here really wants it."

Jim sat up sharply. "Doesn't *want* it? In what way?"

"I'm not sure that he wants a magazine or paper aimed entirely at himself; in its way *Drum* is a form of apartheid too. It would be a different thing in the reserves, with unsophisticated readers. If we could take people there a magazine in their own language, I think they'd buy it—those that could afford a magazine at all. But the African in the cities seems to have got past a separate paper. I think what he really wants is the honest and straightforward treatment of his own interests and opinions in a paper everybody reads. After all, what are the ones he really goes for? The *Star* and *The Sunday Times*—two 'white' newspapers."

"You're not suggesting turning *Drum* into a magazine for all races?"

"No; and unfortunately we couldn't if we wanted. Other races will never bring themselves to buy a paper which has been 'black' so long."

"Then what *are* you suggesting?"

"To fight a holding action here, and put our real effort into building up the other editions—in places where they're really wanted. East Africa first, and then the Federation. You feel that what stops us selling more copies here is my 'highbrow' ideas. But in West Africa the level of the magazine is far higher than it is here—and we sell nearly twice what we sold three years ago."

Jim sighed. "We can go back to East Africa some time in the future —but the problem there is lack of advertising. It's here the advertisers have the money, so it's here we have to build the magazine." He held up a piece of paper. "I've worked out a basic formula to be followed every month. If you'll keep to this, and avoid the highbrow, political kind of story, then I'm sure we can carry the price increase—and we shall also be on much safer ground in our future dealings with the Government. . . ."

* * * * *

Outside my office as I got back, two heavily-built Africans were sitting. A thug and his henchman, one could see at a glance. One of the engaging—and also maddening—features about life on *Drum* was that the place was used as a kind of general headquarters by many Africans, who would come in for a smoke or a chat with one of the staff, to do a bit of typing, or to make a few free telephone calls. Sometimes the place seemed more like the entrance to a railway station than a newspaper office.

"What are you doing here?" I would ask someone I'd never seen before, who was busily tapping away at Nat's or Casey's typewriter.

"Don't you know me, sir? I'm Casey's friend"; or, "I'm just waiting to see Nat"; or even, "Don't you know me, sir? I once asked you for a job and you told me you wouldn't give me one."

There was little or no protection from the outside world; people wanting jobs, wanting money, wanting their novels read and criticised; men who'd been beaten up on farms and wanted to show their scars; beaten up by gangsters and wanted the gangsters' names and addresses published in the paper . . . at different times they'd all just pushed their way in and appeared on the far side of my desk. These two didn't look like ones who'd been beaten up, however.

As I closed one door, Casey slipped in through the other.

"I'm in a bit of trouble, sir." This direct approach and serious look were unlike Casey.

"What kind of trouble?"

"You remember the article 'On the Beat'—the one about going down to Durban?" I nodded. "You remember the character I called 'Kid Sportswear', because of his flashy sort of get-up? Well—he' recognised himself."

"Well, if that's all, Casey, what's it matter? It's no libel to say chap likes smart clothes."

"It isn't that, sir. I said he was down in Durban with a cherry—which he was. Now his wife's read the article, and she's real mad."

"But he can't be identified just by your calling him 'Kid Sportswear'."

"He can by his wife, sir," said Casey shrewdly.

"He looks big enough to cope with his wife."

Casey gave me a pitying look. "It isn't a question of size. She's making his life hell."

"Well—what does he want us to do? Publish a note that Mr. So-and-so was *not* down in Durban with a cherry? I'll do that if he likes."

"What he wants to do is to carve me up—he says he's going to, too."

"Here in the office?"

"No, sir, after I get home."

"Okay, Casey, bring him in."

Casey went to the door and beckoned. He came back with the couple I had seen outside, a tall, heavily-built African who looked like a fighter going to seed, with an extremely sulky expression, such as a child puts on when it wants its bad temper to be noticed. I held out my hand. He took it reluctantly, then sat down, looking away from me. He was attended by a short, thickset pug who sat down with his hat between his knees, and gazed steadily at the carpet.

"I'm fed up, sir. That's what I am. *Fed up.*"

"Why? What's the matter?"

"I think this man Casey is my friend, sir. Now I see that he is *not* my friend."

"Why, what has Casey done?"

"What Casey has done, sir, is to write about me in your paper. He writes about me in a way that causes me much trouble. He has made my life a hell."

"I'm told you think you are 'Kid Sportswear'. But how can anyone identify you just by that? When I read Casey's piece I thought he was writing about Peter Lafolo."

Casey looked grateful for this happy thought, but added: "It's his friends and family, sir. Some of them think 'Kid Sportswear' is meant for him."

"But even so, what harm is there in that?"

The big man banged his ham fist on the desk. "This Casey man has hurt me, sir. And for that I am intending to hurt him."

It looked all too easy for him to hurt Casey, I thought, as I leaned across and said sternly: "I called you in here to see what I could do to help you. I'm still quite prepared to help you. But I won't have you threaten a member of my staff. That's not going to help you. Just the opposite. That would really cause some trouble."

"I wasn't threatening Casey. I just say I intend to *hurt* him."

"That's what I call threatening," I said, "and you can cut it out. If any trouble comes to Casey, several people here will know who's responsible. Bear *that* in mind. Now, as regards your complaint, what would you like us to do? D'you want a notice in the magazine next month saying some people have mistakenly thought 'Kid Sportswear' was you—and that the story was purely imaginary?"

"It isn't public trouble I've got, sir. It's worse—it's *private* trouble. That's why I'm going to cause . . ."

"No more of *that*. If you've had trouble with your relatives, I'll go and see them if you want me to. If you've had trouble with an employer, I'll go and see him. I'll write you a letter which you can show—if that's what you want."

"Well . . . I don't know . . ."

"Think it over. Talk it over with your friends. There's no hurry. The next edition won't go to press for a fortnight. Decide what you want doing, and come back in a week—if it's something reasonable, we'll do it."

He rose to his feet, still slowly, but mollified. The pug rose at the same time as if coupled with him on a string. Casey, relieved but not yet reassured, slid down off the filing cabinet where he had been perched and escorted the big man out. The pug, who had not yet opened his mouth, shuffled silently after; at the door he turned, looked round at me, and his mouth opened for the first time, but he thought better of it and no sound came out.

After five minutes Casey was back.

"Can you get eight pounds, sir?"

"Why—what for?"

"It's 'Crasher', sir, the man you were just talking to."

"What does Crasher want eight pounds for?"

"Well, sir, it's his car."

"What about his car?"

"Sir, he always uses someone else's insurance disc. It's a point of honour with him. He always does it. He's paid far more in fines than the cost of an insurance—but he just won't get one of his own. He takes the disc off any car he sees and sticks it on his windscreen. He says he was caught again on the way here and they're fining him eight quid."

"Casey," I said, "I guess Crasher has assessed the loss to his dignity and reputation arising from your article at eight quid or your dead body, and since he can't carve you he's levying a small fine of that amount."

"No, sir, no." Casey was visibly concerned for his friend's reputation. "No, he wouldn't do *that*, sir. He's a gangster. That's not his line. Anyway he tried to borrow the money first from Theo—only Theo hadn't got eight quid. That's the only reason he asked me. I'm certain he'll bring it back—it'll be here to-morrow without fail."

"Okay," I said. "If it's here to-morrow, we can have a drink. And if it isn't, we'll split the loss."

*   *   *   *   *

A few days later I got a letter from Jim Bailey: "Following the outline formula I gave you for the new *Drum* at ninepence, here is a detailed list of the stories that should go into every issue. . . . The magazine needs youthfulness, hard stories and a rapport with its public. . . . So for the next 6–12 months can we avoid being highbrow and work out the strong, sensational stories which our public goes for. . . ."

I wrote back that I had no faith in these new proposals, or the calculations on which they were based and, that being so, I could not honestly try to carry out the programme. I suggested that he found an editor who could.

In the course of the next week we had one more talk, in which Jim asked me to say what were my difficulties, and why I was unwilling to continue in the job. I hesitated. Should I try once more to bridge the gap between our different ideas of what the magazine should be—which was essentially an incompatibility between our natures? The time for that had gone.

"They really all boil down to one," I said, "that we never discuss anything to do with the magazine. Important steps—such as this price increase, or the question of what should go into the paper to sell it at the new price—are all settled by you on the basis of hunches. You pass your hunch on to me in a note, and I'm then left with the task of either carrying out the hunch—whether I think it's bad or good—or of trying to dissuade you from an action on which you've already set your mind."

"I don't think it's true that I don't discuss things," Jim replied. "On the contrary, I *like* discussing things. I only don't discuss them with you because of your extreme touchiness. I assure you I discuss everything with Cecil Eprile, and he discusses everything with me. It's only you who are difficult to talk to."

"I have reasons for everything I do," I said, "and when you produce criticisms, I naturally produce my answers. But I'm not talking about criticisms, I'm talking about discussions, plans for the future. I certainly shouldn't feel touchy about whether the paper is going to cost nine-pence or a shilling—but I *should* like to talk it out. Our firm isn't so rich in talent and experience that we can ignore one another's views."

"What arrangement are you proposing for the future?"

"We've reached an impasse—and I want to go. You believe that if the paper were made in accordance with your formula and your ideas you'd soon be selling twice as many copies. I think you're wrong—and that you'll sell fewer. But you can't try it out because I'm standing in the way. *I* believe we should now be pressing on hard in other parts of Africa. But it's your money not mine, and you don't think that's the best way to use it. So we're stuck. At present neither of us gets what he wants, but if I go you will at least find out whether your own plan works—which will be something."

"Well—if that's how you feel," said Jim, "perhaps it's best. And I would like you to know that I appreciate what you've done to give the magazine coherence, and to improve its looks."

"And I'm grateful to you for bringing us out here, and for the chance to travel around."

* * * * *

And so the experiment came to an end; in the six months I had still to serve, we should see very little of each other.

CHAPTER XXXV

ROLL ON THE YEAR 2000!

I WAS NOW drawing near to the end of my time with *Drum* and everything had begun to take on the poignancy which attaches—against one's will and common sense—to work one will soon not be doing, places one will no longer be familiar with, and people one is seeing, perhaps, for the last time. Dorothy and I had no intention of leaving South Africa, which we now regarded as our home, but I realised very well that, once I gave up the office, I should have other contacts and other demands, and so would the people I had known and worked with for so long. This stretch of life would be over.

Even the letters from readers—normally a chore to be disposed of quickly so as to get down to the problems of the magazine—now seemed like voices, friendly and appealing, almost always odd, and soon to be cut off; expressed sometimes so vividly that they came over, not as letters at all, but as private musings which had got themselves down on paper.

Greeting to you, Mr. DRUM,

I am one of the girls who read DRUM every month and I am not satisfied to see other girl on the covers. And please Mr. DRUM help me to be a cover girl too and one thing is this Mr. DRUM I am the Kit who does not have her father and Mother, and I am suffering about Mr. Wrong. I can't get Mr. Right, and please Mr. DRUM I wish one of our readers can help me to get Mr. Right, because I don't want to be Miss M—— for ever, no marriage.

So now we pray

Our father and mother who are in town hallowed be thy name

C———— M————

Amen

Sir,

Though, I have got it in my mind to be contributing to the editions of your monthly Journal some important and interesting stories, but circumstances has seized the gateway of that for me during the past period.

Now, I wish to be doing so, and I hope you will assist me as per my request. The first one for trial, I enclose herein for you to treat as necessitated.

I remain to be,

Yours sincerely,

Clement O———.

It did not need the address to tell me that one came from West Africa, where a rotund eighteenth-century English—freely interspersed with modern business terms and fragments of officialese—is a favoured style. Very different was this one from South West Africa.

Father Tom H Kingson

You see, I dont know wat can I do according to this Drum Contest. My heart fall sore, Because I'm not learn to march (too much) as a schoolboy. Just look what I'm doing in that Contest, just wrong or correct I don't now.

My heart burning in my body. And my human body am very very narrow indeed.

Now, I'm kneeling under the tree. I pray for my Lord to help me with a good luky. Our father in heaven please help boy Ranko he is Poverty as a church mouse.

Just help me with a peac of honey God,, once of a day.

I'm Poverty little Ranko who born under the ant-hill, a man

Ranko D———

c/o Post Rasetent, South West Africa.

There was a note from Peter—brief and to the point as were all his communications:

Dear Sir

I have a knob on the right of my stomach so I have gone to consult a doctor

Peter.

There was another letter, also, which I read through carefully twice.

Dear Sir

I hereby apply for the position of a reporter on the staff of the *Drum*. I am 30 years of age, married, in excellent health, and so deeply interested in news reporting that I would never accept a job not somehow connected with it.

Although I have little direct experience of reporting, I am familiar with the procedure, since for the past ten years I have been in official service, and am fully experienced in making notes, drawing up reports etc.

All this has been done to the full satisfaction of my superiors, and now that I have resolved to enter the journalistic world, I approach you before anyone else, having regard to your reputation and to that of the magazine you edit.

I am told that I have a flair for quick and easy writing, and the expression of clear statements. I believe I can make a useful and impressive contribution to your paper. I have always admired the *Drum* and should welcome the opportunity of being associated with it.

I believe in working hard, and have learned to work constructively with others. I ask for the favour of an interview in which you can form your own opinion of my appearance and personality.

Sincerely yours
K—— P——

I could hear Nat chatting away outside the door, so called him in.

"What d'you make of that, Nat?"

He read it through, and suddenly began to laugh. "He's got a nerve, hasn't he?"

"Why—what d'you mean?"

"Well, he's a police spy, isn't he? He wants a job on *Drum*, and he writes what he thinks is a good letter, but he gives the game away all along."

"Where?"

"Well, look at his language—'familiar with procedure', 'in official service', 'fully experienced in drawing up reports', 'writing and expression of clear statements'—that means taking down what the prisoner said. . . ."

"H'm. And d'you think the chap wrote it himself?"

Nat looked again. "No. Certainly he didn't. It was dictated to him by his officer. What shall you do with it?"

"Tell him that as a responsible magazine we only take on fully-trained journalists with the highest qualifications. And add that, as he's made such a promising start in an official career, I advise him to keep on with it, and earn promotion by satisfying his superiors."

Nat laughed. "There are big changes in the cops. Perhaps this is part of the new system."

"What new system?"

"They say they've had some top London bobby sent out here to give them good advice. Everyone's very upset about it."

"In what way?"

"We-e-e-ell . . . With the cops you always used to know just where you were. They beat you up and pushed you in the cells. Next day you were brought into court and the magistrate automatically fined you £1 to £3. You were given a kick in the behind and told to go home. Quite often the cop who was supposed to charge you forgot to turn up in court, so you were let off. The whole thing was quite simple and straightforward."

"And now?"

"Well someone must have been telling them that you don't get information from people by knocking them around. Now they're polite. I was asked to *sit down* the other day. They ask for your reference book, take down your name and address, and then start asking you a whole lot of questions you don't properly follow. You have the feeling they're slowly framing something together on you, and before long they'll have a full-dress case, with a judge and jury and lawyers and the rest. They're much more cunning, and it makes you feel they're cooking something up. A lot of us have noticed it. It isn't only me. All the same . . ."

"All the same what?"

"All the same, if they're trying to get one of their chaps in here it means they haven't got one here already—which is something. Or if they *have* got one he doesn't tell them all they want."

*   *   *   *   *

When Nat had gone and, in a desultory half-hearted way, I was turning out one or two drawers, I came across some scraps of paper. One lot of scraps held the records of loans, for the most part trivial, which I had jotted down and dropped into a folder. Most, I saw, had long since been repaid, and I remembered the words of an African reporter on *Golden City Post* who had come in one day with a pound or two towards the sum of £10 which he had needed in some emergency.

"You don't understand the African temperament, Mr. Hopkinson. Really you do *not*. I come here and ask you to borrow me £10, you say 'Yes okay'. But when you borrow me something you mustn't just leave it like that—you must keep coming to me and asking for it back. And you should charge interest. If you don't do these things, I think you are not worried over the money. So I forget it too."

"But you don't forget, Wilson," I said. "Here you are bringing it to me of your own accord."

He scratched his head. "I bring it to you, sir, because I feel uneasy not to. But who knows? Next time you borrow someone, maybe he won't be so careful. Then you lose. You must study the African temperament, Mr. Hopkinson."

In a folder in the same drawer were a number of scribbled notes in my own writing which at first I didn't recognise; then I saw they were records of things my staff had said to me at different times about myself. I'd written them down soon after they were said, so as not to lose them. I had put no names against any of them in case someone rummaged in the drawers, which were always open, but I could remember who had said each, and the occasion.

"We'd like to ask you to come drinking with us, sir, but you seem too old. They say you drink a hell of a lot when you feel like it, all the same . . ."

"Sir, you are *too* reasonable. That's your trouble. You're always seeing both sides. For us there's only one side—and we don't want to be told about the other."

"Why are you bothering me, sir? Why can't you leave me alone? I'm not drunk. Really, I'm not drunk. I tell you I'm *not* drunk. I'm just lying here in this gutter."

"You know it all, I suppose. But you haven't taught us a thing. *Not* a thing. You take damn good care to keep it all to yourself."

"You're my boss, sir. I work for you. If someone tells you to do something and you think it's the wrong thing to do—you just won't do it. That's why I'm saying I work for you."

Over the telephone: "This is your favourite son speaking, sir X—— Y——."

And, strangest of all, the one I thought about most often, because it seemed to sum up the whole ambivalence of black and white to one another in South Africa, was the following. It had been said to me on the balcony of our flat in Hillbrow, seven floors up, after dinner and a few drinks, by someone swaying, unsteady, and for that reason perhaps all the more truthful: "You like us, Mr. Hopkinson—we know that. And you do the best for us you can, your way of thinking. But one day you and me will be standing here on this balcony—see? Like we're standing now. Then I shall just give you one big push . . ." and he swayed heavily towards me.

Reading these notes and fragments, I started to jot down a balance sheet, what had been done, achieved, and what had not been done at all. On the asset side were two or three things I thought worth while —above all the progress of some half-dozen members of the staff. Nat was now a trained reporter, fit to work on any paper in the world; sharp, alert, but also tolerant and thoughtful, he had come a long way in three years. Peter, who had always possessed ability and courage, now had confidence as well, and a much firmer basis of technique. Moreover his name as a photographer was beginning to become known abroad. Casey's writing was all his own, and always had been, but at least he had now a profession as sub-editor which would help him to live in New York—which I thought of as his spiritual home and where I believed he was likely to end up, if his demon didn't get the better of him first. In West Africa Matthew Faji and Christian Gbagbo had developed their talents faster than they might have done without me; and Nelson, whose ability was formed already, had gained recognition in the firm more quickly from having someone who believed in and supported him from the first.

What else? In three and a half years we had published a dozen or two articles which were worth publishing, and we had given some readers—perhaps a few thousand altogether—the feeling that their views and attitudes were respected; that we made the magazine for them to the utmost of our ability, and did not turn out something cheaper or sillier or more vulgar because they were black.

Overseas the paper's reputation had been extended; and the fame which was coming to Ian Berry had come through his association with the magazine.

Moreover, now that the new price had been introduced in South Africa, and with sales for the moment holding up, all editions of *Drum* were paying for the first time in their history; but though I was glad that they should pay, I had not worked as I had for these last years in order to turn a minus on balance-sheets into a plus. The larger aims cherished had not merely not been achieved, they hadn't even been approached.

I had hoped to make a magazine which the African reader would take to with enthusiasm, and then, having captured his interest, to use it to give him a much fuller picture of the outside world, to break down his isolation, to widen his tiny location-bound horizon. In South Africa we had not got started; in West Africa we had got little further than to be successful from a business point of view.

And the second great hope I had, which was to use the magazine as a training-ground for Africans in journalism, had not been realised either. Perhaps half the people I had originally started with had made

[11] Mike Phahlane, Hopkinson, and Peter Magubane in the *Drum* office.

progress—one or two notably; others had made none, and some had fallen by the wayside.

Had I, I wondered, learned anything myself? Certainly I had found a new home and a new continent; life, instead of contracting, as would have been normal at my age, had expanded vastly. I had travelled in new countries, and made a number of new friends. Since so little was known about Africa and its problems at first-hand, the knowledge of places and people I had acquired—even though so much of it was superficial—would be valuable to me in my profession as a journalist. But what did I really *know* that I had not known before?

Perhaps only two things. First, there is no simple solution to the difficulties of a continent that has been left behind by history and is now trying to catch up. I had never believed that apartheid could be a solution, but I could see now that nobody else believed it either. Sixty years ago, and at enormous cost, it might have been attempted; now it was as impossible as it was undesirable—and nobody, not even its ardent supporters, was seriously trying to put it into practice. All they were doing was to use its supposed existence in the future as an excuse for refusing to meet difficulties here and now; much as the promise of heavenly bliss had been used, over much of the world, to justify the torments of the damned during earthly life.

Equally "one man, one vote" seemed to me silly, when there are still some millions of Africans who have no idea of what a vote is and who, if they had one to-morrow, would gladly exchange it for a mealie. A vote is useless, and even dangerous, without the background of experience—above all of cynicism and distrust—which must guide one in making use of it; and the conferring of a vote before a people is able to make use of it with judgement, is a curse and not a benefit; just as the withholding of it after the right moment is a crime.

Differences of development are real, just as our common humanity is real; and no lasting order can be founded which does not take account of both. This may be an unpalatable fact to those who would like to be rid of all responsibility towards the African by the single act of liberation—that is by simply handing him over to himself. But a fact does not vanish through being ignored.

Looking back, it seemed to me that almost everyone I had met and talked to in the last four years, had a solution, knew exactly what should be done. Their only difficulty was to get other people to let them carry out what they knew to be correct. The answer was federation, or it was votes for all; it was "separate development", or it was education. It was the revival and encouragement of the Africans' own civilisation. It was négritude, and the elimination of white influence. It was loans from America, scholarships to Europe, or stronger barriers against Communist infiltration. So far from having any solution, either to the particular problems of South Africa or the far wider problems of the continent, I felt less assured by far than when I first came out.

The second piece of knowledge I had gained was a faith in the urban African. It is common practice in South Africa—as among administrators in colonial or ex-colonial territories—to divide Africans into two classes; there is the "simple native", the "blanket-boy", the tribesman from the reserves, who is *good*. Respectful, obedient, docile, knowing his place; grateful and devoted to the particular white man under the shadow of whose wing he pecks his scanty livelihood. As against him is the urban African, who is *bad*. Cheeky (the favourite word, with its Afrikaans equivalent "parmantig"), ungrateful, grasping; he is nothing more than the simple native who has been "spoiled". And to get over the difficult fact that it is contact with the white man which has spoiled him, it is necessary to argue that, by an innate depravity, he chooses always what is worst in white civilisation—juke-boxes and alcohol, instead of Christianity and space travel. If only those millions of urbanised chickens could be levered back into their tribal shells and made eggs again, all would be well.

For myself, my experience of the last years had been precisely with the urban African, and with a specialised section of the urbanised, the intellectuals; that is, the class most casually dismissed by white officialdom as "unrepresentative", so long as they confine themselves to private interests; or most ruthlessly harried as "troublemakers" if they apply themselves to the problems of their people. And to me the urban African does not appear as a spoiled rustic to be re-tribalised by forcibly turning back the clock; on the contrary, he is the Man of To-morrow, but still painfully entangled with the past and still forcibly fettered in the present.

I believe in the future of the urban African; but I also believe in the civilisation I have inherited, and I believe the African can only find his true future through this civilisation which, in affecting him, will itself be profoundly modified. This it needs, because our civilisation, with all it has achieved and has still to offer, has walked into a dead end. Western man has lost the capacity to be spontaneously happy. The damning thing about his culture, his religion, his way of life, is that through them he does not find happiness. Content, once, to expect this happiness as a reward hereafter, he has begun to lose faith in the hereafter. Still more has he lost faith in himself as entitled to a heavenly reward, since he knows in his heart that the test of his religion, as well as of his material life, is the ability to be happy here and now, and that the failure to achieve happiness on earth is the denial of true religion; not its implementation.

The African—though much of his superficial gaiety is allied to despair—has not lost the capacity for immediate response and ready happiness. He lives now, in the present, on this earth. It is a bitter complaint among many whites that the African "won't work"; that he is "lazy"; that even if you offer him extra pay he doesn't always rush to earn it. Sometimes indeed, when you offer him more money, he will actually round on you and declare that if you're willing to pay him £20 a month now, you must have been underpaying him all those years when you paid him only £12.

It is not strictly true that the African "won't work" or is "lazy". What is true is that he does not think work the end of life. He can work extremely hard; but he can also actively enjoy doing nothing, whereas Western man feels guilty the moment he is idle. The African does not believe man came into the world in order to get through so much farming, labouring or factory drudgery. His derisive comment on the white man is that he "doesn't know how to enjoy himself by day or night".

In short, the black man—with his love of play, his enjoyment of the moment, his humour, his strong sense of drama and the boisterous freedom he gives to his emotions—is not the opposite of the white man, but his complement. Equally the white man—with his long-term vision, his power to subordinate present to future, his stern control and the arid nature of his private life—is the necessary complement of the more easy-going, freedom-loving black. It is this fact that, mentally and spiritually, the races complement each other which makes nonsense of artificial schemes for segregation, since each race knows in its heart that it needs what the other has to offer; and it is significant that in South Africa it is the Afrikaner—with his passion for order, his insistence on segregation, his rejection of our common humanity as "a sickly liberalistic concept", and his Calvinist beliefs in the basic guilt and wickedness of man—who is most irresistibly attracted to the African.

I believe, then, that the races need each other; not that black needs white to tell him what to do, and white needs black to do the donkey-work. But that the races need each other as day needs night, or rain the sunshine. At present the black man is still prepared, on the whole, to make this admission; still, and for a while to come. But the white man's vanity will not allow it; he claims to be all-sufficient. "Anything he can do, I can do better." Anything, that is, except possibly to live.

Meantime, the black man's adaptability, his quickness to assimilate Western knowledge, manners, techniques are making nonsense of all attempts to keep him down by regulations; to force him into a tribal pattern he is not merely outgrowing, but forgetting; to limit the education he may absorb, and the type of employment he is allowed to fill. Every day, thanks to Western instruction, the lead the Westerner has gained grows smaller. No vast distance over the horizon lies the day when the African will be the equal of the white man in the white man's own fields.

He will be faced on that day with a choice, to revenge himself or to co-operate. Which course he follows then depends largely, I believe, on how we—the whites—act in the present. If his course is to revenge himself, Africa, fifty years hence, can be the next great menace before which the peoples tremble.

If, however, the course is for co-operation, the life of man may become something quite different from the pitiful, fear-ridden and guilty life we know to-day, since the values we have expelled will be restored. The return the African will make for the rapid mental and economic progress which he is now, with Western assistance, beginning to achieve, is to give back to Western man what he most deeply misses—the capacity to enjoy his term on earth. And the Gods will smile when they look down at the earth, instead of weeping; for from Africa, man will learn an extension of his values. He will learn that life was never intended to be merely an arduous progress—by way of examinations, overwork, increases in salary, stomach ulcers and heart attacks—to a final commemorative slab. With, as achievement, the manufacture or distribution of some unnecessary article, or the defacement of some corner of the natural world.

From Africa, man will recover the knowledge that life was above all intended to be enjoyed. Roll on the year 2,000! Not only for the sake of Africa and Africans, but for the sake of all mankind—neurotic, hygienic, ulcerated, bewildered, guilty and overworked mankind—roll on the year 2,000!

* * * * *

I was roused from this reverie by someone in the room. It was Cecil Eprile.

"Have you heard?"

"No, what?"

"I'm taking over *Drum* from you, and going to be Editor-in-Chief of all the papers."

I paused as if waiting for him to say it again. I paused, opened my mouth, and remained speechless. I knew this was a moment calling for congratulations, handshakes and approval, but I could say nothing. After looking at me enquiringly for a moment, Cecil turned and went out of the room.

It was not that I thought badly of Cecil's ability; still less that I disliked him. We had always got on easily. He had been the editor of *Golden City Post* since it was launched, and any success it had had was due to him. He had wide journalistic experience, and a much greater knowledge of the South African scene than I was ever likely to acquire. I had often sought his opinion where my own was insufficient.

It was simply that we had different ideas of what journalism means, and of the purpose for which one labours to produce a newspaper or magazine. *Drum* under his control might, or might not, be more successful, but its aims would be entirely changed.

Without criticising Cecil or what he stood for, his appointment as my successor put the final seal of failure on my three and a half years' work.

CHAPTER XXXVI

LAST PARTY

IT WAS MY last evening in the office. I had asked the staff to come round for drinks at their favourite shebeen. Casey was to organise things so that we got a room to ourselves, and to ask Can and anyone else from *Golden City Post* who might care to come along as well.

"There's rather a lot of us," Casey said, "so don't all rush in at once. Drift up in twos and threes, and if there's a cop anywhere around I'll warn you off."

When I "drifted" past the door with Nat, Casey looked out and beckoned us in. It was a bare room, just behind the shop; it would have been a store-room if the shop had been run seriously and not just as a blind. It had a cement floor, with a strip of carpet on it, which was a relief since the cement was cold, and the windows—high-up in one wall—were completely pasted over with brown paper so that no one could look in. There was a door which locked, and on which someone posted himself as guard to decide who should be allowed in and who kept out, a big chair into which I was put, and various stools, chairs (I recognised a couple which had vanished some while before from the office), oil-drums and boxes with newspaper spread over them. One corner was full of domestic objects belonging to the owner's family, among other things a folding-pram and a bicycle. The handlebars of the bicycle stuck into my back between the shoulder-blades; it irritated me for the first five minutes, after that I never looked round or thought of moving, and it was only when I got up to go that I realised I had had one handle pressing into me for the last two hours.

People kept drifting in, until finally we had all assembled. From *Drum* there was Peter, Nat, Casey, John Taukobong the driver, Victor who had succeeded Joshua as office messenger, and a comparative new-comer, Mike Phahlane, who wrote a column of jazz criticism called "Swingcerely Yours"; from *Post* there was Can and the sports editor, Theo, who had done work for us from time to time; there was also a free-lance writer, Duke Ngcobo; a musician known as "General" Duse, and two or three others whom I knew less well—about fifteen in all.

Casey called me to the door and, in his quick urgent whisper which still, after three and a half years, I found so difficult to catch, asked what drink he should order. We settled for two big case bottles of brandy and a dozen or so quarts of beer to start with, since I knew from previous outings that my guests liked to drink spirits and beer alternately, and that the favourite spirit was "mahog", usually a sticky sweetish brandy which you could feel easing its claws into your liver and stomach as soon as it got inside. General took charge of the bar and poured everyone out a slug of brandy, holding the glasses up to the light to make sure they were all equal; the beer we took as we pleased. After a while came another carefully measured slug, and another free-for-all session with the beer. At first there was an opener, but this soon vanished, and from that time on General opened the beer bottles with his teeth, hooking the metal caps deftly off against a single tusk in his lower jaw, which must have been designed and inserted by nature for that purpose.

Once while he was doing this there was an ugly crack and I thought he had broken it. This gave me the shivers because I knew if he had he would do nothing about it, but simply wait until the stump fell out, or wore smooth in course of time—but luckily he had only bitten a piece of glass off the top of the bottle together with the metal cap. We poured that bottle out more carefully than the rest and went on drinking.

Meantime Mike Phahlane had got to work to entertain us. Mike was short-legged and thick-set, about thirty years old, with an orange-complexion and a fringe of black whiskers all round his face, ending in a tuft beneath his chin. He had a laughing black eye and a jovial expression, which he could smoothe in a flash into contrition and anxiety when I asked him what had happened to a missing photograph or block. With his swaggering walk and air of cheerful effrontery, with his black suit and black hat, stuck flat on top of his head and turned up all round, he looked like a dissolute chaplain in some African Navy of the future. Mike had a remarkable ear for dialects, forms of expression and tones of voice, and was always enacting scenes of himself being interviewed by cops who had stopped him on the way home. As a rule he could twist them round his finger, and if he happened to be dealing with someone stupid, could insult him to his face with a submissive voice and smiling countenance.

Mike began by giving us the meeting—which had then lately taken place—between Kennedy and Khruschev, doing both the men speaking and their two interpreters. His "Russian" got great applause. He went on to do imitations of us all—Casey, summoned back from the shebeen by the news that I'm looking for him. Casey, frail, with his hunched shoulders, swaying slightly, puffing furiously at a cigarette to try to drown the smell of drink. Benson, with his trick of clapping his hand to his forehead, as he comes out with some thumping lie as to why he wasn't at work yesterday, and the important political enquiries which had detained him. He also imitated exactly what I must suppose to be my own soft voice and quiet manner, my way of holding a finger up to claim somebody's attention and saying: "*Nat* —just a second, please"; "*Casey*—if you're not too busy"; "*Edna*— just one or two letters", and "Oh, by the way, where's Benson?" He gave Victor getting into an entanglement with his girl-friend on the telephone, and himself approaching the management for a loan of £100.

Mike was a natural mimic, and his impersonations began brilliantly, but as he became more and more sloshed, all the characters spoke alike, and Victor was soon chatting to his girl in a mixture of Khruschev's Russian and Tshombe's French. By now it had become dark and the room was lit only by a single hanging bulb in the centre, casting strange shadows on the lower part of all our faces. We looked like creatures in a Daumier lithograph, prisoners perhaps, with our heads rising up out of the darkness of a cell, black shiny heads and a single white one.

We were all at least partly drunk. I saw Can surreptitiously push away a further case bottle of brandy, as though fearful of its effect upon us all once it began to circulate; the General had spotted it, however, and it was soon being measured out as carefully as water to a shipwrecked crew. From time to time someone rattled on the door, and was either allowed in or told bluntly to clear off. Mike, in one of his impersonations, kicked over the big plate in the middle which was serving us as a general ash-tray. The butts that were still alight started to burn holes in the carpet, and we all stamped on them inaccurately, or splashed beer on to the smouldering edges.

Henry, the shebeen-keeper, a smooth and prosperous African in a light beige suit, kept coming in to see if all was well, and he now brought a further supply of beer which General got to work on, a certain order being maintained amid the noise and growing confusion by the military precision with which he collected and stacked away the empties.

And now the tensest part of the evening was beginning. Mike— who would never willingly yield the floor to anyone—was pulled down, and Duke took his place. Duke was a plumpish Zulu from

Natal, with a round face and a missing tooth. "Mr. Hopkinson," he started in, "you have been with us more than three years. We are all glad you are going because of this party, but we are all sorry for the occasion of this party. I am going to say to you now what the Zulu wife says to her husband who is going away . . ." And he recited a long piece, half-poem, half-prayer, in which the husband is urged by the wife to go since he has to go, but to come back one day and to "come back clean".

"We hope you will come back and work with us one day again. We don't know what you are going to do now—but we look forward to the day of your return." Duke spoke with a kind of easy eloquence, rather like the chairman at a company meeting.

Mike, who had endured Duke's speech with difficulty, now sprang up again: "No, no—I must speak. I want to speak. I have something I *must* say"—and he brushed off all restraining hands. He spoke for some time, ending up . . . "Sir, you are our father." Anxious to calm down our general emotion, I said, "Thank you, Mike. But I don't think I *am* your father."

Looking at me with large pained eyes, he began, "But you are, you *have* to be. . . ."

I pushed him down on to the floor beside me, and said that now I wanted to say something. I told them the past few years had been mixed ones; that there were things to think of with pleasure, and other things with disappointment . . . "The work of an editor isn't to do things himself, it's to extract them from other people. He has to gather around him a team, a group of people of varying abilities—such as yourselves—and try to produce a climate, an atmosphere, in which they can work without feeling bullied or intimidated; without quarrelling with each other; without getting bored or fed-up; without too much worry over their jobs; without idling.

"When Casey wrote a really funny story, Peter took a good set of pictures, or Nat made some complicated subject clear and readable—then that was my success, and I was happy. . . . The opposite was true as well."

I found I was talking almost to myself, looking fixedly down at the carpet; when I paused and the silence got too acute, I looked up and saw eyes gazing at me through the smoke as though our lives depended on attention.

I told them what I had hoped we should achieve: *Drums* springing up all over Africa; the office a training-ground for journalists and cameramen, from which papers not yet in existence would one day draw their staffs. For the fact that these dreams would not be realised, I could not blame them—but there were two things for which I felt they had responsibilities. "I should have liked to hand over to an African editor. We have no African editor. If one day he is to come, only you can produce him. And lastly—a joint failure—I should have liked to have got far more out of you all. You speak of my coming back one day to work with you again. I would be happy to come back under conditions which made it possible for us to achieve the things we failed to do in these last years. But I warn you that, if ever I come back—much as I value and appreciate what you have done—it will be to demand far more from you all. Far, far more from everyone."

Casey, pressing his glass between his hands and with eyes both angry and appealing, was trying to speak. Whatever he said would cost him a prodigious effort, and I tried, by looking neutrally towards him, to reduce the tension and the effort.

"Mr. Hopkinson," he began, with a slow and careful articulation, as though he found it physically difficult to enunciate, as perhaps by now he did: "I don't agree with everything that's been said. Not at all. Some things I don't accept. But I say two things. *Two* things. One, when all of us has a trouble, we have come to you. You don't care if a man is black or yellow, bald or covered with fur. You listen to him. If you are able to help him, then you do. That's why Mike, who talked a lot of bull-shit, called you the father of the paper. Well, you were. . . .

"The second thing is—you talk of disappointments. Yes, I'm sure you have had disappointments. Big disappointments. Sometimes from us. Sometimes not from us. But I tell you this. When we go on a job and there are troubles, and we want to pack up or go off on the booze, then we would think, 'Better not disappoint the old man'!"

Casey looked across at me. I was experiencing an intense strain; it was not concerned with what he said, but that he should be able to get it out, as though, if he failed to say what he wanted, he would be left carrying some painful load around inside him.

The words "old man" evidently struck him as needing some explanation: "We call you that, you understand, not exactly because you are an old man yet—more perhaps oldish, at least compared to us—but because of your position. We feel—'Get done what the old man says we have to do'. . . . Well," he said, looking down into his glass and automatically passing it over to the General to be refilled, "I guess that's all I have to say. We're glad you've been here; we're sorry you're going. And that's all."

We passed the bottle round. Since some had taken in all they could hold, the rest were now free to help themselves. One or two had slipped out and gone home. Henry, the shebeen-owner, his other customers having long since vanished, had now settled down with us.

Peter got up. He spoke in an abrupt and jerky manner, not so much addressing us as flinging out sentences for anyone who cared to pick up.

"What I want to say to you fellows is just one thing. You think you're the same fellows you were when you were sitting in this room three years ago. You're not. You may feel the same, but I'm telling you that you are *not* the same. None of us is the same. Nat here is not the same. Casey is not the same. I am not the same. We're different people from what we were. We think differently. We work in a different way. We are not the same. . . ."

"No," I said, "and I am not the same either. Nothing like the same."

It was growing late, and there would be problems, as always for Africans, about getting home. We straightened ourselves, shook hands all round, and I went through into the back to settle up with Henry.

"So much for the brandy," he said, "and so much for the beers."

"It ought to be more. You've left out the last lot of beers you brought."

"Oh," he said, "that was my own contribution."

I thanked him, and went out through the dark store. All the rooms were now dark and empty, and a tremendous reek of smoke and drink flowed out of the room where we had been sitting. In the dark street hovered a group of shadowy forms.

"Has everyone got transport? Can everyone get home?"

"Yes—we're okay," the voices shouted. "Good-night."

"Good-night."

My car was over on a deserted parking lot; John and Victor came with me to carry my two cases full of books and papers from the office. I fumbled with the keys and dropped them.

"I'm all right, John," I said. "You think I can't get home, but I shall."

I climbed in and called goodbye. Once at the wheel I knew the car would take me home. Inside myself I felt completely empty as though the whole contents of my body had been extracted. For the last hour or so, I realised, I had been shivering all over; the room had been stuffy and crowded, and I was swimming in drink, but it seemed as though all warmth had been drained out of me.

NOTE

READERS WHO HAVE got as far as this may care to know what has happened since to some of the characters in this book.

Casey, Nat, Peter, John Taukobong and Victor are still with *Drum* in Johannesburg; so are Nelson Ottah, Christian Gbagbo and Matthew Faji in West Africa.

Benson Dyantyi, Mike Phahlane and Ian Berry left at the same time I did, or soon after. Sidney Andrews had left some time before. Ian Berry, now with the "Magnum" agency in Paris, was described in a recent issue of *Photography* as "the world's greatest news photographer".

Can Themba, married and with a small daughter, was for a time the sober and capable news editor of *Post*, and has now gone back to being a schoolmaster.

Todd Matshikiza is working in London in television; and Matthew Nkoana is believed to have left South Africa, on his way to Ghana and the outside world.

Humphrey Tyler, to whom my thanks are due for permission to reprint his account of the Sharpeville shootings—the only eye-witness account by any journalist—is working on a newspaper in Durban.

Jim Bailey remains in control of his two papers *Drum* and *Post*—formerly known as *Golden City Post*.

And it should be added that, without his financial support, sustained over ten years and often in difficult conditions, there would have been no such magazine as *Drum* for us to argue over.